WITHDRAWN FROM THE EVAN
LIBRARY AT FMCC

DATE DUE

E446.P35
PEASE
ANTISLAVERY ARGUMENT

08
6.0

Date Due

OCT 18 '67			
NOV 29 '67			
DEC 10 '69			
OCT 28 1970			
NOV 4 1970			
NOV 3 1971			
APR 12 '05			
DEC 15 06			

FULTON-MONTGOMERY COMMUNITY
COLLEGE LIBRARY

PRINTED IN U.S.A.

THE

American Heritage

Series

UNDER THE GENERAL EDITORSHIP OF

LEONARD W. LEVY AND ALFRED YOUNG

The Antislavery Argument

EDITED BY

WILLIAM H. PEASE
University of Alberta, Calgary

AND

JANE H. PEASE
University of Alberta, Calgary

08453

THE BOBBS-MERRILL COMPANY, INC.
A Subsidiary of Howard W. Sams & Co., Inc.
PUBLISHERS • INDIANAPOLIS • NEW YORK • KANSAS CITY

Copyright © 1965 by the Bobbs-Merrill Company, Inc.
Printed in the United States of America
Library of Congress Catalog Card Number: 65-22346
Designed by Stefan Salter Associates
First Printing

The Antislavery Argument

THE AMERICAN HERITAGE SERIES

Foreword

There would be much less meaning to the study of the history of American democracy but for the antislavery movement, incomparably the most important reform movement in this nation's past. It was also inevitable, given this nation's religious roots, its democratic aspirations, its legacy of freedom, and its unbounded hope for the future of man. Indeed, slavery will be attacked wherever men are free, or hope to be. In the United States the argument against slavery, which Mr. and Mrs. Pease present in systematic and analytical form, was remarkably varied and complex. It was religious and secular, moral and political, ethical and legalistic, philosophical and self-interested, Northern and Southern. As the Peases note, the mosaic pattern of the argument is most impressive.

The value of this volume, wholly apart from its illuminating introduction, is that it places in the hands of students and scholars, as no other volume has, representative selections that reflect the many dimensions and varieties of antislavery thought, from the eighteenth century to Emancipation. No other collection is remotely as complete and comprehensive as this one, nor does any study focus so intensively on ideology. Here are Quakers, Garrisonians, colonizationists, gradualists, politicians, constitutional lawyers, free Negroes and former slaves, Southerners, New England aristocrats, revivalist preachers, moral philosophers, crusading reformers, and many, many others, and here are all the different kinds of arguments used by them to oppose slavery. The Peases have placed us all in their debt by their tireless research in the old tracts, sermons, speeches, books, proceedings, poetry, and other forms of expression in which the antislavery argument was advanced.

This book is part of a series whose aim is to provide the essential sources of the American experience, especially of American thought, from the colonial period to the present. When completed, the series will constitute a documentary library of our history. Many of these volumes will fill a need among scholars, students, libraries, and general readers, for authoritative collections of original materials that illuminate the thought of significant individuals, such as James Madison or Louis Brandeis; or of groups, such as Puritan political theorists or American Catholic leaders on social policy; or, of movements, such as the Antifederalists or the Populists. There are a surprising number of subjects traditionally studied in American history for which there are no documentary anthologies. This series will be the most comprehensive and authoritative of its kind. It will also have the distinction of presenting representative pieces of substantial length, documents that have not been condensed into meaningless snippets.

Leonard W. Levy
Alfred Young

Contents

Foreword
VII

Introduction
XXIII

Chronology
LXXXV

Selected Bibliography
XCI

Editors' Note
XCV

I

Arguments for Philanthropic and Gradual Emancipation

ANTHONY BENEZET ATTACKS THE SLAVE TRADE.

From *Observations on the Inslaving, Importing and Purchasing of Negroes* . . . (1748).

1

JOHN WOOLMAN PREACHES AGAINST SLAVEHOLDING.
From "Some Considerations on the Keeping of Negroes . . ." (1762).

5

THE AMERICAN CONVENTION FOR PROMOTING
THE ABOLITION OF SLAVERY ADVOCATES
GRADUAL EMANCIPATION.
From *Address . . . to the People of the United States* (1804).

14

II

Arguments Concerning Colonization

ROBERT GOODLOE HARPER DEFENDS AFRICAN
COLONIZATION.
From Letter [to the American Colonization Society] . . . (1817).

18

COLORED AMERICANS OBJECT TO COLONIZATION.
From [Responses to Schemes for African Colonization], in William Lloyd Garrison, *Thoughts on African Colonization* . . . (1817 and 1831).

32

FRANCES WRIGHT PRESENTS A COLONIZATION PLAN.
From "A PLAN *for the Gradual Abolition of Slavery* . . ." (1825).

38

JAMES G. BIRNEY DESPAIRS OF EQUAL RIGHTS
FOR NEGROES.
From . . . *Address to the Free Colored People, Advising Them to Remove to Liberia* (1852).

43

FRANCIS P. BLAIR, JR., TURNS COLONIZATION
TO POLITICAL ADVANTAGE.

From *The Destiny of the Races of This Continent* . . . (1859).

49

III

Argument for Immediate Emancipation

NEW ENGLAND ANTI-SLAVERY SOCIETY
DEFINES IMMEDIATE EMANCIPATION.

From *Annual Report* . . . (1833).

60

AMERICAN ANTI-SLAVERY SOCIETY
DECLARES ITS SENTIMENTS.

From "Declaration [of Sentiments] of the National Anti-Slavery Convention . . ." (1833).

65

AMOS A. PHELPS SUPPORTS IMMEDIATE ACTION.

From *Lectures on Slavery and its Remedy* (1834).

71

IV

Argument from Sentiment

LYDIA MARIA CHILD PLAYS UP THE ATROCITY THEME.

From *An Appeal in Favor of That Class of Americans Called Africans* (1833).

86

---

xii *Table of Contents*

JAMES A. THOME CONDEMNS LICENTIOUSNESS.
From "Speech . . . Delivered at the Annual Meeting of the American Anti-Slavery Society . . ." (1834).

91

THEODORE DWIGHT WELD SHOWS SLAVERY AS IT IS.
From *American Slavery As It Is* . . . (1839).

94

JOHN G. WHITTIER STIRS SYMPATHY FOR THE FUGITIVES.
"The Hunters of Men" (1830-1838).

102

HARRIET BEECHER STOWE DESCRIBES SLAVERY'S HORRORS IN FICTION.
From *Dred* . . . (1856).

105

V

Arguments from Religion

LEONARD BACON PLEADS FOR MODERATION.
From "Slavery" (1833).

111

WILLIAM ELLERY CHANNING OPPOSES SLAVERY ON RATIONAL RELIGIOUS GROUNDS.
From *Slavery* (1836).

114

JOHN RANKIN ASSERTS THAT RELIGIOUS TEACHING IS AGAINST SLAVERY.
From *Letters on American Slavery* . . . (1824).

118

JOHN G. WHITTIER RENDERS A VIVID SLAVERY SCENE
AT THE NORTH.
"A Sabbath Scene" (1855).
123

WILLIAM LLOYD GARRISON DEFENDS
ABOLITIONIST "INFIDELITY."
From *The "Infidelity" of Abolitionism* (1860).
128

STEPHEN S. FOSTER DAMNS THE
PRO-SLAVERY CHURCHES.
From *The Brotherhood of Thieves . . .* (1843).
134

VI

Arguments from Economics

ELIAS HICKS URGES PEOPLE NOT TO BUY
SLAVE-PRODUCED GOODS.
From *Observations on the Slavery of the Africans and Their Descendants . . .* (1811).
143

AMERICAN AND FOREIGN ANTI-SLAVERY SOCIETY
ADDRESSES THE NON-SLAVEHOLDERS OF THE SOUTH.
From *Address to the Non-Slaveholders of the South . . .* (1843).
148

HINTON ROWAN HELPER ADDRESSES THE
NON-SLAVEHOLDERS OF THE SOUTH.
From *The Impending Crisis . . .* (1857).
163

CHARLES C. BURLEIGH EMPHASIZES
ECONOMIC ADVANTAGE FOR THE NORTH.
From *Slavery and the North* (1855).
172

WILLIAM HENRY SEWARD WARNS OF AN
IRREPRESSIBLE ECONOMIC CONFLICT.
From "The Irrepressible Conflict" (1858).
177

VII

Argument for Direct Action

BERIAH GREEN COUNSELS NORTHERN MEN
ABOUT WHAT TO DO.
From *Things for Northern Men to Do* ... (1836).
182

THE AMERICAN ANTI-SLAVERY SOCIETY ADMONISHES
THE NEGROES HOW TO ACT.
From *Address to the People of Color* ... (1834).
191

WILLIAM KING PLANS A NEGRO SETTLEMENT.
From "Scheme for improving the Coloured People of Canada" (1848).
196

ELIHU BURRITT PROPOSES COMPENSATED EMANCIPATION.
From "A Plan of Brotherly Copartnership of the North and South ..." (1856).
200

MARIA WESTON CHAPMAN URGES SUPPORT OF THE
AMERICAN ANTI-SLAVERY SOCIETY.

From *"How Can I Help to Abolish Slavery?"* ... (1855).

205

THE NEW ENGLAND ANTI-SLAVERY CONVENTION
EXHORTS THE SLAVES TO DIRECT ACTION.

From *Address of the New England Anti-Slavery Convention to the Slaves of the United States* ... (1843).

212

VIII

Argument from Natural Rights and Natural Law

CHARLES FOLLEN LINKS EQUALITY
WITH NATURAL RIGHTS.

From "Speech before the Anti-Slavery Society ..." (1836).

224

JAMES FORTEN, JR., PLEADS FOR NEGRO RIGHTS.

From *An Address Delivered before the Ladies' Anti-Slavery Society of Philadelphia* ... (1836).

233

WILLIAM ELLERY CHANNING DEFINES THE
USE OF THE HIGHER LAW.

From *The Duty of the Free States* ... (1842).

240

THEODORE PARKER WARNS OF THE DANGERS WHICH THREATEN THE RIGHTS OF MAN.

From "A Sermon of the Dangers which Threaten the Rights of Man in America . . ." (1854).

246

IX

Argument from Civil Liberties

GERRIT SMITH DEFENDS FREE SPEECH AS A GOD-GIVEN RIGHT.

From "Speech . . ." in the New York Anti-Slavery Convention *Proceedings of the . . . [Utica] Convention . . .* (1835).

257

JOHN QUINCY ADAMS DEFENDS THE RIGHT OF PETITION.

From *Letters . . . to his Constituents . . .* (1837).

260

EDWARD BEECHER EXAMINES THE ALTON AFFAIR.

From *Narrative of Riots at Alton . . .* (1838).

268

COLORED MEN OF AMERICA DEMAND EQUAL RIGHTS AS AMERICANS.

From *Proceedings of the Colored National Convention . . .* (1853).

273

CHARLES SUMNER ARGUES FOR SCHOOL DESEGREGATION.

From "Equality before the Law . . . in the Case of Sarah C. Roberts v. The City of Boston . . ." (1849).
280

X

Argument for Racial Equality

DAVID WALKER PROPOSES ACTIVISM AND REVOLUTION.

From *Walker's Appeal* . . . (1829).
298

JAMES RUSSELL LOWELL CONDEMNS THE PREJUDICE OF COLOR.

"The Prejudice of Color" (1845).
310

NATHANIEL P. ROGERS RIDICULES THE BLUE COLLAPSE STAGE OF PREJUDICE.

"Color-Phobia" (1838).
315

MARTIN DELANY EXHORTS THE NEGRO TO STRAIGHTEN HIS SHOULDERS AND RAISE HIS EYES.

From *The Condition, Elevation, Emigration, and Destiny of the Colored People of the United States* . . . (1852).
319

HOSEA EASTON CONDEMNS COLOR PREJUDICE AGAINST THE NEGROES.

From *A Treatise on the Intellectual Character, and Civil and Political Conditions of the Colored People of the U. States* . . . (1837).

330

CHARLES REMOND CONDEMNS DISCRIMINATION IN PUBLIC TRANSPORTATION.

From "Remarks of Charles Lenox Remond," (1842).

335

XI

Arguments on the Constitution

WILLIAM I. BOWDITCH CONDEMNS THE CONSTITUTION AS PROSLAVERY.

From *Slavery and the Constitution*. (1849).

343

FREDERICK DOUGLASS ASSERTS THAT THE CONSTITUTION IS ANTISLAVERY.

From *The Constitution of the United States* . . . (1860).

348

WILLIAM GOODELL ARGUES THE ANTISLAVERY NATURE OF THE CONSTITUTION ON A VARIETY OF GROUNDS.

From *Views of American Constitutional Law* . . . (1844).

360

ROBERT RANTOUL, JR., INTERPRETS THE CONSTITUTION STRICTLY AND CONCLUDES IT IS ANTISLAVERY.

From *The Fugitive Slave Law* . . . (1851).

370

SALMON P. CHASE ARGUES IN DEFENSE OF AN
UNDERGROUND RAILROAD OPERATOR.

From *Reclamation of Fugitives from Service* ... (1847).

384

XII

Argument for Political Action: Regular Parties

THE MASSACHUSETTS ANTI-SLAVERY SOCIETY ADDRESSES
MASSACHUSETTS ABOLITIONISTS ON THE
SUBJECT OF POLITICAL ACTION.

From *An Address to the Abolitionists of Massachusetts* ... (1838).

395

JOSHUA R. GIDDINGS SUPPORTS ANTISLAVERY ACTION
THROUGH MAJOR PARTIES.

From *The Rights and Privileges of the Several States in Regard to Slavery* ... (1842).

411

XIII

Argument for Political Action: Third Parties

ARNOLD BUFFUM LAUDS THE ANTISLAVERY
THIRD PARTY.

From *Lecture Showing the Necessity for a Liberty Party* ... (1844).

418

WILLIAM GOODELL ENDORSES A MANY-PLANKED POLITICAL PLATFORM.

From *Address of the Macedon Convention* . . . (1847).

427

CHARLES SUMNER EXPLAINS THE DUTIES OF MASSACHUSETTS DURING THE KANSAS-NEBRASKA CRISIS.

From *Duties of Massachusetts at This Crisis* . . . (1854).

439

CHARLES FRANCIS ADAMS CONDEMNS THE KNOW-NOTHINGS.

From *What Makes Slavery a Question of National Concern?* . . . (1855).

445

FREDERICK DOUGLASS DENOUNCES DISUNION AS A FUTILE ANTISLAVERY DEVICE.

From *The Anti-Slavery Movement* . . . (1855).

452

XIV

Argument Against Political Action

WENDELL PHILLIPS VIGOROUSLY ESCHEWS POLITICAL ACTION.

From *Can Abolitionists Vote or Take Office* . . . (1845).

459

STEPHEN S. FOSTER IS SURE THAT REVOLUTION
IS THE ONLY REMEDY.
From *Revolution the Only Remedy* ... (n.d.).
474

XV

Emancipation and the War Power

ABRAHAM LINCOLN DECREES EMANCIPATION.
480

THE EMANCIPATION PROCLAMATION (1862).
481

THE THIRTEENTH AMENDMENT ENDS SLAVERY IN
THE UNITED STATES (1865).
483

Introduction

That the day in 1619 on which the first Negro laborer arrived in Virginia should have been so fateful a day in American history was the consequence of a distinctive economic and social situation. The seventeenth-century American South was largely wilderness, extending westward as far as the eye could see and the imagination could reach. There the temptation to move was great, the opportunity for an independent livelihood ever present. Where labor was scarce and land was free the bonds of formal contract were lightly held. Neither indentured service nor free labor provided a stable working force. Nor did Indian servitude prove successful, for the Indian was an unwilling and indifferent laborer. Thus the coming of the Negro seemed a Godsend to the economic mind of America; the imported African was able and apparently willing to labor, inexhaustible in supply, and, because of his color, always identifiable, easily controlled. Soon, therefore, Negro slavery both as economic fact and as social system fastened itself upon the American community. If it was concentrated in the South, this bespoke neither northern squeamishness nor southern obtuseness but the simple fact of economic utility.

The predominantly English legal system provided, however, no adequate rubric for slavery. Absent in the English tradition, slavery had not given rise to a formal body of law to deal with it. In simple fact, therefore, there was neither social convention nor legal guarantee to protect the slave or to give him a defined status in society. In the absence of prior usage, slavery in

America became, by the end of the seventeenth century, defined by the "chattel principle," the ownership of the body and labor of the slave as property.

The chattel principle may have answered political and economic necessity; it did not satisfy men's consciences. In a religious age, the questions posed were often in religious terms. If the slave became a Christian, as indeed he should, ought he then to be freed as a child of God? Did not the very inhumanity of the slave trade make it un-Christian? Quakers, in increasing numbers, answered Yes, condemning the Middle Passage and the barbarities of its practice. By the mid-eighteenth century, Quakers like schoolteacher Anthony Benezet of Philadelphia, and John Woolman, tailor of Mount Holly, New Jersey, were arguing fervently against the trade, traveling, speaking, and writing on behalf of Christian treatment for the Negro.

The devotion of the Quakers was paralleled in other denominations; and their argument was reinforced, toward the end of the century, by equally impressive secular arguments drawn from the intellectual complex of the Enlightenment. While the English reformer and antislavery leader, Granville Sharp, said that slavery was contrary to the precepts of common law, Thomas Jefferson in America urged that the importation of slaves be listed as a grievance in the Declaration of Independence. Spurred on by the excitement of the American Revolution, opposition to slavery grew rapidly in the northern and southern states alike. In his *Notes on Virginia* Jefferson spoke of the "great political and moral evil" of slavery. The universal appeal of that pronouncement was reflected in the formation of early antislavery societies chiefly in the South; in the founding of the first national antislavery society in 1794; in the adoption of at least gradual abolition of slavery in every state north of the Mason-Dixon Line by 1804; and in the ordinance which declared that the entire Northwest Territory was to be forever free from slavery.

These public actions were reinforced by individual acts of emancipation. Many slaveholders freed their human chattels by the terms of their wills, for, as John Randolph of Roanoke declared, "*my conscience tells me they are justly entitled*" to it.[1] Some men, like Edward Coles, who had been private secretary to James Madison, emancipated their slaves during their own lifetimes. Coles took his slaves to Illinois and settled with them, later becoming an antislavery leader in the state. At Nashoba, in West Tennessee, Frances Wright, the English reformer, established a settlement which provided southern slaveholders a place to which they might send slaves whom they wished to manumit, and which, observed George Flower, himself a reformer and communitarian, would "divest emancipation of its usual difficulties."[2]

Ironically it was a Connecticut Yankee whose invention of the cotton gin made these early efforts at emancipating and elevating the Negro not only pathetically inadequate but also largely irrelevant. At the end of the eighteenth century slavery was a dying institution. After Eli Whitney's invention of 1793, however, it revived and became seemingly indispensable.[3] Less and less, therefore, was emancipation an accepted aim; more and more the free Negro presented a danger. In addition, Southerners, faced with a growing Negro population, marked the revolt in San Domingo and feared that their own slaves would be roused to insurrection by free blacks. With ever greater vigilance, therefore, southern law restricted voluntary emancipation. And in 1831, after Nat Turner had struck terror

---

[1] Excerpts from the will of John Randolph printed in *Liberator,* August 13, 1836.

[2] George Flower to the Editor, August 25, 1826, *Genius of Universal Emancipation,* September 30, 1826.

[3] Whether slavery was really dying has been challenged by Melvin Drimmer in a provocative paper presented at the American Historical Association's annual meeting in December 1964. If further elaboration fully substantiates his point, the roles of Eli Whitney and of the early Southern antislavery movement will have to be reassessed.

into the heart of Virginia, all hope for general and voluntary emancipation became largely an ideal of the past.

The Colonization Movement

In this context the African colonization movement took shape. As early as the 1770's the Rhode Island clergyman Samuel Hopkins and his friend William Thornton, a Quaker physician, had toyed with the idea of colonizing free Negroes. And Ferdinando Fairfax of Virginia had urged Congressional appropriations to that end. Thomas Jefferson himself urged that freed Negroes "should be colonized to such place as the circumstances of the time should render most proper" and be supplied with tools and animals by the government until they had become a "free and independent people."[4]

Then, in the fall of 1816, a young New Jersey schoolmaster unveiled his plan. The Negro, said Robert Finley, was capable of improvement; but he could not hope to achieve equality among whites. Colonization not only would best answer the interests of the Negro but would also promote the general welfare of the United States by removing a generally undesirable element of the population. It would help Christianize and civilize the African natives themselves and would be a source of profitable trade and commerce. Colonization, he averred, would be good for "patriotism and benevolence."[5] By January of 1817, Finley's exhortations bore fruit with the founding of the American Colonization Society; and, with some assistance from the American government, the Society had established, by 1821, the colony of Liberia.

Commanding considerable attention both North and South,

---

[4] Thomas Jefferson, *Notes on the State of Virginia* (Boston: Wells & Lilly, 1829), p. 144. Information on colonization from Philip J. Staudenraus, *The African Colonization Movement 1816–1865* (New York: Columbia University Press, 1961).

[5] *Ibid.*, pp. 19–22.

the Society's program claimed to be the only antislavery activity which could enlist the support of southern slaveholders, whose cooperation was essential if antislavery was to be effective. For them it provided a way of getting rid of troublesome free Negroes, whose presence in the South was a constant threat to social tranquillity. In Virginia, especially, colonization sentiment was strong. During the 1820's, the roster of the Society's leaders included such names as Bushrod Washington, James Madison, James Monroe, and John Marshall. In the North, too, there was significant support, even among those who would later become abolitionists and anticolonizationists—Gerrit Smith, Amos A. Phelps, Samuel J. May, Joshua Leavitt, Arthur Tappan, and Salmon Chase among them.

It was the lot of the American Colonization Society, however, quickly to lose its commanding position in the antislavery crusade. Many in the South, pointing out that its support came largely from the Border States, suspected the Society of being an abolition organization in disguise. And in the North antislavery enthusiasts became quickly disillusioned by proslavery colonization argument, by the limited success of Liberia, and by the hostility of the Negroes themselves. "The belief has of late obtained pretty rapidly at the North," wrote Gerrit Smith in 1833, "that our Society is an obstacle in the way of emancipation, in the way of the precious cause of universal freedom."[6]

The failure of the American Colonization Society to win antislavery approval for more than a few years did not mean that the idea of colonization was wholly abandoned. It appeared as a continual refrain throughout the course of the antislavery crusade. Almost universally, however, this refrain emphasized colonization within the confines of the North American continent. During the 1820's, for example, North Carolina Friends attempted to settle manumitted slaves in Indiana.

---

[6] American Colonization Society, *Seventeenth Annual Report* quoted in *ibid.*, p. 221.

Farther to the south, Benjamin Lundy, Quaker antislavery leader, early colleague of William Lloyd Garrison, and editor of the *Genius of Universal Emancipation,* attempted, in the 1830's, to establish a Negro settlement in the Mexican state of Tamaulipas. Far to the north, Cincinnati's free Negroes purchased land in Canada, whence several hundred of them moved in 1830 and founded the Wilberforce community. Finally, in 1859, Senator Frank Blair devised a plan to establish a Negro state in Central America; four years later, President Lincoln himself considered a similar plan.

Blair had argued that it was imperative to remove the Negroes from the South, otherwise slave labor would drive out free, the blacks would drive out the whites, and southern oligarchs would try to fasten their system on the nation from motives of pure profit. Thus the greatness of the South would decline, as that of Virginia already had. These arguments were not in themselves either new or startling. But when Blair added that colonization was "the deliverance of two incongruous races from an unnatural connection, and setting both free[;] [t]hat [the] sable race, bred in the pestilence of Africa, is a blot on the fair prospect of our country," he showed just how far colonization arguments had moved from the purpose of the antislavery crusade.[7]

But it did not require Blair's bluntness. The fact was that the idea of colonization had little lasting appeal to Americans, North or South, white or black.

The Emergence of Immediate Abolition

By the early 1830's a new intensity and enthusiasm had entered the antislavery movement. Propelled in part by the

---

[7] Frank P. Blair, Jr., *The Destiny of the Races of This Continent. An Address Delivered before the Mercantile Library Association of Boston, Massachusetts, on the 26th of January, 1859* (Washington: Buell and Blanchard, 1859), p. 21.

humanitarian zeal which defined so much of the reform of the Middle Period, this intensity was closely allied to the religious revivalism which emerged at the same time. No one better expressed the revivalist quality than Charles Grandison Finney, who preached across the Burned Over District, expostulating against sin, urging upon "earnest young people predisposed to morality and reform" conversion and the Lord's Way.[8] No matter what the denomination, a significant portion of Protestant Americans shared a like dedication to God's will. "Forego sin and seek repentance and ye shall be saved." So ran the charge. It took little imagination, therefore, to understand that the antislavery crusade marched under the banner of the Lord, for slavery was admittedly sinful. "I do not depend on anyone as an abolitionist," wrote William Jay, antislavery lawyer of New York and son of Chief Justice John Jay, "who does not act from a sense of religious obligation."[9]

The 1820's and 1830's were also a period of humanitarian reform. Among the British, whose antislavery actions so frequently served as models for the American cause, the crusade had been given impetus in 1824 with the doctrine of immediatism—rid the empire of slavery at once and in full. By 1830 British antislavery people had completely adopted the immediatist position and had introduced it to their American colleagues. Slaveholders, they felt, were unwilling to cooperate in any program of gradual emancipation. Slave revolts, actual and threatened, made definitive action seem ever more imperative. And, finally, as Professor David Davis points out, immediatism provided a "simple, emotional slogan" whose very simplicity gave a distinct strategic advantage.[10]

---

[8] Gilbert H. Barnes, *The Antislavery Impulse, 1830–1844* (New York: D. Appleton-Century Co., 1933), p. 25.

[9] Louis Filler, *The Crusade Against Slavery 1830–1860* (New York: Harper and Brothers, 1960), p. 23.

[10] David B. Davis, "The Emergence of Immediatism in British and American Antislavery Thought," *Mississippi Valley Historical Review*, XLIX (September 1962), 209–230; quotation p. 227.

For American abolitionists the way was clearly marked by the ending, in 1833, of slavery throughout the British Empire. What had been only antislavery before 1820 became, by 1830, decidedly abolitionist. Committed, by its humanitarianism and its religious zeal to the moral imperative of antislavery, the movement readily absorbed and was reinforced by a contemporary romanticism and optimism which, Davis observes, saw issues sharply etched, clearly defined, simplistically stated. Hence immediatism, which was, from the beginning, implicit in abolitionism, provided an uncomplicated and total answer to a problem which had theretofore defied solution.

Considered generically, this emerging doctrine of a pious and righteous reformism was the common property of sober and responsible men. It had found ample expression in the benevolent societies, which dominated American reform during the period. Organized by dedicated men of God, though not of the cloth, the benevolent societies, centered largely in New York, undertook a massive and interlocking program to convert the nation to Christian righteousness and pious living. The major societies were five in number, the American Sunday School Union, the American Bible Society, the American Tract Society, the American Home Missionary Society, and the American Education Society. Through their agents and their publications they flooded the country with admonitions to follow the ways of the Lord, who, of course, "wished all men to obey His laws as the stewards interpreted them."[11] The "benevolent empire," as it has been called, was led by a small, closely-knit group of men including the New York merchants Arthur Tappan and his brother Lewis, Gerrit Smith, wealthy landowner and reform enthusiast of upstate New York, and the lawyer William Jay. By the beginning of the 1830's they were ready to extend the empire to embrace the antislavery crusade. As it

---

[11] Clifford S. Griffin, *Their Brothers' Keepers* (New Brunswick: Rutgers University Press, 1960), p. xii.

turned out, however, the man who pushed the hardest and the one who forced their hand was an obscure newspaperman from Boston.

Nat Turner's rebellion in 1831 had seemed, to the benevolent leaders, good reason to proceed slowly. But, if he gave it a thought, William Lloyd Garrison concluded that it was a cue to move rapidly forward. He was long since committed to action. Born in Newburyport, Massachusetts, in 1805, Garrison had early entered the ranks of the abolitionists. As a young printer he published his first antislavery article in 1826. Two years later he went to Bennington, Vermont, where he edited for a season the *Journal of the Times,* launching, through its pages, a fierce attack on slavery. In a Fourth of July oration in 1829, Garrison further spelled out his views. He spoke fervently of the horrors of slavery and demanded "education and freedom [which] will elevate our colored population to a rank with the white—making them useful, intelligent and peaceable citizens." And he took that extreme stand which was to be a Garrisonian hallmark for the next thirty years. All actions, even in defiance of the Constitution, he asserted, must be used to destroy slavery. ". . . If we must share in the guilt and danger of destroying the bodies and souls of men, *as the price of our Union;* if the slave States will haughtily spurn our assistance, and refuse to consult the general welfare; then the fault is not ours if a separation eventually take place. . . ."[12]

Then, after a year in Baltimore working on the *Genius of Universal Emancipation* with Lundy, Garrison returned, in 1830, to Boston and started his own antislavery paper. In its first issue, January 1, 1831, the *Liberator* carried a message which became Garrison's shrill but accurate boast for the rest of his antislavery career. "I will not equivocate—I will not

---

[12] Quoted in Wendell Phillips Garrison and Francis Jackson Garrison, *William Lloyd Garrison, 1805–1879; the Story of His Life as Told by His Children,* I (New York: The Century Co., 1885–1889), 130, 133.

excuse—I will not retreat a single inch—AND I WILL BE HEARD."
And heard he was.

The Formation of Antislavery Societies

Within the year Garrison, together with a group of antislavery colleagues, had formed the New England Anti-Slavery Society. If it was, as Garrison's recent biographer observes, "simply a forum for individuals to bear their testimony against slavery,"[13] it was at least a starting point from which to advance. Still needed, of course, was a national organization. Spurred on by the progress of British antislavery, a group of antislavery leaders in New York, led by those stalwarts of the benevolent empire, the Tappan brothers, met in October of 1833 to form the New York Anti-Slavery Society. The mob which harassed this meeting led the New Yorkers to delay forming a national society. But Garrison, recently returned from England where he had been lionized as the principal spokesman of American antislavery, demanded the formation of an American antislavery society in the very year of British emancipation.

Garrison's imperiousness did not inspire universal enthusiasm. Still, his insistence was not without its point. The issue, in fact, was drawn between the younger and more impetuous Garrison, who demanded immediate abolition unqualified, and the older and more practical New York leadership, who supported an "*immediate* emancipation which is gradually accomplished."[14]

Who was victor in this altercation is an open question. Garrison got, in 1833, an American Anti-Slavery Society. And Garrison largely wrote the Society's Declaration of Sentiments. Still, the founding meeting was held in Philadelphia, far from

---

[13] John L. Thomas, *The Liberator, William Lloyd Garrison, A Biography* (Boston: Little, Brown and Company, 1963), p. 142.

[14] *Zion's Herald*, VI, 21, quoted in Barnes, *Antislavery Impulse*, p. 49.

the center of Garrisonian influence; and the Society itself was dominated by the New York group. But Garrison, never particularly concerned about organization, was chiefly interested in propaganda and action. In that he was still free, although the reins of formal societal activity were held in New York. At best it seemed a compromise—at worst it proved an irreconcilable stalemate.

There were others, in addition to the Garrisonians and the New Yorkers, who also played a distinct role in the new American Anti-Slavery Society. These were the western abolitionists. They were represented in Philadelphia principally by Beriah Green, President of the Oneida Institute in upstate New York. Green, earlier a professor at Western Reserve College in Ohio, had been so outspokenly abolitionist that, in 1833, he was forced out of the College; not, however, before he and some colleagues had converted the young Theodore Weld, a Finney-trained revivalist, to "aggressive abolitionism."[15] Though he had refused to attend the Philadelphia convention, Weld became the leading western abolitionist. "God," he had written to the New York leadership at the time of the Convention,

has committed to every moral agent the privilege, the right and the responsibility of *personal ownership*. This is God's plan. Slavery annihilates it, and surrenders to avarice, passion and lust, all that makes life a blessing. It crushes the body, tramples into the dust the upward tendencies of intellect, breaks the heart and kills the soul.[16]

---

[15] Benjamin P. Thomas, *Theodore Weld, Crusader for Freedom* (New Brunswick: Rutgers University Press, 1950), p. 36. Here Thomas refutes Barnes, *Antislavery Impulse*, pp. 39–40, who maintains that Weld converted Green, Charles B. Storrs, the President of Western Reserve College, and Elizur Wright, Jr., professor of mathematics.

[16] Theodore Weld to Arthur Tappan, Joshua Leavitt, and Elizur Wright, Jr., in Anti-Slavery Convention, Philadelphia, *Proceedings of the Anti-Slavery Convention Assembled at Philadelphia, Dec. 4, 5, 6, 1833* (New York: Dorr & Butterfield, 1833).

Introduction

The revivalist training which Weld had received from Finney and the conversion to immediatism which he experienced at the hands of Green and other Western Reserve professors had done their work. When he entered Lane Seminary in Cincinnati to complete his theological training, he was already a dedicated antislavery worker. The very next spring (1834) he organized the Lane Debates to discuss slavery and colonization. The debates were, in reality, old-fashioned revivalist meetings devoted to bearing witness against the evils, the sin, of slavery. So ardent were the spirits of the Lane students that, opposed in antislavery activity by the seminary administration, most of them resigned in a body and later transferred to Oberlin, just then beginning its career and pledged to accept both men and women, whites and Negroes. The Debates were important because they were the genesis of organized abolitionism in the western part of the country. From those Lane students came, in large part, the first generation of traveling agents of the American Anti-Slavery Society. Increased in number and called the "Seventy" after 1837, these agents lectured widely in the Western Reserve and as far east as New England, converting their hearers in substantial numbers to the abolitionist cause, preaching the New York doctrine of immediate emancipation gradually achieved.[17] The work of the Seventy, of whom over fifty were Weld-trained antislavery revivalists, made of the western territory perhaps the most active center of antislavery work.

To speak of these groups of antislavery workers as three separate entities is to point up their different backgrounds and methods. The Garrisonians were peculiarly a New England group, largely radicals, devoted to religion and yet before long actively anticlerical.The moderate New York group hovered

---

[17] Barnes, *Antislavery Impulse,* p. 77. See also Dwight L. Dumond, *Antislavery Origins of the Civil War in the United States* (Ann Arbor, Michigan: University of Michigan Press, Ann Arbor Paperback, 1959), p. 34.

about the metropolis, for here were its leaders, here its business connections, here the center of the benevolent empire of which it was so intimate a part. In the West the Weld-Finney abolitionists were crusaders whose labors had a peculiarly beatific quality about them, whose crusade was almost what Finney had hoped for—a religious revival. Emphasize these variations as one will, however, there was little difference in the brands of abolitionism that they taught.

The Doctrine of Immediatism

There was nonetheless considerable discussion among the abolitionists about the nuances of immediatism; and historians have been set by the ears trying to sort them out. The British had had the first word in the 1820's. Immediatism for them meant that emancipation should not only be immediately enacted but that it should not be followed by any transition period of apprenticeship nor complicated by any sort of colonization. Immediatism also implied an immediate moral purging of personal involvement in the sin of slavery.[18] This was what all the abolitionists had in mind. Yet they qualified and hedged the term, immediatism, in so many ways that while they may have satisfied themselves, they most assuredly left everybody else badly confused.

Garrison, for example, one of the loudest trumpeters of the doctrine of immediatism, tempered his definition with his own brand of realism. "Urge immediate abolition as earnestly as we may, it will, alas! be gradual abolition in the end. We have never said that slavery would be overthrown by a single blow; that it ought to be, we shall always contend."[19]

It was not as simple as that. Garrisonian immediatism extended only to the abolition of slavery as a formal system. What

---

[18] Davis, "The Emergence of Immediatism," pp. 209–210.
[19] Quoted in W. P. and F. J. Garrison, *William Lloyd Garrison*, I, 228n.

happened thereafter was another problem entirely. "Immediate abolition does not mean," he wrote in 1832, "that the slaves shall immediately exercise the right of suffrage, or be eligible to any office, or be emancipated from law, or be free from the benevolent restraints of guardianship." This is twice unclear, because even the terms are of different orders. What indeed did Garrison mean? "We contend," he added,

> for the immediate personal freedom of the slaves, for their exemption from punishment except where law has been violated, for their employment and reward as free laborers, for their exclusive right to their own bodies and those of their own children, for their instruction and subsequent admission to all trusts, offices, honors and emoluments of intelligent freemen. . . . Nor does immediate abolition mean that any compulsory power, other than moral, should be used in breaking the fetters of slavery.[20]

Jumbled as it was, Garrison's statement meant an instant end of slavery followed by a carefully hedged grant of the rights of normal citizenship.

William Goodell, antislavery leader of upstate New York and editor of antislavery and reform papers, argued that immediate and unconditional emancipation was "prudent, safe and beneficial," and added that the crime and sin of slavery should be immediately repented. To that he added that "there are, at the present time, the highest obligations resting on the people of the free states to remove slavery, by moral and political action, as prescribed in the Constitution of the United States."[21]

The New York abolitionists further changed the emphasis. Both they and the westerners talked of "immediate emancipation, gradually accomplished," or, as the westerners put it, "gradual emancipation, immediately begun." Some of the Lane

---

[20] Quoted in *ibid.*, pp. 294–295.

[21] William Goodell, *Slavery and Anti-Slavery; a History of the Great Struggle in Both Hemispheres; with a View of the Slavery Question in the United States* (New York: W. Harned, 1852), p. 398.

people thought this meant that "the master's control over the Negro was to cease at once; the freedman was to be employed as a laborer but 'placed under a benevolent and disinterested supervision . . . until ready for intellectual and moral equality with whites.'"[22]

Professor Gilbert H. Barnes has pointed out that, after the publication of Horace Kimball's and James Thome's history of emancipation in the West Indies, the New York doctrine of "immediate emancipation, gradually accomplished" gave way to real immediatism. But he added that the difference was significant only to the devoted antislavery workers, that everyone else thought that "real immediatism" was what had been meant all along.[23] Thus insignificant was the distinction that successfully badgered not only the antislavery crusaders themselves but also their interpreters from that day to this.

Disseminating the Doctrine

Commenting on the founding of the Boston Female Anti-Slavery Society in the middle 1830's, Charles Francis Adams wrote that "the new organization contemplated only the single proposition, that slavery, 'because in direct violation of the laws of God,' ought to be abolished. But," he added, "it devised no means to reach that end, beyond the dissemination of the reasons of this belief among those whom it was essential to convert. It specified no direction of its labors, excepting the general one of slavery, wherever found."[24] It was one of the central problems of the abolitionists that they never devised a practical program. They were so concerned with sin and mor-

---

[22] Russel B. Nye, *William Lloyd Garrison and the Humanitarian Reformers* (Boston: Little, Brown, 1955), p. 95.

[23] Barnes, *Antislavery Impulse*, pp. 138–139.

[24] Charles Francis Adams, *What Makes Slavery a Question of National Concern? A Lecture Delivered . . . at New York, January 30 . . . 1855* (Boston: Little, Brown, 1855), pp. 11–12.

ality that they failed to grapple with the physical reality of the slave who was presumably their first concern. Their preoccupation with theory and nuance not only vitiated their energies in fruitless discussion of ideology but also contributed to their failure to unite in action.

But, for all their internal bickering, they did generate a significant consensus. As a propaganda organization they were superlatively abrasive. Particularly in the East their major weapon was often the press. Garrison's *Liberator*, begun in 1831, set the pace; and, for the next thirty years, some thirty or forty different antislavery newspapers preached abolition to America. Many of them were founded, flourished for a day, and collapsed; but a few had long and distinguished careers in the antislavery crusade. Among the most famous and successful papers, in addition to the *Liberator*, were the *Philanthropist*, the *Anti-Slavery Bugle*, the *National Anti-Slavery Standard*, the *Emancipator*, the *National Era*, the *Herald of Freedom*, and the *Pennsylvania Freeman*.[25] In addition there were numerous antislavery magazines, tracts, and other periodical and monthly publications. *The Anti-Slavery Record*, for example, was a magazine for adults; *The Slave's Friend*, a journal for juveniles. Among the tract series was the *Anti-Slavery Examiner*, and among the annuals, the *Liberty Bell*, filled with essays, poems, and other matter. There were also the annual reports of the various local, state, and national organizations. And, finally, there were the exposés of slavery: compilations,

---

[25] *Liberator*, Boston, 1831–1865; *Philanthropist*, New Richmond and Cincinnati, 1836–1843, eds. James G. Birney, Gamaliel Bailey; *Anti-Slavery Bugle*, New Lisbon, Ohio, 1845–1861, eds. B.S. and Elizabeth H. Jones, Marius Robinson; *National Anti-Slavery Standard*, New York, 1840–1870, eds. *inter alia* Lydia Maria and David Lee Child, Sydney Gay; *Emancipator*, New York, 1833–1841, Boston, 1841–1850, eds. William Goodell, Joshua Leavitt; *National Era*, Washington, 1847–1860, ed. Gamaliel Bailey; *Herald of Freedom*, Concord, New Hampshire, 1835–1846, eds. J. H. Kimball, N. P. Rogers, Parker Pillsbury; *Pennsylvania Freeman*, Philadelphia, 1836–1854, eds. J. G. Whittier, C. C. Burleigh, J. M. McKim.

some reliable, others not, of the conditions of the slave, calculated to shock the iron-stomached and reduce to pulp the sentimental, to win both to the abolitionist position. Of the exposés, the most famous and probably the most carefully done was Weld's *Slavery As It Is*, a remarkable collection of the facts and figures of slavery, designed to cut raggedly into the conscience.

Despite the vigor with which it was disseminated, the printed word was not sufficient. Often the threats hurled against the abolitionists did more to persuade than the content of the papers themselves. In 1836 the office of James G. Birney's *Philanthropist* was sacked, and antislavery men in Cincinnati, where the paper was published, were warned to avoid him. Birney, himself a southerner and former slaveholder who had been converted to abolition by Weld two years earlier, had been constantly threatened. "Must we trample," he asked in defiance, "on the liberty of white men here because they have trampled on the liberty of black men at the South? Must we forge chains for the *mind* here, because they have forged them for the *body* there? Must we extinguish the right to *speak*, the right to *print* in the North, that we may be in unison with the South?" His answer: "No, never."[26] Yet, only a year later, in Alton, Illinois, Elijah Lovejoy's press was destroyed, and Lovejoy was murdered by the mob. These were deplorable extralegal actions, but they were blessings in disguise for the cause. Lovejoy's brother, Owen, suggested that Elijah dead was worth more than Elijah alive. Alive he was only a Lovejoy. Dead he was a martyr.[27]

These attacks on freedom of the press rallied to the antislavery cause many who before had been only mildly sympathetic. In Boston, Unitarianism's grand old man, William Ellery

---

[26] Quoted in Betty Fladeland, *James Gillespie Birney: Slaveholder to Abolitionist* (Ithaca: Cornell University Press, 1955), p. 138.

[27] Owen Lovejoy to Henry G. Chapman, December 9, 1837, Weston Papers, Antislavery Collections, Boston Public Library.

Channing, in a long letter to Birney, admitted his personal distaste for the abolitionists (whose tactics and virulence he deplored), but staunchly defended a free press in particular and civil liberties in general. And that applied to abolitionists as well as to those whose acts Channing approved. In Ohio, too, the rising young lawyer, Salmon P. Chase, came to the support of the free press and abolitionism.

The major difficulty with the printed word was that it failed to reach the unconverted. In this respect, the antislavery lecturer had much the edge. If initially he went unnoticed, his continued presence in any community quickly became an issue of moment. Here the platform techniques of the revivalist and the orator were at a premium. Often the lecturers were at their best in the country town and village, where religious revivalism had its strongest hold. But, whether in hamlet or city, village or town, they followed carefully prescribed tactics. If their delivery and manner were individual—and they were vastly so—the fundamentals of their strategy were the same. Seek out the clergy in each community, try to establish rapport with them at once, and conduct antislavery meetings with their help. Once on the platform, keep the principle of immediate abolition in the forefront; eschew detailed plans for they only lead to endless objection and argument; be sure to have facts ready and stick carefully to them. Weld, Finney-trained, represented the best of the lecturing technique. "If your hearts ache and bleed," he urged with religious excitement,

> we want you, you will help us; but if you merely adopt our principles as dry theories, do let us alone: we have millstones enough swinging at our necks already. Further, if you join us merely out of a sense of *duty*, we pray you keep aloof and give place to those who leap into our ranks because they cannot keep themselves out; who instead of whining about duty, shout "privilege", "delight"![28]

---

[28] From the *Emancipator*, July 28, 1836, quoted in Barnes, *Antislavery Impulse*, p. 79.

It was not easy going. Many towns turned upon these abolitionists as disturbers of the peace. Assaulted with eggs, nails, and stones, charged by enraged citizens, booed and hissed, the intrepid crusaders stood their ground when they could, fled when they had to. Throughout the North they found it ever more difficult to find halls, churches, or other buildings in which to hold their meetings. Constantly they were subjected to abuse and violence. Certainly it was very dramatic that, in the spring of 1838, the meetings of the Anti-Slavery Convention of American Women were disrupted when the newly completed Pennsylvania Hall, built in Philadelphia especially for reform meetings, was burned down around them. But the events of late October of 1835 had been more significant. In Utica, New York, the state antislavery convention was routed by the mob and had to retire to Gerrit Smith's estate at nearby Peterboro; and on the same day, in Boston, the meeting of the Boston Female Anti-Slavery Society was broken up and Garrison, seized by the mob, was led through the streets in an attempted lynching. These events had important repercussions. In Peterboro, Smith, long a supporter of colonization, drew more closely to the abolitionists; in Boston, George B. Emerson, Henry I. Bowditch, and Wendell Phillips, nabobs all, cast their patrician lot with the abolitionist forces. Once again mob action against abolitionists had netted distinguished recruits for their cause.

Taking Practical Action

To win converts to antislavery was one thing; to be able to do something directly about slavery was quite another. Unable to challenge the system directly the antislavery people did, nevertheless, find a partial substitute by assisting the free Negroes already in the North. In 1832, for example, the New England Anti-Slavery Society urged the establishment of vocational apprenticeships for young Negro boys and the establishment of schools where Negroes might receive a basic education. It urged action against the kidnaping of Negroes. In Massachusetts it supported the repeal of a law prohibiting interracial marriage. In 1831, antislavery crusaders tried to establish a manual labor school in New Haven; and, two years later, in Canterbury, Connecticut, a young white woman, Prudence Crandall, attempted to educate Negroes in her school for young ladies. Although both these efforts failed, not all attempts to provide education for Negroes were unsuccessful. Gerrit Smith, in Peterboro, opened a manual labor school for Negroes in 1834 because he thought that "it is the duty of the whites to elevate the condition and character of the colored people." At Oberlin College in Ohio Negroes were admitted. Farther west, in Indiana, Augustus Wattles, one of the Lane students, ran the Emlen Institute, for the "support and education in school learning and the mechanics arts and agriculture, [of] such colored boys, of African and Indian descent, whose parents would give them up to the institute." In New York, the American Anti-Slavery Society sponsored the Phoenix Society, whose purpose was, in various ways, to uplift the Negroes and to encourage them "to improve their minds and to abstain from every vicious and demoralizing practice."[29]

What to a later generation would seem the automatic weapon of economic retaliation and boycott received only the scantest attention of antislavery crusaders. While they were generally willing to support the notion of purchasing goods made only with free labor and to encourage the establishment of stores in which such goods were sold, substantial support came only from the Quakers. Most people seem to have agreed with Gar-

---

[29] *New Haven Journal of Freedom,* August 20, 1834, quoted in *African Repository and Colonial Journal,* X (December 1834), 312. Wattles quoted in "Transplanting Negroes to Ohio," *Journal of Negro History,* I (July 1916), 308. "Objects of the Phoenix Society of New York," in American Anti-Slavery Society, *Address to the People of Color, in the City of New York. By Members of the Executive Committee of the American Anti-Slavery Society* (New York: S. W. Benedict & Co., 1834), p. 8.

rison, who commented that such action was only a "subordinate" way of fighting slavery and not really very effective. And Garrison's colleague, Samuel May, Jr., thought that "persons may fritter away great energies & respectable powers in controversies about yards of cotton-cloth & pounds of sugar. . . . [T]o urge this [free produce argument], as a principal weapon of offense, would be very like bailing out the Atlantic with a spoon. . . ." Still, it might mean that free labor would have a real opportunity to demonstrate its worth in competition with slave labor. If one felt strongly about slavery, there was a justification in the analogy about receiving stolen goods; and one might suppose, as Angelina Grimké Weld did, that, if everybody refused to buy slave-produced cotton goods, the slaveholders would have either to give up slavery or give up selling cotton.[30]

There were other arguments as well. The American and Foreign Anti-Slavery Society, addressing the Non-Slaveholders of the South, argued that slavery adversely affected population growth, lowered the standards and extent of education, acted as a brake upon economic expansion, and subjected the South to an unsatisfactory attitude toward the laboring class. To this list Boston Unitarian Theodore Parker added soil exhaustion, depressed land values, fewer internal improvements in the South, and limited immigration into the South.[31] Probably the most popular economic argument, however, was that which

---

[30] Samuel May, Jr., to J. B. Estlin, May 2, 1848, May Papers, Antislavery Collections, Boston Public Library. Angelina G. Weld to Lewis Tappan, August 8, 1841, in Gilbert H. Barnes and Dwight L. Dumond, eds., *Letters of Theodore Dwight Weld, Angelina Grimké Weld and Sarah Grimké, 1822–1844,* II (New York: D. Appleton-Century Co., 1934), 872–876.

[31] American and Foreign Anti-Slavery Society, *Address to the Non-Slaveholders of the South, on the Social and Political Evils of Slavery* (New York: S. W. Benedict, 1843). Theodore Parker, "A Letter on Slavery [December 22, 1847]" *The Slave Power* ed James K. Hosmer (*The Centenary Edition of the Works of Theodore Parker*) (Boston: American Unitarian Association, [1907–1913]), pp. 60–72.

pointed out the evil collusion between northern capital and southern agriculture. All the other arguments, which Hinton Rowan Helper also echoed in his *Impending Crisis*, could not match that which Charles Sumner, Wendell Phillips, and others called the alliance between the lords of the lash and the lords of the loom. "Slavery," declaimed Senator William H. Seward, in his March 11, 1850, speech, setting forth the loom and lash argument, "has . . . a natural alliance with the aristocracy of the North and with the aristocracy of Europe. So long as Slavery shall possess the cotton-fields, the sugar-fields, and the rice-fields of the world, so long will Commerce and Capital yield it toleration and sympathy. Emancipation is a democratic revolution. It is Capital that arrests all democratic revolutions."[32] But the fact remained that free produce and boycotts interested few but the Quakers; and that Seward's dramatic challenge interested few but later generations of economic determinists.

Still, the crusaders did try to nibble away at the peculiar institution. In the District of Columbia, because it was Federal territory, they demanded the abolition of slavery and the slave trade. Repeatedly they sent petitions to Congress, thus precipitating a major debate which, before the petition campaign had ended, enlisted the sympathies of many more Northerners than the antislavery crusade had previously been able to do. Beginning this venture after 1835 and continuing it unabated for the remainder of the decade and long after, antislavery enthusiasts collected petitions with zeal, presented them to Congress by the thousands. Not only did they agitate over the District of Columbia, they prayed also against the annexation of Texas, for the forbidding of slavery in the territories, against admitting any new slave states, and for abolishing interstate commerce in slaves. Although other antislavery work contin-

---

[32] William H. Seward, *Speech on the Admission of California. Delivered in the Senate of the United States, March 11, 1850* (Washington: Buell & Blanchard, 1850), p. 42.

ued, particular stress was placed upon the petition activities. These, as Beriah Green indicated in 1836, were the "Things for Northern Men To Do. . . ."

The importance of the petition campaign lay not, however, in its attack on slavery, although this had been the principal purpose. Rather it lay in arousing those whose interest in antislavery had been only indifferent. When southern forces in the House of Representatives adopted the Gag Rule, they were, on the one hand, presumably fulfilling the Constitutional provision that all citizens had a right to be heard by their government without, on the other hand, subjecting the government to the unpleasant task of having to listen to what was being said. Although the Rule itself was essentially a procedural maneuver, John Quincy Adams, crusty ex-President and Representative from Massachusetts, challenged it as a frontal assault on civil liberties. For eight years, therefore, Adams presented the petitions to the Congress as fast as his northern constituency could send them on to him, battling at every turn for the principle and practice of free speech. So important was the fight over petitions that it grew to a major issue and solidly united the antislavery Congressmen. Although these men were not strong enough to be a major political force, still they were important enough to draw Weld to Washington to act as their researcher and assistant. The irony of the whole affair was that, while the antislavery coterie did yeoman service in the Congress, it was Adams, never an orthodox abolitionist, who, by his defense of civil rights, gave to the crusade its most effective outlet during the first decade of organized activity.

The Defense of Civil Liberties

The antislavery crusade admittedly made progress during the decade of the 1830's in its identification with the issue of civil rights. William Seward, just beginning a great political career, had the prescience to understand what was happening. "The clamor about Abolitionists," he wrote in 1835,

> will, as such *violent* efforts in favor of *moderation* always do, produce reaction. . . . The very fact that no honorable or highminded or reputable man in the North, even in the very excitement of mass meetings, will lend his sanction to the monstrous claims of the South for Legislation against abolitionists, and the still more monstrous conduct of the Post Office Department [in confiscating antislavery literature], proves that if the South persist the issue will be changed[,] fearfully changed[,] for them.[33]

Within the year Seward's prognosis bore fruit. "We are becoming abolitionists at the North fast," wrote Sumner in 1836; "riots, the attempts to abridge freedom of discussion, and the conduct of the South generally, have caused many to think favorably of immediate emancipation who have never before been inclined to it." And, at the South, Senator William Cabell Rives of Virginia commented ruefully that "Southern fanatics . . . are now likely to do more injury to our cause than five hundred men such as Garrison, Tappan, Thompson, Adams, and Slade."[34]

Some of those fanatics of the North looked unfavorably upon what was happening. The popular women's novelist and antislavery writer, Lydia Maria Child, was "disheartened sometimes to see how few of the *nominal* abolitionists are *real* ones. Many in this region [around Northampton, Massachusetts,] for instance," she observed with dismay, "have 'their dander up' (as some express it) about their own rights of petition, etc., but

---

[33] William H. Seward to Thurlow Weed, September 8, [1835], Thurlow Weed Papers, Rush Rhees Library, University of Rochester.

[34] Quoted in Russel B. Nye, *Fettered Freedom: Civil Liberties and the Slavery Controversy, 1830–1860* (East Lansing: Michigan State College Press, 1949), pp. 53–54. George Thompson was the English abolitionist; William Slade was a Representative from Vermont.

few really sympathize with the slave." But Child, and her like, lived too frequently disembodied from political reality. "The contest is becoming—has become," wrote the more astute Birney to Gerrit Smith,

one, not alone of freedom for the *black*, but freedom for the *white*. It has now become absolutely necessary, that Slavery should cease in order that freedom may be preserved to any portion of our land. The antagonist principles of liberty and slavery have been roused into action and one or the other must be victorious. There will be no cessation of the strife, until Slavery shall be exterminated, or liberty destroyed.

"It is not only for the emancipation of the enslaved among us that we are contending," he added a year later; "the very principles of republican freedom are menaced with overthrow! The liberty of those yet free is in imminent peril!"[35]

Conflict With the Churches

The political emphasis of the antislavery crusade became paramount only after 1840. More critical during this first decade was the internal dissension which racked the movement. By 1840 all semblance of a unified antislavery crusade was shattered. That the movement had stressed close connections with the churches was not an unmixed blessing. Very early the demands of antislavery belief ran afoul the tenets of church doctrine and church unity. By 1840 the Hicksite Friends, themselves a liberal wing of Quakerism, had split over the antislavery issue. In New England, antislavery Methodists and Baptists both separated themselves from their national church

---

[35] Lydia Maria Child to Theodore Weld, December 29, 1838, in Barnes and Dumond, eds., *Weld-Grimké Letters*, II, 735. James G. Birney to Gerrit Smith, September 13, 1835, in Dwight L. Dumond, ed., *Letters of James Gillespie Birney, 1831–1857*, I (New York: D. Appleton-Century Company, 1938), 243; Birney to Ezekial Webb, Thomas Chandler, Darius C. Jackson, October 6, 1836, in *ibid.*, I, 362.

organizations and, fearful of being overshadowed in secular antislavery organizations, organized their own antislavery societies. The Presbyterian doctrinal split of 1837 was closely linked to antislavery activity. Although the initial dispute was between the orthodox Old School, strong in the South, and the liberal New School, strongest in the North, the attitudes toward slavery held by each group exacerbated the problem.

More important still in the antislavery movement was the struggle between conservative churches and congregations as such and the abolitionists. The dispute, which emerged between 1835 and 1840, was not confined to New England; but its center lay among the Garrisonians of Boston. The churches thought the Garrisonians extremists; the Garrisonians thought the churches indifferent. The churches condemned the Garrisonians as intolerantly un-Christian toward any who disputed them; the Garrisonians branded the churches proslavery. The Reverend Leonard Bacon, New England Congregationalist and long an ardent antislavery worker within the ranks of the American Colonization Society, expressed the view of moderate churchmen. To solve the slavery question, he asserted, was not easy. It depended upon many factors. Therefore, merely to own slaves was not, in the phrase of the day, a *malum in se*. The abolitionists, on the other hand, thought otherwise. John Putnam's congregation in Dunbarton, New Hampshire, by a church vote in 1838, decided to "exclud[e] all slaveholding ministers from their pulpits, and slaveholding church members from their communion."[36] As far as the Garrisonians were concerned, anyone who did not take that position was wrong. They agreed heartily with one of their most colorful brethren, Stephen S. Foster, who happily damned the American churches and their clergy as a "brotherhood of thieves."

---

[36] John M. Putnam, *Sermon on Holding Communion with Extortioners: Preached at Dunbarton, N.H., October 14, 1838* (Concord, N.H.: John R. French, 1838), p. 12.

While Garrison and his friends thus read out the clergy and organized religion, moderate churchmen formed their own organization to combat the growing heresy. In 1834, largely through the efforts of Lyman Beecher, then President of Lane Seminary and a leading Congregational clergyman, the Massachusetts Association of Clergymen adopted a stance which straddled antislavery and colonization. And, when Garrison damned it as "proslavery subservience," the Association retaliated with the American Union for the Relief and Improvement of the Colored Race. Under the particular leadership of John and Charles Tappan in Boston, the Union was supported by the city's Congregational ministry. Try as it might, however, it did not succeed; died, in fact, a speedy death: "a soulless organization," Garrison jeered, "with a sounding title."[37]

The failure of the American Union, however, merely marked the beginning of a major crisis. By 1836 most of the Congregational churches in central New England had closed their doors to abolitionist speakers; and, in 1837, the Church's General Association of Massachusetts closed its pulpits to "itinerant agents and Lecturers" who advanced "sentiments . . . of an erroneous or questionable character."[38] That the ban was general was unfortunate; that it excluded the abolitionists, however, was thought to justify it. The following year the dispute broke into open warfare. A number of clergymen, some of them known as abolitionists, issued a Clerical Appeal, denouncing Garrison's actions and his attack against the clergy for their fellowshipping with slaveholders and their opposition to him. Although there was nothing particularly new in the Appeal, it did crystallize the issue. The Garrisonians of course were delighted. "Tell brother Stanton," crowed Maria Weston Chapman of Boston, "that (to use one of his own felicitous expres-

---

[37] Barnes, *Antislavery Impulse*, pp. 92, 61; quoted in Thomas, *The Liberator*, p. 195.

[38] Quoted in Barnes, *Antislavery Impulse*, p. 96.

sions) 'we are taking the starch out of their sanctified linen' by the dozen." Others, however, were less pleased. Elizur Wright, Secretary of the American Anti-Slavery Society, to whom Mrs. Chapman addressed her remarks, had taken a more judicious view.

I think you must have rated the weight and calibre of Messrs "Woodbury, Fitch & co" [the authors of the Clerical Appeal] far higher than ever I did, to make so serious a matter of their retreat, or whatever else you may please to call it, from the anti slavery ranks. Nor can I see how Garrison stands in any need of our aid—for he seems to have left all his enemies thrice dead behind him, even if he has not killed some of his friends. The truth is, that as much as I regretted and abominated the "appeal"—and I did so most cordially—I was sorry to see Garrison & Phelps expend upon it those annihilating batteries which ought to have been directed to another quarter.

But Elizur Wright was from New York, and his comments did little to heal the now gaping wounds.[39]

Conflict With Other Reforms

Tilting with the clergy was only one part of the compounding confusion. Garrison's interest, more and more, embraced not only antislavery but a whole roster of reforms. As he saw himself and his followers increasingly as universal reformers, by just that degree he complicated the antislavery crusade and confused its adherents. When the American Anti-Slavery Society was organized, in 1833, the efforts of the women were duly noted; and the convention heartily recommended establishing "Ladies' Anti-Slavery Societies as the harbinger of a brighter day."[40] By 1837 numerous regional female antislavery societies

---

[39] Maria Weston Chapman to Elizur Wright, Jr., October 19, 1837, Weston Papers; Elizur Wright, Jr. to M. W. Chapman, September 15, 1837, *ibid.*
[40] *Proceedings of the Anti-Slavery Convention . . . 1833*, p. 17.

had been formed. They were united that year in the Anti-Slavery Convention of American Women. These women did excellent work in the cause, distributing petitions, collecting signatures, writing essays, lecturing, and carrying out the necessary clerical work that such an effort always entails. What rankled many people, however, was that a women's crusade seemed to be getting in the way of the antislavery crusade. Angelina Grimké not only spurred on the women of the South to help overthrow slavery but lectured in the North to audiences which included men. Both Angelina and her sister Sarah actively pursued their women's rights in their prosecution of antislavery work. Startling it was, indeed, to many to see women take on what were assumed to be the prerogatives of men. But, expostulated Maria Weston Chapman about the forthcoming meetings of the American Anti-Slavery Society in 1839, "If a word is said about woman's rights &c I hope the party uttering it will be called to order[,] this being not a question of *Woman's* rights . . . but *Members* rights—*persons* rights."[41] To the conservatives, however, it was mighty disturbing to see those women getting out of line and performing in public.

Women's rights were, indeed, only one of the extraneous reform ventures. After 1835 Garrison became interested in the Perfectionism of John Humphrey Noyes and his Oneida Community. By 1840 he not only rejected government use of force but had espoused a firm nonresistance position. Dissatisfied with the American Peace Society he, Henry Wright, an agent of the American Anti-Slavery Society and the most radical of the nonresistants, and other extremists, founded the New England Non-Resistance Society. But at this even Theodore Weld, most tolerant and generous of abolitionists, balked. He is, wrote Abby Kelley, a not impartial Garrisonian, "unsparingly severe

---

[41] Maria Weston Chapman, draft of letter, [1839], Weston Papers, Vol. I, no. 48.

upon us—Says all that Garrison, M. W. Chapman and all others who have adopted the will a wisp delusions of non-resistance, can possibly do for the emancipation of the slave, will be undermined and counteracted by their idle notions on this subject —Yet not *idle, pernicious* is even too soft a name. . . . Yet," she added with an implicit sigh, "he respects our sincerity and is all toleration."[42]

Conflict Over Political Action

It was confusing enough to have the Garrisonians espouse universal reformism; it was positively ironic that, the more they devoted themselves to those particular will-o'-the-wisps of non-resistance and no-government, the more they ran counter to the growing tendency within the antislavery movement to turn to political action. In fact, incongruous as it seems, the Garrisonians themselves worked both sides of the street. It was, after all, their women who too collected the signatures and circulated the petitions that John Quincy Adams untiringly laid before the Congress.

Significantly, however, politicians who ignored the petitions were likely to find themselves in trouble in their constituencies; the antislavery crusaders were beginning to threaten selective voting in favor of those who supported their cause. The aspiring office-seeker was confronted with probing questions to which he had to give not only formal but also correct answers, as William Seward had reason to know when, in 1838, he received such a questionnaire from New York State abolitionists. The letter that accompanied the questions observed that "the answer with which we may be favored will be promptly and without exception communicated to the public."[43]

---

[42] Abby Kelley to Anne W. Weston, May 28, 1839, Weston Papers.

[43] Copy of a letter from William Jay and Gerrit Smith to William H. Seward, October 1, 1838, in Seward to Thurlow Weed, [October 5], 1838, Weed Papers.

It was perfectly evident that politics was a useful device in the antislavery cause. Its utility was not overlooked even in Garrison's bailiwick. The Massachusetts Anti-Slavery Society noted, in 1838, that, while the slavery question was a moral issue, politics was a branch of morals; political activity, therefore, could legitimately be antislavery activity. Although it eschewed the idea of specific antislavery parties, it felt, as Ellis Gray Loring, Boston lawyer and antislavery Brahmin, said, that "We cannot be justified in abandoning any wide field of action, be it moral, social, religious or political" which, as James G. Birney qualified it, "endeavor[s] to purify both the present parties."44

At the antislavery convention in Cleveland in October, 1839, newspaper editor Myron Holley of Rochester, New York, went further, and moved, though unsuccessfully, the nomination of antislavery presidential and vice-presidential candidates for the 1840 elections. Nor did his subsequent success in achieving support for such nominations at the Monroe County Anti-Slavery Convention in Rochester and again at the larger convention in Warsaw, New York, survive the nominees' rejection of the nominations. That he failed, however, was less significant than that he had tried. The time was not yet quite ripe.

The stalwart Garrisonians were less than enthusiastic about political action. Samuel J. May remained, for the entire decade between 1836 and 1846, "a total-abstinent from politics, viewed in a party light"; but Garrison equivocated and said that a man might vote if his conscience so dictated. The issue was becoming hopelessly confused. "Great efforts are making to form an abolition party in this country," wrote Lewis Tappan to the

---

44 Massachusetts Anti-Slavery Society, *An Address to the Abolitionists of Massachusetts, on the Subject of Political Action* ([Boston]: n.p., [1838]), p. 6. Although the address is signed by Francis Jackson for the Board of Managers, the copy in Widener Library of Harvard College has Loring's name penned in, presumably by Charles Sumner. James G. Birney to Salmon P. Chase, June 5, 1837, Chase Papers, Library of Congress, quoted in Filler, *Crusade against Slavery*, p. 141.

English abolitionist, John Scoble, late in 1839. "The number of abolitionists is now so large here, and their voices on many points so various, that it will be impossible, I think, to have them united long. In fact they are disunited already. There will probably be an abolition political party—a religious association—a Garrison party, &c &c."[45]

Finally, in the spring of 1840, at the annual meeting of the American Anti-Slavery Society, the real drama took place. Determined that the New York moderates should no longer control the Society, Garrison and a boatload of supporters from Boston and vicinity sailed, in festive holiday mood, to New York, there to pack the sessions, and there, in the end, to capture the American Anti-Slavery Society for themselves. Though fraught with all the passionate melodrama of the best horse-opera tradition, this episode did little except proclaim publicly a schism already well developed. For the New Yorkers were moderate, the Bostonians were militant. The New Yorkers were conservative; the Bostonians, radical. The former worked closely with the churches, the latter damned them. New York welcomed political action, Boston remained skeptical or hostile. And, lest there be any doubt, the Bostonians welcomed the women with open arms; but Lewis Tappan testily observed that "women have equal rights with men, and therefore they have a right to form societies of women only. Men have the same right. *Men* formed the Amer. Anti S. Society."[46] With such malediction on the folk in Boston the New York faction walked out of the convention, surrendered the American Anti-Slavery Society to the Garrisonians, and founded, the very next day, the American and Foreign Anti-Slavery Society.

---

[45] Samuel May, Jr. to J. B. Estlin, February 26, 1846, May Papers. W. P. and F. J. Garrison, *William Lloyd Garrison*, II, 290. Lewis Tappan to John Scoble, December 10, 1839, Tappan Papers, Library of Congress, quoted in Filler, *Crusade against Slavery*, p. 152.

[46] Lewis Tappan to Theodore Weld, May 26, 1840, Barnes and Dumond, eds., *Weld-Grimké Letters*, II, 836.

Neither group effectively survived the surgery thus attempted. From then on the American Anti-Slavery Society declined in status, and its rival organization never achieved significant power. The antislavery movement had, in reality, passed out of the control of the moral reformers and into the hands of the politically-minded antislavery men.

The Emergence of Political Antislavery

"If the Anti Slavery organizations cannot find better business in [the] future than they have been engaged by, for a year or two back, they will assuredly die." Ellis Gray Loring was not quite right in that prediction for both the American and the American and Foreign Anti-Slavery Societies limped on through the 1840's and 1850's. But "all hopes of fusing into one the main divisions of the anti-slavery host" were, Theodore Weld thought, "utterly vain." The reasons, he noted presciently, were "personal animosities and repulsions."[47] 1843 was particularly calculated to demonstrate the point. In May the Boston and New York factions of the American Anti-Slavery Society argued over whether they ought to give up the New York headquarters. They eventually made peace. The New York committee remained as the organization's front, while the real power was transferred to Boston. But they made little progress. In June, at the New England Anti-Slavery Convention, Stephen Foster excoriated the Executive Committee in general and Lydia Maria Child in particular, blasted the churches, and damned Frederick Douglass' lack of anticlerical vigor. In a subsequent clash between Foster and Edmund Quincy, the President of the convention, only the pleas of Wendell Phillips

---

[47] Ellis Gray Loring to Lydia M. Child, April 29, 1841, in Loring Letterpress Book, Houghton Collection, Harvard College Library. Theodore Weld to Lewis Tappan, February 3, 1843, quoted in Barnes, *Antislavery Impulse*, p. 194.

and Garrison for order saved the meeting from uproarious dissolution.

Nor was 1843 the only bad year. Four years later, for example, Frederick Douglass fell out with Garrison over his insistence upon establishing a new antislavery paper. Dissuaded from setting up in Boston after "the leading antislavery friends" had convinced him that it would "draw away support from the Anti Slavery journals now established" and would "be likely . . . to keep up the colored distinction," Douglass went off to Rochester and started a paper anyway.[48] The fact was that Douglass was moving away from the radicals and toward political antislavery.

There was less bickering within the American and Foreign Anti-Slavery Society; but, Samuel May, Jr., said, it was "scarcely more than 'a shadow of a name.'" By 1850 it was too poor to employ a single agent. And, by 1852, when it was reorganized, it had ceased to be more than a "paper organization."[49] In the political arena, however, things were better. The petition campaign had been waged with good success; and in 1844 the Whigs, with some northern Democratic support, voted down the Gag. Meanwhile Joshua Giddings, antislavery Representative from Ohio, had demonstrated in dramatic fashion the growing importance of the abolitionist faction in Congress. Censured by the House in 1842 for his antislavery resolutions presented during the discussion of the Creole Case,[50] Giddings resigned his seat, stood for re-election, and was triumphantly returned to Washington. Thereafter his Whig colleagues toler-

---

[48] Samuel May, Jr. to J. B. Estlin, May 29, 1847, May Papers.

[49] *Ibid.*, February 25, 1847. Filler, *Crusade against Slavery*, p. 261n.

[50] The Creole Case concerned a coastal slaver going from Hampton Roads to New Orleans. The slaves seized the ship and took her to the British port of Nassau. There nineteen of the slaves were charged with murder; the rest were set free. The liberation of the slaves became a diplomatic issue between the United States and Britain, and the status of slaves on the high seas was debated in Congress.

ated his antislavery views in return for his vote on other issues.

Giddings' action symbolized the dilemma that political antislavery would have to face. To work through politics meant to adopt the techniques of compromise, to work within the framework of the possible, to temper ardent devotion to principle with a keen eye for the voting tallies. Giddings was quite aware of that when, campaigning in Ohio in 1842, he urged antislavery people to work within the major political parties, to avoid political splits whenever possible; when he urged that Henry Clay need not be rejected just because he was a slaveholder. Slavery, after all, was legal in the South, explained Giddings; Clay, after all, was a Whig.

No major political figure of the 1840's and 1850's recognized political reality better than New York's William Seward. "It is not in human nature," he wrote in 1845, "that all who desire the abolition of slavery should be inflamed with equal zeal, and different degrees of fervor produce different opinions concerning the measures proper to be adopted." If some, like William Ellery Channing, feared involvement in political issues, or like Francis LeMoyne, who rejected the vice-presidential nomination of the Liberty Party in 1839, feared that political involvement might tempt men from "high and holy principle of right"; still more and more antislavery crusaders were drawn to political action.[51]

Constitutional Theory

Effective political action, however, had to be grounded in an adequate political and Constitutional theory. Did the provisions

---

[51] [Joshua R. Giddings], *The Rights and Privileges of the Several States in Regard to Slavery; Being a Series of Essays, Published in The Western Reserve Chronicle, (Ohio,) after the Election of 1842* (n.p.: n.p., [1842]). William H. Seward to Salmon P. Chase et al, May 1845, in Frederick W. Seward, *William H. Seward; an Autobiography from 1801 to 1834. With a Memoir of his Life and Selections from his Letters...*, I (New York: Derby and Miller, 1891), 742. Francis J. LeMoyne to James G. Birney, December 10, 1839, in Dumond, ed., *Birney Letters*, I, 514.

of the Declaration of Independence relating to equality and to inalienable rights govern the interpretation of the Constitution? Were they part of the fundamental law of the land? Did the three-fifths compromise in the Constitution recognize slavery or did it relate only to taxation and representation? Did the Constitutional provision against ending the slave trade before 1808 and the fact that in 1808 the trade was abolished make the Constitution a slavery or an antislavery instrument? Was the provision for the return of fugitives from service a federal recognition of property rights in slaves or was it concerned solely with interstate executive relations? Clearly these were questions of import to the antislavery crusade. Clearly they demanded answers.

Those who argued that the Constitution was an antislavery document did not rely solely upon axiomatic truths grounded in antislavery convictions but examined political institutions and theory as well and analyzed the Constitution in detail. John Quincy Adams was exceedingly pragmatic about the whole affair. Unwilling to accept the position that the Constitution was already antislavery, he proposed to limit and gradually to abolish slavery by Constitutional amendment. Adams' viewpoint insisted that, though the Constitution was not *ipso facto* antislavery, it could be made so. From a different vantage point William Jay noted that, since the Constitution did not specifically sanction slavery, it existed only by toleration. This meant, as Weld observed, that slavery was a local or municipal institution and that government might either refuse to support it or, more actively, legislate against it. Pushing still further some argued that slavery had been abolished by the Declaration of Independence, that it had never been re-established, and that it was therefore illegal everywhere. The slave, consequently, had been deprived of Constitutional guarantees of due process of law and should be set free by the courts. William Goodell observed that Congress' right to regulate interstate commerce gave it the power to abolish slavery; and that the

Constitutional requirement of republican government automatically outlawed the despotism of slavery. Finally, there were those who urged that the Government, under the war powers of the Constitution as well as under the general welfare clause, had ample forces to cope, as Birney put it, with a "vicious and dangerous state of things existing in the community generally."[52]

Robert Rantoul, young Democratic reformer of Boston, on the other hand, construed the Constitution narrowly and still came to antislavery conclusions. He urged that if, with a strict interpretation of the Constitution, slavery was outside its bounds, then all proslavery arguments on the federal level would be pointless. Rantoul maintained that the three-fifths ratio was a political compromise which pertained only to taxation. Insisting that the injunction to deliver up fugitives was addressed to the states, he concluded that the federal government had no authority to legislate concerning fugitive slaves. The purpose of the Constitution was to protect liberty; that of the Union, to guarantee independence. Clearly, then, the Constitution must be an antislavery document. In a different argument, yet taking the same strict view, Frederick Douglass contended that, Madison's journals and court decisions notwithstanding, the Constitution meant exactly what it said and nothing more.

Not all the antislavery crusaders, however, construed the Constitution as an antislavery document. The Garrisonians, in particular, were adamantly certain that the Constitution was a proslavery document. Whether or not their assessment was any more simplistic than that of the *anti*slavery interpretation, their arguments made it seem so. Slavery, they contended, existed under the Constitution, therefore the Constitution must be a proslavery document. The three-fifths ratio, the time limit on

---

[52] James G. Birney to the Hartford Committee, August 15, 1844, *ibid.*, II, 834.

ending the slave trade, the provisions for returning fugitives, all recognized slavery and in that recognition tarred the Constitution with the sinfulness of the institution. The Constitution, proclaimed the Garrisonians, was a "Covenant with Death and an agreement with Hell." It followed that no abolitionist could support the Constitution. And from that followed the Garrisonian doctrine of disunion. As early as 1842 Garrison had written, "I go . . . for the repeal of the union between the North and the South." And even so *un*Garrisonian a person as William Ellery Channing, contemplating the possible annexation of Texas, declared, "So I say, let the Union be dissevered rather than receive Texas into the confederacy. . . . The free States should declare that the very act of admitting Texas will be construed as a dissolution of the Union"; for, if it were not so construed, then the North would have to play soldier and policeman for slavery itself.[53] In 1845 Wendell Phillips spelled out the ramifications of the argument in answer to his title question, "Can Abolitionists Vote or Take Office?" The answer, he replied, was No. To take office and to vote implied support of the government and Constitution in their entirety. Partial support and private interpretation were untenable, because they ran counter to the very basis of organized society. The only alternative was to withhold support completely. It was a long and involved argument, but the point was clear. Ultimately one would be driven beyond nonparticipation and no-government to explicit disunion and to implicit revolution.

It was a timid quibbling when, in 1857, Phillips observed that disunion meant political disunion only and would not affect trade, commerce, or the enforcement of legal contracts. More realistic was the rejoinder offered by those whose antislavery zeal was less doctrinaire. Very early William Goodell raised his voice against disunion. It would get nowhere, he

---

[53] William L. Garrison to George W..Benson, March 22, 1842, in W. P. and F. J. Garrison, *William Lloyd Garrison*, III, 49. William E. Channing quoted in *ibid.*, III, 61.

asserted, because it begged the issue of antislavery. To break away in disunion, he pointed out, was only to abandon the slave to the South and leave untouched those men in the North who were proslavery still. Disunion, he continued, would not alter the Black Codes of the North. If the end of antislavery was to exorcise evil from society, then disunion only left evil in control. "I think," wrote William Seward, cutting to the heart of the palaver, "that a disseverence of the American Union . . . would be a calamity to be deplored equally by the free states and the slave states and disastrous to the hopes of the lovers of freedom and humanity throughout the world."[54] That comment was directed squarely at the Garrisonians.

In line with the desire for practical action, a resolution among the constitutional arguments seemed imperative—and the easiest resolution was to ignore the clash and remove the argument to another level. Whether or not the Constitution was antislavery became largely irrelevant if one looked to natural law and natural rights as the cornerstone of any political system. In the middle 1830's Charles Follen had argued for the universal equality of men and women, native-born and foreigners, Negroes and whites alike. And Edward Beecher, clergyman and President of Illinois College, had observed, in his commentary on the Alton riots, that, despite chattel slavery, the Negro was a human being still. "We are to exert ourselves," urged Beriah Green in 1846, "for the enfranchisement of the Slave, not because he is a *Negro,* but because he is a MAN. On the same principle, we are to exert ourselves to secure to ALL our fellow-citizens the free enjoyment of all their rights. Otherwise, lacking consistency, we shall lose our power." Then, speaking on the admission of California before the Senate in 1850, Seward noted dramatically that "there is a higher law

---

[54] Draft of letter from William H. Seward to [Thomas W. Higginson, *et. al.*], January 3, 185[7], William H. Seward Papers, Rush Rhees Library, University of Rochester.

than the Constitution, which regulates our authority over the domain, and devotes it to the same noble purposes [as the Constitution]."[55] Potent words, indeed. For those who did not find the Constitution thoroughly antislavery and yet sought political action without revolution, the Higher Law provided a way out.

The Liberty Party

Rejecting Garrisonian disunion, resting wherever possible on an antislavery interpretation of the Constitution, occasionally appealing to the Higher Law exclusively, those who undertook antislavery action formed parties separate from the old Whig and Democratic Parties, which seemed increasingly wedded to proslavery views. Political action had been better than inaction. Hopefully action through antislavery parties would achieve, if not immediate emancipation, at least such mitigation of the worst evils of slavery as was possible in the real world.

The earlier attempts of Myron Holley to form an antislavery third party finally came to fruition in the Albany, New York, convention of the National Liberty Party in 1840, which nominated James Birney and Thomas Earle of Pennsylvania its presidential and vice-presidential candidates. Since colonization, church action, petitions, pressure on the major parties, and all other forms of antislavery action had failed, Alvan Stewart, Liberty Party leader, asserted, it was necessary to create a new political party: a party, as Professor Dwight L. Dumond summarized it, based upon the Bible, the Higher Law, the principles of equality and inalienable rights, and the antislavery interpretation of the Constitution.[56] That was enough to satisfy the most diverse tastes.

---

[55] Beriah Green to James G. Birney, December 17, 1846, Dumond, ed., *Birney Letters*, II, 1032. William H. Seward, *Speech on the Admission of California*, pp. 27-28.

[56] Dwight L. Dumond, "Introduction," *Birney Letters*, I, x–xi.

Within a year, however, the more astute political abolitionists questioned the efficacy of an exclusively antislavery party and wondered whether the better part of wisdom and the more successful part of valor did not consist of putting the new party into the mainstream of politics, of giving it a broader base from which to draw votes. The issue of success in the real world plagued the new party. As early as 1841, after the disappointing 7,000 votes cast for Birney in 1840, it became imperative to decide what blend of political expediency and antislavery idealism would make the Liberty Party a significant political antislavery force. Salmon Chase gave the politician's view, saying that "we think it better to limit our *political action* by the *political power*, explicitly and avowedly, rather than run the risk of misconstruction by saying that we aim at *immediate and universal emancipation by political action.*" Birney considered such opportunism sheer heresy, yet even he came to realize that a party based only on abolition had little chance for political success. So the old argument of 1840 about combining antislavery activity with other issues was revived within the Liberty Party. By 1846 even Lewis Tappan, who had refused to tolerate such a mixture within the American Anti-Slavery Society, came reluctantly to agree "that the Liberty party, in order to accomplish much, must be a *reform* party" and "include other subjects of reformation" than antislavery.[57] Birney, cheered by his vote of 62,000 in 1844, agreed.

Candidates as well as principles were involved in third party politics. Should only staunch antislavery men be Liberty Party candidates or should the party seek experienced politicians who were sympathetic to the antislavery position? Choosing to experiment with the latter course, the party had then to find candidates willing to risk themselves and their careers as its standard-bearers. Thrice, indeed, did William Henry Seward,

---

[57] Salmon P. Chase, quoted in W. P. and F. J. Garrison, *William Lloyd Garrison*, III, 61. Lewis Tappan to James G. Birney, March 10, 1846, Dumond, ed., *Birney Letters*, II, 1006-1007.

already well-known for his antislavery stand as Governor of New York, reject the party's invitation to be its 1844 presidential candidate, yet not before the offer pointed up dissension within the party. On the one hand, as Beriah Green later noted in speaking for the purists, "to offer (vote) office or accept of office on any other ground and for any other purpose, than to furnish a true *medium,* thro' which the throne of the Messiah may be reflected, is exceedingly absurd and immeasurably wicked. It is high treason. It is Devil-worship." On the other hand, the more pragmatic Michigan editor, Theodore Foster, observed rather testily of this ministerial point of view that too many Liberty Party speakers and leaders were clergymen who "are mostly opposed to venturing out politically: they will not do it: and they will keep the men with them."[58]

The Free Soil Party

Though the Liberty Party experienced internal dissension and had a short life, its experience did establish third parties as a mode of antislavery action. The issue of the annexation of Texas and the subsequent war with Mexico gave considerable impetus to the general antislavery cause and added additional fuel to the political fire. It intensified an already growing fear that the South and its northern capitalist minions—the "Slave Power Conspiracy" as it was dramatically called—were seizing control of the nation's destiny. Specifically the issue crystallized in 1847 over the disposition of territory taken from Mexico. Out of it emerged the Free Soil Party, whose purpose was to keep slavery from the newly acquired territory. There was more to it than that, however, for the Free Soilers also absorbed several dissident political factions: the radical Barnburners in the New York Democracy, the political activists of the Liberty

---

[58] Beriah Green to James G. Birney, April 6, 1952, *ibid.,* II, 1143; Theodore Foster to Birney, August 1, 1946, *ibid.,* II, 1025.

Party, and a number of major antislavery Democrats such as Charles Sumner of Massachusetts and Salmon P. Chase of Ohio. Sumner himself, in 1848, had, in most striking language, linked the lords of the loom with those of the lash; and, by implication, Democratic principle with antislavery belief. Whether the connection was well-founded may be doubted. But without much question the Free Soil Party seemed to have filled the need for an antislavery party related to broader political issues and to have moderated idealism with a good measure of expediency. In 1848, Martin Van Buren, its antiabolitionist presidential candidate, received 291,000 votes.

Early in the free soil agitation Joshua Leavitt, New York abolitionist and a leader of the Free Soil Party, remarked that "the Liberty party is not dead but TRANSLATED"; a translation suggested by the Free Soil motto, "FREE SOIL, FREE SPEECH, FREE LABOR, AND FREE MEN." That this broader political movement won no more support from the Garrisonians than had the Liberty Party is not surprising since Massachusetts orthodoxy had condemned the Liberty Party for compromising antislavery principle with political ambition. Its one redeeming feature, Garrison remarked caustically, was that the Free Soil Party was leading "inevitably" to disunion and "hence I hail it as the beginning of the end." But Samuel May, Jr., pointed out that the Liberty Party had moved en bloc into the "so-called Free Soil Party"; that "they [the Liberty Party] are utterly annihilated as a party, and their leaders . . . will soon fall to their true level of shame; the more they are known, the less will they be trusted." Political activist though he was, Frederick Douglass likewise feared that the free soil movement was a compromising bit of political action sure to lead to "folly and hypocrisy, without advancing the cause of freedom at all." The fact of the matter, as Professor Louis Filler correctly states, was that "the Free-Soil party was not an expansion of Liberty-party principles, but a catch-all political platform for abolitionists and antiabolitionists."[59] That the Compromise of 1850, by resolving the territorial issue, could kill the party only indicated its remoteness from real antislavery dedication. After a Free Soil vote of only 156,000 in 1852, the party did not recover its strength two years later during the Kansas-Nebraska debate. The Free Soil Party had also failed.

The Republican Party

The problems which bedeviled the Liberty and then the Free Soil parties were but opposite sides of the same coin. In the former case political reality had been largely sacrificed for an idealistic moral principle. In the latter case moral principle had been lost in a welter of passing political expediencies. Only with the formation of the Republican Party in 1854 did there seem to be a viable marriage between the moral and practical wings of antislavery thought. Drawing to its ranks not only the former following of the Liberty and Free Soil parties but also the antislavery remnant of shattered Whiggery and the staunchly antislavery Democrats disillusioned by the Kansas-Nebraska Act, the Republican Party appeared at the right time to capitalize upon the disruption of the old parties and to absorb not only their antislavery components but also their ambitious leaders and dissatisfied supporters. Although the dramatic pyrotechnics of the party, both in the Senate and in Kansas, seemed to identify it largely with antislavery, its fundamental principles were anti-extension and the protection of northern economic interests both in the territories and in the

---

[59] Leavitt quoted in Griffin, *Their Brothers' Keepers*, p. 171. Garrison to Helen B. Garrison, July 26, 1848, in W. P. and F. J. Garrison, *William Lloyd Garrison*, III, 231. Samuel May, Jr., to J. B. Estlin, September 19, 1848, May Papers. Frederick Douglass, "What Good Has the Free Soil Movement Done?" in Philip S. Foner, ed., *The Life and Writings of Frederick Douglass*, I (New York: International Publishers, 1950–1955), 367. Filler, *Crusade against Slavery*, p. 191.

Congress. The anti-extension potential of the party was, however, eliminated in 1857 by the Dred Scott Decision, which denied that Congress had the right to legislate about slavery in the territories. With a Constitutional amendment on slavery a political impossibility, the Republican Party was, therefore, left with no means to carry out its anti-extension principle except by appealing to the Higher Law or by relying on the municipal nature of slavery. At the very moment, therefore, when a viable political mechanism for antislavery emerged, the avenues for legal political action were closed. That Kansas, the scene of bloody civil conflict, was the focus of political antislavery tragically emphasized the frustration of the fifties.

Civil Rights and Negro Equality

In addition to the question of slavery in the territories, the twin issues of guaranteeing civil rights for the free Negro and of protecting the fugitive slave were central to the antislavery crusade during the 1850's. Both, of course, had been constant concerns of antislavery people from the very beginning. The idea of immediate emancipation carried with it the implicit assumption that the Negro was entitled to the same civil rights as the white man. Though this assumption was often obscured or denied in the 1830's by the equivocation over the meaning of immediate emancipation, support for it did accompany the birth of the American Anti-Slavery Society and increased as the abolitionist ranks grew. The abolitionists' rejection of African colonization rested largely on the ground that it violated the Negroes' right to civil equality. And, of course, the Negroes, regarding colonization as forced emigration, rejected it for precisely the same reason. Meeting in national convention in Philadelphia in 1833 they affirmed that they preferred not to emigrate at all; but that, if necessary, they might go to the American West, "where the *plough-share* of prejudice has as yet been unable to penetrate the soil," or to Canada.[60] At least they insisted that such emigration be within the American continent, for they considered America their native land and themselves citizens of the United States—and entitled to the rights thereof.

Nor did Negroes docilely accept discrimination at home. In 1832, for example, Philadelphia Negroes petitioned the State legislature to implement their civil liberties by not enforcing the Fugitive Slave Act of 1793; and six years later an "Appeal of 40,000 Citizens," written for the committee by the Negro leader, Robert Purvis, argued against a change in the Pennsylvania Constitution which would disfranchise the Negroes, who had long been able to vote in the state. The antislavery societies also actively fought for Negro rights. The Declaration of Sentiments of the American Anti-Slavery Society affirmed that Negroes, as well as whites, were entitled to receive education, to hold property, and to enjoy full civil rights.

The abolitionists did not confine themselves to the issue of civil equality as solely a legal problem but early came to probe its connection with racial prejudice. "The duty of the whites in regard to this cruel prejudice [against the Negroes]," said the American Anti-Slavery Society, "is not to indulge it, but to repent and overcome it." Abolitionists also saw that law, especially Northern Black Codes, reinforced prejudice. "The repeal of all laws, making a difference because of *Color* or *descent* is indispensible," argued Birney in the middle 1840's. "Without this no effectual or permanent improvement of the great body of colored people can be brought about." If men would only, "in their social intercourse," he argued, "treat the colored people just as Christian gentlemen ought to treat them were they not colored people, they will do more in ten years toward

---

[60] American Society of the Free Persons of Colour, *Minutes and Proceedings of the Third Annual Convention for the Improvement of the Free People of Colour in the United States* (New York: n.p., 1833), p. 28.

making them virtuous and moral, happy and useful, than by centuries of labor bestowed on them as a separate class."[61]

Nonetheless, despite Garrison's assertion, in 1837, that the abolitionists were for total abolition and, "as a just consequence, [for] the complete enfranchisement of our colored countrymen," the preference among the antislavery crusaders remained the rather more general wish "to elevate the character and condition of the people of color, by encouraging their intellectual, moral, and religious improvement. . . ." To implement their wish, the movement frequently sponsored vocational training for the Negroes. The short-lived American Union for the Relief and Improvement of the Colored Race, for example, hoped to "begin the education and industrial training of Negroes."[62] Frederick Douglass was convinced that the Negroes primarily needed sound preparation in the mechanical arts to enable them to earn respectable livings and to demonstrate to their white fellow-countrymen that they were indeed capable. The National Colored Convention in 1848 urged the Negro to eschew menial tasks as a badge of slavery, but to prepare himself as a mechanic, tradesman, or skilled artisan.

One group of Negroes and whites attacked the problem in somewhat more systematic fashion, founding and running a number of Negro communities in Canada and in the western states. The Wilberforce, Dawn, Elgin, and Refugee Home Society settlements in western Ontario, as well as several lesser ones in Ohio and Michigan, tried, according to definite plan, to train their Negro residents to be self-dependent. If, in the end, these communities enjoyed very limited success, nevertheless

---

[61] American Anti-Slavery Society to Theodore Weld, 1834, in Barnes and Dumond, eds., *Weld-Grimké Letters*, I, 126. James G. Birney to William Wright, June 20, 1845, in Dumond, ed., *Birney Letters*, II, 945, 947.

[62] Quoted in W. P. and F. J. Garrison, *William Lloyd Garrison*, II, 199. American Anti-Slavery Society, Constitution, Article III, in *Proceedings of the Anti-Slavery Convention. . . 1833*, p. 7. Barnes, *Antislavery Impulse*, p. 62.

their academic education and more thorough agricultural training did demonstrate that positive action by the friends of the Negro was not impossible. Unfortunately, however, these communities, like the Underground Railroad which led toward them, were often disparaged by antislavery people, particularly the Garrisonians, for dealing with a few Negroes directly and missing the rest, when, by the more favored way of propagandizing and moral earnestness, millions presumably would be assisted. It was the perennial issue of the abolitionist crusade—limited practical action or general pious exhortation.

Despite their limitations, however, the antislavery crusaders did accomplish some extension of rights for free Negroes in the North. Sharing with their fellow-countrymen a boundless faith in the efficacies of education, they directed much of their energy to extending school opportunities for Negroes. And here, more than in any other area, perhaps, the importance of civil rights became evident. Though vandalism forced Prudence Crandall to close her school, and the argument of William W. Ellsworth failed to win her acquittal in the lower court, still his argument in her defense and against Connecticut's law restricting education in the state for any "person of color" not a resident of the state was fundamental to the whole issue. That the Negro paid taxes and fulfilled other obligations of citizenship meant, contended Ellsworth, that the Negro was a citizen. As a citizen he was entitled to an education. To deny him the franchise or to argue that he resided in another state could not impair his citizen's right to an education. Ellsworth's argument was only the beginning. Although never more than in token numbers during the next three decades, Negroes were admitted to schools of the country; and increasingly the emphasis was against segregation. Maria Weston Chapman came straight to the point when she insisted that *"exclusive* instruction, teaching for *blacks,* a school founded on color, a church in which men are herded ignominiously apart from the refining influence of association with the more highly educated and accomplished—what are they? A direct way of fitting white men for tyrants, and black men for slaves."[63]

The same issue presented itself in 1849 in the Roberts Case in Boston. Charles Sumner, arguing eloquently, if unsuccessfully, in behalf of the Negro girl, Sarah Roberts, held that the idea of equality developed in the Enlightenment meant essentially the idea of equal rights. Separate schools, he argued, created a caste system; and caste, he continued, was a heathenish and monstrous institution. Separation in education, he therefore concluded, was not equal. Consequently, he pleaded, it was the duty of the court to declare against segregated schools. Similar arguments were used elsewhere. James Wheaton, a member of the Committee on Education of the General Assembly of the State of Rhode Island, in his Minority Report of 1851, argued that segregated education meant civil decapacitation, inferior schooling, unfair taxation, and social stigma. Neither Wheaton nor Sumner represented, in the event, the victor. Yet time seemed on their side; for, in Massachusetts, separate schools were abolished in 1855; and, in Rhode Island, ten years later.

Even though the abolitionists did not succeed in overcoming all prejudice against the Negro, they struggled valiantly against this most insidious form of discrimination. They argued against the assertion that the Negro was an inferior creature, damned by virtue of his color. John Rankin said, for example, that the Negro was really white—like all other men—and that his blackness was caused by his living in the torrid zone, which caused "a coagulated substance" between the epidermis and the dermis to turn black from exposure to the sun. And the *Quarterly Anti-Slavery Magazine* for January 1837 carried a piece about the different intensities of color in plants, men, and animals, ascribing them to geography and particularly to

---

[63] Maria Weston Chapman, *"How Can I Help to Abolish Slavery?" or, Counsels to the Newly Converted* (Anti-Slavery Tract No. 14) (New York: American Anti-Slavery Society, [1855], pp. 4–5.

the heat needs of the organisms. Others argued against prejudice in simpler terms. Garrison, Frederick Douglass recalled, simply said that *"Prejudice against color was rebellion against God."*[64]

Most importantly, of course, the abolitionists realized that, while prejudice was a sin to be repented of, still they could scarcely complain about the South's treatment of the slaves if they did little to improve the Negroes' lot in the North. Time and again Garrison demanded an end to discrimination in public transportation and in church pews as well as in schools. He fought for the repeal of a Massachusetts law against interracial marriage. He urged Negroes to fight discrimination in the courts and to use their right of franchise or, where it was denied them, to work to get that right. Adin Ballou, in his *Discourse on Slavery*, admonished Americans to restore the slave to manhood by insuring his right to own property and to benefit from equal treatment before the law. In 1848 the American and Foreign Anti-Slavery Society prepared a pamphlet on the northern Black Codes; and many antislavery societies insisted, with the New England Anti-Slavery Society, that free Negroes should have equal "civil and political rights and privileges with the whites." On the whole, they were as good as their word, refusing to exclude Negroes from their organizations. "Those Societies that reject colored members, or seek to avoid them," resolved the Anti-Slavery Women's Convention in New York in 1837, "have never been active or efficient.... The abandonment of prejudice is required of us as a proof of our sincerity and consistency."[65]

Yet that the issue came up at all tells something of the strength of prejudice even among the abolitionists; and Martin Delany's contention that the Negro was frequently crowded off the antislavery stage is not without validity. Negroes, sometimes feeling themselves excluded or at least downgraded,

---

[64] Quoted in W. P. and F. J. Garrison, *William Lloyd Garrison*, II, 292.

[65] Quoted in Louis Ruchames, "Race, Marriage and Abolition in Massachusetts," *Journal of Negro History*, XL (July 1955) 254–255.

Introduction lxxiii

actively sought a more conspicuous role in the antislavery crusade. They not only contributed directly to the general antislavery movement, but also established independent organizations and created their own press.

The antislavery societies made great effort to publicize, laud, and employ the Negro in the crusade. They made much of individual, talented Negroes, particularly if they were bona-fide ex-slaves, as writers and lecturers, and exhibited them for all mankind to admire. Frederick Douglass, Charles Remond, William C. Nell, and William Wells Brown were all lecturers in the antislavery vineyard. And among those who wrote their own narratives were Douglass (probably the most articulate) and Brown; of those whose autobiographies were ghosted, probably the best known was Uncle Tom's prototype, Josiah Henson of the Dawn Community in Ontario.

Frequently, however, friction developed between these Negroes and the white antislavery leadership. Frederick Douglass, for example, split with the Garrisonians. Not only was there the substantive issue over political action when Douglass became an active supporter of the Liberty Party; Douglass further offended by publishing his own paper. Very irritating to the Negro activists was the patronizing air which so many whites adopted toward them. Maria Weston Chapman, for example, undertook indirectly to coach Douglass in appropriate conduct during a lecture tour he made in England, worrying lest he be bribed and weaned away by the anti-Garrisonians of the British and Foreign Anti-Slavery Society. And the minister, Henry Highland Garnet, resented what he considered Mrs. Chapman's insufferable attempts to interfere in his affairs.[66]

These and similar frictions caused many Negroes to rely more and more upon their own resources. During the 1850's,

---

[66] The Weston Papers contain significant examples of both the patronizing air and Negro abolitionist response. See especially Frederick Douglass to Maria Weston Chapman, March 29, 1846. Filler, *Crusade against Slavery*, p. 143.

therefore, they organized a series of colored conventions, hopeful of accomplishing for themselves what they feared the whites would not accomplish. They were, in a way, latter-day successors, though of a milder sort, to David Walker, who in his *Appeal* of 1829 had exhorted the Negroes to direct action and, implicitly, to violence. In some cases the Negroes even showed a renewed interest in colonization. Martin Delany organized a primitive black nationalist movement—back to Africa—bitterly chastising the antislavery movement as a whole for excluding the Negro from its activities. Even Birney, who had earlier supported colonization and then rejected it, was disillusioned by the Negroes' failure to achieve justice in the United States and urged them to return to Africa as the only place where they could avoid prejudice and inequality.

The Fugitive Slave Cases

The general question of Negro civil rights was dramatized in the specific issue of the fugitive slave. The issue had existed since the very early days of the antislavery crusade. The Federal Act of 1793 had provided for the return of escaped slaves, and early antislavery action on behalf of fugitives grew out of the terms of that Act. It was a prime concern to thwart the "kidnapers," as they were called, who pursued the fugitives into the North and carried them back to the South. The first significant challenge to the Act of 1793 did not come, however, until 1837, in the case of Prigg *vs.* Pennsylvania, which concerned the seizure and return to Maryland of a Negro escaped from his master and fugitive in Pennsylvania. The court's decision in 1842—the case had gone to the Supreme Court by the common agreement of both states—was a mixed victory for antislavery forces. The Pennsylvania law which guaranteed the fugitive regular judicial proceedings was declared unconstitutional because it interfered with federal statute. But, by thus separating state and federal function, the decision allowed states to forbid their officials to enforce the Fugitive Slave Act, now the sole responsibility of federal officers. This point of the court's decision became the basis of later personal liberty laws forbidding state officials to assist in enforcing the 1793 statute.

In another case, in 1839, Governor William H. Seward of New York refused to surrender to Virginia three sailors demanded by that state for their part in helping to free a slave. Seward argued that slave stealing was not a crime in New York and therefore he could not accede to Virginia's request—a position he maintained through several years of mutual recriminations and retaliations.

Still another case, in 1841, involved slaves aboard a Spanish vessel, the *Amistad,* who had mutinied and seized the vessel. It was later boarded by the crew of an American naval vessel and brought to New Haven where the Negroes were interned. The Spanish government demanded that the Negroes be returned. The abolitionists challenged the request in federal district and circuit courts. Eventually the case went to the Supreme Court where John Quincy Adams won freedom for most of the Negroes on various grounds of technical error, of faulty Spanish diplomatic methods, and, most importantly, of the right of *habeas corpus* and the principles of the Declaration of Independence. In all of these cases the civil rights of Negroes were at stake. In each instance, the antislavery forces won a substantial victory.

Other fugitive slave cases revolved around the Underground Railroad and illegal assistance given escaping slaves. The justification for such action was, of course, that the Higher Law condoned lawbreaking in the interests of a greater moral good. "I agree with you fully," wrote Amos Phelps to Charles Torrey, who subsequently died while imprisoned for helping slaves escape, "in the doctrine that the slave laws & all other wicked laws, are to be habitually & everywhere *disobeyed.* In their *requirements & prohibitions they are in equity & before God, a nullity & are to be treated as such.*"⁶⁷ Many were the stalwart antislavery folk, both North and South, who wholeheartedly agreed and who flouted the laws.

Only in the North, however, could violations provide significant test cases of the Fugitive Slave Law. Illustrative of these tests was the case of John Van Zandt of Ohio. Van Zandt had harbored a fugitive slave and was sued by the slave's owner, Wharton Jones. The case went to the Supreme Court. Both Salmon P. Chase and William H. Seward, counsels for Van Zandt, argued their case not only on the grounds of faulty evidence but on the more significant grounds that the Act of 1793 violated the Northwest Ordinance and that it conflicted with the Constitution. To plug any loopholes they also appealed to the Higher Law. Few were surprised, however, when Van Zandt lost his case.

With the passage of the Fugitive Slave Act as part of the Compromise of 1850, the fugitive slave's protection was further undermined. Special commissioners were appointed to determine whether an accused Negro was a fugitive. They were paid on a piecework basis—paid twice as much to find the Negro a fugitive as to find him not. Furthermore the Act explicitly obliged all citizens to assist in the return of fugitives. Finally, the accused Negro was denied judicial process and the means to make his defense.

The reaction of the antislavery legions to the new law was instantaneous and unequivocal. Arguing from natural right and God's law, asserting that people intuitively knew right from wrong, and stating that any law favoring slavery was unconstitutional, the Garrisonian clergyman Charles Beecher stoutly defended "the duty of disobedience to wicked laws." Joshua Giddings, resting his case on the legal contention that slavery was a state, not a federal concern, and on the moral assumption

---

⁶⁷ Amos A. Phelps to Charles T. Torrey, December 10, 1844. Phelps Papers, Antislavery Collections, Boston Public Library.

that the Higher Law was prior to specific statute, found disobedience the true constitutional position.[68]

The law was defied, therefore, with monotonous frequency. In 1851 Thomas Sims was brought before the commissioner in Boston. Antislavery forces immediately went into action. It was *opera bouffe* in this case. Thomas Wentworth Higginson, adventurous young Bostonian abolitionist, hatched a great plot. Sims was to escape confinement by leaping out of a courthouse window into a mattress and then being spirited away. The window, however, was nailed shut before the plan could be put into effect. Meanwhile, Robert Rantoul and Ellis Gray Loring argued for Sims before the commissioner. They pointed out that the commissioner was performing a judicial function although he was not legally a judge; that in cases involving either personal liberty or property, the law demanded trial by jury; and that no judicial examination of evidence had established that the accused was actually "held to service." Loring, in his brief, added also that the rights of personal security and civil liberty were at stake, and that the requirement that Negroes carry identification papers was a discriminatory burden not required of white persons. When all else failed, Wendell Phillips tried to bribe the captain of the vessel assigned to carry Sims back to the South. He, too, failed. To the disgust of the abolitionists, Sims was returned South.[69]

---

[68] Charles Beecher, *The Duty of Disobedience to Wicked Laws. A Sermon on the Fugitive Slave Law* (New York: John A. Gray, 1851). Joshua R. Giddings, "Speech on the Annual Message of the President, of December, 1850," in *Speeches in Congress* (Boston: John P. Jewett & Co., 1853), pp. 420–444.

[69] Anna M. Wells, *Dear Preceptor: The Life and Times of Thomas Wentworth Higginson* (Boston: Houghton Mifflin, 1963), p. 74. Deborah Weston to Anne W. Weston, April 15, 1851, Weston Papers. *Trial of Thomas Sims, on an Issue of Personal Liberty, on the Claim of James Potter of Georgia, against him, as an Alleged Fugitive from Service. Arguments of Robert Rantoul, jr. and Charles G. Loring...* (Boston: W. S. Damrell, 1851). Leonard W. Levy "Sims' Case: the Fugitive Slave Law in Boston in 1851," *Journal of Negro History*, XXXV (January 1950), 39–74.

The same year, in Syracuse, Samuel J. May, Unitarian minister, Garrisonian, and earlier defender of Prudence Crandall, led the antislavery forces in the rescue of Jerry McHenry. In March of 1851 May had shown his position when he had challenged an antislavery meeting "respecting the fugitive slave law, and these five [fugitive Negro] persons [whom May had harbored and now presented to the meeting]. Would they resist the Law? Would they shield the wanderers? Would they defend them at all hazards?"[70] May answered those questions the following October when he and other antislavery leaders led a mob which seized Jerry from the clutches of the law and spirited him off to Canada. May's only regret was that the charges brought against the rescuers were never pressed: there would have been publicity indeed, for William H. Seward, by then a United States Senator, had offered to go bond for the men and to act as their defense lawyer.

Of all the fugitive slave cases, however, none was more renowned than the rendition of Anthony Burns in 1854. The Boston abolitionists were determined that the Sims fiasco would not be repeated. They organized a vigilance committee; but it could not agree on a plan of action beyond meeting in Faneuil Hall on May 26. Frustrated, Higginson, together with Lewis Hayden, a Boston Negro, and Martin Stowell of the Jerry Rescue in Syracuse, organized an attack upon the courthouse. Higginson had told Theodore Parker, the Unitarian clergyman and abolitionist, and Samuel Gridley Howe, the reformer, on their way to the Faneuil Hall meeting, that the idea was to rescue Burns. Nobody, however, got the plans straight, and no one came from the meeting when Higginson, with twenty-five men and twelve axes, assaulted the courthouse. They were driven back by the police, but not before one of the policemen

---

[70] George Thompson to Anne W. Weston, March 7, 1851, Weston Papers.

had been killed and Stowell arrested. Action having been thus precipitated, Burns was, the next day, marched, under guard of federal troops, to the waterfront and there shipped off for the South. Some, like Charles Francis Adams, "applauded the effort" to seize Burns. Lydia Maria Child, however, had only the heartiest contempt for the incredible muddle which the abolitionists had made of the affair.[71]

The attitude demonstrated by all this sound and fury was more significant than the accomplishment. The antislavery crusade had reached the point of open resistance to law. It was clear that unless the law was changed only trouble could ensue. The change that occurred was the Dred Scott decision, which was rather conclusively a change in the wrong direction, for it ended the hope of any judicial protection for the Negro, slave or free.

The Appeal to Revolution and Disunion

The disunion-revolution theme of the Garrisonians began, as a consequence of Chief Justice Roger Taney's *obiter dictum,* to command a renewed attention. To uphold the Constitution, declared the Garrisonian, Charles E. Hodges, in 1855, even before Taney made his remarks, was to surrender the "final and universally-conceded right of revolution." Since Constitution and government support the slaveholder, advised Stephen Foster, the private citizen must "renounce his allegiance to the government. His only choice is between slaveholding and revolution." ". . . [L]et us strike for revolution," cried Henry C. Wright. "Let us drive slavery from our soil, and never allow a man to be put on trial on the question whether he is a man or a

---

[71] Wells, *Dear Preceptor,* pp. 85–89. Samuel Shapiro, "The Rendition of Anthony Burns," *Journal of Negro History,* XLIV (January 1959), 43. Lydia M. Child to Francis G. Shaw, June 3, 1854, Houghton Collection.

beast."⁷² Still nonresistant, Garrison argued rather in the milder terms of simple disunion. But, disunion only or violence as well, a moral revolution of major dimensions was coming to a head.

Among the Negroes, too, direct action was urged. In a virtually unique document the New England Anti-Slavery Convention as early as 1843 had addressed the slaves themselves, encouraging them to escape from their masters. In the same year, the Negro clergyman Henry Highland Garnet made a much stronger appeal to violence at the Buffalo Convention of Colored Citizens.

Brethren, arise, arise! Strike for your lives and liberties. Now is the day and the hour. Let every slave throughout the land do this and the days of slavery are numbered. Rather die freemen than live to be slaves. . . . Awake, Awake, millions of voices are calling you! Let your motto be resistance; no oppressed people have secured their liberty without resistance.⁷³

Six years later George Thompson, English antislavery leader who knew the American scene at first hand, envisaged "death to the slave-catchers" and "saw no help but in the slaughter of some of the villians [sic] who were the chief conspirators against the rights of the colored man. . . ." By the middle of the 1850's exhortation had increasingly become action. Fighting raged in Kansas, and in Boston firebrands like Higginson, the supporters of the Emigrant Aid Society, and the suppliers of Beecher's Bibles gave to the antislavery crusade a character

---

⁷² Charles E. Hodges, *Disunion, Our Wisdom and Our Duty* (Anti-Slavery Tract No. 11) (New York: American Anti-Slavery Society, [1855]), p. 2. Stephen S. Foster, *Revolution the Only Remedy for Slavery* (Anti-Slavery Tract No. 7) (New York: American Anti-Slavery Society, [1855]), p. 16. Wright quoted in W. P. and F. J. Garrison, *William Lloyd Garrison*, III, 424.

⁷³ Quoted in John Hope Franklin, *From Slavery to Freedom* (New York: Alfred A. Knopf, 1956), p. 250.

which it had not had before. Then, in 1859, encouraged by men like Gerrit Smith, Higginson, and Theodore Parker, John Brown, back from Kansas, launched his attack at Harpers Ferry. The country was stunned. Some, like Seward, called it a "mad invasion"; others, like Lydia Maria Child, deplored "such violent attempts to right wrong" because they were "both injudicious and evil."[74] Abolitionists in general, however, gave their blessing to the man if not to the endeavor.

The final act was national civil war. The arts of political manoeuver, through which the antislavery crusade had tried to work in the fifties, had failed to find the avenues necessary to avoid armed struggle. Once war came, even nonresistants like Wendell Phillips and Garrison supported the government, demanding that it use the war power to abolish slavery. Within two years the pressures of moral reform and the needs of political strategy led President Abraham Lincoln to issue the Emancipation Proclamation. When Generals John C. Frémont and David Hunter had, earlier in the War, proclaimed emancipation in the military zones which they controlled, Lincoln had countermanded their orders. And even the Emancipation Proclamation freed no slaves since, at its promulgation, it concerned slaves only in areas then outside Federal control. The real point, however, had been made. And on December 18, 1865, with the adoption of the Thirteenth Amendment, the Negro was in law universally free from involuntary servitude in America.

The American Anti-Slavery Society continued, after the war, debating its role and haggling over the women's rights question. Even at this late date, internal dissension beclouded the issue of realizing the other half of abolition—full civil rights for freedmen. Nonetheless, the antislavery crusade had ended.

---

[74] George Thompson to Anne W. Weston, March 7, 1851, Weston Papers. William H. Seward to Frances Miller Seward, November 15, 1859, Seward Papers. Lydia M. Child to Sarah Shaw, November 4, 1859, Houghton Collection.

The Dilemma of the Antislavery Crusade

Looking back over the antislavery movement, one is at once impressed by the mosaic pattern of it all. How many and how varied were the people in it. The elite of Boston's Brahmin caste like Edmund Quincy and Wendell Phillips; lower class leaders like Benjamin Lundy and William Lloyd Garrison; clerical spokesmen like Theodore Parker and Charles Grandison Finney; antislavery anticlericals like Parker Pillsbury and Stephen Foster; philanthropists like Gerrit Smith and Arthur Tappan; political advocates like James G. Birney and Joshua Giddings. The antislavery crusade also embraced much of the nation, from the Garrisonians of Boston to the Moderates of New York and the revivalist-oriented Lane debaters in the Western Reserve. Even in the South, there were those who were interested in the crusade: early colonizationists like Robert Harper; later, men like James Thome of Kentucky and William King of Louisiana. Nor were the crusaders white only. The antislavery ranks included numerous Negroes: David Walker and Nat Turner, Josiah Henson and Martin Delany, Henry Highland Garnet and Hosea Easton, Robert Purvis and Charles Remond, the James Fortens, father and son, and Frederick Douglass.

Despite their diversity, the antislavery enthusiasts agreed on one thing: slavery was wrong and ought to be ended. That, however, was about the only thing on which they could agree. About the *what* there was no dissension; over the *how* there was no unity. That lack of unity is evidenced not only by the movement itself but also by the wide variety of interpretations which have been made of it. It is that lack, in the final analysis, which must qualify any judgment of success which one may be tempted to make about the crusade.

One can say that antislavery bespoke moral suasion, that it comprised a dedicated effort to convert America to the belief that slavery was sinful, that to support slavery was sinful, that to fail to oppose it was sinful, that any involvement with the peculiar institution, directly or indirectly, burdened one with guilt which demanded atonement. In this sense the antislavery movement was a religious phenomenon, and those who emphasize the close connection between it and religious revivalism emphasize an important point. But moral suasion was not enough. By the 1840's many had turned to political action as the best way to effect useful and lasting social change. In the end, however, political action, too, was inadequate. From the Compromise of 1850 through the Dred Scott decision antislavery political action was constantly frustrated. Gradually all channels of action were blocked. Moral suasion was ineffective and inadequate to end slavery as an institution. None of the programs for practical action through education, vocational training, communitarianism, and the like, proved more than partial expedients. And, finally, the last and best hope, political action, had led up a blocked, though not in principle blind, alley.

The antislavery crusade, however, did not die out in political frustration. Behind the plans for political action was the moral issue which became ever more intense and imperative throughout the entire antislavery era. When all channels for effective action, for fulfilling the real-world aims which gave the moral stance external reality, were cut off, the consequences became explosive. In a sense, perhaps, the frustrations were predictable, for the antislavery crusade had never penetrated the South, never reached the slaveholders, who alone of all Americans could have ended the peculiar institution either through or without national political action. When, in 1861, warfare broke out, it seemed to have been predictable if not inevitable as far back, perhaps, as 1850. The firing on Fort Sumter demonstrated symbolically the consequence of an irresistible moral force meeting an immovable political fact. When all the instruments of practical accommodation had failed, there was left only bloody catharsis

Still one thing remained to be noted. It was odd, perhaps, that those who had insisted on disunion in the 1840's and 1850's should, when the war came, have so frequently demanded the preservation of the Union and insisted that the rule of war be made the instrument for ending the slavery that they so deplored but had been unable to abolish. The Union, as it turned out, was saved; as a legal matter, slavery was ended. It is the irony of history that the equally important issue, the moral commitment to the rights of the Negro as a man, went down to so cruel a defeat.

Chronology

1619 The first Negro laborer was imported into Virginia.
1754 John Woolman addressed his fellow Quakers in *Some Considerations of the Keeping of Negroes.*
1775 The first Quaker antislavery society, the Society for the Relief of Free Negroes Unlawfully Held in Bondage, was organized in Philadelphia.
1777–1804 Gradual abolition laws were passed in the northern states: Vermont, Massachusetts, New Hampshire, Pennsylvania, Rhode Island, Connecticut, New York, New Jersey.
1785 The New York City Manumission Society was organized by John Jay and Alexander Hamilton.
1787 The Northwest Ordinance banned slavery in the Northwest Territory.
1789 The Pennsylvania Abolition Society was organized by Benjamin Franklin.
1793 The first Federal fugitive slave act provided for the return of slaves escaped across state boundaries.
1794 The first national antislavery society, the American Convention for Promoting the Abolition of Slavery, was founded.
1807 Congress passed the law prohibiting the importation of slaves into the United States after January 1, 1808.
1817 The American Colonization Society was founded to settle free Negroes in Africa.
1820 The Missouri Compromise admitted Missouri as a slave

state but prohibited slavery in the Louisiana Territory thereafter above 36° 30' north latitude.

1821 The Quaker, Benjamin Lundy, started publishing his antislavery paper, the *Genius of Universal Emancipation.*

1822 A slave revolt occurred in Charleston, South Carolina, led by the free Negro, Denmark Vesey.

1831 The *Liberator* was founded by William Lloyd Garrison.

1831 The Nat Turner Rebellion occurred in Virginia.

1831 The New England Anti-Slavery Society was founded in Boston.

1831–1832 Emancipation was narrowly defeated in the Virginia constitutional convention.

1832 William Lloyd Garrison's *Thoughts on African Colonization* was published. It marked a turning point of antislavery against colonization.

1833 Slavery was ended in the British Empire.

1833 The American Anti-Slavery Society was founded in Philadelphia.

1834 Debates on colonization and slavery were held at Lane Seminary in Cincinnati.

1834 The moderate and church-oriented American Union for the Relief and Improvement of the Colored Race was founded by Massachusetts Congregational ministers.

1834 Prudence Crandall's school for Negro girls in Canterbury, Connecticut, was closed by vandalism and mob destruction.

1835 The near lynching of Garrison occurred in Boston.

1836 The office of James G. Birney's *Philanthropist* was sacked in Cincinnati.

1836–1844 The campaign against the Gag Rule, restricting the reception of antislavery petitions, was carried on in the House of Representatives by John Quincy Adams.

1837 "The Seventy" were sent out to preach antislavery by the American Anti-Slavery Society.

- 1837 Elijah Lovejoy's press was destroyed, and Lovejoy was killed in Alton, Illinois.
- 1838 Pennsylvania Hall, built for meetings of reform groups, was burned during the Anti-Slavery Convention of American Women in Philadelphia.
- 1838 Abolitionists initiated a program of questioning political candidates on slavery-related issues.
- 1839 *American Slavery As It Is: Testimony of a Thousand Witnesses*, edited by Thedore D. Weld, was published. It exposed atrocities and the bad conditions of slavery.
- 1840 The American Anti-Slavery Society started the publication of the *National Anti-Slavery Standard*.
- 1840 The Liberty Party was organized and nominated James G. Birney for President.
- 1840 The American and Foreign Anti-Slavery Society was formed in a split of the moderates from the Garrison-dominated American Anti-Slavery Society.
- 1840 The World Anti-Slavery Convention was held in London. Women from the American delegation were denied seats on the floor.
- 1841 The Amistad Case, involving the status of certain slaves who had mutinied and were brought to Connecticut, was tried in Federal courts.
- 1842 Prigg v. Pennsylvania found a state guarantee of judicial process to fugitives unconstitutional, but freed state officials from enforcing the Federal Fugitive Slave Act.
- 1843 The Buffalo Convention of Colored Citizens marked a turning point in Negro separate organization and militancy.
- 1845 The annexation of Texas gainsaid abolitionist warnings and added a new issue to the cause.
- 1846–1848 United States victory in the Mexican War presented a new issue of the permitting of slavery in the Mexican Cession (opposed by the Wilmot Proviso) and

of the admitting of California as a free state. A temporary resolution was achieved in the Compromise of 1850.

1847 Frederick Douglass started publication of the *North Star*.

1848 The Free Soil Party was organized and nominated Martin Van Buren its presidential candidate.

1849 The Roberts Case, in which Charles Sumner unsuccessfully challenged segregation in Boston public schools, was argued.

1850 The Fugitive Slave Act, part of the Compromise of this year, further curtailed the civil guarantees of those seized as fugitives.

1851 The fugitive Jerry McHenry was rescued from the "slave catchers" in Syracuse, New York.

1851 The alleged fugitive Thomas Sims was returned to Georgia under the new fugitive slave law.

1852 Harriet Beecher Stowe's *Uncle Tom's Cabin* was published. It epitomized the sentimental popularization of antislavery.

1854 The Kansas-Nebraska Bill was passed. It fomented civil war in Kansas Territory over the slavery issue.

1854 The New England Emigrant Aid Company was organized to settle antislavery men in Kansas and to make it a free state.

1854 The Republican Party was established. It absorbed antislavery Whigs and Democrats and the remnants of the Free Soil Party.

1854 The fugitive slave, Anthony Burns, was returned from Boston to Virginia.

1857 Hinton Rowan Helper's *The Impending Crisis of the South*, addressed to the self-interest of non-slaveholding whites, was published.

1857 By the Dred Scott decision Negroes—slave or free— were effectively denied rights as American citizens; and

Congress was denied the right to legislate on slavery in the territories.
1858 Abraham Lincoln condemned slavery in his "House Divided" speech.
1858 Stephen Douglas proposed the Freeport Doctrine in answer to the Dred Scott decision.
1858 William H. Seward delivered his "Irrepressible Conflict" speech at Rochester, New York.
1859 John Brown raided Harpers Ferry to foment and support a revolt of slaves.
1861 The Civil War began.
1863 The Emancipation Proclamation was issued.
1865 The Thirteenth Amendment was ratified.

Selected Bibliography

The principal problem confronting the bibliographer of the antislavery movement is that either as a whole or in its various facets the movement has not been subjected to thorough study. Any bibliography of the movement, therefore, must be partial, revealing large areas where adequate studies simply do not exist. For those undertaking study in this area three general guides are particularly useful. Louis Filler, *The Crusade against Slavery, 1830–1860*. New York: Harper and Brothers, 1960, is up-to-date, broad in its coverage, and provides as good a bibliographical introduction to the area as can be found. It should be supplemented with Dwight L. Dumond, *A Bibliography of Antislavery in America*. Ann Arbor: The University of Michigan Press, 1961, which is a substantial collection of major primary antislavery literature, marred unfortunately by errors and by the inclusion of some irrelevant material. Philip M. Hamer, ed., *A Guide to the Archives and Manuscripts in the United States*. New Haven: Yale University Press, 1961, should be consulted by the student whose interest is primarily professional.

Among the more general studies of the antislavery movement are Mary S. Locke, *Anti-Slavery in America, 1619–1808*. Boston: Ginn and Co., 1901; Alice D. Adams, *The Neglected Period of Anti-Slavery in America, 1808–1831*. Boston: Ginn & Co., 1908; Dwight L. Dumond, *Antislavery Origins of the Civil War in the United States*. ca. 1939. Paperback edition, Ann Arbor: University of Michigan Press, 1959; Gilbert H.

Barnes, *The Antislavery Impulse, 1830-1844.* Ca. 1933. Reprinted, Gloucester, Massachusetts: Peter Smith, 1957; Dwight L. Dumond, *Antislavery. The Crusade for Freedom in America.* Ann Arbor: University of Michigan Press, 1961; Louis Filler, *The Crusade Against Slavery;* and Russel B. Nye, *William Lloyd Garrison and the Humanitarian Reformers.* Boston: Little, Brown, 1955.

Good biographies of antislavery leaders and lieutenants are, lamentably, in very short supply. Among the more useful are Wendell Phillips Garrison and Francis Jackson Garrison, *William Lloyd Garrison, 1805-1879; The Story of His Life as Told by His Children.* 4 vols. New York: The Century Co., 1885-1889; Walter M. Merrill, *Against Wind and Tide; A Biography of William Lloyd Garrison.* Cambridge: Harvard University Press, 1963; John L. Thomas, *The Liberator; William Lloyd Garrison. A Biography.* Boston: Little, Brown and Company, 1963; Benjamin P. Thomas, *Theodore Weld, Crusader for Freedom.* New Brunswick: Rutgers University Press, 1950; Betty Fladeland, *James Gillespie Birney: Slaveholder to Abolitionist.* Ithaca: Cornell University Press, 1955; Irving H. Bartlett, *Wendell Phillips: Brahmin Radical.* Boston: Beacon Press, 1961; Oscar Sherwin, *Prophet of Liberty: The Life and Times of Wendell Phillips.* New York: Bookman Associates, 1958; Henry S. Commager, *Theodore Parker,* 2nd ed. Boston: Beacon Press, 1947; Anna Mary Wells, *Dear Preceptor: The Life and Times of Thomas Wentworth Higginson.* Boston: Houghton Mifflin Co., 1963; Lewis Tappan, *The Life of Arthur Tappan.* New York: Hurd and Houghton, 1870; Samuel F. Bemis, *John Quincy Adams and the Union.* New York: Alfred A. Knopf, 1956; Martin B. Duberman. *Charles Francis Adams, 1807-1886.* Boston: Houghton, Mifflin Co., 1961; Albert Bushnell Hart, *Salmon Portland Chase.* Boston: Houghton Mifflin Co., 1899; David Donald, *Charles Sumner and the Coming of the Civil War.* New York: Alfred A. Knopf, 1960; David L. Smiley, *Lion of White Hall: The Life* of *Cassius Clay*. Madison: University of Wisconsin Press, 1962; Merton L. Dillon, *Elijah P. Lovejoy. Abolitionist Editor*. Urbana: The University of Illinois Press, 1961; Ralph Volney Harlow, *Gerrit Smith: Philanthropist and Reformer*. New York: Henry Holt and Co., 1939; Arthur W. Brown, *Always Young for Liberty: A Biography of William Ellery Channing*. Syracuse: Syracuse University Press, 1956; Otelia Cromwell, *Lucretia Mott*. Cambridge: Harvard University Press, 1958; Amelia Mott Gummere, ed., *The Journals and Essays of John Woolman . . . with a Biographical Introduction*. New York: The Macmillan Co., 1922; and Benjamin Quarles, *Frederick Douglass*. Washington: The Associated Publishers, 1948; and Frederick W. Seward, *William H. Seward. . . .* New York: Derby and Miller, 1891. Two collections of letters stand out as models of usefulness and careful scholarship: Gilbert H. Barnes and Dwight L. Dumond, eds., *Letters of Theodore Dwight Weld, Angelina Grimké Weld and Sarah Grimké, 1822–1844*. 2 vols. New York: D. Appleton-Century Co., 1934, and Dwight L. Dumond, ed., *Letters of James Gillespie Birney, 1831–1857*. 2 vols. New York: D. Appleton-Century Co., 1938.

Much of the best work on special facets of the antislavery movement is to be found in monographs and journal articles. Among those which may be cited for their importance to antislavery interpretation or for their contributions to particular problems and areas within the movement are Avery O. Craven, "An Unorthodox Interpretation of the Abolition Movement," *Journal of Southern History*, VII (February 1941), 57–58; David Donald, "Toward a Reconsideration of Abolitionists," in *Lincoln Reconsidered: Essays on the Civil War Era*. New York: Alfred A. Knopf, 1956, 19–36; Hazel C. Wolf, *On Freedom's Altar: The Martyr Complex in the Abolition Movement*. Madison: University of Wisconsin Press, 1952; Martin B. Duberman, "The Abolitionists and Psychology," *Journal of Negro History*, XLVII (July 1962), 183–191; Merton L. Dillon, "The Failure of American Abolitionists," *Journal of Southern His-*

tory, XXV (May 1959), 159–177; C. Vann Woodward, "The Antislavery Myth," *The American Scholar*, XXXI (Spring 1962), 312–328; Betty Fladeland, "Who Were the Abolitionists?" *Journal of Negro History*, XLIX (April 1964), 99–115; David B. Davis, "The Emergence of Immediatism in British and American Antislavery Thought," *Mississippi Valley Historical Review*, XLIX (September 1962), 209–230; Larry Gara, *The Liberty Line: The Legend of the Underground Railroad*. Lexington: University of Kentucky Press, 1961; Howard H. Bell, "Expressions of Negro Militancy in the North, 1840–1860," *Journal of Negro History*, XLV (January 1960), 11–20, and "National Negro Conventions of the Middle 1840's: Moral Suasion vs. Political Action," *ibid.*, XLII (October 1957), 247–260; Leon F. Litwack, *North of Slavery. The Negro in the Free States, 1790–1860*. Chicago: University of Chicago Press, 1961; William H. Pease and Jane H. Pease, *Black Utopia. Negro Communal Experiments in America*. Madison: The State Historical Society of Wisconsin, 1963; P. J. Staudenraus, *The African Colonization Movement, 1816–1865*. New York: Columbia University Press, 1961; and Russel B. Nye, *Fettered Freedom. Civil Liberties and the Slavery Controversy, 1830–1860*. East Lansing: Michigan State College Press, 1949; Joseph Nogee, "The Prigg Case and Fugitive Slavery, 1842–1850," *Journal of Negro History*, XXXIX (July 1954), 185–205; Leonard W. Levy and Harlan B. Phillips, "The *Roberts* Case: Source of the 'Separate But Equal' Doctrine," *American Historical Review*, LVI (April 1951), 510–518; James M. McPherson, "The Fight Against the Gag Rule: Joshua Leavitt and Antislavery Insurgency in the Whig Party, 1839–1842," *Journal of Negro History*, XLVIII (July 1963), 177–195; Douglas H. Maynard, "The World's Anti-Slavery Convention of 1840," *Mississippi Valley Historical Review*, XLVII (December 1960), 452–471.

Editors' Note

In an edition of documents such as this, certain technical procedures need explaining. Throughout the volume we have, with few exceptions, retained the original form of each selection. We have, therefore, not used the designation *sic* except where clarity seemed to demand it. We have corrected obvious typographical errors, but not errors of any other kind. The old-fashioned ʃ we have replaced with a modern s. We have capitalized the first letter of a word when it appears as the first word of an excerpt, even though in the original text it was lower case. Finally, we have eliminated all footnotes from the texts except those few which particularly contribute to clarity and which add fundamental information. All other footnotes are editorial and are so indicated.

Many people and numerous libraries have helped us in preparing this volume. All merit our thanks, though we can mention only the principal ones. Nearly all the documents used here are from original texts available in the New York State Library in Albany, or from the Harvard College Library. A few are from originals in the Boston Public Library and several from university libraries. We thank them all for their assistance. We owe a particular debt to the Library of Rensselaer Polytechnic Institute, Troy, New York, whose inter-library loan service obtained original texts for us on many occasions and whose Xerox service made working reproductions of nearly all our material.

Finally, we wish especially to acknowledge permission kindly given us by the Public Archives of Canada to reproduce sections from William King's "Scheme for improving the Coloured People of Canada [1848]"; and to acknowledge that, by the courtesy of the Trustees of the Boston Public Library, we have been permitted to quote brief passages, individually identified in the notes, from various manuscripts in the Library's Antislavery Collections.

Eagle Mills, New York.   W. H. P.
June 25, 1965   J. H. P.

I

Arguments for Philanthropic and Gradual Emancipation

ANTHONY BENEZET ATTACKS THE SLAVE TRADE

By the middle of the eighteenth century Americans were voicing concern over the problems of slavery. As was also the case in England, their concern was particularly directed toward the African slave trade and its attendant evils. Among the most eloquent spokesmen in America against the slave trade was Anthony Benezet (1713–1784), a Philadelphia Quaker, schoolteacher, and reformer. In the selection which follows, Benezet attacked both the antisocial and un-Christian character of the slave trade.

From Anthony Benezet, *Observations on the Inslaving, Importing and Purchasing of Negroes; With Some Advice Thereon, Extracted from the Epistle of the Yearly-Meeting of the People Called Quakers, Held at London in the Year 1748* (Germantown: Christopher Sower, 1760), pp. 3–10.

In ancient Times it was the Practice of many Nations, when at war with each other, to sell the Prisoners they made in Battle, in order to defray the Expences of the War. This unchristian or rather inhuman practice, after many Ages continuance, is at length generally abolished by the Christian Powers of Europe, but still continues among some of the Nations of Asia and Africa, and to our sad Experience we find it also practised by the Natives of America. In the present war,[1] how many of our poor Country Men are dragged to Bondage and sold for Slaves; how many mourn, a Husband, a Wife, a Child, a Parent or some near Relation taken from them; and were we to follow them a little farther, and see them exposed to sale and bought up to be made a Gain of, what Heart so hard that would not melt with Sympathy and Sorrow: And could we hear the Purchasers, for the sake of Gain, pushing on the Savages to captivate our People, what inhuman wretches should we call them, what Punishment should we think their Guilt deserved! But while our Hearts are affected for our Brethren and Relations, while we feel for our own Flesh and Blood, let us extend our Thoughts to others, and allow me, gentle Reader! to recommend to thy serious Consideration, a Practice that prevails among several Nations who call themselves Christians, and I am sorry to say it, in which we as a Nation are deeply engaged, and which is of such a Nature, as that nothing can be more inconsistent with the Doctrines and Practice of our meek Lord and Master, nor stained with a deeper Dye of Injustice, Cruelty and Oppression, I mean the *Slave Trade,* the purchasing and bringing the poor Negroes from their Native Land, and subjecting them to a State of perpetual Bondage, and that often the most cruel and oppressive. And this carried on chiefly at the instigation of those to whom

---

[1] King George's War, the American phase of the War of the Austrian Succession (1740–1748). [Eds.]

the Promulgation of the merciful, pure, and holy Gospel of Christ Jesus was committed. Will not the just Judge of all the Earth visit for all this? Or dare we say, that this very Practice is not one Cause of the Calamities we at present suffer; and that the Captivity of our People is not to teach us to feel for others, and to induce us to discourage a Trade, by which many Thousands are Yearly captivated? Evils do not arise out of the Dust, nor does the Almighty willingly afflict the Children of Men; but when a People offend as a Nation, or in a publick Capacity, the Justice of his moral Government requires that as a Nation they be punished, which is generally done by War, Famine or Pestilence. I know there are many Arguments offered in favour of the Purchasers, but they are all drawn from Avarice or ill founded, none will stand the Test of that divine Rule: *To do unto all Men, as we would they should do unto us.* Without Purchasers, there would be no Trade; and consequently every Purchaser as he encourages the Trade, becomes partaker in the Guilt of it. . . .

. . . Let any consider what it is to lose a Child, a Husband or any dear Relation, and then let them say what they must think of those who are ingaged in, or encourage such a Trade. By the fore mentioned Accounts it appears, how by various perfidious, and cruel Methods, the unhappy Negroes are inslaved, and that mostly, by the Procurement of those called Christians, and violently rent from the tenderest Ties of Nature, to toil in hard Labour, often without sufficient Supplies of Food, and under hard Taskmasters, and this mostly to uphold the Luxury or Covetousness of proud selfish Men, without any Hope of ever seeing again their native Land; or an end to their Miseries. Oh ye cruel Taskmasters! Ye hard-hearted Oppressors, will not God hear their Cry? And what shall ye do, when God riseth up, and when he visiteth; what will ye answer him? *Did not he that made you, make them? and did not one fashion you in the Womb?*

Hitherto I have considered the Trade as inconsistent with the Gospel of Christ, contrary to natural Justice, and the common feelings of Humanity, and productive of infinite Calamities to many Thousand Families, nay to many Nations, and consequently offensive to God the Father of all Mankind. Yet it must be allowed, there are some well minded Persons, into whose Hands some of the Negroes have fallen, either by Inheritance, Executorship, or even some perhaps purely from Charitable Motives, who rather desire to manage wisely for their good, than to make Gain by their Labour; these I truly sympathize with, for considering the general situation of those unhappy People, they have indeed a difficult Path to tread.

I might next consider the Trade as it is destructive of the Welfare of human Society, and inconsistent with the Peace and Prosperity of a Country, as by it the number of natural Enemies must be encreased, and the Place of those taken up who would be its support and security. Or I might shew from innumerable Examples, how it introduces Idleness, discourages Marriage, corrupts the Youth and ruins and debauches Morals. I might likewise expose the weakness of those Arguments, which are commonly advanced in Order to vindicate the Purchasers, such, as their being Slaves in their own Country, and therefore may be so to us, or that they are made acquainted with Christianity in lieu of their Liberty, or that the last Purchaser will use them better than they formerly were: But not to mention, that these are only vain pretences, that the true Motive of encouraging the Trade is selfish Avarice; to say nothing of the weakness of the Argument: That because others do ill, we may do so too; or the absurdity of recommending the Christian Religion by Injustice and disregard to the Rights and Liberties of Mankind, or the Encouragement that every new Purchaser gives to a Trade altogether unjust and iniquitous. What is already said, will I hope be sufficient to prevent any considerate Christian from being, in any Degree, defiled with a Gain so full of Horrors, and so palpably inconsistent with the Gospel of our blessed Lord and Saviour Jesus Christ, which breaths nothing but Love and Good will to all Men of every Nation, Kindred, Tongue and People.

Under the Mosaic-Law Man-stealing was the only Theft punishable by Death: It is thus expressed in Exodus Chap. 21, 16. *He that stealeth a Man and selleth him, or if he be found in his Hand, he shall surely be put to death.*

JOHN WOOLMAN

PREACHES AGAINST SLAVEHOLDING

Like his contemporary and fellow Quaker, Anthony Benezet, John Woolman (1720–1772) devoted much of his life to preaching and writing against slaveholding. By trade a tailor and shopkeeper in Mt. Holly, New Jersey, Woolman traveled throughout the southern colonies convincing Friends and others of the un-Christian evils of slaveholding. The selection which follows is from his most famous antislavery writing.

Some who keep slaves, have doubted as to the equity of the practice; but as they knew men, noted for their piety, who were in it, this, they say, has made their minds easy.

To lean on the example of men in doubtful cases, is difficult:

From John Woolman, "Some Considerations on the Keeping of Negroes. Recommended to the Professors of Christianity of Every Denomination. Part the Second. First Printed in the Year 1762," in *The Works of John Woolman* (Philadelphia: Joseph Crukshank, 1774), pp. 295–308.

for only admit, that those men were not faithful and upright to the highest degree, but that in some particular case they erred, and it may follow that this one case was the same, about which we are in doubt; and to quiet our minds by their example, may be dangerous to ourselves; and continuing in it, prove a stumbling block to tender-minded people who succeed us, in like manner as their examples are to us.

But supposing charity was their only motive, and they not foreseeing the tendency of paying robbers for their booty, were not justly under the imputation of being partners with a thief, Prov. xxix. 24.[1] but were really innocent in what they did, are we assured that we keep them with the same views they kept them? If we keep them from no other motive than a real sense of duty, and true charity governs us in all our proceedings toward them, we are so far safe: but if another spirit, which inclines our minds to the ways of this world, prevail upon us, and we are concerned for our own outward gain more than for their real happiness, it will avail us nothing that some good men have had the care and management of Negroes.

Since mankind spread upon the earth, many have been the revolutions attending the several families, and their customs and ways of life different from each other. This diversity of manners, though some are preferable to others, operates not in favour of any, so far as to justify them to do violence to innocent men; to bring them from their own to another way of life. The mind, when moved by a principle of true love, may feel a warmth of gratitude to the universal father, and a lively sympathy with those nations, where divine Light has been less manifest.

This desire for their real good may beget a willingness to undergo hardships for their sakes, that the true knowledge of God may be spread amongst them: but to take them from their

---

[1] "Whoso is partner with a thief hateth his own soul: he heareth cursing, and bewrayeth it not." [Eds.]

own land, with views of profit to ourselves, by means inconsistent with pure justice, is foreign to that principle which seeks the happiness of the whole creation. Forced subjection, of innocent persons of full age, is inconsistent with right reason; on one side, the human mind is not naturally fortified with that firmness in wisdom and goodness, necessary to an independent ruler; on the other side, to be subject to the uncontroulable will of a man, liable to err, is most painful and afflicting to a conscientious creature.

It is our happiness faithfully to serve the divine Being, who made us: his perfection makes our service reasonable; but so long as men are biassed by narrow self-love, so long an absolute power over other men is unfit for them.

Men, taking on them the government of others, may intend to govern reasonably, and make their subjects more happy than they would be otherwise; but, as absolute command belongs only to him who is perfect, where frail men, in their own wills, assume such command, it hath a direct tendency to vitiate their minds, and make them more unfit for government.

Placing on men the ignominious title SLAVE, dressing them in uncomely garments, keeping them to servile labour, in which they are often dirty, tends gradually to fix a notion in the mind, that they are a sort of people below us in nature, and leads us to consider them as such in all our conclusions about them. And, moreover, a person which in our esteem is mean and contemptible, if their language or behaviour toward us is unseemly or disrespectful, it excites wrath more powerfully than the like conduct in one we accounted our equal or superior; and where this happens to be the case, it disqualifies for candid judgment; for it is unfit for a person to sit as judge in a case where his own personal resentments are stirred up; and, as members of society in a well framed government, we are mutually dependent. Present interest incites to duty, and makes each man attentive to the convenience of others; but he whose will is a law to others, and can enforce obedience by punishment; he whose wants are supplied without feeling any obligation to make equal returns to his benefactor, his irregular appetites find an open field for motion, and he is in danger of growing hard, and inattentive to their convenience who labour for his support; and so loses that disposition, in which alone men are fit to govern.

The English government hath been commended by candid foreigners for the disuse of racks and tortures, so much practised in some states; but this multiplying slaves now leads to it; for where people exact hard labour of others, without a suitable reward, and are resolved to continue in that way, severity to such who oppose them becomes the consequence; and several Negroe criminals, among the English in America, have been executed in a lingering, painful way, very terrifying to others.

It is a happy case to set out right, and persevere in the same way: a wrong beginning leads into many difficulties; for to support one evil, another becomes customary; two produces more; and the further men proceed in this way, the greater their dangers, their doubts and fears; and the more painful and perplexing are their circumstances; so that such who are true friends to the real and lasting interest of our country, and candidly consider the tendency of things, cannot but feel some concern on this account.

There is that superiority in men over the brute creatures, and some of them so manifestly dependent on men for a living, that for them to serve us in moderation, so far as relates to the right use of things, looks consonant to the design of our Creator.

There is nothing in their frame, nothing relative to the propagating their species, which argues the contrary; but in men there is. The frame of men's bodies, and the disposition of their minds are different; some, who are tough and strong, and their minds active, chuse ways of life requiring much labour to support them; others are soon weary; and though use makes labour more tolerable, yet some are less apt for toil than others, and their minds less sprightly. These latter labouring for their subsistence, commonly chuse a life easy to support, being content with a little. When they are weary they may rest, take the most advantageous part of the day for labour; and in all cases proportion one thing to another, that their bodies be not oppressed.

Now, while each is at liberty, the latter may be as happy, and live as comfortably as the former; but where men of the first sort have the latter under absolute command, not considering the odds in strength and firmness, do, sometimes, in their eager pursuit, lay on burthens grievous to be borne; by degrees grow rigorous, and, aspiring to greatness, they increase oppression, and the true order of kind Providence is subverted.

There are weaknesses sometimes attending us, which make little or no alteration in our countenances, nor much lessen our appetite for food, and yet so affect us, as to make labour very uneasy. In such case masters, intent on putting forward business, and jealous of the sincerity of their slaves, may disbelieve what they say, and grievously afflict them.

Action is necessary for all men, and our exhausting frame requires a support, which is the fruit of action. The earth must be laboured to keep us alive: labour is a proper part of our life; to make one answer the other in some useful motion, looks agreeable to the design of our Creator. Motion, rightly managed, tends to our satisfaction, health and support.

Those who quit all useful business, and live wholly on the labour of others, have their exercise to seek; some such use less than their health requires; others chuse that which, by the circumstances attending it, proves utterly reverse to true happiness. Thus, while some are divers ways distressed for want of an open channel of useful action, those who support them sigh, and are exhausted in a stream too powerful for nature, spending their days with too little cessation from labour.

Seed sown with the tears of a confined oppressed people,

harvest cut down by an overborne discontented reaper, makes bread less sweet to the taste of an honest man, than that which is the produce, or just reward of such voluntary action, which is one proper part of the business of human creatures.

Again, the weak state of the human species, in bearing and bringing forth their young, and the helpless condition of their young beyond that of other creatures, clearly shew that Perfect Goodness designs a tender care and regard should be exercised toward them; and that no imperfect, arbitrary power should prevent the cordial effects of that sympathy, which is, in the minds of well-met pairs, to each other, and toward their offspring.

In our species the mutual ties of affection are more rational and durable than in others below us; the care and labour of raising our offspring much greater. The satisfaction arising to us in their innocent company, and in their advances from one rational improvement to another, is considerable, when two are thus joined, and their affections sincere. It however happens among slaves, that they are often situate in different places; and their seeing each other depends on the will of men, liable to human passions, and a bias in judgment; who, with views of self-interest, may keep them apart more than is right. Being absent from each other, and often with other company, there is a danger of their affections being alienated, jealousies arising, the happiness otherwise resulting from their offspring frustrated, and the comforts of marriage destroyed.—These things being considered closely, as happening to a near friend, will appear to be hard and painful.

He who reverently observes that goodness manifested by our gracious Creator toward the various species of beings in this world, will see, that in our frame and constitution is clearly shewn that innocent men, capable to manage for themselves, were not intended to be slaves. . . .

. . . Through the force of long custom, it appears needful to speak in relation to colour.—Suppose a white child, born of parents of the meanest sort, who died and left him an infant, falls into the hands of a person, who endeavours to keep him a slave, some men would account him an unjust man in doing so, who yet appear easy while many black people, of honest lives, and good abilities, are enslaved, in a manner more shocking than the case here supposed. This is owing chiefly to the idea of slavery being connected with the black colour, and liberty with the white:—and where false ideas are twisted into our minds, it is with difficulty we get fairly disentangled.

A traveller, in cloudy weather, misseth his way, makes many turns while he is lost; still forms in his mind, the bearing and situation of places, and though the ideas are wrong, they fix as fast as if they were right. Finding how things are, we see our mistake; yet the force of reason, with repeated observations on places and things, do not soon remove those false notions, so fastened upon us, but it will seem in the imagination as if the annual course of the sun was altered; and though, by recollection, we are assured it is not, yet those ideas do not suddenly leave us.

Selfishness being indulged, clouds the understanding; and where selfish men, for a long time, proceed on their way, without opposition, the deceiveableness of unrighteousness gets so rooted in their intellects, that a candid examination of things relating to self-interest is prevented; and in this circumstance, some who would not agree to make a slave of a person whose colour is like their own, appear easy in making slaves of others of a different colour, though their understandings and morals are equal to the generality of men of their own colour.

The colour of a man avails nothing, in matters of right and equity. Consider colour in relation to treaties; by such, disputes betwixt nations are sometimes settled. And should the father of us all so dispose things, that treaties with black men should sometimes be necessary, how then would it appear amongst the princes and ambassadors, to insist on the prerogative of the white colour?

Whence is it that men, who believe in a righteous omnipotent Being, to whom all nations stand equally related, and are equally accountable, remain so easy in it; but for that the ideas of Negroes and slaves are so interwoven in the mind, that they do not discuss this matter with that candour and freedom of thought, which the case justly calls for?

To come at a right feeling of their condition, requires humble serious thinking; for, in their present situation, they have but little to engage our natural affection in their favour.

Had we a son or a daughter involved in the same case, in which many of them are, it would alarm us, and make us feel their condition without seeking for it. The adversity of an intimate friend will incite our compassion, while others, equally good, in the like trouble, will but little affect us.

Again, the man in worldly honour, whom we consider as our superior, treating us with kindness and generosity, begets a return of gratitude and friendship toward him. We may receive as great benefits from men a degree lower than ourselves, in the common way of reckoning, and feel ourselves less engaged in favour of them. Such is our condition by nature; and these things being narrowly watched and examined, will be found to center in self-love.

The blacks seem far from being our kinsfolks, and did we find an agreeable disposition and sound understanding in some of them, which appeared as a good foundation for a true friendship between us, the disgrace arising from an open friendship with a person of so vile a stock, in the common esteem, would naturally tend to hinder it.—They have neither honours, riches, outward magnificence nor power; their dress coarse, and often ragged; their employ drudgery, and much in the dirt: they have little or nothing at command; but must wait upon and work for others, to obtain the necessaries of life; so that, in their present situation, there is not much to engage the friendship, or move the affection of selfish men: but such who live in the spirit of true charity, to sympathise with the afflicted in the lowest stations of life, is a thing familiar to them.

Such is the kindness of our Creator, that people, applying their minds to sound wisdom, may, in general, with moderate exercise, live comfortably, where no misapplied power hinders it.—We in these parts have cause gratefully to acknowledge it. But men leaving the true use of things, their lives are less calm, and have less of real happiness in them.

Many are desirous of purchasing and keeping slaves, that they may live in some measure conformable to those customs of the times, which have in them a tincture of luxury; for when we, in the least degree, depart from that use of the creatures, for which the Creator of all things intended them, there luxury begins.

And if we consider this way of life seriously, we shall see there is nothing in it sufficient to induce a wise man to chuse it, before a plain, simple way of living. If we examine stately buildings and equipage, delicious food, superfine cloaths, silks and linens; if we consider the splendour of choice metal fastened upon raiment, and the most showy inventions of men; it will yet appear that the humble-minded man, who is contented with the true use of houses, food and garments, and chearfully exerciseth himself agreeable to his station in civil society, to earn them, acts more reasonably, and discovers more soundness of understanding in his conduct, than such who lay heavy burdens on others, to support themselves in a luxurious way of living. . . .

. . . In true gospel simplicity, free from all wrong use of things, a spirit which breathes peace and good will is cherished; but when we aspire after imaginary grandeur, and apply to selfish means to attain our end, this desire, in its original, is the same with the Picts in cutting figures on their bodies; but the evil consequences attending our proceedings are the greatest.

A covetous mind, which seeks opportunity to exalt itself, is a great enemy to true harmony in a country: envy and grudging usually accompany this disposition, and it tends to stir up its likeness in others. And where this disposition ariseth so high, as to embolden us to look upon honest industrious men as our own property during life, and to keep them to hard labour, to support us in those customs which have not their foundation in right reason; or to use any means of oppression; a haughty spirit is cherished on one side, and the desire of revenge frequently on the other, till the inhabitants of the land are ripe for great commotion and trouble; and thus luxury and oppression have the seeds of war and desolation in them.

THE AMERICAN CONVENTION FOR PROMOTING THE ABOLITION OF SLAVERY ADVOCATES GRADUAL EMANCIPATION

The assumptions about liberty and equality implicit and explicit in the American Revolution and the founding of the American Republic caused many people to question the legitimacy of slaveholding. Relatively early most northern states adopted legislation to abolish slavery, and interested citizens formed private associations to end slavery throughout the country by gradual emancipation. One such group, meeting in the Quaker stronghold of Philadelphia early in 1804, published its conclusions in an address "to the PEOPLE *of the* UNITED STATES" *in which it condemned the evils of slave trading and slaveholding and advocated a program of general emancipation. It was characteristic of such organizations that they failed clearly to define the means by which to achieve their aims.*

From American Convention for Promoting the Abolition of Slavery and Improving the Condition of the African Race, Assembled at Philadelphia, in January, 1804, *Address. . . to the People of the United States* (Philadelphia: Solomon W. Conrad, 1804), pp. 4–8.

A principal object of our concern, is to rouse the attention of the public to the continued—may we not say—increasing necessity of exertion. We fear many have taken up an idea, that there is less occasion now than formerly, for active zeal in promoting the cause of the oppressed African: but when it is remembered that there are about nine hundred thousand slaves in our country! that hundreds of vessels do annually sail from our shores, to traffic in the blood of our fellow men! and that the abominable practice of kidnapping is carried on to an alarming extent! surely it will not be thought a time for supineness and neglect. Ought not rather every faculty of the mind to be awakened? and in a matter wherein the reputation and prosperity of these United States are so deeply involved, is it possible that any can remain as indifferent and idle spectators?

The gross and violent outrages committed by a horde of kidnappers, call aloud for redress. We have reason to believe, there is a complete chain of them along our sea coast, from Georgia to Maine. Like the vulture, soaring in apparent indifference, while watching for his prey, these shameless men, disguised in the habiliments of gentlemen, haunt public places, and at night seize and carry off the victims of their avarice. The Convention are informed of some of their insidious manoeuvres. They generally have vessels moored in small rivers and creeks, and after stealing the unprotected, they decoy by stratagem and allure by specious offers of gain, such free persons of colour as they find susceptible of delusion. Others residing near the seacoast, are continually purchasing slaves in the middle states, to sell at an advanced price to their compeers in infamy. For the victims of this shocking business, they find a ready market among the southern planters. The design of this detail, must be obvious: It is to excite the vigilance of every friend to humanity and to virtue, in the detection and punishment of these monsters in the shape of men.

To complain of injusice, or petition for redress of grievances, cannot be mistaken for rebellion against the laws of our country. We lament therefore the existence of statutes in the state of North Carolina, prohibiting individuals the privilege of doing justice to the unfortunate slave, and to their own feelings, by setting him at liberty; and we learn with the deepest regret, that the state of South Carolina has recently repealed the law prohibiting the importation of slaves from Africa into that state. Such appears to be the melancholy fact; but we cannot restrain the involuntary question—Is this possible? Is the measure of iniquity not yet filled? Is there no point at which you will stop? Or was it necessary to add this one step, to complete the climax of folly, cruelty, and desperation? Oh legislators! we beseech you to reflect, before you increase the evils which already surround you in gloomy and frightful perspective!

Beholding with anxiety the increase rather than diminution of slavery and its dreadful concomitants, we earnestly request the zealous co-operation of every friend to justice and every lover of his country. It is an honourable, a virtuous, and a humane cause in which we have embarked. Much good has already been effected, but much remains to be done; and, under the divine blessing, may we not confidently hope, that in proportion to the sincerity of our motives, and the temperate, firm, and persevering constancy of our exertions, will be our success, and peaceful reward. Those who live contiguous to the sea-ports, in particular, we wish may be stimulated to vigilance, that none of those shameful acts of atrocity adverted to, may elude deserved punishment; and our fellow citizens of the eastern states are respectfully invited to pay attention to the clandestine traffic in slaves, carried on from some of their ports. Such daring infractions of the laws of our country require prompt and decisive measures.

Many aspersions have been cast upon the advocates of the freedom of the Blacks, by malicious or interested men; but, conscious of the rectitude of our intentions, and the disinterestedness of our endeavours, we hope not to be intimidated by censure from performing the part assigned to us. We frankly own, that it is our wish to promote a general emancipation; and, in doing this, it is our belief we essentially promote the true interests of the state: Although many inconveniencies may result from a general liberation of the People of Colour; yet those which flow from their continuance in slavery, must be infinitely greater, and are every day increasing. It is, therefore, in our estimation, desirable that this object should be brought about with as much speed as a prudent regard to existing circumstances, and the safety of the country, will admit: But in all our endeavours for its accomplishment, we hope to move with care and circumspection. We pointedly disavow the most distant intention to contravene any existing law of the states collectively or separately—We will not knowingly infringe upon the nominal rights of property, although those rights may only be traced to our statute-books; and while we desire to be supported in our endeavours to defend the cause of the oppressed, we hope that discretion and moderation will characterize all our proceedings. We feel with others the common frailties of humanity, and, therefore cannot expect an exemption from error. The best intentions are sometimes inadvertently led astray; a lively zeal in a good cause may occasionally overleap the bounds of discretion: although therefore individuals may, in some instances, have suffered their zeal to exceed knowledge, yet we repeat, that the line of conduct which we approve, and which is consonant with the spirit and design of our institutions, is in strict conformity with a due submission to existing laws, and to the legal claims of our fellow citizens. On this ground we think we have a just claim to the countenance and support of all liberal minds—of all who delight in the real prosperity of their country, and in the multiplication of human happiness.

We conclude in the expression of a hope, that the Supreme Disposer of events, will prosper our labours in this work of justice, and hasten the day, when liberty shall be proclaimed to the captive, and this land of boasted freedom and independence, be relieved from the opprobrium which the sufferings of the oppressed African now cast upon it.

II

Arguments Concerning Colonization

ROBERT GOODLOE HARPER
DEFENDS AFRICAN COLONIZATION

One of the first organizations in the antislavery movement to attack the whole issue of slavery with a concrete program was the American Colonization Society, founded in December, 1816–January, 1817. Although its activity consisted primarily in colonizing free American Negroes in Africa, its contention was that such a plan would facilitate the eventual ending of slavery in the United States. Among its earliest supporters was Robert Goodloe Harper (1765–1825), ex-Senator, lawyer, and a first citizen of Baltimore. In a letter addressed to Elias B. Caldwell, first Secretary of the American Colonization Society, a letter which became an important document in the Society's propaganda, Harper rehearsed the major arguments for African colonization.

From Robert Goodloe Harper, Letter [to the American Colonization Society], Baltimore, August 20, 1817, in Amercian Colonization Society, *First Annual Report* (n.p.: n.p., [1817]), pp. 14–23.

In reflecting on the utility of a plan for colonizing the free people of color, with whom our country abounds, it is natural that we should be first struck by its tendency to confer a benefit on ourselves, by ridding us of a population for the most part idle and useless, and too often vicious and mischievous. These persons are condemned to a state of hopeless inferiority and degradation by their color, which is an indelible mark of their origin and former condition, and establishes an impassable barrier between them and the whites. This barrier is closed forever by our habits and our feelings, which perhaps it would be more correct to call our prejudices, and which, whether feelings or prejudices, or a mixture of both, make us recoil with horror from the idea of an intimate union with the free blacks, and preclude the possibility of such a state of equality, between them and us, as alone could make us one people. Whatever justice, humanity, and kindness, we may feel towards them, we cannot help considering them, and treating them, as our inferiors; nor can they help viewing themselves in the same light, however hard and unjust they may be inclined to consider such a state of things. We cannot help associating them in our feelings and conduct, nor can they help associating themselves, with the slaves, who have the same color, the same origin, and the same manners, and with whom they or their parents have been recently in the same condition. Be their industry ever so great, and their conduct ever so correct, whatever property they may acquire, or whatever respect we may feel for their characters, we never could consent, and they never could hope, to see the two races placed on a footing of perfect equality with each other; to see the free blacks, or their descendants, visit in our houses, form part of our circle of acquaintance, marry into our families, or participate in public honors and employments. This is strictly true of every part of our country, even those parts where slavery has long ceased to exist, and is held in abhorrence. There is no State in the Union where a negro or mulatto can ever hope to be a member of Congress, a judge, a militia officer, or even a justice of the peace; to sit down at the same table with the respectable whites, or to mix freely in their society. I may safely assert that Paul Cuffee,[1] respectable, intelligent, and wealthy as he is, has no expectation or chance of ever being invited to dine with any gentleman in Boston; of marrying his daughter, whatever may be her fortune or education, to one of their sons; or of seeing his son obtain a wife among their daughters.

This circumstance, arising from the difference of color and origin between the slaves and the free class, distinguishes the slavery of America from that of every other country, ancient or modern. Slavery existed among almost all the ancient nations; it now exists throughout Asia, Africa, and America, and in every part of the Russian and Turkish dominions in Europe; that is, in more than three-fourths of the world. But the great body of the slaves every where, except in North and South America, are of the same race, origin, color, and general character, with the free people. So it was among the ancients. Manumission therefore, by removing the slave from the condition of slavery, exempted him from its consequences, and opened his way to a full participation in all the benefits of freedom. He was raised to an equality with the free class, became incorporated into it with his family, and might, by good fortune or good conduct, soon wash out the stain, and obliterate the remembrance, of his former degraded condition.

But in the United States this is impossible. You may manumit the slave, but you cannot make him a white man; he still remains a negro or a mulatto. The mark and the recollection of his origin and former state still adhere to him; the feelings produced by that condition in his own mind, and in the minds of the whites, still exist; he is associated, by his color and by these recollections and feelings, with the class of slaves; and a

---

[1] Paul Cuffee (1759?–1817), a native of Massachusetts, was part Indian, part Negro. He became a sea captain in the Atlantic coastal trade and later was active in promoting trade and colonization in Africa. [Eds.]

barrier is thus raised between him and the whites, that is, between him and the free class, which he can never hope to transcend. With the hope he gradually loses the desire. The debasement, which was at first compulsory, has now become habitual and voluntary. The incitement to good conduct and exertion, which arises from the hope of raising himself or his family in the world, is a stranger to his breast. He looks forward to no distinction, aims at no excellence, and makes no effort beyond the supply of his daily wants; and the restraints of character being lost to him, he seeks, regardless of the future, to obtain that supply by the means which cost him the least present trouble. The authority of the master being removed, and its place not being supplied by moral restraints or incitements, he lives in idleness, and probably in vice, and obtains a precarious support by begging or theft. If he should avoid those extremes, and follow some regular course of industry, still the habits of thoughtless improvidence, which he contracted while a slave himself, or has caught from the slaves among whom he is forced to live, who of necessity are his companions and associates, prevent him from making any permanent provision for his support by prudent foresight and economy, and, in case of sickness, or of bodily disability from any other cause, send him to live as a pauper at the expense of the community. . . .

. . . It is not in themselves merely that the free people of color are a nuisance and burden. They contribute greatly to the corruption of the slaves, and to aggravate the evils of their condition, by rendering them idle, discontented, and disobedient. This also arises from the necessity, under which the free blacks are, of remaining incorporated with the slaves, of associating habitually with them, and forming part of the same class in society. The slave, seeing his free companion live in idleness, or subsist, however scantily or precariously, by occasional and desultory employment, is apt to grow discontented with his own condition, and to regard as tyranny and injustice the authority which compels him to labor. Hence, he is strongly incited to elude this authority, by neglecting his work as much as possible, to withdraw himself from it altogether by flight, and sometimes to attempt direct resistance. This provokes or impels the master to severity, which would not otherwise be thought necessary; and that severity, by rendering the slave still more discontented with his condition, and more hostile towards his master, by adding the sentiments of resentment and revenge to his original dissatisfaction, often renders him more idle and more worthless, and thus induces the real or supposed necessity of still greater harshness on the part of the master. Such is the tendency of that comparison which the slave cannot easily avoid making between his own situation and that of the free people of his own color, who are his companions, and in every thing, except exemption from the authority of a master, his equals, whose condition, though often much worse than his own, naturally appears better to him; and, being continually under his observation, and in close contact with his feelings, is apt to chafe, goad, and irritate him incessantly. This effect, indeed, is not always produced; but such is the tendency of this state of things, and it operates more extensively, and with greater force, than is commonly supposed.

But this effect, injurious as it must be to the character and conduct of the slaves, and consequently to their comfort and happiness, is far from being the worst that is produced by the existence of free blacks among us. A vast majority of the free blacks, as we have seen, are and must be an idle, worthless, and thievish race. It is with this part of them that the slaves will necessarily associate the most frequently and the most intimately. Free blacks of the better class, who gain a comfortable subsistence by regular industry, keep as much as possible aloof from the slaves, to whom in general they regard themselves as in some degree superior. Their association is confined as much as possible to the better and more respectable class of slaves; but the idle and disorderly free blacks naturally seek the society of such slaves as are disposed to be idle and disorderly too, whom they encourage to be more and more so by their example, their conversation, and the shelter and means of concealment which they furnish. They encourage the slaves to theft, because they partake in its fruits; they receive, secrete, and dispose of the stolen goods, a part, and probably much the largest part, of which they often receive as a reward for their services; they furnish places of meeting and hiding places in their houses for the idle and the vicious slaves, whose idleness and vice are thus increased and rendered more contagious. These hiding places and places of meeting are so many traps and snares for the young and thoughtless slaves who have not yet become vicious; so many schools, in which they are taught, by precept and example, idleness, lying, debauchery, drunkenness, and theft. The consequence of all this is very easily seen, and I am sure is severely felt, in all places where free people of color exist in considerable numbers. That so many resist this contagion, that the free blacks themselves, as well as the slaves, do not become still more generally profligate, is a strong and consoling proof that the race possesses a fund of good dispositions, and is capable, in a proper situation, and under proper management, of becoming a virtuous and happy people. To place them in such a situation, to give them the benefit of such management, is the object of your noble enterprise; and surely no object is more entitled to approbation.

Great, however, as the benefits are which we may thus promise ourselves from the colonization of the free people of color, by its tendency to prevent the discontent and corruption of our slaves, and to secure to them a better treatment, by rendering them more worthy of it, there is another advantage, infinitely greater in every point of view, to which it may lead the way. It tends, and may powerfully tend, to rid us, gradually and entirely, in the United States, of slaves and slavery: a great moral and political evil, of increasing virulence and extent, from which much mischief is now felt, and very great calamity in future is justly apprehended. It is in this point of view, I confess, that your scheme of colonization most strongly recommends itself, in my opinion, to attention and support. The alarming danger of cherishing in our bosom a distinct nation, which can never become incorporated with us, while it rapidly increases in numbers and improves in intelligence; learning from us the arts of peace and war, the secret of its own strength, and the talent of combining and directing its force—a nation which must ever be hostile to us, from feeling and interest, because it can never incorporate with us, nor participate in the advantages which we enjoy; the danger of such a nation in our bosom need not be pointed out to any reflecting mind. It speaks not only to our understandings, but to our very senses; and however it may be derided by some, or overlooked by others, who have not the ability or the time, or do not give themselves the trouble to reflect on and estimate properly the force and extent of those great moral and physical causes which prepare gradually, and at length bring forth, the most terrible convulsions in civil society, it will not be viewed without deep and awful apprehension by any who shall bring sound minds and some share of political knowledge and sagacity to the serious consideration of the subject. Such persons will give their most serious attention to any proposition which has for its object the eradication of this terrible mischief lurking in our vitals. I shall presently have occasion to advert a little to the manner in which your intended colony will conduce to this great end. It is therefore unnecessary to touch on it here. Indeed, it is too obvious to require much explanation.

But, independently of this view of the case, there is enough in the proposed measure to command our attention and support on the score of benefit to ourselves.

No person who has seen the slaveholding States, and those where slavery does not exist, and has compared ever so slightly their condition and situation, can have failed to be struck with the vast difference in favor of the latter. . . .

Arguments Concerning Colonization 25

... Where slavery exists, the slave labors as little as possible, because all the time that he can withdraw from labor is saved to his own enjoyments; and consumes as much as possible, because what he consumes belongs to his master; while the free white man is insensibly but irresistibly led to regard labor, the occupation of slaves, as a degradation, and to avoid it as much as he can. The effect of these combined and powerful causes, steadily and constantly operating in the same direction, may easily be conceived. It is seen in the striking difference which exists between the slaveholding sections of our country and those where slavery is not permitted.

It is therefore obvious that a vast benefit would be conferred on the country, and especially on the slaveholding districts, if all the slave laborers could be gradually and imperceptibly withdrawn from cultivation, and their place supplied by free white laborers—I say gradually and imperceptibly, because, if it were possible to withdraw, suddenly and at once, so great a portion of the effective labor of the community as is now supplied by slaves, it would be productive of the most disastrous consequences. It would create an immense void, which could not be filled; it would impoverish a great part of the community, unhinge the whole frame of society in a large portion of the country, and probably end in the most destructive convulsions. But it is clearly impossible, and therefore we need not enlarge on the evils which it would produce.

But to accomplish this great and beneficial change gradually and imperceptibly, to substitute a free white class of cultivators for the slaves, with the consent of the owners, by a slow but steady and certain operation, I hold to be as practicable as it would be beneficial; and I regard this scheme of colonization as the first step in that great enterprise.

The considerations stated in the first part of this letter have long since produced a thorough conviction in my mind that the existence of a class of free people of color in this country is highly injurious to the whites, the slaves, and the free people of color themselves. Consequently, that all emancipation, to however small an extent, which permits the persons emancipated to remain in this country, is an evil which must increase with the increase of the operation, and would become altogether intolerable, if extended to the whole, or even to a very large part, of the black population. I am therefore strongly opposed to emancipation, in every shape and degree, unless accompanied by colonization.

I may perhaps on some future occasion develop a plan, on which I have long meditated, for colonizing gradually, and with the consent of their owners, and of themselves, where free, the whole colored population, slaves and all; but this is not the proper place for such an explanation, for which indeed I have not time now. But it is an essential part of the plan, and of every such plan, to prepare the way for its adoption and execution, by commencing a colony of blacks, in a suitable situation and under proper management. This is what your society propose to accomplish. Their project therefore, if rightly formed and well conducted, will open the way for this more extensive and beneficial plan of removing, gradually and imperceptibly, but certainly, the whole colored population from the country, and leaving its place to be imperceptibly supplied, as it would necessarily be, by a class of free white cultivators. In every part of the country this operation must necessarily be slow. In the Southern and Southwestern States it will be very long before it can be accomplished, and a very considerable time must probably elapse before it can even commence. It will begin first, and be first completed, in the Middle States, where the evils of slavery are most sensibly felt, the desire of getting rid of the slaves is already strong, and a greater facility exists of supplying their place by white cultivators. From thence it will gradually extend to the South and Southwest, till, by its steady, constant, and imperceptible operation, the evils of slavery shall be rooted out from every part of the United States, and the slaves themselves, and their posterity, shall be converted into a free, civilized, and great nation, in the country from which their progenitors were dragged, to be wretched themselves and a curse to the whites.

This great end is to be attained in no other way than by a plan of universal colonization, founded on the consent of the slaveholders and of the colonists themselves. For such a plan, that of the present colonization society opens and prepares the way, by exploring the ground, selecting a proper situation, and planting a colony, which may serve as a receptacle, a nursery, and a school, for those that are to follow. It is in this point of view that I consider its benefits as the most extensive and important, though not the most immediate.

The advantages of this undertaking, to which I have hitherto adverted, are confined to ourselves. They consist in ridding us of the free people of color, and preparing the way for getting rid of the slaves and of slavery. In these points of view they are undoubtedly very great. But there are advantages to the free blacks themselves, to the slaves, and to the immense population of middle and southern Africa, which no less recommend this undertaking to our cordial and zealous support.

To the free blacks themselves the benefits are the most obvious, and will be the most immediate. Here they are condemned to a state of hopeless inferiority, and consequent degradation. As they cannot emerge from this state, they lose by degrees the hope and at last the desire of emerging. With this hope and desire they lose the most powerful incitements to industry, frugality, good conduct, and honorable exertion. For want of this incitement, this noble and ennobling emulation, they sink for the most part into a state of sloth, wretchedness, and profligacy. The few honorable exceptions serve merely to show of what the race is capable in a proper situation. Transplanted to a colony composed of themselves alone, they would enjoy real equality: in other words, real freedom. They would become proprietors of land, master mechanics, shipowners, navigators, and merchants, and by degrees schoolmasters, justices of the peace, militia officers, ministers of religion, judges, and legislators. There would be no white population to remind them of and to perpetuate their original inferiority; but, enjoying all the privileges of freedom, they would soon enjoy all its advantages and all its dignity. The whites who might visit them would visit them as equals, for the purposes of a commerce mutually advantageous. They would soon feel the noble emulation to excel, which is the fruitful source of excellence in all the various departments of life; and, under the influence of this generous and powerful sentiment, united with the desire and hope of improving their condition, the most universal and active incitements to exertion among men, they would rise rapidly in the scale of existence, and soon become equal to the people of Europe, or of European origin, so long their masters and oppressors. Of all this the most intelligent among them would soon become sensible. The others would learn it from them; and the prospect and hope of such blessings would have an immediate and most beneficial effect on their condition and character; for it will be easy to adopt such regulations as to exclude from this colony all but those who shall deserve by their conduct to be admitted: thus rendering the hope of admission a powerful incentive to industry, honesty, and religion.

To the slaves, the advantages, though not so obvious or immediate, are yet certain and great.

In the first place, they would be greatly benefited by the removal of the free blacks, who now corrupt them, and render them discontented: thus exposing them to harsher treatment and greater privations. In the next place, this measure would open the way to their more frequent and easier manumission; for many persons, who are now restrained from manumitting their slaves by the conviction that they generally become a nuisance when manumitted in the country, would gladly give them freedom, if they were to be sent to a place where they might enjoy it usefully to themselves and to society. And, lastly, as this species of manumission, attended by removal to a country where they might obtain all the advantages of freedom, would be a great blessing, and would soon be so considered by the slaves, the hope of deserving and obtaining it would be a great solace to their sufferings, and a powerful incitement to good conduct. It would thus tend to make them happier and better before it came, and to fit them better for usefulness and happiness afterwards.

Such a colony, too, would enlarge the range of civilization and commerce, and thus tend to the benefit of all civilized and commercial nations. In this benefit our own nation would most largely participate; because, having founded the colony, and giving it constant supplies of new members, as well as its first and principal supply of necessaries and comforts, its first connexions would be formed with us, and would naturally grow with its growth and our own, till they ripened into fixed habits of intercourse, friendship, and attachment.

The greatest benefit, however, to be hoped from this enterprise, that which, in contemplation, most delights the philanthropic mind, still remains to be unfolded. It is the benefit to Africa herself, from this return of her sons to her bosom, bearing with them arts, knowledge, and civilization, to which she has hitherto been a stranger. Cast your eyes, my dear sir, on this vast continent; pass over the northern and northeastern parts, and the great desert, where sterility, ferocious ignorance, and fanaticism, seem to hold exclusive and perpetual sway; fix your attention on Soudan, and the widely extended regions to the south; you see there innumerable tribes and nations of blacks, mild and humane in their dispositions, sufficiently intelligent, robust, active, and vigorous, not averse from labor or wholly ignorant of agriculture, and possessing some knowledge of the ruder arts, which minister to the first wants of civilized man; you see a soil generally fertile, a climate healthy for the natives, and a mighty river, which rolls its waters through vast regions inhabited by these tribes, and seems destined, by an all wise and beneficent Providence, one day to connect them with each other, and all of them with the rest of the world, in the relations of commerce and friendly intercourse. What a field anity, which colonies of civilized blacks afford the best and is here presented for the blessings of civilization and Christi- probably the only means of introducing. These colonies, composed of blacks already instructed in the arts of civilized life and the truths of the gospel, judiciously placed, well conducted, and constantly enlarged, will extend gradually into the interior, will form commercial and political connexions with the native tribes in their vicinity, will extend those connexions to tribes more and more remote, will incorporate many of the natives with the colonies, and in their turn make establishments and settlements among the natives, and thus diffuse all around the arts of civilization, and the benefits of literary, moral, and religious instruction. . . .

. . . An objection, of some plausibility, is frequently urged against this scheme of colonizing the free people of color, which it may be proper in this place to notice. These people, it is said, especially the industrious and estimable part of them, will not go to the new colony. That many of them will decline to go at first, and some always, cannot be doubted. It is even probable, and may be safely admitted, that but few of them now think favorably of the project; for men, especially ignorant men, venture unwillingly upon great changes, the extent, nature, and consequences of which they are little capable of understanding. But it by no means follows that the same unwillingness or hesitation will continue, after the ground shall have been broken, the way opened, and the settlement formed. In the first instance, none will engage but the most industrious, intelligent, and enterprising, who are capable of discerning the advantages of the undertaking, and have resolution and energy enough to encounter its first hardships and risks. This is the case with all colonies, and especially those formed in distant, unknown, or unsettled countries. Some resolute and adventurous spirits first embark, and they open and prepare the way for others. It is stated and believed, on evidence better known to you than to me, that a sufficient number of such persons stand ready at this time to commence the colony, as soon as the necessary previous arrangements can be made. I have no doubt of the fact, not only from information, but from general reasoning on the human character, and my knowledge of many individuals among the free blacks. When this first step is taken, (and in most enterprises the greatest difficulty lies in the first step,) when a settlement of free blacks shall have actually been formed, the way opened, and the first difficulties surmounted, others will soon be disposed to follow. If successful and prosperous, as it certainly will be if properly conducted, its success will quickly become known to the free blacks in every part of the country.

However distrustful of the whites, they will confide in the reports made to them by people of their own color and class. The prosperity of the settlement, and the advantageous condition of the settlers, will soon be universally understood and believed; and, indeed, will be far more apt to be exaggerated than undervalued. The most ignorant and stupid of the free people of color will speedily understand or believe that, in the colony, they may obtain a state of equality, opulence, and distinction, to which they can never aspire in this country: hence the desire to join their friends and equals there may be expected soon to become general among them; nor is it too much to hope and anticipate that this desire will speedily grow into a passion; that the difficulty will be not to find colonists, but to select them; and that the hope of being received into the favored number, for whom it may be practicable to provide annually, will ere long become a most powerful and operative incentive to industry, sobriety, and general good conduct, among the whole class from which the selection will be annually made.

COLORED AMERICANS OBJECT TO COLONIZATION

Although the American Colonization Society strove vigorously to attract free Negroes to settle in Africa, it received less than enthusiastic support from the proposed recipients of its benevolence. Various groups in the North periodically castigated the whole colonization idea in resolutions and addresses. Of the two illustrations reproduced below, the first is the response of the Philadelphia Negro community to the organization of the Society in 1816–1817. It set the tone for subsequent Negro responses elsewhere. The second is the more militant response of Pittsburgh Negroes in 1831, inspired, partly at least, by William Lloyd Garrison's campaign against the American Colonization Society. In 1832 Garrison published an attack on the Society entitled Thoughts on African Colonization *in which he printed many of these Negro responses. The two printed here are from this volume.*

From [Responses to Schemes for African Colonization], in William Lloyd Garrison, *Thoughts on African Colonization: Or an Impartial Exhibition of the Doctrines, Principles and Purposes of the American Colonization Society. Together with the Resolution, Addresses and Remonstrances of the Free People of Color* (Boston: Garrison and Knapp, 1832), Part II, pp. 10–13, 34–35.

To the humane and benevolent Inhabitants of the city and county of Philadelphia.

The free people of color, assembled together, under circumstances of deep interest to their happiness and welfare, humbly and respectfully lay before you this expression of their feelings and apprehensions.

Relieved from the miseries of slavery, many of us by your aid, possessing the benefits which industry and integrity in this prosperous country assure to all its inhabitants, enjoying the rich blessings of religion, by opportunities of worshipping the only true God, under the light of Christianity, each of us according to his understanding; and having afforded to us and to our children the means of education and improvement; we have no wish to separate from our present homes, for any purpose whatever. Contented with our present situation and condition, we are not desirous of increasing their prosperity but by honest efforts, and by the use of those opportunities for their improvement, which the constitution and laws allow to all. It is therefore with painful solicitude, and sorrowing regret, we have seen a plan for colonizing the free people of color of the United States on the coast of Africa, brought forward under the auspices and sanction of gentlemen whose names give value to all they recommend, and who certainly are among the wisest, the best, and the most benevolent of men, in this great nation.

If the plan of colonizing is intended for our benefit; and those who now promote it, will never seek our injury; we humbly and respectfully urge, that it is not asked for by us; nor will it be required by any circumstances, in our present or future condition; as long as we shall be permitted to share the protection of the excellent laws and just government which we now enjoy, in common with every individual of the community.

We, therefore, a portion of those who are the objects of this plan, and among those whose happiness, with that of others of our color, it is intended to promote; with humble and grateful acknowledgments to those who have devised it, renounce and disclaim every connexion with it; and respectfully but firmly declare our determination not to participate in any part of it.

If this plan of colonization now proposed, is intended to provide a refuge and a dwelling for a portion of our brethren, who are now held in slavery in the south, we have other and stronger objections to it, and we entreat your consideration of them.

The ultimate and final abolition of slavery in the United States, by the operation of various causes, is, under the guidance and protection of a just God, progressing. Every year witnesses the release of numbers of the victims of oppression, and affords new and safe assurances that the freedom of all will be in the end accomplished. As they are thus by degrees relieved from bondage, our brothers have opportunities for instruction and improvement; and thus they become in some measure fitted for their liberty. Every year, many of us have restored to us by the gradual, but certain march of the cause of abolition—parents, from whom we have been long separated—wives and children whom we had left in servitude—and brothers, in blood as well as in early sufferings, from whom we had been long parted.

But if the emancipation of our kindred shall, when the plan of colonization shall go into effect, be attended with transportation to a distant land, and shall be granted on no other condition; the consolation for our past sufferings and of those of our color who are in slavery, which have hitherto been, and under the present situation of things would continue to be, afforded to us and to them, will cease for ever. The cords, which now connect them with us, will be stretched by the distance to which their ends will be carried, until they break; and all the sources of happiness, which affection and connexion and blood bestow, will be ours and theirs no more.

Nor do we view the colonization of those who may become emancipated by its operation among our southern brethren, as capable of producing their happiness. Unprepared by education, and a knowledge of the truths of our blessed religion, for their new situation, those who will thus become colonists will themselves be surrounded by every suffering which can afflict the members of the human family.

Without arts, without habits of industry, and unaccustomed to provide by their own exertions and foresight for their wants, the colony will soon become the abode of every vice, and the home of every misery. Soon will the light of Christianity, which now dawns among that portion of our species, be shut out by the clouds of ignorance, and their day of life be closed, without the illuminations of the gospel.

To those of our brothers, who shall be left behind, there will be assured perpetual slavery and augmented sufferings. Diminished in numbers, the slave population of the southern states, which by its magnitude alarms its proprietors, will be easily secured. Those among their bondmen, who feel that they should be free, by rights which all mankind have from God and from nature, and who thus may become dangerous to the quiet of their masters, will be sent to the colony; and the tame and submissive will be retained, and subjected to increased rigor. Year after year will witness these means to assure safety and submission among their slaves, and the southern masters will colonize only those whom it may be dangerous to keep among them. The bondage of a large portion of our brothers will thus be rendered perpetual.

Should the anticipations of misery and want among the colonists, which with great deference we have submitted to your better judgment, be realized; to emancipate and transport to Africa will be held forth by slaveholders as the worst and heaviest of punishments; and they will be threatened and successfully used to enforce increased submission to their wishes, and subjection to their commands.

Nor ought the sufferings and sorrows, which must be produced by an exercise of the right to transport and colonize such only of their slaves as may be selected by the slaveholders, escape the attention and consideration of those whom with all humility we now address. Parents will be torn from their children—husbands from their wives—brothers from brothers—and all the heart-rending agonies which were endured by our forefathers when they were dragged into bondage from Africa, will be again renewed, and with increased anguish. The shores of America will, like the sands of Africa, be watered by the tears of those who will be left behind. Those who shall be carried away will roam childless, widowed, and alone, over the burning plains of Guinea.

Disclaiming, as we emphatically do, a wish or desire to interpose our opinions and feelings between all plans of colonization, and the judgment of those whose wisdom as far exceeds ours as their situations are exalted above ours; *we humbly, respectfully, and fervently intreat and beseech your disapprobation of the plan of colonization now offered by 'the American Society for colonizing the free people of color of the United States.'*—Here, in the city of Philadelphia, where the voice of the suffering sons of Africa was first heard; where was first commenced the work of abolition, on which heaven has smiled, for it could have had success only from the Great Maker; let not a purpose be assisted which will stay the cause of the entire abolition of slavery in the United States, and which may defeat it altogether; which proffers to those who do not ask for them what it calls benefits, but which they consider injuries; and which must insure to the multitudes whose prayers can only reach you through us, MISERY, *sufferings, and perpetual slavery.*

JAMES FORTEN, Chairman.

Resolved, That 'we hold these truths to be self-evident: that all men are created equal, and endowed by their Creator with certain inalienable rights; that among these are life, liberty, and the pursuit of happiness'—Liberty and Equality now, Liberty and Equality forever!

Resolved, That it is the decided opinion of this meeting, that African colonization is a scheme to drain the better informed part of the colored people out of these United States, so that the chain of slavery may be rivetted more tightly; but we are determined not to be cheated out of our rights by the colonization men, or any other set of intriguers. We believe there is no philanthropy in the colonization plan towards the people of color, but that it is got up to delude us away from our country and home to the burning shores of Africa.

Resolved, That we, the colored people of Pittsburgh and citizens of these United States, view the country in which we live as our only true and proper home. We are just as much natives here as the members of the Colonization Society. Here we were born—here bred—here are our earliest and most pleasant associations—here is all that binds man to earth, and makes life valuable. And we do consider every colored man who allows himself to be colonized in Africa, or elsewhere, a traitor to our cause.

Resolved, That we are freemen, that we are brethren, that we are countrymen and fellow-citizens, and as fully entitled to the free exercise of the elective franchise as any men who breathe; and that we demand an equal share of protection from our federal government with any class of citizens in the community. We now inform the Colonization Society, that should our reason forsake us, then we may desire to remove. We will apprise them of this change in due season.

Resolved, That we, as citizens of these United States, and for the support of these resolutions, with a firm reliance on the protection of divine providence, do mutually pledge to each other our lives, our fortunes, and our sacred honor, not to support a colony in Africa nor in Upper Canada, not yet emigrate to Hayti. Here we were born—here will we live by the help of the Almighty—and here we will die, and let our bones lie with our fathers.

Resolved, That we return our grateful thanks to Messrs Garrison and Knapp, publishers of the Liberator, and Mr Lundy, editor of the Genius of Universal Emancipation, for their untiring exertions in the cause of philanthropy.

Resolved, That the proceedings of this meeting be signed by the Chairman and Secretary, and published in the Liberator.

J. B. VASHON, Chairman.

FRANCES WRIGHT

PRESENTS A COLONIZATION PLAN

Of all the attempts to solve the issue of slavery by colonization, the Nashoba settlement near Memphis, in West Tennessee, was one of the most bizarre. Frances Wright (1795–1852), fiery and controversial English feminist and reformer, undertook as her first major American reform the establishment, in 1825, of Nashoba as a way to facilitate gradual emancipation and to achieve the ultimate external colonization of all American Negroes. Nashoba's career was short. Its aims as unstable as its founder's interest, it soon became an anti-marriage, anti-religion, Utopian community in which the whites discussed and the slaves worked. By 1830 the community was totally defunct. The selection that follows was the prospectus for the settlement, which appeared in a leading antislavery paper, the Genius of Universal Emancipation, *in October 1825.*

From Frances Wright, "A PLAN *For the gradual abolition of slavery in the United States, without danger or loss to the citizens of the south,*" Genius of Universal Emancipation, October 15, 1825.

Arguments Concerning Colonization 39

It appears superfluous, in proposing a plan for the general abolition of slavery from the United States, to observe upon the immensity of the evil, and the gloomy prospect of dangers it presents to the American people—disunion, bloodshed, servile wars of extermination, horrible in their nature and consequences, and disgraceful in the eyes of the civilized world.

It is conceived that any plan of emancipation, to be effectual, must consult at once the pecuniary interests and prevailing opinions of the southern planters, and bend itself to the existing laws of the southern states. In consequence, it appears indispensable, that emancipation be connected with colonization, and that it demand no pecuniary sacrifice from existing slaveholders, and entail no loss of property on their children. The following plan is believed to embrace all these objects, and is presented to some southern and northern philanthropists, in the hope that, if meeting with their approbation, it will also meet with their support. It was originally suggested by the consideration of the Germany society, lately conducted by Mr. Rapp, at Harmony, Indiana, and (since the purchase of that property, by Mr. Owen,) at Economy, Pennsylvania.[1]

The great advantages of united, over individual labor, have been evinced by the practice of several religious communities—Moravians, Shaking Quakers,[2] and Harmonites.—The latter people furnish a most striking evidence in favor of this system. Ten years since, after the purchase of the congress lands in Indiana, Mr. Rapp's society had to struggle with all the inconveniencies arising from a total deficit of any monied capital whatsoever. The society, now, is in possession of superabundant wealth, and comprises within itself, all the varieties of human industry.

---

[1] George Rapp (1757–1847) established the "Harmony Society," a communal religious group, in his native Würtemberg; and moved it in 1804 to America. He established communities at Harmony, Indiana (1814–1824), and Economy, Pennsylvania (1824–1905). [Eds.]

[2] Usually called simply Shakers. [Eds.]

In directing the attention to the advantages of a co-operative system of labor, as practiced in the above named societies, it is necessary, at the same time, to compare those advantages with the disadvantages of existing slave labor.

It is conceived to be an admitted truth, that slave labor, as considered in itself, independent of the nature of the produce it is employed in raising, is profitless. In Maryland and Virginia, and in other states and districts, where slave labor is brought in direct competition with the free labor of the north, agriculture yields indifferent profit. It is only where the produce, raised by slave labor, is secured from such competition, that its value is certain.—This is the case with respect to the three great staples of the more southern states—cotton, sugar and rice; which articles are, as yet, produced by free labor in no part of the world, in sufficient quantities to interfere with the gains of the American and West Indian planters. It is probable, that the proposed investment of British capital, with a view to raising tropical productions, by free labor, in the East Indies and South America, will at no distant period, affect the present value of southern property. This effect, whenever and by whatever produced, will tend towards the adoption of some other mode of labor, even in that section of the union, where reform may at present appear the least practicable. It is thought, however, that if a more humane and profitable system should be brought to bear in any one state, the example must gradually extend through all.

To render these advantages more immediately apparent, and to bring the first experiment within the reach of a small capital, it is proposed:

To purchase two sections of congress lands, within the good south western cotton line—say in some tract bordering on Tennessee, either in Alabama, or Mississippi, unless within Tennessee itself, or elsewhere, some suitable and advantageous purchase of improved property, should present itself.

To place on this land from fifty to one hundred negroes, [the greater the number, the more will the advantages of a system of united labor be apparent,]³ and to introduce a system of co-operative labor, conducted as far as shall be advisable in the given case, on the plan of the German and other communities above mentioned, holding out, as the great stimulus to exertion, the prospect of liberty, together with the liberty and education of the children.

To open a school of industry which, on the Lancasterian plan,⁴ shall carry order and co-operation from the school room into the field, the children working, under the direction of their monitors, with such intermission as shall keep their minds cheerful, and their bodies vigorous. It is believed that, on a cotton plantation, such a system will raise the value of youthful, to nearly that of mature labor. The same may apply, also, to such establishments as shall hereafter combine manufacture with agriculture.

It appears unnecessary to enlarge on the probable effect, which a mild but steady system of order and economy, together with the improved condition and future destinies of the children, and an induced personal and family interest in the thriving of the establishment, will produce on the dispositions and exertions of the parents. The better to insure those effects, the parents will be gradually brought to understand, in weekly evening meetings, the object of the establishment, and taught orally [in simple language] the necessity of industry, first for the procuring of liberty, and afterwards the value of industry when liberty shall be procured. Any deficiency of exertions, or other misconduct, may also be explained to them as charged to their account, and binding them to a further term of service.

The duration of the term of service must be somewhat de-

---

³ The brackets occur, throughout this selection, in the original. [Eds.]

⁴ The Lancastrian plan, popular in the early nineteenth century, involved training a group of older pupils, who were then assigned to teach younger pupils. Thus one adult teacher could service a larger number of pupils. [Eds.]

cided by experience. It must cover the first purchase money; the rearing of infancy, and loss by sickness or other accidents; and bring replacing labor into the community. . . . To prevent the separation of families, it would be proposed to value the labor, not by heads, but by families, retaining the parents for an additional number of years, rather than manumitting them and retaining the children to a certain age. It would be advisable also, to continue the labor for an additional year or years, the profits of which should defray the expences of removal, and supply implements of husbandry and other necessaries to the colonists. . . .

. . . It is hoped that, after one successful experiment, a similar establishment will be placed in each state; and that when the advantages of the system shall be ascertained, many planters will lease out their property, to be worked in the same way, receiving an interest equal or superior to that returned at present, while the extra profits may be devoted to the forwarding of the general system.

The experiment farm, which it is proposed to establish by subscription, will, as it is hoped, among other advantages, offer an asylum and school of industry for the slaves of benevolent masters, anxious to manumit their people, but apprehensive of throwing them unprepared into the world.

It may not be superfluous to observe, that due care shall be taken to prevent all communication between the people on the proposed establishment, and laborers on the plantations. And to prevent this more effectually, it may be advisable, that the property shall be somewhat isolated. Of course every possible facility to be afforded to planters and other strangers, for examination of the property and the principles on which it shall be conducted. . . .

. . . It is thought unnecessary, at present, to specify any place, or country, for the reception of the colonists.—Many ideas prevail on this subject; and all, perhaps, may be consulted. Independent of Hayti, there is the Mexican territory of

Texas, touching the line of United States, free to all colors, with a climate suited to the complexion of the negro race, with a fine region beyond the rocky mountains, within the jurisdiction of the United States.

This plan, proposed in a spirit of equal good will to master and slave, is intended to consult the interests of both. To prepare the latter for liberty, but in accordance with the laws of the state, by removal out of the state.—To remove, by gradual and gentle means, a system fraught with danger, as well as crime—To turn labor to account, which is, in many places, worse than profitless, and every where to heighten its value. To assimilate the industry of the south to that of the north, and enable it to multiply its productions, and improve all the rich advantages of the southern soil and climate—To open also the field of industry to free white labor, now in a great measure closed throughout a large portion of this magnificent country.

JAMES G. BIRNEY

DESPAIRS OF EQUAL RIGHTS FOR NEGROES

James Gillespie Birney (1792–1857), a native of Kentucky and in his early career a slaveholding lawyer in Alabama, was an early supporter of the American Colonization Society. Largely through the efforts of Theodore Dwight Weld, however, he had been, by 1834, won over to the abolitionist point of view and became an early leader in the American Anti-Slavery Society. The continued failure of the free Negroes to achieve equal status in the United States discouraged him, however. The passage of the Fugitive Slave Bill in 1850 and the court's decision in the case of Strader, Gorman and Armstrong v. Christopher Graham that a free Negro, returning to a state where he had previously been a slave, became again a slave led Birney to reassert his earlier colonization ideas. In the selection which follows Birney argued that the Negroes' position in the United States had constantly deteriorated from 1787 to 1850 and that, since there appeared no likelihood of any improvement, they might better emigrate, preferably to Africa.

. . . You will soon have to make an election—an inevitable one, too,—depending on the open deeds of your class, rather than on their more secret thoughts. The election to which I refer is contained in this question, which each of you may ask himself—"*shall I, if I am able, emigrate from this country?*" If you have made up your minds *not* to emigrate, there will be no use in your determining to what country you should go. I am not unaware of the noble resolution passed in your meetings some years ago—that you would remain here, and abide the destiny of your colored friends in slavery. Neither am I unaware, that when this resolution was made known, your presence and good conduct among us were thought might be made serviceable in gaining liberty for the enslaved. But that day is passed by—that expectation—apparently so well founded—is vain. The state of case that rendered your resolution magnanimous has changed. Your presence here, now, can be of no service to your enslaved brethren. By remaining, you only destroy yourselves. Your submitting, suffering, ultimately dying here can effect nothing on the hearts and determination of your oppressors and the oppressors of your brethren. The nobleness

---

From James G. Birney, *Examination of the Decision of the Supreme Court of the United States, in the Case of Strader, Gorman and Armstrong vs. Christopher Graham, Delivered at its December Term, 1850: Concluding with an Address to the Free Colored People, Advising them to Remove to Liberia* (Cincinnati: Truman and Spofford, 1852), pp. 43–46.

of your conduct may extract the remark that *"such a fellow ought to have gone to Liberia—he would have been a great acquisition there."* But no more influence on those who could serve him than the last gasp of a worn out German would, on the petty despots of his oppressed countrymen, or, of an Irishman, on the tyrannous rulers of his brethren. We think more highly of them, *coming over to this country,* than of their wilting, and at length sinking down ingloriously at home:—especially do we, if, by their self-restraint they *save* something, and send to their friends to get *them* away too. A plan is prepared by your enemies,—it is this, *they are determined to get you away that they may maintain slavery* more undisturbed. As parts of this plan, they are resolved—(and when did they fail in any project to support slavery)—to extend it—to bring more persons to be interested and implicated in it, and thus to make all the mighty power of the government subservient to its existence and confirmation.

Superiority on the part of the whites will always be vaunted over you—*as a class, inferiority* will always be acknowledged by you. There are *individuals* who will be exceptions, but they will be rare, and *exceptions* only. But the frame of mind that these tempers are well qualified to beget, will, as a general thing, and in the long run, become habitual. To this, I know of no exception. We are told that *white* Americans, with all their high democratic notions, become the most listless and degraded beings, when reduced to slavery—as they formerly were by the corsairs of the Mediterranean. It would seem, indeed—as if to show how odious a thing slavery is—that, just in proportion as the feelings and honor of men are elevated in freedom, they become low and abject in slavery.

As long as there was any well-founded hope that the principles of our government would prevail, and that they would in the end exterminate slavery, I wished you to remain here. While I feel still convinced that—should we advance in population and wealth as we have done for the last fifty years—

slavery will finally disappear, as it now has in almost all European countries, its abolition will not be brought about by the *principles* of the government, but by the causes mentioned and others united with them. Slavery is a most expensive thing, in a dense state of population. When this is the case, freeman will perform, and perform better than slaves, the offices to which the latter are often called. Should it ever be submitted to me, for instance, whether a friend should go to purgatory—from which, it is said he *may* be gotten out—or to hell, from which they say no one can get out—I should have no hesitation in advising him to try the former. . . .

. . . But let us suppose that you have answered the first question in the affirmative, and that you have fully made up your minds to remove. The next that naturally arises is, '*to what country shall I go?*' There are three countries, Canada, the British West Indies, and Liberia, to which you can go, and to the last two you may be said to be *invited*.

Canada, at best, is a cold and wintry country, with a climate farther north and colder than those in which most of you have been brought up. The most desirable part of it, too, the southern, is already occupied by the whites, and the lands are at a higher price than you could afford to pay. Almost of necessity, you will be pushed into the bleak and hyperborean regions of it. Besides, a spirit of contempt and hostility against the colored man, akin to our own, prevails much in Canada. They have their Provincial legislature in which white men, mostly of the Anglo-Saxon race, bear sway. While I would say, go anywhere to get rid of this country, go not there, if you can help it. If you do, you go as an *inferior class*, and many of the ills you suffer here, you will continue to suffer there. Nor do we know —and such a thing is not to my mind more improbable, than was, two or three years ago, the passing of the Fugitive Slave Act in Congress—that a negotiation may not be successfully made by this country with Great Britain, in which may be contained a provision for your being delivered up to this government, or to its proxy, the slave-catcher. Remember, too, that you are to assist in building up the nation into which you go, and of which you and your descendants are to constitute a part. On that account if you do not think you owe it to yourselves, you certainly do to them, not to emigrate to any land where you will, *by caste,* be an inferior portion of it, and always remain such. And it may be, too—and if I read the signs of the times right, it will be—that before very long Canada will be separated from Great Britain, and constitute, in all likelihood, a part of this government.

Many of our remarks about Canada will also apply to the British West Indies. They too, have their Provincial legislatures, though they are not so inaccessible to the colored man as the one in Canada. But the whites there, once were slaveholders, and when compelled to relinquish slavery, they did not relinquish the unjust and domineering spirit of the master. This spirit is seen in their multifarious oppressions of the emancipated people *under color of law.* They seem to be mad at being forced to give up their dominion over the slaves, and, in this cowardly way, to take their revenge, as far as they can. The climate is sultry, warm, tropical—warmer, indeed, than many of you have been accustomed to. But it is one of the kind providences of God, that our physical constitutions become more and more adapted to the climate in which we live—especially if it be a warm one. . . .

But I have said, you were *invited* there. 'Tis true, it may be so said. But why? To *labor* for them. That you may assist them in making more sugar than they now have, and in giving new value to old and neglected estates. It is very true that all the honors that can be bestowed there are accessible to the colored man, and that public opinion against him is not so prevalent as it is in Canada. In this respect they may be superior to Canada—but you are *invited,* because they expect you will be inferior, *as a class.* If you were not to be laborers *for the planters,* you would occasion disappointment. So you would, too, should you emigrate to those islands solely for the sake of bettering your own condition, or of setting up for yourselves. The British West Indies will gain but little distinction till the majority rule there, and till they of that majority show themselves, also, friends of popular rights, and qualified in every way to bear office and transact business.

There is another reason which ought not to be omitted, and which would, probably, have some influence in dissuading you from settling down in the British West Indies. Like other old slave holding colonies, they are much in debt and the taxes are high. Taxes, to be sure, are paid, as we all know, by different interests; but every where, and under all governments, they are paid by *labor*, in some form. I know of no exemption that you could claim, were you to fix your residence there.

Of Liberia, I intend to say but little. She is now, and she has been for the last four years, politically detached from this government. She is entirely free and her national independence has been recognized by France and Great Britain. What is true of it, has been as well said as I could say it—perhaps, much better. It would be strange, indeed, if its warm advocates had not, in commending it, gone a good deal beyond the truth. That Liberia is no *elysium* is very clear to my mind. Should you conclude to emigrate to it, I would not have you to imagine that you are going to any such place. In saying this, I intend no disparagement of Liberia, below other *new* countries, but they all testify to the truth of the remark. In going there you are going to a land—rich and fertile I believe it to be—in which much *work*—particularly of the rough kind—is to be done, before the conveniences and advantages you leave behind, can be had; where *labor* of the right kind is scarce and hard to be obtained; where society is rude and uncouth, and where, after struggling with difficulties for a life-time, you will die, leaving things, it is to be hoped, better than you found them. There may be some exceptions, but I speak not of them, but of the general social condition. . . .

. . . It would not much surprise me, if the counsel I have thought it well to offer were, *at first* rejected by you all. Indeed, it would more surprise me, if it were not—although you must see that it is offered for *your* good—that it springs from the oppressive principle that gave birth to the Colonization Society, and from the wrongs inflicted on you by the whites—wrongs that you are unable to resist. I am fully prepared, too, for *permanent* opposition on the part of two classes of the colored people. 1. Those who have made money, however small in amount, it must be when compared with the whites, and wish to enjoy it here, content that they and their families suffer all the impositions they now suffer, impositions that, if the belief I entertain is true, will be aggravated in future. 2. Those who have not more energy or force of character than will suffice them to run their chance of getting enough in this country to eat and wear.

To these two classes—knowing it would be useless—I have nothing to say. But to the more noble-minded—to those who wish to get from under the pressure of irresistible, unjust power —to those who wish to give full sweep to the faculties which God has given to all his children—to those who wish to make MEN of themselves—to those, the sooner the idea is proposed the better.

FRANCIS P. BLAIR, JR.,
TURNS COLONIZATION
TO POLITICAL ADVANTAGE

Like many other antislavery politicians in the 1850's and early 1860's, Abraham Lincoln included, Francis P. Blair, Jr., (1821–1875) of Missouri hoped at once both to eliminate slavery and to remove the free Negro population to some part of the Western Hemisphere outside the United States. Thus at one stroke Blair would expunge the issue of race and the harmful economic effects of the slave system, obviate the problem created by the Dred Scott decision (1857), which effectively denied all rights to the free Negroes, and, in the bargain, aid American expansion southward by establishing client states populated with American-oriented Negroes. These views he set forth in a speech in Boston in 1859 while serving as a Free Soil Representative from Missouri.

[Southerners] see and feel the ruin around them in the poverty and despair of their unemployed countrymen and in the wasted face of the country. They know that mischief must fall on their posterity, when the land is surcharged with hosts of slaves wielding the physical energy of the country, and an oppressed white race, which may at some time turn the hatred now nurtured against the instruments which deprive them of their bread, to those whose opulence and power is founded on the subjection of both subordinate classes. The growing evil is marked by the far-seeing forecaste of the oligarchy, not only on the census tables, but in the atmosphere that sighs around them. But they meet it in the spirit of daring men—political ambition whispers, and as from the beginning, its inaudible breathing swells the bosom of the proud and aspiring with the thought—"Evil, be thou my good." This malady of the South is now to be cured, the chevaliers think, by the sword. Its first movement was by combination and diplomacy to make Presidents, prostitute aspirants at the North, break compacts, seize Kansas, make a black line across the continent, and spread the contagion of Slavery over all the south of the continent and its islands, and make an Occidental Empire, in imitation of the Oriental Empires of Timour and Mohammed. Success seemed to answer to the first well-directed push, but Kansas at last

---

From Frank P. Blair, Jr., *The Destiny of the Races of This Continent. An Address Delivered before the Mercantile Library Association of Boston, Massachusetts, on the 26th of January, 1859* (Washington: Buell and Blanchard, 1859), pp. 20–28.

proved a stumbling-block, and now schemes of direct and immediate aggression, under Executive auspices, with arms, are meditated. The shades of Cortez and Pizarro visit in dreams the couches of numberless military chieftains with the spoils of Mexico, South America, and Cuba, in their hands; and Satrapies, with crowds of vassals held of some victorious conqueror, rise in visions to put our plain confederated Republic of free citizens to shame.

But this age, unhappily for all military meteors, is utilitarian. The sober minds of our countrymen see no advantage in ravaging Mexico or Cuba; nor do they think Slavery such a blessing that they should incur the disgrace of buccaneering to bring a free people under the yoke. It is against the genius of our Republic, born of Freedom and Toleration, to provoke by flagrant wrong, and especially by a wrong having a still greater one for its purpose, the establishment of Slavery in a neighboring Republic, which fought bravely and successfully to abolish it. This scheme for alleviating our plague, by visiting it upon another people, is not just, nor will it succeed.

There is another remedy, deriving its force from the nature of our Constitution. It is, indeed, its healing principle, curing wounds otherwise irremediable. It is Freedom. It is the deliverance of two incongruous races from an unnatural connection, and setting both free. That sable race, bred in the pestilence of Africa, is a blot on the fair prospect of our country. The institution which grows up out of its servitude is a poisonous excrescence, which sucks the vitality out of those to whom it clings. It is an institution which, in making the aliment of the whole society in which it exists depend on the growth of Slavery, makes this at last the lot of all who are not the masters.

Deliverance therefore from a people who cannot assimilate with our people, the subjects of an institution utterly abhorrent to our free institutions, is the natural and easy mode of restoring symmetry to our political systems, and equality among the people and States of the Union.

How happily might the genius and generous enthusiasm of

the leading spirits of the South accomplish this grand result, if the patriotism which lies at the bottom of their hearts could hold in check their heady ambition? Even the soaring flight which would carry the flag of this country over all the surrounding islands of the Gulf and nations of our continent, might prove fortunate, if in the fullness of our strength we carried along with it the wisdom, justice, freedom, and love of liberty, that first unfurled it. But no! buccaneering abroad—threats, violence, and sinister intrigue, at home—are the auspices under which these vast designs are inaugurated.

> "O for a Falconer's voice
> To lure these tassel gentles back again,
> But bondage is hoarse, and may not speak aloud."

If there is no commanding voice to bring these high-flyers back again to the just, wise, and peaceful policy that once characterized our Government, if the two races of the impoverished whites and enslaved blacks, with mutual hate, subject each other to a common oppression, and "dare not speak aloud," the first heavy calamity that comes from either the perverted ambition that would usurp power over the weaker nations around us, or the weaker class among us, will awaken a new sense of patriotism. The counsels of Washington, Jefferson, Macon, and Gaston, of Lowndes, the elder Gadsden of the Revolution, Crawford,[1] and all the lights of the South, that led

---

[1] Nathaniel Macon (1757–1837), North Carolina planter, member of the House of Representatives and of the Senate, old school agrarian republican, believed that white and Negro could never assimilate in America; William Gaston (1778–1844), North Carolinian, Federalist Representative in Washington (1813–1817), judge of the North Carolina Supreme Court (1834–1844); William Lowndes (1782–1822), Representative from North Carolina, argued the States' Rights position on behalf of the South during the Missouri Compromise debates (1820–1821); Christopher Gadsden (1724–1805), South Carolina, served in the First Continental Congress, was an officer in the Revolutionary Army and was active in South Carolina politics; William Henry Crawford (1772–1834), Senator from Georgia, served both as Secretary of War (1815–1816) and of the Treasury (1816–1825), candidate for President (1824). [Eds.]

the way to homogeneous institutions to make our Union perpetual, will again prevail, and Mr. Calhoun's sectionalism will abate its presumption. The patriotism of the South will then scan the cause of the growth of the North, and will gradually open the way to that prime element of its prosperity—Free Labor. The reform will be gradual, as all mighty movements, to be safe, must be slow. Whenever a region is acquired within our tropics to make a permanent home for our American freedmen, emancipation will take place rapidly all along the line of slave States bordering on the free. Our slaves might even be allowed to make compositions with their masters, and work out their own freedom, in the rich countries of the tropics, where the labor of a man adapted to the climate is worth four times as much as in Virginia or Kentucky. And, whether this be done or not, I am satisfied that if such a refuge is provided for the blacks, and the argument that emancipation will place them on an equality, within the States, with the laboring white man, is thus taken out of the mouths of the supporters of the institution, the same class of men, whose prejudices, aroused by the fact that they have been injured by the competition of slave labor, has been made the means to perpetuate the slavery of the instruments of their ruin, will in turn demand that the slave shall be removed—they will vote his emancipation when they know that emancipation includes removal from the State.

It is only by the joint action of the State and National Governments that emancipation can be effected. President Monroe, an eminently practical statesman, gave this as his opinion in the Virginia Convention in 1829, and when it was suggested that the National Government could not interfere in this delicate matter, he declared that it could do so in aid of the State Governments, and that emancipation was not practicable without such aid. "And," he says, "if we find that this evil (Slavery) ' has preyed upon the vitals of the Union, and has been preju- ' dicial to all the States where it has existed, and is likewise ' repugnant to their several State Constitutions and Bills of

'Right, why may we not expect that they will unite with us in 'accomplishing its removal?" The Indians have been removed from the different States at the expense of the General Government, and new homes provided for them; and as there are free negroes in every one of the States, and the subject is thus brought home to the people of all, what is to prevent the Federal Government from offering to all of that class, who are willing to accept it, a home in a climate congenial to their natures, and throwing around them its protection, as has been done for the Indians? I do not propose that any man should be constrained to go there, but that we should offer them the inducement to go, precisely as we do with the people of our own race, when we acquire for them regions like California, in which they can better their condition. Without further action on the part of our Government than to secure homesteads to those who are now free, or may hereafter become so, either by the act of the State Government or individuals, and the guaranty of their civil and political rights, (as England has done for her subjects in portions of Honduras,) emigrants in thousands would soon find their way to freedom—to the rich soil, where the people of their own color prevail, although just emerging from Slavery, over the Spanish and aboriginal race, making the main strength of the country, and holding office both in church and state. Can any doubt that the American-born and American-instructed African, carrying with him the intelligence, the industry, the progressive impulse, acquired by all engaged in the agriculture of this country, would fail to carry success with them to their new abodes? It imparts new energy to a plant, to transplant it in a better and more congenial soil. By the gradual transfer of four millions of our freedmen to the vacant regions of Central and South America; invigorated by a fresh sense of liberty; with lands of their own before them to improve; with immense forests of mahogany and all the precious woods of the tropics, the dye stuffs, the medicinal plants, and varieties of fruits, which make up of themselves a rich commerce, growing spontaneously, and to be had simply for the labor of preparation; with mines of silver and gold shut up simply because of the exhaustion of the race that opened them—a race unsuited to the climate in which they are found—who can doubt that the transplantation of the negro from our temperate zone to that hot climate, that infuses immense vigor into all the animal life as well as vegetable growth that is native to it, would not only create wealth, but establish a great national power, for the benefit of that under the patronage and protection of which it arose?

All the Spanish States of this continent have, in their new organization, made our Government their exemplar. The relics of despotism inherent in their old forms, and possibly the inveterate habit of that people, will not permit them to settle, and the machinery to move easily and in order. A dependency of our Government, composed of a people addicted to respect it, and accustomed to its forms, aided by a multitude of our own race, whose enterprise and interest would induce them to embark their capital and skill in building up a new power to appropriate the riches of the tropics, would form a Republic to give law to all of their caste within the reach of its influence. I have no doubt that all the nations and islands of the Gulf would fall under the influence and make a league with such a dependency of the United States as I have contemplated, and that the whole would necessarily look to our Union for protection. The contiguity of the United States, and the relations which its commerce and overshadowing power would create, and the very posture of the country, enveloped in the waters poured out from our land and the Gulf stream that washes our shores, must make the people who inhabit it with us, though not of us. It would, in fact, become our India, but under happier auspices; for, instead of being governed by a great company, to drive the people to despair and insurrection by its exactions, it would have its own Government, which would owe a fealty to ours, as Canada does to England, which is governed by its own representative Assemblies and by a Governor and Cabinet, which, however appointed, recognise conformity to public opinion declared by the representative body to be a duty. The Crown is but a symbol of authority. Its power and that of the British Parliament is felt only in aiding the improvement of the country and protecting it. The tie between them is a triple cord of increased power, happiness, and glory, the growth of their union. And I believe such will be the bond to bind to the car of our Union as dependencies the free Republics of African Americans now in embryo in our tropics, and the Indian Republics of Mexico, in which the red race now constitutes seven-eighths of the population.

It is the true mission of a superior and enlightened race to protect and establish with well-founded institutions the feebler races within the reach of its influence. The general welfare requires this, and renders it the exalted duty of powerful nations. England, France, and Russia, though subject to selfish monarchies, yet feel the impulse of this enlightened age; and we see the Czar giving freedom and personal rights to his sixty millions of serfs, and spreading civilization over all the north of Europe and Asia. England and France hold up besotted Turkey, and endeavor to instil life again by imparting freedom and toleration to the masses. England extends her principles of representative government, in greater or less degree, to her dependencies; and France, propagating her power in Africa and Asia, carries with it the refinement, intelligence, and skill, which may at some time elevate the people she civilizes in the scale of nations. Shall the mighty State of this hemisphere—the pioneer of the liberal principle of the greatest good to the greatest number—be known to the red and black races struggling into existence, under liberal forms of government, in neighboring climes suited to their caste, only as a depredator and enslaver? They seem to have been committed to our guardianship by the gracious Providence that has conferred so many blessings upon us in the achievement of our own liberties. Shall we abuse the power thus conferred by establishing bondage as the law for all whom we can master?

I dare not speak for all the States, but for that in which I live I can assert that there is a strong feeling among the masses to absolve Missouri from the shame of countenancing the slave trade, foreign or domestic, or of increasing the burden upon the Union by emptying the Treasury and creating a national debt to buy islands of slaves, *en masse,* for others' uses, or even of continuing the abuse within its own limits, to foster the pride of a few at the expense of the interests of the many. But there are difficulties in accomplishing this last point, that the people of the free States do not seem to estimate; and yet, when nearly one-half of these States have laws on their statute books prohibiting the immigration of free negroes into them, they should understand why it is that almost every man repels any scheme of emancipation which would let loose a hundred thousand negroes in Missouri, either to prey upon the community as paupers, or to become competitors with the free white laborer for wages. The removal of the manumitted slaves is a *sine qua non* in every State that looks to deliverance from Slavery.

The alternatives through which this inexorable condition is to be reached ought to be well considered by every friend of emancipation. Missouri may be delivered by selling the slaves in a Southern market, or by sending them, as the Indians were sent, to freeholds abroad, at the expense of the General Government. The riddance to be obtained by selling the slaves of Missouri, their owners would recoil from with commendable repugnance. It is a great error to impute to slave-owners generally, but especially to those of the farming States, a want of feeling for their slaves. The hearts of Southern men, though slaveholders, are alive to as generous and tender emotions as any on earth, and they feel family ties bind them to the slaves who have been associated in its cares and labors, almost as strongly as the ties of consanguinity. It is the reluctance to subject them to more intense labor under overseers, without the family sympathies to make them lenient, that forms an obstruction to Missouri's becoming a free State by the sale of that class of her people. As freedmen, neither the North nor the South will receive them; and unless a better home is made for them abroad, the process now going forward in Missouri to emancipate the State must consign them to the cotton region. The immense accession to her white population from the East, during the last year and this, has put in motion a mass of another hue toward the South, and more light will pursue this dark retreating body, as it follows the shadow of a cloud passing from our fields. The temptation held out by Missouri—the middle pathway of nations—inviting emigration from all the world, is now too great to be resisted by its comparatively small body of slaves. . . . It is madness to suppose that she will long endure the decreptitude of Slavery. And while her slaves and those of the Southern States within the temperate zone are an encumbrance to them, if set free, and seated within the tropics, they would be worth much to the nation and to the world. The value of a dependency there, made up of our emancipated blacks, may be estimated by the readiness of some of our statesmen to pay $300,000,000 for the island of Cuba, which the law of gravitation, that attracts feeble countries to their strong neighbors, will bring to us before long without payment, and which, if we should now purchase it, could only be the right of unrestricted trade, and not the land and slaves, which would still belong to their present owners. . . .

. . . How grandly our nation would loom up in the eyes of the world, if, abandoning the policy which makes it the taskmaster of slaves, it should lay its hands to the work not only of restoring freedom to the race which has so long and so faithfully served us and our fathers, but to recompense them for their long servitude, by giving them all homes in regions congenial to their natures, and guarantying to them a free government of their own, in which, without ceasing to be a part of this country, they should still be to themselves, and escape the presence of that social subordination and inferiority inseparable from the contact of different races in the same community. The moral power and grandeur of the act would challenge the admiration of the world, and make our later fame surpass the glory of the great struggle which gave us a place among nations.

III

Argument for Immediate Emancipation

THE NEW ENGLAND ANTI-SLAVERY SOCIETY DEFINES IMMEDIATE EMANCIPATION

In December, 1831, William Lloyd Garrison (1805–1879) and a small group of fellow Bostonians organized the New England Anti-Slavery Society. The aim of the Society and of the "Garrisonians," as they were soon called, was immediate emancipation. It was a radical concept and was soon variously interpreted. In its Annual Report *of January 1833, the Society explained what it—and Garrison—meant by this term.*

From New England Anti-Slavery Society, "Annual Report, Extracts," *The Abolitionist*, I (January 1833), 21–22.

What, then, is meant by IMMEDIATE ABOLITION?

It means, in the first place, that all title of property in the slaves shall instantly cease, because their Creator has never relinquished his claim of ownership, and because none have a right to sell their own bodies or buy those of their own species as cattle. Is there any thing terrific in this arrangement?

It means, secondly, that every husband shall have his own wife, and every wife her own husband, both being united in wedlock according to its proper forms, and placed under the protection of law. Is this unreasonable?

It means, thirdly, that parents shall have the control and government of their own children, and that the children shall belong to their parents. What is there sanguinary in this concession?

It means, fourthly, that all trade in human beings shall be regarded as felony, and entitled to the highest punishment. Can this be productive of evil?

It means, fifthly, that the tremendous power which is now vested in every slaveholder to punish his slaves without trial, and to a savage extent, shall be at once taken away. Is this undesirable?

It means, sixthly, that all those laws which now prohibit the instruction of the slaves, shall instantly be repealed, and others enacted, providing schools and instruction for their intellectual illumination. Would this prove a calamity?

It means, seventhly, that the planters shall employ their slaves as free laborers, and pay them just wages. Would this recompense infuriate them?

It means, eighthly, that the slaves, instead of being forced to labor for the exclusive benefit of others by cruel drivers, and the application of the lash upon their bodies, shall be encouraged to toil for the mutual profit of themselves and their employers, by the infusion of new motives into their hearts, growing out of their recognition and reward as men. Is this diabolical?

It means, finally, that right shall take the supremacy over wrong, principle over brute force, humanity over cruelty, honesty over theft, purity over lust, honor over baseness, love over hatred, and religion over heathenism. Is this wrong?

This is our meaning of Immediate Abolition.

Having thus briefly defined the extent of immediate abolition, it may be useful to state some of its probable, nay, certain benefits.

It will remove the cause of bloodshed and insurrection. No patrols at night, no standing army, will be longer needed to keep the slaves in awe. The planters may dismiss their fears, and sleep soundly; for, by one act, they will have transformed their enemies into grateful friends and servants.

It will give protection to millions who are now at the mercy of a few irresponsible masters and drivers: every man and every woman may then find redress at law.

It will annihilate a system of licentiousness, incest, blood and cruelty.

It will open an immense market to our mechanics and manufacturers; for these two millions of free persons will need, and will make every exertion to obtain, hats, bonnets, shoes, clothes, houses, lands, &c. &c. of which they are now to a great extent, and while they remain in bondage must be destitute.

It will afford facilities for educating them in morals, science and literature, *which can never be granted to them as slaves.*

It will permit us to supply every one of them with a Bible, and bring them into the house of God.

It will extinguish the fires of division between the North and the South, and make the bonds of our Union, (which is now held by a hair, if that be not separated at this moment,) stronger than chains of iron.

It will enable us to take the one hundred thousand infants, who are annually born of slave parents, and doomed to a life of ignorance and servitude,—place them in infant schools, and transfer them into primary and sabbath schools; from these into high schools and Bible classes; and, by the assistance of the Holy Spirit, from Bible classes into the christian church. Thus they will become ornaments to society—capable men, good citizens, devoted christians—instead of mere animals.

It will banish the poverty of the South, reclaim her barren soil, and pour new blood into all her veins and arteries. The transformation of two millions of slaves into free laborers, animated in view of a just recompense for their voluntary toil, will renovate the whole frame of society. There is not a slave State but will exhibit the flush of returning health, and feel a stronger pulse, and draw a freer breath. It is, indeed, often urged that the slaves, if freed, would not work. But they, who cherish this belief, disregard the nature of mind. The slaves, in their present condition, have surely no motives for exertion; and men without motives are mere machines, mere animals, to be watched and driven by physical force: the natural consequence is, they are as indolent as possible: knowing that, whether they toil much or little, the fruits of their labor will be enjoyed by their masters, they are improvident and lazy. Then comes the whip upon their bodies *to make them industrious*, every stroke of which puts vengeance into their hearts, to be repaid, an eye for an eye, a tooth for a tooth, and blow for blow, at the first favorable moment. Compensate them fairly for their labor, and every stone in the earth would be a magnet to attract them. They would have all the hopes, and desires, and feelings of men. And here it is proper to refer to a wild notion which is prevalent in this country. Many persons seem to be wonderfully perplexed and appalled, in view of immediate abolition. They talk as if the slaves, on being liberated, must be driven into the woods, or become drones or vagabonds in society. In the first place, this expulsion is physically impracticable; and, secondly, the planters are unable to dispense with their labor. The liberated slaves would be placed under wholesome regulations, and encouraged to act well; there would, of *necessity*, be few changes of masters, but every thing would go on as peaceably as in the case of the slaves in St. Domingo, who, for eight years after their liberation, continued to work with untiring industry, maintaining the utmost order, and were only roused to deeds of violence by the attempt of Napoleon to reduce them again to servitude.[1] The labor of the blacks is invaluable—the south cannot flourish without them;—and their expulsion would bring great and everlasting reproach upon the American name.

The immediate abolition of slavery will purify the churches at the south, which are now red with innocent blood, and 'filled with all unrighteousness.' It is impossible that religion should prosper, where the pastors and members of churches trade in the souls of men. 'How is the gold become dim! how is the most fine gold changed! The whole head is sick, and the whole heart faint.' Now, abolish slavery, and the gospel will have free course, run, and be glorified; salvation will flow in a current broad and deep; and for a short time only can it be reproachfully said that there exist two millions of slaves in a christian land.

In fine, immediate abolition would save the lives of the planters, enhance the value of their lands, promote their temporal and eternal interests, and secure for them the benignant smiles of Heaven. It would destroy the market for slaves, and, consequently, to a certain extent, destroy the foreign slave trade; for when the Africans cannot be sold, they will not be stolen.

---

[1] Although there was considerable agitation in France during the Revolution to end slavery in the colonies, including the foundation of societies like *Les Amis des Noirs,* its suppression remained more formal than actual. Resistance of planters in Haiti (the French part of the island of San Domingo) made any effective ending of slavery impossible. It was not until Haiti had broken completely with France in 1804 that slavery in fact ended. The description given here by the abolitionists would appear to contradict the fact of rather extensive uprisings and bloodshed throughout the 1790's and up to 1804. [Eds.]

THE AMERICAN ANTI-SLAVERY SOCIETY DECLARES ITS SENTIMENTS

The year 1833 was critical for the world-wide antislavery movement. On August 1 of that year slavery was ended in the British Empire. William Lloyd Garrison (1805–1879), who returned to the United States from a trip to England where he had been lionized as the American antislavery leader, insisted that an American antislavery society should be formed before the end of 1833. He also wished it to follow the British precedent and espouse both immediate and uncompensated emancipation. A convention met, therefore, in Philadelphia in December. The members, dominated by the New York followers of Arthur and Lewis Tappan, assigned to Garrison, Samuel J. May, and John G. Whittier the writing of a "Declaration of Sentiments." According to May and Whittier, Garrison wrote the document by himself. It was adopted by the convention in the form in which it appears below, after a long denunciation of the American Colonization Society, which the convention found objectionable in tone, had been excised.

The Convention, assembled in the City of Philadelphia to organize a National Anti-Slavery Society, promptly seize the opportunity to promulgate the following DECLARATION OF SENTIMENTS, as cherished by them in relation to the enslavement of one-sixth portion of the American people.

American Anti-Slavery Society, "Declaration [of Sentiments] of the National Anti-Slavery Convention . . . assembled in the City of Philadelphia, [December 4, 1833]," *The Abolitionist,* I (December 1833), 178–180.

More than fifty-seven years have elapsed since a band of patriots convened in this place, to devise measures for the deliverance of this country from a foreign yoke. The cornerstone upon which they founded the TEMPLE OF FREEDOM was broadly this—'that all men are created equal; that they are endowed by their Creator with certain inalienable rights; that among these are life, LIBERTY, and the pursuit of happiness.' At the sound of their trumpet-call, three millions of people rose up as from the sleep of death, and rushed to the strife of blood; deeming it more glorious to die instantly as freemen, than desirable to live one hour as slaves. They were few in number—poor in resources; but the honest conviction that TRUTH, JUSTICE and RIGHT were on their side, made them invincible.

We have met together for the achievement of an enterprise, without which, that of our fathers is incomplete, and which, for its magnitude, solemnity, and probable results upon the destiny of the world, as far transcends theirs, as moral truth does physical force.

In purity of motive, in earnestness of zeal, in decision of purpose, in intrepidity of action, in steadfastness of faith, in sincerity of spirit, we would not be inferior to them.

Their principles led them to wage war against their oppressors, and to spill human blood like water, in order to be free. *Ours* forbid the doing of evil that good may come, and lead us to reject, and to entreat the oppressed to reject, the use of all carnal weapons for deliverance from bondage—relying solely upon those which are spiritual, and mighty through God to the pulling down of strong holds.

Their measures were physical resistance—the marshalling in arms—the hostile array—the mortal encounter. *Ours* shall be such only as the opposition of moral purity to moral corruption—the destruction of error by the potency of truth—the overthrow of prejudice by the power of love—and the abolition of slavery by the spirit of repentance.

Their grievances, great as they were, were trifling in comparison with the wrongs and sufferings of those for whom we plead. Our fathers were never slaves—never bought and sold like cattle—never shut out from the light of knowledge and religion—never subjected to the lash of brutal taskmasters.

But those, for whose emancipation we are striving,—constituting at the present time at least one-sixth part of our countrymen,—are recognized by the laws, and treated by their fellow beings, as marketable commodities—as good and chattels—as brute beasts;—are plundered daily of the fruits of their toil without redress;—really enjoy no constitutional nor legal protection from licentious and murderous outrages upon their persons;—are ruthlessly torn asunder—the tender babe from the arms of its frantic mother—the heart-broken wife from her weeping husband—at the caprice or pleasure of irresponsible tyrants;—and, for the crime of having a dark complexion, suffer the pangs of hunger, the infliction of stripes, and the ignominy of brutal servitude. They are kept in heathenish darkness by laws expressly enacted to make their instruction a criminal offence.

These are the prominent circumstances in the condition of more than TWO MILLIONS of our people, the proof of which may be found in thousands of indisputable facts, and in the laws of the slaveholding States.

Hence we maintain—

That in view of the civil and religious privileges of this nation, the guilt of its oppression is unequalled by any other on the face of the earth;—and, therefore,

That it is bound to repent instantly, to undo the heavy burden, to break every yoke, and to let the oppressed go free.

We further maintain—

That no man has a right to enslave or imbrute his brother—to hold or acknowledge him, for one moment, as a piece of merchandise—to keep back his hire by fraud—or to brutalize his mind by denying him the means of intellectual, social and moral improvement.

The right to enjoy liberty is inalienable. To invade it, is to usurp the prerogative of Jehovah. Every man has a right to his own body—to the products of his own labor—to the protection of law—and to the common advantages of society. It is piracy to buy or steal a native African, and subject him to servitude. Surely the sin is as great to enslave an AMERICAN as an AFRICAN.

Therefore we believe and affirm—

That there is no difference, *in principle*, between the African slave trade and American slavery;

That every American citizen, who retains a human being in involuntary bondage, as his property, is [according to Scripture][1] a MAN-STEALER.

That the slaves ought instantly to be set free, and brought under the protection of law;

That if they had lived from the time of Pharaoh down to the present period, and had been entailed through successive generations, their right to be free could never have been alienated, but their claims would have constantly risen in solemnity;

That all those laws which are now in force, admitting the right of slavery, are therefore before God utterly null and void; being an audacious usurpation of the Divine prerogative, a daring infringement on the law of nature, a base overthrow of the very foundations of the social compact, a complete extinction of all the relations, endearments and obligations of mankind, and a presumptuous transgression of all the holy commandments—and that therefore they ought to be instantly abrogated.

We further believe and affirm—

That all persons of color who possess the qualifications which are demanded of others, ought to be admitted forthwith to the enjoyment of the same privileges, and the exercise of the same prerogatives, as others; and that the paths of preferment, of

---

[1] Brackets occur in the original. [Eds.]

wealth, and of intelligence, should be opened as widely to them as to persons of a white complexion.

We maintain that no compensation should be given to the planters emancipating their slaves—

Because it would be a surrender of the great fundamental principle, that man cannot hold property in man;

Because SLAVERY IS A CRIME, AND THEREFORE IT IS NOT AN ARTICLE TO BE SOLD;

Because the holders of slaves are not the just proprietors of what they claim;—freeing the slaves is not depriving them of property, but restoring it to the right owner;—it is not wronging the master, but righting the slave—restoring him to himself;

Because immediate and general emancipation would only destroy nominal, not real property: it would not amputate a limb or break a bone of the slaves, but by infusing motives into their breasts, would make them doubly valuable to the masters as free laborers; and

Because if compensation is to be given at all, it should be given to the outraged and guiltless slaves, and not to those who have plundered and abused them.

We regard, as delusive, cruel and dangerous, any scheme of expatriation which pretends to aid, either directly or indirectly, in the emancipation of the slaves, or to be a substitute for the immediate and total abolition of slavery.

We fully and unanimously recognise the sovereignty of each State, to legislate exclusively on the subject of the slavery which is tolerated within its limits. We concede that Congress, *under the present national compact,* has no right to interfere with any of the slave States, in relation to this momentous subject.

But we maintain that Congress has a right, and is solemnly bound, to suppress the domestic slave trade between the several States, and to abolish slavery in those portions of our territory which the Constitution has placed under its exclusive jurisdiction.

We also maintain that there are, at the present time, the highest obligations resting upon the people of the free States to remove slavery by moral and political action, as prescribed in the Constitution of the United States. They are now living under a pledge of their tremendous physical force to fasten the galling fetters of tyranny upon the limbs of millions in the southern States;—they are liable to be called at any moment to suppress a general insurrection of the slaves;—they authorise the slave owner to vote for three-fifths of his slaves as property, and thus enable him to perpetuate his oppression;—they support a standing army at the south for its protection;—and they seize the slave who has escaped into their territories, and send him back to be tortured by an enraged master or a brutal driver.

This relation to slavery is criminal and full of danger: IT MUST BE BROKEN UP.

These are our views and principles—these, our designs and measures. With entire confidence in the overruling justice of God, we plant ourselves upon the Declaration of our Independence, and upon the truths of Divine Revelation, as upon the EVERLASTING ROCK.

We shall organize Anti-Slavery Societies, if possible, in every city, town and village in our land.

We shall send forth Agents to lift up the voice of remonstrance, of warning, of entreaty and rebuke.

We shall circulate, unsparingly and extensively, anti-slavery tracts and periodicals.

We shall enlist the PULPIT and the PRESS in the cause of the suffering and the dumb.

We shall aim at a purification of the churches from all participation in the guilt of slavery.

We shall encourage the labor of freemen over that of the slaves, by giving a preference to their productions;—and

We shall spare no exertions nor means to bring the whole nation to speedy repentance.

Our trust for victory is solely in GOD. *We* may be personally defeated, but our principles never. TRUTH, JUSTICE, REASON, HUMANITY, must and will gloriously triumph. Already a host is coming up to the help of the Lord against the mighty, and the prospect before us is full of encouragement.

Submitting this DECLARATION to the candid examination of the people of this country, and of the friends of liberty all over the world, we hereby affix our signatures to it;—pledging ourselves that, under the guidance and by the help of Almighty God, we will do all that in us lies, consistently with this Declaration of our principles, to overthrow the most execrable system of slavery that has ever been witnessed upon earth—to deliver our land from its deadliest curse—to wipe out the foulest stain which rests upon our national escutcheon—and to secure to the colored population of the United States, all the rights and privileges which belong to them as men and as Americans—come what may to our persons, our interests, or our reputations—whether we live to witness the triumph of JUSTICE, LIBERTY and HUMANITY, or perish untimely as martyrs in this great, benevolent and holy cause.

AMOS A. PHELPS

SUPPORTS IMMEDIATE ACTION

Amos A. Phelps (1805–1847), a Boston clergyman, was one of the first agents employed by the American Anti-Slavery Society to spread the antislavery message throughout New England and to organize local antislavery societies. His Lectures on Slavery and its Remedy *contains an extended definition of the meaning of immediate emancipation. Although he supported the view that the antislavery crusade should be preached from the pulpit, he broke with Garrison, in the late 1830's, over the latter's intemperate denunciation of those clergymen who did not welcome the crusaders to their pulpits.*

Different schemes of emancipation take their names from the different *doctrines* on which they are based, rather than from their actual operation. Thus the scheme of Immediate Emancipation is built upon the doctrine; that *immediate emancipation is the duty of the master and the right of the slave,* and takes its name accordingly. All schemes of Gradual Emancipation are built upon the doctrine, *that gradual emancipation is the duty of the master and the right of the slave,* and take their name accordingly. Now the actual operation of the doctrine of immediate emancipation may be gradual on the community, taken as a community—just as is the doctrine of immediate repentance. Indeed, the doctrine of immediate emancipation is nothing more or less than that of immediate repentance, applied to this particular sin; and therefore in this case, as in others, its actual operation on the community as such, may be gradual. It may in point of fact become the power of God to the actual repentance of one here and another there, and not of the whole community at once. And if any are disposed to rate out at this, that after all it is nothing but a scheme of gradual emancipation, then I have only to say *first,* if this be so, that there is no such thing as immediate repentance in respect to any sin, and the the doctrine that teaches it is false; and *second,* that if this scheme be gradual, then schemes that are built on the doctrine of gradual emancipation, are not

---

From Amos Augustus Phelps, *Lectures on Slavery and its Remedy* (Boston: New-England Anti-Slavery Society, 1834), pp. 154–187.

schemes of emancipation at all, but rather schemes of perpetual and everlasting servitude; and *third,* that there are none so blind as those who will not see.

The distinction I have made is a most obvious one. The veriest child can see and understand it. On the one scheme, I come to the conscience of the community as a community, and of the individual as an individual, with the pressure of immediate duty—duty now—duty on the spot; and if, in point of fact, it be only here and there one at a time who yields to that pressure and repents—what then? Am I to be cashiered as a gradualist, and my scheme of repentance as mere gradualism? Not by men of sense and candor.

My remark then is this, that slavery can never be remedied by any schemes of gradual emancipation—i. e. by any schemes which are built, and which act on the principle that gradual emancipation is the duty of the master and the right of the slave. And the plain reason is, the *principle of reform,* with which they start and on which they proceed, is a wrong principle. It does not teach the *'vital power'* of the mischief. This is clear; for in the first place, the doctrine on which these schemes are built is a *false doctrine.* It expressly asserts that present emancipation is not duty, and therefore virtually asserts that present slaveholding is duty, and is not therefore sin. It asserts this to day. The morrow comes, and it asserts the same to-morrow. The next day comes, and it still asserts the same. Weeks, months, years roll on, and still the doctrine is evermore the same—present emancipation is not duty, and present slaveholding is not sin. Duty and guilt are always crowded into the morrow, and thus to all intents and purposes crowded out of existence. And now I affirm that the doctrine which does this is a false doctrine. It admits, perhaps, that there is guilt somewhere, but it always screens the culprit. It cannot therefore be true.

And farther, it is a *wicked doctrine,* and all schemes built upon it are therefore wicked. It is so, because it respects the assumed rights and imagined interests of the master, in preference to the real rights and interests of the slave. If either party is to be favored in the work of remedy in preference to the other, most obviously it should be the injured. But the doctrine of gradual emancipation, and all schemes built upon it, go on the assumption that the rights and interests of the injurer are to be consulted first. They take the ground, therefore, that the rights and interests of the slave are of secondary importance, and that the rights and interests of the master, though usurped and imaginary, are to be the *primary* standard of decision, in respect to the time when and the mode in which the wrested and trampled rights of the slave are to be restored. Now I maintain that such doctrine and such schemes are *wicked*. They do not lift a finger in the way of breaking the rod of the oppressor. On the contrary, they take sides with him against the oppressed. They justify him in the present retention of his usurped authority and power. They even give his continued oppression the sanction of their authority. They license his present retention of the wages of iniquity, and authorize its continuance, until such time as he, himself being judge, can give them up without inconvenience; and thereby, they frame an excuse behind which, if disposed, he may entrench himself forever.

This leads me therefore to say, that the doctrine in question is an *inefficient doctrine*. How can it be otherwise? False and wicked, what efficacy can it have in the work of remedying falsehood and wickedness? It throws the charge of guilt back upon the past, or on upon the future, and brings in a plea of innocence for the present. How then can it awaken conviction of guilt—the indispensible prerequisite to all genuine repentance and real reformation? It pushes emancipation, too, into the distant future, and talks of it as duty at some time and in some way; but it always talks of doing duty to-morrow, and doing it gradually even then. But what child does not know, that to-morrow never comes—that the duty of the morrow is never the duty of to-day?

But this is not the worst; this doctrine gives up the whole ground of debate between freedom and slavery, and virtually takes the side of slavery. For it admits the principle, that in some cases it is lawful to hold man as property, leaving it to the slaveholder to decide whether his be such a case or not; or rather, deciding for him, that it is. It yields therefore the whole ground in debate. It admits the very principle out of which all slaveholding has grown; by which it is perpetuated; on which the slaveholder, in his present practice, acts; under which he ever finds an apology for his sin, and for which, therefore, as the fundamental principle and only safeguard of continued slaveholding he warmly contends. What power on the conscience, what influence on the life, then, can such a doctrine have? Can you change a man's opinions and practice on a subject, so long as you yield him the main and fundamental principle in debate? Can you make the slaveholder quit his slaveholding, so long as you admit to him, that in some cases, himself being judge, it is right for him to practice it? As soon might you think to stop the slave-traffic, and yet admit to the slave-trader that in some cases, himself being judge in the case, it is perfectly right to carry it on. He would be very sure not to find a case in which it would be wrong for him to do it, whatever might be true of others. You never would find him condemning himself as a pirate. He would understand the law of self-preservation, if not the law of interest, too well for that. Such doctrine would never reach the case. It would be the extreme of impotency. . . .

. . . *The only true and effectual scheme of remedy, is that of Immediate Emancipation.* This scheme, as I have said, is so named, because it is built and acts on the doctrine, that immediate emancipation is the duty of the master, and the right of the slave. And I maintain, it is the only true and efficient means of remedy. It is so,

Because it *starts right in theory.* Its doctrine is the *true doctrine.* It takes the ground that slaveholding is, in all cases, wicked; and this, as I have shown, is the true ground. The scheme thus entrenches itself in the omnipotence of truth, and cannot but be an efficient one.

And besides, whether true or not, the doctrine *at the outset, calls in question the starting point and fundamental principle of all slavery.* That principle, as I have shown, is the principle, admitted in theory and acted on in practice, that in *some* cases, at discretion, it is lawful to hold man as property. From this admitted in theory, as the *starting point* has originated, first the demand and market for slaves, then the traffic, and then the system of slavery. Slaveholding, traffic, market, all are but parts of the same system of iniquity and blood. They all originated from, and are all perpetuated by the one principle, admitted in theory, and acted on in practice, that in *some* cases at discretion, it is lawful to hold man as property. This one principle, then, is the originating and the sustaining principle of all slavery. This once denied and abandoned as a principle of action, and all slaveholding would be at an end. Now the doctrine of immediate emancipation, and therefore the scheme built upon it, *begins* its operations here. It calls this principle in question at the outset, and pronounces it false and wicked. It thus lays the axe at the root of the tree. It admits not as valid, either the fundamental principle of slavery, or the objections urged in apology for it. It denies the whole, and pronounces the whole matter of slaveholding wicked, both in theory and practice. Slaveholding and all its connected sins began by *starting wrong in theory*—on a wrong and wicked principle of action; and its iniquities are perpetuated by continued action on that principle. And now the doctrine of immediate emancipation proposes that the remedy shall begin at the same spot—viz. *by starting right in theory*—i.e. with the denial and abandonment of that wrong principle of action, out of which all slaveholding has grown. Of course, true or not, if this doctrine prevails, slavery is demolished. Its efficacy on slavery must of necessity be radical and mighty.

And more, this scheme of immediate emancipation starts

right in theory in another respect—viz. *it assails slavery in its true character, as a moral, rather than a physical evil.* All moral evils, it is true, have more or less of physical evil connected with them, and growing, as a necessary consequence, out of them. . . . But to speak of slavery, taken as a whole, as *an* EVIL, meaning by it a mere physical evil, or at best, nothing more than a physical moral evil; to speak of it as a calamity, an unfortunate system, &c. &c., is to talk utter nonsense. It is to misrepresent its character. Slavery, in its true and real character in the sight of God, is a moral evil—a sin—a crime, and not a mere undefined evil, or calamity, or misfortune. And every man who is in any way implicated in the matter, is implicated in a sin, and not merely in a misfortune or calamity. If, therefore, this sin is ever remedied, it must be assailed and remedied in this, *its true character.* To assail it in any other is certain defeat. . . .

. . . We may talk of it as a calamity, an unfortunate state of society, a great evil, &c. until dooms-day, if we will, and have our talking for our pains. Nay, we may weep tears of blood over the matter, and so long as we regard and speak of it in this light merely, have our crying for our pains. Satan can never be dislodged from this strong hold in this way. It is as a moral evil—a sin then, that this matter is to be assailed, and remedied, if remedied at all. To talk about it, and operate on it as a mere physical evil, or if moral, as moral only to generations past, is utter folly. You can never reach the difficulty in this way. It is a moral evil, and must therefore be so regarded and acted on, if you would act to the purpose. Removal, colonization—what is it but a mere physical operation? What, but a mere *carting off* of slavery? . . . To think of remedying slavery thus, is absurd. Do your utmost, and the spirit of slavery, its fundamental principles, yet live. If you would act to purpose, you must assail it in its true character—as a moral evil, for the existence of which, moral agents are responsible and guilty.

Now it is in this character, especially, that the scheme of

immediate emancipation assails it. The fundamental doctrine of this scheme is, that slaveholding is wicked. As certain, then, as it is, that truth is power, so certain is it that this doctrine, laying the axe as it does at the root of the tree, will sooner or later become mighty, through God, to the pulling down of this strong hold.

There is every reason, then, for supposing that the scheme in question is the only efficient one. *It starts right in theory.* Its doctrine is just what it needs to be, in order to make it efficient. It is the true doctrine. It calls the fundamental principle of slavery in question at the outset, and pronounces it wrong and wicked; and finally, it assails the matter in its true character— as a sin, and not as a calamity or evil merely. No theory could be better fitted to secure its end, and therefore, the scheme that is built upon it, cannot but be of mighty efficacy.

. . . This scheme is the only true and effectual one, because *it starts right in practice.* Right theory generally leads to right practice. It is so in this case. Other schemes of emancipation content themselves with lopping off the branches, in the hope that in this way the tree will ultimately die. And perhaps it would, but for the fact, that the branches grow faster than they are, or can be cut off. This scheme, however, aims its blows at the root. It first corrects the wrong and wicked *theory,* out of which all slaveholding in practice has grown, and by which it is perpetuated. It then proceeds to apply its principles to the right spot—viz. *that practice itself.* Now this is beginning in the application of its principles just where it should begin. It assails the practice first and directly; and does it on the principle, that all indirect attacks are fruitless. What! abolish slavery indirectly, by a mere incidental influence, or rather by no influence, save just letting it alone to its own 'calm and dispassionate reflections'!! Leviathan is not so tamed. There never was a grander mistake than has been made on this subject. Philanthropists in England and America once thought that if they could succeed in putting a stop to the Foreign slave trade, slavery would ultimately die, of its own accord. And so they wasted their energies in the tedious, though at length successful efforts for its abolition. The civilized world, with one consent, pronounced the traffic a crime, and forbade it under the severest penalties. And what was the result? Did slavery die? Was the monster starved, for want of new supplies? Nay, were his supplies diminished a whit? The truth is, they went to work the wrong way. They began at the wrong place. It has been so proved by the actual experiment. The whole matter thus far is a comparative failure. . . .

. . . In the remedy of all such prevailing sins, you must begin where the sins themselves begin. You must dry up the fountain, or you can never dry up the stream. You must shut up the market, or you can never cut off supply. Abolish slavery, by abolishing the traffic in slaves! Shut up the market by cutting off supplies! Yes, truly, if it *could* be done. But it cannot. Cover the ocean with your fleets, and the shores of Africa with your colonies, if you will, but you cannot stop that traffic. So long as the market exists, and cries 'give,' 'give,' it will be supplied. The traffic will go on. You cannot prevent it. . . .

. . . Now the scheme of immediate emancipation does this. It begins with the market. It takes the ground that all slaveholding is wicked, and demands therefore that it cease. It plies the conscience with the doctrine of immediate duty, and rests not until the master has yielded his assent. In this way it abolishes the practice of holding slaves, and of course shuts up the market, annihilates the traffic, and puts an end to the whole system of slavery, and its connected iniquities and woes. I say, then, that the scheme of immediate emancipation is the only true and efficient scheme of remedy for slavery. It is the only scheme that starts right in theory, and in practice too. Let it once become the prevalent scheme, let its doctrine once become the prevalent doctrine in our land, and slaveholding, and with it, the slave traffic is abolished forever. The rod of the oppressor is broken. The cry of violence ceases. The oppressed go free.

The shouts of jubilee are heard. The judgments of heaven are turned back, and God, in mercy, smiles on us again. . . .

. . . Let the pulpit and the press speak out with all their power, and the years will not be many before jubilee will be proclaimed throughout our land, and the world be permitted, in millions of slaves emancipated, to see a living witness to the power and efficacy of the scheme of IMMEDIATE EMANCIPATION.

But you will say, perhaps, 'all this *sounds* very well; but after all, it is a most absurd and Quixotic scheme—"the wildness of fanaticism" itself. What! turn two millions of slaves out upon the community at once'!

By no means. Nothing is farther from our designs and wishes. We would not turn them adrift on society, if we could. So far from it, we are opposed to such a measure. We insist, even, that the master has no right thus to set them afloat on society, unlooked after and uncared for. He may not add insult to injury in this way, any more than by retaining them in bondage, or giving them their freedom on condition of expatriation.

'Well, then, what would you do? What does your immediate emancipation mean?'

It means simply and only an immediate emancipation from slavery, not from all its consequences. It is simply, that the slaves be at once delivered from the control of arbitrary and irresponsible power, and, like other men, put under the control of equitable laws, equitably administered. Slavery, as I have shown, is the principle that man, in some cases, at his own discretion, may hold his fellow man as property. This, adopted as a *practical principle,* is slavery. Rejected as a *practical principle,* is slavery rejected. Immediate Emancipation, then, means that slaveholders, as individuals, and as a community, should at once give up this as a principle of action, and so doing, give up all that treatment which is based upon it, and thus put their slaves on the footing of men, and under the control of motive and law. It is, for example, that England should at once yield the *principle* of taxing us at pleasure, without our consent; and in this *one* act, yield of course, all the treatment growing out of, and based upon that principle.

Or more specifically, immediate emancipation means,

1. That the slaveholder, so far as he is concerned, should cease at once to hold or employ human beings as property.

2. That he should put them at once, in his regard and treatment of them, on the footing of men, possessing the inalienable rights of man.

3. That instead of turning them adrift on society, uncared for, he should offer to employ them as free hired laborers, giving them, however, liberty of choice whether to remain in his service or not.

4. That from this *starting point—this emancipation from slavery itself,* he should at once *begin* to make amends for the past, by entering heartily on the work of qualifying them for, and elevating them to all the privileges and blessings of freedom and religion;—thus doing what he can to emancipate them from their ignorance, degradation, &c.—in other words, from the *consequences* of slavery, as well as from the thing itself.

Thus much in respect to the individual. In respect to the community as such, the scheme means,

1. That, in its collective capacity, it should yield the principle of property in man, and thus cease to recognize any human being as the property of another.

2. That, by wise and equitable enactments, suited to the various circumstances of the various classes of its members, it should recognize them, all alike, as men—as subjects of equal law, under its, and only its control, to be deprived of 'life, liberty and the pursuit of happiness,' on no account but that of crime, and then, by due and equitable process of law.

And farther, in respect to those slaves, who might be disposed to leave their master's service, and become idle vagrants in society, the scheme means,

1. That they should come under the control of vagrant laws—just as white vagrants do.

2. That, if they commit crimes, they should be tried and condemned, like other vagrants, by due process of law.

And finally, in respect to non-slaveholders, the scheme means,

1. That they, acting as individuals, should *yield the principle of slavery,* and so doing, yield all that supineness and inaction on the subject, which grows out of its virtual, if not professed admission.

2. That they should adopt its opposite as *their* principle of action, and so doing, *begin* at once, in every lawful and practicable way, to enlighten the public mind, to change the tone of public sentiment, to organize and concentrate its energies, and, in this and other ways, do what they can to convince slaveholders of their duty, and persuade them to do it. In a word, in respect to all the parties concerned, the scheme means, *a yielding up of the* PRINCIPLE *of slavery as a practical principle—a basis of action, and the adoption of its opposite.* This one act is emancipation from slavery. All that follows is the carrying out of the new principle of action, and is to emancipation just what sanctification is to conversion; or just what a subsequent sober life, the recovery of health, reputation, property, &c., are to the adoption, as a basis of action, of the principle of entire abstinence from ardent spirit. . . .

. . . The evil to be remedied is a moral evil, and we propose therefore to remedy it as such. In the first place, then, we disclaim all physical force, and all unconstitutional legal interposition.

We disclaim all trickery, either in doctrines or measures. We have no idea of playing the hypocrite. We would not, if we could, frame a set of doctrines, or adopt a system of measures, which should say one thing here and another there, or which should profess one thing, viz. to let slavery alone, and yet at the same time aim to overthrow it. We are for being frank, open, plain-hearted. We mean to think out, and speak out our opinions and designs. If we really think the present slaveholder guilty, we mean to tell him so frankly, and not lull him to sleep, and lead him to perdition by the soothing lullaby of entailment, present innocence and future repentance. And if our *real* design is the overthrow of slavery, we mean to avow it, and, from what we know of our Southern friends, we believe they will like us the better for our frankness. We have no idea of catching the slaveholder asleep on this subject, and, by honied words and smooth speeches, tricking him out of his slaves, before he knows it. He will not let them slip through his fingers so easily. This is a case that demands plain dealing. Nothing else will answer. And, therefore, we intend frankly to avow our design; and then, in order to accomplish it, we mean,

To preach the truth, the whole truth, on the subject. The grand obstacle in the way is, the *will* of the slaveholder. This being changed, there would of necessity be a change in all those laws and other obstacles which have grown out of it; and this will, if changed at all, is to be changed by 'light and love' on this subject, as well as on others. So, by God's blessing, we intend to change it; and therefore, instead of concealing our light, and showing out our love in honied words and smooth speeches, we intend to go on the principle that 'faithful are the *wounds* of a friend,' and believing that 'open rebuke is better than secret love,' speak out clearly and distinctly, and let in on the slaveholder's conscience the concentrated light and authority of the pulpit and the press. In this way we hope to reach him, and at the same time organize, and concentrate a public sentiment on the subject, that shall strike off every chain, break every yoke, and sweep away, in its onward and resistless progress, every vestige of slavery. Such things have been done in other cases, and we trust they can be done in this.

And now do you say, that this is not telling how?— that here is no plan? It is the how, and the plan of Jesus Christ, in respect to all sin—slavery not excepted. It is the plan on which he has been acting, and is now acting, in conjunction with his people, for the conversion of the world. It is simply the application of his plan for the abolition of every sin to the abolition of a particular one. How does Christ propose to change the will of the world and convert it from all sin to himself? Not by magic —not by miracle; but by the humble, yet mighty instrumentality of his people and his ministers, living out, speaking out, printing out, and preaching out the *truth*—the one great truth, to which all others are subservient, that 'God now commandeth all men, every where, to repent.' This, is the grand weapon in the warfare, and, through God, it is mighty to the pulling down of strong holds, and will yet bring the world into captivity to Christ. We propose to try it in the present case, and we doubt not its efficacy will be such as to show that its temper is etherial.

And now, do you say still that this is all talk—that it does not go into the detail of the plan at all? Let us come then to the detail? We propose,

1. A national Society, whose special business it shall be to superintend this great movement, to collect facts, print tracts and send them abroad upon the winds, to enlist the press and the pulpit, to employ agents and send them abroad to confer with influential individuals, address popular assemblies, assemblies of clergymen, form auxiliaries, &c. &c.; in a word, to throw out an influence, steady, strong and increasing on the subject, until every section of the land shall be pervaded with it, and the *people* with one consent, shall rise and say to the oppressed, 'Go free.'

And in carrying this operation into effect, we propose—

2. To begin where the influence of slavery is least felt, and there are, therefore, fewest obstacles to success. Of course, we shall begin with Northern ministers and Northern men, and among these, with those who are not committed on the side of slavery, but whose minds are most open to conviction. And by the time we get these right, we shall expect to find that other minds have become open to conviction, and long before the work is thoroughly done up at the North, if we mistake not,

the leaven will have begun to work at the South. Minds there will be open to conviction. We shall then go there, and first address ourselves to the ministers of the gospel, then to other good men, then to the community generally, and among others, to those broken-hearted mothers and deserted wives, who are doomed to weep day and night over sons and husbands that have fallen victims to the shameless licentiousness, which slavery every where begets. In this way we expect to proceed, and what is more, *succeed*. . . .

. . . The thing proposed, then, can be done. To say that it cannot, is to deny the efficacy of the gospel. It is to distrust the readiness and power of God to give it effect. It is to be treacherous to ourselves, treacherous to our country, treacherous to the cry of the oppressed, treacherous to God. Away, then, with the plea, that nothing can be done—that the consummation, so devoutly to be wished, cannot be realized.

IV

Argument from Sentiment

LYDIA MARIA CHILD
PLAYS UP THE ATROCITY THEME

One of the most effective of the early books of antislavery teachings was that by the popular author, Lydia Maria Child (1802–1880), entitled An Appeal in Favor of That Class of Americans Called Africans *and first published in 1833. Because of her following, Mrs. Child's message gained readier access to the homes of the unconverted than abolitionist tracts usually did. Nevertheless, like many other such tract writers, she played up the atrocities which slave owners not only could but did inflict on their chattels. These references were repeated over and over in the propaganda of the movement.*

From Lydia Maria Child, *An Appeal in Favor of That Class of Americans Called Africans* (New York: John S. Taylor, 1836), pp. 26–29.

Argument from Sentiment 87

The following account was originally written by the Rev. William Dickey, of Bloomingsburgh, to the Rev. John Rankin, of Ripley, Ohio. It was published in 1826, in a little volume of letters, on the subject of slavery, by the Rev. Mr. Rankin, who assures us that Mr. Dickey was well acquainted with the circumstances he describes.
"In the county of Livingston, Kentucky, near the mouth of Cumberland river, lived Lilburn Lewis, the son of Jeferson's sister. He was the wealthy owner of a considerable number of slaves, whom he drove constantly, fed sparingly, and lashed severely. The consequence was, they would run away. Among the rest was an ill-grown boy, about seventeen, who, having just returned from a skulking spell, was sent to the spring for water, and, in returning, let fall an elegant pitcher, which dashed to shivers on the rocks. It was night, and the slaves were all at home. The master had them collected into the most roomy negro-house, and a rousing fire made." (Reader, what follows is very shocking; but I have already said we must not allow our nerves to be more sensitive than our consciences. If such things are done in our country, it is important that we should know of them, and seriously reflect upon them.) "The door was fastened, that none of the negroes, either through fear or sympathy, should attempt to escape; he then told them that the design of this meeting was to teach them to remain at home and obey his orders. All things being now in train, George was called up, and by the assistance of his younger brother, laid on a broad bench or block. The master then cut off his ancles with a broad axe. In vain the unhappy victim screamed. Not a hand among so many dared to interfere. Having cast the feet into the fire, he lectured the negroes at some length. He then proceeded to cut off his limbs below the knees. The sufferer besought him to begin with his head. It was in vain—the master went on thus, until trunk, arms, and head, were all in the fire. Still protracting the intervals with lectures, and threatenings of like punishment, in case any of them were disobedient, or ran

away, or disclosed the tragedy they were compelled to witness. In order to consume the bones, the fire was briskly stirred until midnight: when, as if heaven and earth combined to show their detestation of the deed, a sudden shock of earthquake threw down the heavy wall, composed of rock and clay, extinguished the fire, and covered the remains of George. The negroes were allowed to disperse, with charges to keep the secret, under the penalty of like punishment. When his wife asked the cause of the dreadful screams she had heard, he said that he had never enjoyed himself so well at a ball as he had enjoyed himself that evening. Next morning, he ordered the wall to be rebuilt, and he himself superintended, picking up the remains of the boy, and placing them within the new wall, thus hoping to conceal the matter. But some of the negroes whispered the horrid deed; the neighbors tore down the wall, and finding the remains, they testified against him. He was bound over to await the sitting of the court; but before that period arrived, he committed suicide."

"N. B. This happened in 1811; if I be correct, it was on the 16th of December. It was on the Sabbath."

Mr. Rankin adds, there was little probability that Mr. Lewis would have fallen under the sentence of the law. Notwithstanding the peculiar enormity of his offence, there were individuals who combined to let him out of prison, in order to screen him from justice.

Another instance of summary punishment inflicted on a runaway slave, is told by a respectable gentleman from South Carolina, with whom I am acquainted. He was young, when the circumstance occurred, in the neighborhood of his home; and it filled him with horror. A slave being missing, several planters united in a negro hunt, as it is called. They set out with dogs, guns, and horses, as they would to chase a tiger. The poor fellow, being discovered, took refuge in a tree; where he was deliberately shot by his pursuers.

In some of the West Indies, blood-hounds are employed to

hunt negroes; and this fact is the foundation of one of the most painfully interesting scenes in Miss Martineau's[1] Demerara. A writer by the name of Dallas has the hardihood to assert that it is mere sophistry to censure the practice of training dogs to devour men. He asks, "Did not the Asiatics employ elephants in war? If a man were bitten by a mad dog, would he hesitate to cut off the wounded part in order to save his life?"

It is said that when the first pack of blood-hounds arrived in St. Domingo, the white planters delivered to them the first negro they found, merely by way of experiment: and when they saw him immediately torn in pieces, they were highly delighted to find the dogs so well trained to their business.

Some authentic records of female cruelty would seem perfectly incredible, were it not an established law of our nature that tyranny becomes a habit, and scenes of suffering, often repeated, render the heart callous.

A young friend of mine, remarkable for the kindness of his disposition and the courtesy of his manners, told me that he was really alarmed at the change produced in his character by a few months' residence in the West Indies. The family who owned the plantation were absent, and he saw nothing around him but slaves; the consequence was that he insensibly acquired a dictatorial manner, and habitual disregard to the convenience of his inferiors. The candid admonition of a friend made him aware of this, and his natural amiability was restored.

The ladies who remove from the free States into the slaveholding ones almost invariably write that the sight of slavery was at first exceedingly painful; but that they soon became habituated to it; and, after awhile, they are very apt to vindicate the system, upon the ground that it is extremely convenient to have such submissive servants. This reason was actually

---

[1] Harriet Martineau (1802–1876), English author and reformer; active in antislavery work in England and a commentator on the American antislavery movement. [Eds.]

given by a lady of my acquaintance, who is considered an unusually fervent Christian. Yet Christianity expressly teaches us to love our neighbor as ourselves. This shows how dangerous it is, for even the best of us, to become *accustomed* to what is wrong.

A judicious and benevolent friend lately told me the story of one of her relatives, who married a slave-owner, and removed to his plantation. The lady in question was considered very amiable, and had a serene, affectionate expression of countenance. After several years' residence among her slaves, she visited New-England. "Her history was written in her face," said my friend; "its expression had changed into that of a fiend. She brought but few slaves with her; and those few were of course compelled to perform additional labor. One faithful negro-woman nursed the twins of her mistress, and did all the washing, ironing, and scouring. If, after a sleepless night with the restless babes, (driven from the bosom of their own mother,) she performed her toilsome avocations with diminished activity, her mistress, with her own lady-like hands, applied the cowskin, and the neighborhood resounded with the cries of her victim. The instrument of punishment was actually kept hanging in the entry, to the no small disgust of her New-England visitors. For my part," continued my friend, "I did not try to be polite to her; for I was not hypocrite enough to conceal my indignation."

The following occurred near Natchez, and was told to me by a highly intelligent man, who, being a diplomatist and a courtier, was very likely to make the best of national evils: A planter had occasion to send a female slave some distance on an errand. She did not return so soon as he expected, and he grew angry. At last he gave orders that she should be severely whipped when she came back. When the poor creature arrived, she pleaded for mercy, saying she had been so very ill, that she was obliged to rest in the fields; but she was ordered to receive another dozen lashes, for having had the impudence to speak. She died at the whipping-post; nor did she perish alone—a new-born baby died with her. The gentleman who told me this fact, witnessed the poor creature's funeral. It is true, the master was universally blamed and shunned for the cruel deed; but the laws were powerless.

I shall be told that such examples as these are of rare occurrence; and I have no doubt that instances of excessive severity are far from being common. I believe that a large proportion of masters are as kind to their slaves as they can be, consistently with keeping them in bondage; but it must be allowed that this, to make the best of it, is very stinted kindness. And let it never be forgotten that the negro's fate depends entirely on the character of his master; and it is a mere matter of chance whether he fall into merciful or unmerciful hands; his happiness, nay, his very life, depends on chance.

JAMES A. THOME
CONDEMNS LICENTIOUSNESS

Not only physical torture but sexual immorality served to shock northern readers into a reaction against the side effects of slavery. James A. Thome (1809–1873), a young Kentuckian at Lane Seminary in Cincinnati when the famous debate on slavery shook that institution in 1834, gave evidence from his own background of the moral turpitude connected with the slave system.

From James A. Thome, "Speech of James A. Thome, of Kentucky, Delivered at the Annual Meeting of the American Anti-Slavery Society, May 6, 1834," in Henry B. Stanton, *Debate at the Lane Seminary*... (Boston: Garrison and Knapp, 1834), pp. 8–9.

... Licentiousness. I shall not speak of the far South, whose sons are fast melting away under the unblushing profligacy which prevails. I allude to the slaveholding West. It is well known that the slave lodgings, I refer now to village slaves, are exposed to the entrance of strangers every hour of the night, and that the sleeping apartments of both sexes are common.

It is also a fact, that there is no allowed intercourse between the families and servants, after the work of the day is over. The family, assembled for the evening, enjoy a conversation elevating and instructive.—But the poor slaves are thrust out. No ties of sacred home thrown around them; no moral instruction to compensate for the toils of the day; no intercourse as of man with man; and should one of the younger members of the family, led by curiosity, steal out into the filthy kitchen, the child is speedily called back, thinking itself happy if it escape an angry rebuke. Why this? The dread of moral contamination. Most excellent reason; but it reveals a horrid picture. The slaves, thus cut off from all community of feeling with their master, roam over the village streets, shocking the ear with their vulgar jestings, and voluptuous songs, or opening their kitchens to the reception of the neighbouring blacks, they pass the evening in gambling, dancing, drinking, and the most obscene conversation, kept up until the night is far spent, then crown the scene with indiscriminate debauchery. Where do these things occur? In the kitchens of church members and elders!

But another general fact. After all the care of parents to hide these things from their children, the young inquisitors pry them out, and they are apt scholars truly. It is a short sighted parent who does not perceive that his domestics influence very materially the early education of his children. Between the female slaves and the misses, there is an unrestrained communication. As they come in contact through the day, the courtezan feats of the over-night are whispered into the ear of the unsuspecting girl, to poison her youthful mind.

Bring together these three facts. 1st. That slave lodgings are exposed, and both sexes fare promiscuously. 2d. That the slaves are excluded from the social, moral and intellectual advantages of the family, and left to seek such enjoyments as a debased appetite suggests. And 3d. That the slaves have free interchange of thought with the younger members of the family; and ask yourselves what must be the results of their combined operation.

Yet those are only *some* of the ingredients in this great system of licentiousness. Pollution, pollution! Young men of talents and respectability, fathers, professors of religion, ministers, all classes! Overwhelming pollution! I have facts; but I forbear to state them; facts which have fallen under my own observation, startling enough to arouse the moral indignation of the community.

I would not have you fail to understand that this is a general evil. Sir, what I now say, I say from deliberate conviction of its truth; let it be felt in the North, and rolled back upon the South, that the slave States are Sodoms, and almost every village family is a brothel. (In this, I refer to the inmates of the kitchens, and not to the whites.) And it is well. God be blessed for the evils which this cursed sin entails. They only show that whatever is to be feared from the abolition of slavery, horrors a hundred fold greater cluster about its existence. Heap them up, all hideous as they are, and crowd them home; they will prove an effectual medicine. Let me be understood here.—This pollution is the offspring of slavery; it springs not from the *character* of the *negro,* but from the *condition* of the *slave.*

THEODORE DWIGHT WELD
SHOWS SLAVERY AS IT IS

The shocking impact of horror tales was an attention-getter for antislavery speakers and writers. But, if their central message was to be effective, they had to be sure that their stories were substantiated. In 1839, therefore, Theodore Dwight Weld (1803–1895), a revivalist preacher trained by Charles G. Finney, the leader of the Lane Debates, and a principal antislavery leader in the West, published a collection of exposés "absolutely diabolical" as a source book for Slavery As It Is. *His introduction to the collection indicates some of the excitement his oratory aroused and serves to explain his tremendous success as an antislavery lecturer. Unhappily very little of Weld's oratory was ever recorded.*

READER, you are empannelled as a juror to try a plain case and bring in an honest verdict. The question at issue is not one of law, but of fact—"What is the actual condition of the slaves in the United States?" A plainer case never went to a jury. Look at it. TWENTY-SEVEN HUNDRED THOUSAND PERSONS in this country, men, women, and children, are in SLAVERY. Is slavery, as a condition for human beings, good, bad, or indifferent? We submit the question without argument. You have common sense, and conscience, and a human heart;—pronounce upon it. You have a wife, or a husband, a child, a father, a mother, a brother or

---

From [Theodore Dwight Weld], *American Slavery As It Is: Testimony of a Thousand Witnesses* (New York: American Anti-Slavery Society, 1839), pp. 7–10.

a sister—make the case your own, make it theirs, and bring in your verdict. The case of Human Rights against Slavery has been adjudicated in the court of conscience times innumerable. The same verdict has always been rendered—"Guilty;" the same sentence has always been pronounced, "Let it be accursed;" and human nature, with her million echoes, has rung it round the world in every language under heaven, "Let it be accursed. Let it be accursed." His heart is false to human nature, who will not say "Amen." There is not a man on earth who does not believe that slavery is a curse. Human beings may be inconsistent, but human *nature* is true to herself. She has uttered her testimony against slavery with a shriek ever since the monster was begotten; and till it perishes amidst the execrations of the universe, she will traverse the world on its track, dealing her bolts upon its head, and dashing against it her condemning brand. We repeat it, every man knows that slavery is a curse. Whoever denies this, his lips libel his heart. Try him; clank the chains in his ears, and tell him they are for *him;* give him an hour to prepare his wife and children for a life of slavery; bid him make haste and get ready their necks for the yoke, and their wrists for the coffle chains, then look at his pale lips and trembling knees, and you have *nature's* testimony against slavery.

Two millions seven hundred thousand persons in these States are in this condition. They were made slaves and are held such by force, and by being put in fear, and this for no crime! Reader, what have you to say of such treatment? Is it right, just, benevolent? Suppose I should seize you, rob you of your liberty, drive you into the field, and make you work without pay as long as you live, would that be justice and kindness, or monstrous injustice and cruelty? Now, every body knows that the slaveholders do these things to the slaves every day, and yet it is stoutly affirmed that they treat them well and kindly, and that their tender regard for their slaves restrains the masters from inflicting cruelties upon them. We shall go into no metaphysics to show the absurdity of this pretence. The man who *robs* you every day, is, forsooth, quite too tender-hearted ever to cuff or kick you! True, he can snatch your money, but he does it gently lest he should hurt you. He can empty your pockets without qualms, but if your *stomach* is empty, it cuts him to the quick. He can make you work a life time without pay, but loves you too well to let you go hungry. He fleeces you of your *rights* with a relish, but is shocked if you work bareheaded in summer, or in winter without warm stockings. He can make you go without your *liberty*, but never without a shirt. He can crush, in you, all hope of bettering your condition, by vowing that you shall die his slave, but though he can coolly torture your feelings, he is too compassionate to lacerate your back—he can break your heart, but he is very tender of your skin. He can strip you of all protection and thus expose you to all outrages, but if you are exposed to the *weather*, half clad and half sheltered, how yearn his tender bowels! What! slaveholders talk of treating men well, and yet not only rob them of all they get, and as fast as they get it, but rob them of *themselves*, also; their very hands and feet, all their muscles, and limbs, and senses, their bodies and minds, their time and liberty and earnings, their free speech and rights of conscience, their right to acquire knowledge, and property, and reputation;—and yet they, who plunder them of all these, would fain make us believe that their soft hearts ooze out so lovingly toward their slaves that they always keep them well housed and well clad, never push them too hard in the field, never make their dear backs smart, nor let their dear stomachs get empty.

But there is no end to these absurdities. Are slaveholders dunces, or do they take all the rest of the world to be, that they think to bandage our eyes with such thin gauzes? Protesting their kind regard for those whom they hourly plunder of all they have and all they get! What! when they have seized their victims, and annihilated all their *rights,* still claim to be the special guardians of their *happiness!* Plunderers of their liberty, yet the careful suppliers of their wants? Robbers of their earnings, yet watchful sentinels round their interests, and kind providers for their comfort? Filching all their time, yet granting generous donations for rest and sleep? Stealing the use of their muscles, yet thoughtful of their ease? Putting them under *drivers,* yet careful that they are not hard-pushed? Too humane forsooth to stint the stomachs of their slaves, yet force their *minds* to starve, and brandish over them pains and penalties, if they dare to reach forth for the smallest crumb of knowledge, even a letter of the alphabet!

It is no marvel that slaveholders are always talking of their *kind treatment* of their slaves. The only marvel is, that men of sense can be gulled by such professions. Despots always insist that they are merciful. The greatest tyrants that ever dripped with blood have assumed the titles of "most gracious," "most clement," "most merciful," &c., and have ordered their crouching vassals to accost them thus. When did not vice lay claim to those virtues which are the opposites of its habitual crimes? The guilty, according to their own showing, are always innocent, and cowards brave, and drunkards sober, and harlots chaste, and pickpockets honest to a fault. Every body understands this. When a man's tongue grows thick, and he begins to hiccough and walk cross-legged, we expect him, as a matter of course, to protest that he is not drunk; so when a man is always singing the praises of his own honesty, we instinctively watch his movements and look out for our pocket-books. Whoever is simple enough to be hoaxed by such professions, should never be trusted in the streets without somebody to take care of him. Human nature works out in slaveholders just as it does in other men, and in American slaveholders just as in English, French, Turkish, Algerine, Roman and Grecian. The Spartans boasted of their kindness to their slaves, while they whipped them to death by thousands at the altars of their gods. The Romans lauded their own mild treatment of their bondmen, while they branded their names on their flesh with hot irons, and when old, threw them into their fish ponds, or like Cato "the Just," starved them to death. It is the boast of the Turks that they treat their slaves as though they were their children, yet their common name for them is "dogs," and for the merest trifles, their feet are bastinadoed to a jelly, or their heads clipped off with the scimetar. The Portuguese pride themselves on their gentle bearing toward their slaves, yet the streets of Rio Janeiro are filled with naked men and women yoked in pairs to carts and wagons, and whipped by drivers like beasts of burden.

Slaveholders, the world over, have sung the praises of their tender mercies towards their slaves. Even the wretches that plied the African slave trade, tried to rebut Clarkson's[1] proofs of their cruelties, by speeches, affidavits, and published pamphlets, setting forth the accommodations of the "middle passage,"[2] and their kind attentions to the comfort of those whom they had stolen from their homes, and kept stowed away under hatches, during a voyage of four thousand miles. So, according to the testimony of the autocrat of the Russias, he exercises great clemency towards the Poles, though he exiles them by thousands to the snows of Siberia, and tramples them down by millions, at home. Who discredits the atrocities perpetrated by Ovando in Hispaniola, Pizarro in Peru, and Cortez in Mexico,— because they filled the ears of the Spanish Court with protestations of their benignant rule? While they were yoking the enslaved natives like beasts to the draught, working them to

---

[1] Thomas Clarkson (1760–1846), English reformer; principal figure in the struggle against the slave trade and in the crusade to abolish slavery in the British Empire. With William Wilberforce he deserves large credit for the act of 1807 which abolished the slave trade in the British Empire. [Eds.]

[2] Middle Passage was the name applied to the voyage of slave-carrying vessels from Africa to the West Indies. It was also sometimes used to refer to the close, tight slave quarters on the slave ships, located in the most cramped areas below decks. [Eds.]

death by thousands in their mines, hunting them with bloodhounds, torturing them on racks, and broiling them on beds of coals, their representations to the mother country teemed with eulogies of their parental sway! The bloody atrocities of Philip II., in the expulsion of his Moorish subjects, are matters of imperishable history. Who disbelieves or doubts them? And yet his courtiers magnified his virtues and chanted his clemency and his mercy, while the wail of a million victims, smitten down by a tempest of fire and slaughter let loose at his bidding, rose above the *Te Deums* that thundered from all Spain's cathedrals. When Louis XIV. revoked the edict of Nantz, and proclaimed two millions of his subjects free plunder for persecution,—when from the English channel to the Pyrennees the mangled bodies of the Protestants were dragged on reeking hurdles by a shouting populace, he claimed to be "the father of his people," and wrote himself "His most *Christian* Majesty."

But we will not anticipate topics, the full discussion of which more naturally follows than precedes the inquiry into the actual condition and treatment of slaves in the United States.

As slaveholders and their apologists are volunteer witnesses in their own cause, and are flooding the world with testimony that their slaves are kindly treated; that they are well fed, well clothed, well housed, well lodged, moderately worked, and bountifully provided with all things needful for their comfort, we propose—first, to disprove their assertions by the testimony of a multitude of impartial witnesses, and then to put slaveholders themselves through a course of cross-questioning which shall draw their condemnation out of their own mouths. We will prove that the slaves in the United States are treated with barbarous inhumanity; that they are overworked, underfed, wretchedly clad and lodged, and have insufficient sleep; that they are often made to wear round their necks iron collars armed with prongs, to drag heavy chains and weights at their feet while working in the field, and to wear yokes, and bells, and iron horns; that they are often kept confined in the stocks day and night for weeks together, made to wear gags in their mouths for hours or days, have some of their front teeth torn out or broken off, that they may be easily detected when they run away; that they are frequently flogged with terrible severity, have red pepper rubbed into their lacerated flesh, and hot brine, spirits of turpentine, &c., poured over the gashes to increase the torture; that they are often stripped naked, their backs and limbs cut with knives, bruised and mangled by scores and hundreds of blows with the paddle, and terribly torn by the claws of cats, drawn over them by their tormentors; that they are often hunted with blood hounds and shot down like beasts, or torn in pieces by dogs; that they are often suspended by the arms and whipped and beaten till they faint, and when revived by restoratives, beaten again till they faint, and sometimes till they die; that their ears are often cut off, their eyes knocked out, their bones broken, their flesh branded with red hot irons; that they are maimed, mutilated and burned to death over slow fires. All these things, and more, and worse, we shall *prove*. Reader, we know whereof we affirm, we have weighed it well; *more and worse* WE WILL PROVE. Mark these words, and read on; we will establish all these facts by the testimony of scores and hundreds of eye witnesses, by the testimony of *slaveholders* in all parts of the slave states, by slaveholding members of Congress and of state legislatures, by ambassadors to foreign courts, by judges, by doctors of divinity, and clergymen of all denominations, by merchants, mechanics, lawyers and physicians, by presidents and professors in colleges and *professional* seminaries, by planters, overseers and drivers. We shall show, not merely that such deeds are committed, but that they are frequent; not done in corners, but before the sun; not in one of the slave states, but in all of them; not perpetrated by brutal overseers and drivers merely, but by magistrates, by legislators, by professors of religion, by preachers of the gospel, by governors of states, by "gentlemen of property and standing," and by delicate females moving in the "highest

Argument from Sentiment 101

circles of society." We know, full well, the outcry that will be made by multitudes, at these declarations; the multiform cavils, the flat denials, the charges of "exaggeration" and "falsehood" so often bandied, the sneers of affected contempt at the credulity that can believe such things, and the rage and imprecations against those who give them currency. We know, too, the threadbare sophistries by which slaveholders and their apologists seek to evade such testimony. If they admit that such deeds are committed, they tell us that they are exceedingly rare, and therefore furnish no grounds for judging of the general treatment of slaves; that occasionally a brutal wretch in the *free* states barbarously butchers his wife, but that no one thinks of inferring from that, the general treatment of wives at the North and West.

They tell us, also, that the slaveholders of the South are proverbially hospitable, kind, and generous, and it is incredible that they can perpetrate such enormities upon human beings; further, that it is absurd to suppose that they would thus injure their own property, that self interest would prompt them to treat their slaves with kindness, as none but fools and madmen wantonly destroy their own property; further, that Northern visitors at the South come back testifying to the kind treatment of the slaves, and that the slaves themselves corroborate such representations. All these pleas, and scores of others, are bruited in every corner of the free States; and who that hath eyes to see, has not sickened at the blindness that saw not, at the palsy of heart that felt not, or at the cowardice and sycophancy that dared not expose such shallow fallacies. We are not to be turned from our purpose by such vapid babblings. In their appropriate places, we propose to consider these objections and various others, and to show their emptiness and folly.

The foregoing declarations touching the inflictions upon slaves, are not hap-hazard assertions, nor the exaggerations of fiction conjured up to carry a point; nor are they the rhapsodies of enthusiasm, nor crude conclusions, jumped at by hasty and imperfect investigation, nor the aimless outpourings either of sympathy or poetry; but they are proclamations of deliberate, well-weighed convictions, produced by accumulations of proof, by affirmations and affidavits, by written testimonies and statements of a cloud of witnesses who speak what they know and testify what they have seen, and all these impregnably fortified by proofs innumerable, in the relation of the slaveholder to his slave, the nature of arbitrary power, and the nature and history of man.

JOHN GREENLEAF WHITTIER
STIRS SYMPATHY FOR THE FUGITIVES

Often poetry could appeal more directly to sentiment than the longer and more formidable antislavery article or essay. Of the many abolitionists who contributed poetic efforts to the cause, John Greenleaf Whittier (1807–1892) and James Russell Lowell stand out. Whittier, a Quaker who was discovered by Garrison early in his editing career, edited the Pennsylvania Freeman, *wrote tracts, among which the early* Justice and Expediency *(1833) stands out, and contributed a constant stream of antislavery verse to the cause. In the brief poem which follows Whittier rouses antipathy for the master and sympathy for the runaway slave.*

John Greenleaf Whittier, "The Hunters of Men," in *Poems Written During the Progress of the Abolition Question in the United States, Between the Years 1830 and 1838* (Boston: Isaac Knapp, 1837), pp. 23–25.

THE HUNTERS OF MEN.

Have ye heard of our hunting, our mountain and glen
Through cane-brake and forest—the hunting of men?
The lords of our land to this hunting have gone,
As the fox-hunter follows the sound of the horn:
Hark—the cheer and the hallo! the crack of the
    whip,
And the yell of the hound as he fastens his grip!
All blithe are our hunters, and noble their match—
Though *hundreds* are caught, there are *millions* to
    catch:
So speed to their hunting, o'er mountain and glen,
Through cane-brake and forest—the hunting of men!

Gay luck to our hunters!—how nobly they ride
In the glow of their zeal, and the strength of their
    pride!—
The Priest with his cassock flung back on the wind,
Just screening the politic Statesman behind—
The saint and the sinner, with cursing and prayer—
The drunk and the sober, ride merrily there.
And woman—kind woman—wife, widow and maid—
For *the good of the hunted*—is lending her aid:
Her foot's in the stirrup—her hand on the rein—
How blithely she rides to the hunting of men!

Oh! goodly and grand is our hunting to see,
In this 'land of the brave and this home of the free.'
Priest, warrior, and statesman, from Georgia to Maine,
All mounting the saddle—all grasping the rein—
Right merrily hunting the black man, whose sin
Is the curl of his hair and the hue of his skin!
Wo, now to the hunted who turns him at bay!

Will our hunters be turned from their purpose and
    prey?
Will their hearts fail within them?—their nerves
    tremble, when
All roughly they ride to the hunting of men?

Ho—ALMS for our hunters! all weary and faint
Wax the curse of the sinner and prayer of the saint.
The horn is wound faintly—the echoes are still
Over cane-brake and river, and forest and hill.
Haste—alms for our hunters! the hunted once more
Have turned from their flight with their backs to the
    shore:
What right have *they* here in the home of the white,
Shadowed o'er by *our* banner of Freedom and Right?
Ho—alms for the hunters! or never again
Will they ride in their pomp to the hunting of men!

ALMS—ALMS for our hunters! why *will* ye delay,
When their pride and their glory are melting away?
The parson has turned; for, on charge of his own,
Who goeth a warfare, or hunting, alone?
The politic statesman looks back with a sigh—
There is doubt in his heart—there is fear in his eye.
Oh! haste, lest that doubting and fear shall prevail,
And the head of his steed take the place of his tail.
Oh! haste, ere he leave us! for who will ride then,
For pleasure or gain, to the hunting of men!

HARRIET BEECHER STOWE DESCRIBES SLAVERY'S HORRORS IN FICTION

The novel was an increasingly popular form of antislavery literature in the 1850's, particularly after the successful publication of Harriet Beecher Stowe's (1811–1896) Uncle Tom's Cabin (1852). Mrs. Stowe wrote a second novel, in 1856, on the subject of slavery, Dred, A Tale of the Great Dismal Swamp, *in which, once again, she appealed to the sensibilities of her readers to impress upon them the horrors of slavery.*

"Mr. Gordon has, I think, a sister of Harry's, who came in with this new estate," said Mr. Clayton.[1]

"Yes, yes," said Mr. Jekyl. "She has given us a good deal of trouble, too. She got away, and went off to Cincinnati, and I had to go up and hunt her out. It was really a great deal of trouble and expense. If I had n't been assisted by the politeness and kindness of the marshal and brother officers, it would have been very bad. There is a good deal of religious society,

From Harriet Beecher Stowe, *Dred, A Tale of the Great Dismal Swamp,* in *Dred. . . Together with Anti-Slavery Tales and Papers, and Life in Florida After the War,* II (Boston: Houghton, Mifflin and Company, 1896), 69–74.

[1] Mr. Clayton is the hero of *Dred.* He hated slavery and went to Canada and established a settlement for Negroes there. Mrs. Stowe patterned him on the Reverend William King, whose plan for the Elgin settlement is reproduced in Section 7 of this collection. Mr. Jekyl was a neighbor. In this excerpt Clayton goes to Alexandria to search for Cora Gordon, slave of Mr. Gordon, who has been sold to the slave traders. [Eds.]

too, in Cincinnati; and so, while I was waiting, I attended anniversary meetings."

"Then you did succeed," said Clayton. "I came to see whether Mr. Gordon would listen to a proposition for selling her."

"Oh, he has sold her!" said Mr. Jekyl. "She is at Alexandria now, in Beaton & Burns's establishment."

"And her children, too?"

"Yes, the lot. I claim some little merit for that myself. Tom is a fellow of rather strong passions, and he was terribly angry for the trouble she had made. I don't know what he would have done to her if I had n't talked to him. But I showed him some debts that could n't be put off any longer without too much of a sacrifice; and, on the whole, I persuaded him to let her be sold. I have tried to exert a good influence over him in a quiet way," said Mr. Jekyl. "Now, if you want to get the woman, like enough she may not be sold as yet."

Clayton, having thus ascertained the points which he wished to know, proceeded immediately to Alexandria. When he was there, he found a considerable excitement.

"A slave woman," it was said, "who was to have been sent off in a coffle the next day, had murdered her two children."

The moment that Clayton heard the news, he felt an instinctive certainty that this woman was Cora Gordon. He went to the magistrate's court, where the investigation was being held, and found it surrounded by a crowd so dense that it was with difficulty he forced his way in. At the bar he saw seated a woman dressed in black, whose face, haggard and wan, showed yet traces of former beauty. The splendid dark eyes had a peculiar and fierce expression. The thin lines of the face were settled into an immovable fixedness of calm determination. There was even an air of grave, solemn triumph on her countenance. She appeared to regard the formalities of the court with the utmost indifference. At last she spoke, in a clear, thrilling, distinct voice:—

"If gentlemen will allow me to speak, I'll save them the

trouble of that examination of witnesses. It's going a long way round to find out a very little thing."

There was an immediate movement of curiosity in the whole throng, and the officer said,—

"You are permitted to speak."

She rose deliberately, untied her bonnet-strings, looked round the whole court, with a peculiar but calm expression of mingled triumph and power.

"You want to know," she said, "who killed those children! Well, I will tell you;" and again her eyes traveled round the house, with that same strong, defiant expression; "I killed them!"

There was a pause, and a general movement through the house.

"Yes," she said again, "I killed them! And oh, how glad I am that I have done it! Do you want to know what I killed them for? Because I loved them!—loved them so well that I was willing to give up my soul to save theirs! I have heard some persons say that I was in a frenzy, excited, and did n't know what I was doing. They are mistaken. I was not in a frenzy; I was not excited; and I did know what I was doing! and I bless God that it is done! I was born the slave of my own father. Your old proud Virginia blood is in my veins, as it is in half of those you whip and sell. I was the lawful wife of a man of honor, who did what he could to evade your cruel laws and set me free. My children were born to liberty; they were brought up to liberty, till my father's son entered a suit for us and made us *slaves*. Judge and jury helped him—all your laws and your officers helped him—to take away the rights of the widow and the fatherless! The judge said that my son, being a slave, could no more hold property than the mule before his plough; and we were delivered into Tom Gordon's hands. I shall not say what he is. It is not fit to be said. God will show at the judgment day. But I escaped, with my children, to Cincinnati. He followed me there, and the laws of your country gave me back to him. To-morrow I was to have gone in a coffle and leave these children—my son a slave for life—my daughter"— She looked around the court-room with an expression which said more than words could have spoken. "So I heard them say their prayers and sing their hymns, and then, while they were asleep and did n't know it, I sent them to lie down in green pastures with the Lord. They say this is a dreadful sin. It may be so. I am willing to lose my soul to have theirs saved. I have no more to hope or fear. It's all nothing, now, where I go or what becomes of me. But, at any rate, they are safe. And now, if any of you mothers, in my place, would n't have done the same, you either don't know what slavery is, or you don't love your children as I have loved mine. This is all."

She sat down, folded her arms, fixed her eyes on the floor, and seemed like a person entirely indifferent to the further opinions and proceedings of the court.

She was remanded to jail for trial. Clayton determined, in his own mind, to do what he could for her. Her own declaration seemed to make the form of a trial unnecessary. He resolved, however, to do what he could to enlist for her the sympathy of some friends of his in the city. The next day he called with a clergyman and requested permission to see her. When they entered her cell, she rose to receive them with the most perfect composure, as if they had called upon her in a drawing-room. Clayton introduced his companion as the Rev. Mr. Denton. There was an excited flash in her eyes, but she said calmly,—

"Have the gentlemen business with me?"

"We called," said the clergyman, "to see if we could render you any assistance."

"No, sir, you cannot!" was the prompt reply.

"My dear friend," said the clergyman, in a very kind tone, "I wish it were in my power to administer to you the consolations of the gospel."

"I have nothing to do," she answered firmly, "with ministers who pretend to preach the gospel and support oppression and robbery! Your hands are defiled with blood!—so don't come to me! I am a prisoner here, and cannot resist. But when I tell you that I prefer to be left alone, perhaps it may have some effect, even if I am a slave!"

Clayton took out Harry's letter, handed it to her, and said:—

"After you have read this you will, perhaps, receive me, if I should call again to-morrow at this hour."

The next day, when Clayton called, he was conducted by the jailer to the door of the cell.

"There is a lady with her now, reading to her."

"Then I ought not to interrupt her," said Clayton, hesitating.

"Oh, I suspect it would make no odds," said the jailer.

Clayton laid his hand on his to stop him. The sound that came indistinctly through the door was the voice of prayer. Some woman was interceding, in the presence of Eternal Pity, for an oppressed and broken-hearted sister. After a few moments the door was partly opened, and he heard a sweet voice, saying:—

"Let me come to you every day, may I? I know what it is to suffer."

A smothered sob was the only answer; and then followed words, imperfectly distinguished, which seemed to be those of consolation. In a moment the door was opened, and Clayton found himself suddenly face to face with a lady in deep mourning. She was tall, and largely proportioned; the outlines of her face strong, yet beautiful, and now wearing the expression which comes from communion with the highest and serenest nature. Both were embarrassed, and made a momentary pause. In the start she dropped one of her gloves. Clayton picked it up, handed it to her, bowed, and she passed on. By some singular association, this stranger, with a serious, radiant face, suggested to him the sparkling, glittering beauty of Nina; and it seemed for a moment as if Nina was fluttering by him in the air, and passing away after her. When he examined the emotion more minutely afterwards, he thought, perhaps, it might have been suggested by the perception, as he lifted the glove, of a peculiar and delicate perfume which Nina was fond of using. So strange and shadowy are the influences which touch the dark, electric chain of our existence!

When Clayton went into the cell, he found its inmate in a softened mood. There were traces of tears on her cheek, and an open Bible on the bed; but her appearance was calm and self-possessed, as usual. She said:—

"Excuse my rudeness, Mr. Clayton, at your last visit. We cannot always command ourselves to do exactly what we should. I thank you very much for your kindness to us. There are many who are kindly disposed towards us, but it's very little that they can do."

"Can I be of any assistance in securing counsel for you?" said Clayton.

"I don't need any counsel. I don't wish any," said she. "I shall make no effort. Let the law take its course. If you ever should see Harry, give my love to him,—that's all! And if you can help him, pray do! If you have time, influence, or money to spare, and can get him to any country where he will have the common rights of a human being, pray do, and the blessing of the poor will come on you! That's all I have to ask."

Clayton rose to depart. He had fulfilled the object of his mission. He had gained all the information, and more than all, that he wished.

V

Arguments from Religion

LEONARD BACON
PLEADS FOR MODERATION

The spectrum of the religious antislavery arguments is as varied as any of the antislavery arguments. Leonard Bacon (1802–1881) was an early and prominent ministerial opponent of slavery and an active worker for the American Colonization Society. Like his famous Congregational colleague, Lyman Beecher, he deplored slavery, but, moderate and temperate in approach, he rejected out of hand what he considered the ill-conceived and uncouth extremism of the Garrisonians. The selection which follows was first printed in the Quarterly Christian Spectator *in 1833.*

From Leonard Bacon, "Slavery," in *Slavery Discussed in Occasional Essays, From 1833 to 1846* (New York: Baker and Scribner, 1846), pp. 50–55.

Ought the naked fact, that a certain man is the master of slaves, to exclude him, without farther inquiry, from the communion of the churches? We answer, No. It may be that he came into that relation without any act of his own. It may be that he is doing for the welfare of those slaves, conscientiously and diligently, the most that existing circumstances will allow. It may be that if he emancipates them from under his hand, the sheriff will immediately arrest them, and sell them to the highest bidder. It may be that he is prosecuting a course of measures, which, after less than a seven years' "apprenticeship," will result in their real emancipation. The mere fact that he is invested with a certain legal power over the persons of these individuals, implying a certain legal title to their services, is not necessarily a crime. The author of these letters on slavery, while he was educating his servants to take care of themselves, and providing their outfit to Liberia, was not a criminal, though he was still their master, and as such, responsible for their good government. The question, in each individual instance, is, Whence did this man obtain his power over these his fellow-men? and to what ends is he employing it? On the answer to this question will depend the propriety of allowing his claims to be considered as a servant of Christ. If he makes it a business to breed slaves for market—if he treats rational and immortal things only as if they were cattle—nay, if he does not see carefully, not only that their physical wants are supplied, but that they are restrained from vice, and properly instructed, especially in the things of their everlasting peace; and if, after due admonition, he will not repent of his iniquity, then treat him as a heathen man and a publican. . . .

. . . What ought the slaveholder to do? What ought he to do in regard to his own slaves? Obviously, he ought to do for them just what, on a careful consideration of their character and all their circumstances, he sees will be most for their good; we do not speak here of the public good, because *their* good and the *public* good are, in reference to this question, inseparable. Let him consider, not only their actual condition, but their liabilities. Be it that their master is kind and attentive to all their wants; be it that they are well governed, and supplied with religious instruction; be it even that they are contented with their present lot, and are unwilling to change places with the free blacks around them; all this weighs but little in the scale against their liabilities. They are liable, as chattels, to be attached and sold for their master's debts; and, whatever commercial revolution, whatever accident, involves him in pecuniary embarrassment, is likely to bring on them a distress, compared with which bankruptcy and poverty are nothing. So, on the death of their master, when his estate comes to be settled and divided, they are liable to the same fate; all their connexions may be sundered; and, torn from all that is home to them, they may be consigned to a condition the more terrible for the former alleviations of their lot. What, then, does a wise regard for their welfare—what does imperative justice towards them—demand of their master? Ought he not, if possible, and as soon as possible, to secure them against such contingencies? Against such contingencies they cannot be secured, as the laws now are, but by being made free. Does he ask, How can I make them free? We answer, You can educate them for liberty; and, as fast as they become at all competent to take care of themselves, you can put them in the way of earning a passage to Africa, or let them choose their own course to whatever country will open its doors to receive them.

But what ought the slaveholder to do in regard to the system of slavery? First of all, he ought, on every fit occasion, to bear his testimony against it, and against the legislation which creates and supports it. He ought to declare himself, fearlessly, the enemy of slavery, and the friend of whatever will mitigate the curse, or promote its peaceful abolition. Where such an evil pervades society, offending the heavens with its atrocity, and cursing the very soil with its afflictive influences, if any individual has a right to be silent, that individual is not the slaveholder. His silence respecting such an evil, is approbation; his neutrality, is partisanship. The timidity which seals his lips, makes him, in fact, an abettor and supporter of all those laws, the mere digest of which is enough to make the brow of an American crimson with shame. If all those men in the southern States, who are, in conscience and in judgment, dissatisfied with slavery—who are convinced that it must be abolished, and desire to see that consummation peacefully accomplished—would but speak out like freemen, there would soon be in those States such a demonstration of public opinion, as would make the advocates of slavery cower and hide their heads for shame.

Yet, in order that the slaveholder's testimony against slavery may be complete and effectual, his example must accord with it. If, on his own plantation, he perpetuates the system just as he received it from his predecessors; if his slaves, born, living, dying, in the lowest condition to which humanity can be degraded, transmit that condition unmitigated to their children; if he does not set himself in earnest, and like a working-man, to the work of elevating and blessing those whose destiny is committed to his hands—no matter what opinions he may express hostile to the system—the testimony of his example is recorded for slavery, slavery as it is, slavery forever.

WILLIAM ELLERY CHANNING OPPOSES SLAVERY ON RATIONAL RELIGIOUS GROUNDS

Perhaps because of their religious outlook, perhaps because of their Boston education and training, perhaps because of the tenor of their minds, Unitarian clergymen, when they espoused antislavery, spoke most convincingly in terms of natural law and natural rights. Full of eighteenth century optimism about the goodness—even the divinity—of man, they vigorously rejected slavery as inconsistent with the nature of man. William Ellery Channing (1780-1842), though never a radical abolitionist and while often attacked for his timid moderation by the Garrisonians, furnished a good number of natural rights arguments for reform in general and, from his congregation, a good number of Boston's antislavery leaders as well. This selection illustrates how closely the Unitarian religious argument against slavery matched the secular natural rights argument.

I come now to what is to my own mind the great argument against seizing and using a man as property. He cannot be property in the sight of God and justice, because he is a Rational, Moral, Immortal Being; because created in God's image, and therefore in the highest sense his child; because created to unfold godlike faculties, and to govern himself by a Divine Law written on his heart, and republished in God's Word. His whole nature forbids that he should be seized as property. From his very nature it follows, that so to seize him is to offer an insult to his Maker, and to inflict aggravated social wrong. Into every human being God has breathed an immortal spirit, more precious than the whole outward creation. No earthly or celestial language can exaggerate the worth of a human being. No matter how obscure his condition. Thought, Reason, Conscience, the capacity of Virtue, the capacity of Christian Love, an Immortal Destiny, an intimate moral connection with God,—here are attributes of our common humanity which reduce to insignificance all outward distinctions, and make every human being unspeakably dear to his Maker. No matter how ignorant he may be. The capacity of Improvement allies him to the more instructed of his race, and places within his

---

From William Ellery Channing, *Slavery*, 3rd. ed. Revised (Boston: James Munroe and Company, 1836), pp. 25–29.

reach the knowledge and happiness of higher worlds. Every human being has in him the germ of the greatest idea in the universe, the idea of God; and to unfold this is the end of his existence. Every human being has in his breast the elements of that Divine, Everlasting Law, which the highest orders of the creation obey. He has the idea of Duty; and to unfold, revere, obey this, is the very purpose for which life was given. Every human being has the idea of what is meant by that word, Truth; that is, he sees, however dimly, the great object of Divine and created intelligence, and is capable of ever-enlarging perceptions of truth. Every human being has affections, which may be purified and expanded into a Sublime Love. He has, too, the idea of Happiness, and a thirst for it which cannot be appeased. Such is our nature. Wherever we see a man, we see the possessor of these great capacities. Did God make such a being to be owned as a tree or a brute? How plainly was he made to exercise, unfold, improve his highest powers, made for a moral, spiritual good! and how is he wronged, and his Creator opposed, when he is forced and broken into a tool to another's physical enjoyment!

Such a being was plainly made for an End in Himself. He is a Person, not a Thing. He is an End, not a mere Instrument or Means. He was made for his own virtue and happiness. Is this end reconcilable with his being held and used as a chattel? The sacrifice of such a being to another's will, to another's present, outward, ill-comprehended good, is the greatest violence which can be offered to any creature of God. It is to degrade him from his rank in the universe, to make him a means, not an end, to cast him out from God's spiritual family into the brutal herd.

Such a being was plainly made to obey a Law within Himself. This is the essence of a moral being. He possesses, as a part of his nature, and the most essential part, a sense of Duty, which he is to reverence and follow, in opposition to all pleasure or pain, to all interfering human wills. The great purpose of all good education and discipline is, to make a man Master of Himself, to excite him to act from a principle in his own mind, to lead him to propose his own perfection as his supreme law and end. And is this highest purpose of man's nature to be reconciled with entire subjection to a foreign will, to an outward, overwhelming force, which is satisfied with nothing but complete submission?

The end of such a being as we have described is, manifestly, Improvement. Now it is the fundamental law of our nature, that all our powers are to improve by free exertion. Action is the indispensable condition of progress to the intellect, conscience, and heart. Is it not plain, then, that a human being cannot, without wrong, be owned by another, who claims, as proprietor, the right to repress the powers of his slaves, to withhold from them the means of development, to keep them within the limits which are necessary to contentment in chains, to shut out every ray of light and every generous sentiment which may interfere with entire subjection to his will?

No man, who seriously considers what human nature is, and what it was made for, can think of setting up a claim to a fellow-creature. What! own a spiritual being, a being made to know and adore God, and who is to outlive the sun and stars! What! chain to our lowest uses a being made for truth and virtue! convert into a brute instrument that intelligent nature, on which the idea of Duty has dawned, and which is a nobler type of God than all outward creation! Should we not deem it a wrong which no punishment could expiate, were one of our children seized as property, and driven by the whip to toil? And shall God's child, dearer to him than an only son to a human parent, be thus degraded? Every thing else may be owned in the universe; but a moral, rational being cannot be property. Suns and stars may be owned, but not the lowest spirit. Touch any thing but this. Lay not your hand on God's rational offspring. The whole spiritual world cries out, Forbear! The highest intelligences recognise their own nature, their own rights, in the humblest human being. By that priceless, immortal spirit which dwells in him, by that likeness of God which he wears, tread him not in the dust, confound him not with the brute.

JOHN RANKIN

ASSERTS THAT RELIGIOUS TEACHING IS AGAINST SLAVERY

John Rankin (1793–1886), a Presbyterian minister originally from Tennessee, was an abolitionist as early as 1815. He carried on his antislavery activities from his parish in Ripley, Ohio, and, in 1836, served as one of a group of antislavery agents (called "The Seventy") who spread the message of the American Anti-Slavery Society in the face of mobs and physical violence. In 1824 he had undertaken to explain his position to his Virginia brother and set out a series of basic arguments to demonstrate that the Bible not only does not sanction slavery but actually opposes it.

According to an intimation given in my last, I am to show that the modern system of slavery is prohibited by the book of inspiration. And as many of the abettors of this system pretend to support it by the sacred Scriptures, I deem it necessary to examine the principal arguments which they have drawn from this source.

From John Rankin, "Letter XI," in *Letters on American Slavery, Addressed to Mr. Thomas Rankin, Merchant at Middlebrook, Augusta Co., Va.*, 5th ed. (Boston: Isaac Knapp, 1838), pp. 73–79.

I. I shall first consider the one which is founded upon Noah's curse. It is argued that this curse consigns all the posterity of Ham to perpetual slavery; that the Africans descended from him; and therefore it is right to enslave them.

I consider that this argument is, in several respects, ill founded.

First, it is not true that the curse consigns all the posterity of Ham to perpetual servitude. Let us hear what it says. (Gen. ix. 25.) 'Cursed be Canaan; a servant of servants shall he be unto his brethren.' Thus we see that but one of Ham's sons was included in the curse. Canaan, doubtless was deeply concerned with his father in the guilt which gave rise to this denunciation against him, else why was he so signally marked as the subject of the curse? The rest of Ham's sons it seems were innocent, and consequently were not included in it. The history of the world shows that many of the nations which descended from them have been respectable, and subjected to no calamities but such as are common to the rest of mankind. Hence it is as plain as stubborn fact can make it, that the curse did not include all of Ham's posterity. It was denounced against Canaan, and history shows that it fell upon his posterity. Our Africans did not descend from him, and therefore were not with him consigned to servitude.

2d. The doom was not perpetual. Sacred history shows that the descendants of Canaan became powerful and wealthy nations before the curse was inflicted upon them. It was first inflicted by the Israelites, who descended from Shem, and who had been servants to some of Ham's posterity in Egypt. They destroyed vast numbers of the Canaanites, and eventually reduced the rest of them to very abject circumstances, and made them tributary. And thus they became the tributary servants of those who had been servants. Hence the following predictions of Noah were literally fulfilled. 'Cursed be Canaan; a servant of servants shall he be unto his brethren.' 'Blessed be the Lord God of Shem; and Canaan shall be his servant.'

Again, it is said Japhet 'shall dwell in the tents of Shem; and Canaan shall be his servant.' This was doubtless accomplished when the Greeks and Romans, who were descendants of Japhet, by conquest took possession of the tents of Shem. At this period the remnant of the Canaanites became tributary to the offspring of Japhet, and thus Canaan became the servant of Japhet. Hence the prediction, so far as it related to servitude, has long since had its accomplishment. The Canaanites have mingled with other nations, and so do not now exist as a distinct people, and consequently the term of their servitude must be terminated. And when we consider the manner in which these ancient predictions were fulfilled, we believe that they related not so much to the slavery of individuals as to national subjugation. There were so few of Canaan's posterity reduced to individual slavery, that we cannot reasonably conclude that to be the kind of servitude predicted. It appears from sacred history that fewer of the descendants of Canaan than those of Shem were reduced to individual slavery. People who are subjugated and made tributary, must labor in order to pay their tribute, and therefore are the servants of their conquerors. This kind of servitude the Canaanites endured to great extremes. The Israelites conquered them, and took possession of their cities, their houses, and their lands, and thus enjoyed the fruits of their labor; and those of them that escaped the sword were eventually made tributary. This evidently appears to be the kind of servitude predicted in Noah's curse, and if so, our kind of slavery is not even so much as found in this ancient prediction. The Israelites were not commanded to enslave, but to exterminate the nations of Canaan.

Finally, if the prediction had included all Ham's posterity, and had consigned them to perpetual servitude, still it could not justify our system of slavery. Predictions are not given in Scripture as rules of moral action. It was predicted, and even decreed, that Jesus Christ should be crucified, and yet his crucifiers were full as guilty as they would have been if no such prediction and decree had ever existed. The Israelites did not proceed against the Canaanites on the ground of prediction, but on that of divine command, and that command was not founded upon prediction, but upon the full cup of their iniquities. The Lord gave the Canaanites a dispensation of grace under the ministrations of Melchisedec, and suspended the infliction of the curse until they had long abused his mercy and filled the cup of their iniquities. Hence, their enormous wickedness was the real cause of their calamities, and the means of bringing the curse upon them. But even on the supposition that this prediction were a rule of moral action, still it could not justify our system of slavery, because we have not sufficient proof that our Africans descended from Ham. We suppose they are of his posterity, but this supposition cannot be supported by satisfactory evidence. The revolutions of nations and time have put the matter beyond the possibility of certain proof. Therefore the whole argument for slavery drawn from Noah's curse, is without foundation. It rests wholly upon bold assertion and mere conjecture, and it certainly must be the product of avaricious derangement.

II. I shall consider the argument which the friends of involuntary slavery have adduced from the example of Abraham. It is alledged that Abraham, the father of the faithful, held slaves, and therefore involuntary slavery must be right.

This argument, like the one before considered, appears to me to be inconclusive in several respects.

First: It is not evident that Abraham's servants were held to involuntary servitude. It is true that he had servants born in his house, and servants bought with his money; but these circumstances do not absolutely prove that their servitude was involuntary. Abraham was a prince; the children of Heth addressed him as such; (Gen. xxiii. 6.) 'Thou art a mighty prince among us.' On one occasion he armed three hundred and eighteen trained servants that were born in his house, and with them gained a signal victory over several of the most powerful kings of the age. (Gen. xiv. 1—16.) Hence it appears that the servants born in his house were merely his subjects. Abraham had no fixed residence, and therefore he and his subjects dwelt in tents. 'By faith he sojourned in the land of promise, as in a strange country, dwelling in tabernacles with Isaac and Jacob.' (Heb. xi. 9.) Thus we see that Abraham's house was but a tabernacle or tent; and it was made large enough to shelter him and all his subjects; and this shows how it happened that the three hundred and eighteen before-mentioned servants were born in his house. These were all fit to bear arms; and therefore, according to the nature of human increase, we must conclude that Abraham had many others likewise born in his house, who were too young for military service, and there must have been nearly an equal number of females—and to all these we may add all those bought with his money. From these circumstances it is reasonable to conclude that Abraham's servants, at least, amounted to more than one thousand. Hence it is most absurd to suppose that a single individual while passing from place to place in a strange country, could compel so large a number of persons to involuntary servitude. And would any man in his senses, under such circumstances, arm three hundred and eighteen involuntary slaves, and march them out against his enemies? Would such a number of armed slaves submit to a single man, cheerfully fight his battles, and thus risk their lives in his defence? Abraham was a wandering stranger, unprotected by civil government, and therefore his servants were not restrained by fear of punishment in case of rebellion; consequently we may safely conclude that the service which they rendered him was of the voluntary kind. But the question still recurs, were not those whom he bought with his money slaves? To this I answer that 'Abraham was very rich in cattle, in silver, and in gold;' and was as benevolent as he was rich; of course he would have many strong inducements to redeem miserable captives taken in war; and these, from a sense of gratitude as well as for the sake of protection, would become his subjects; and such being redeemed by their own consent would be under the most solemn obligations to render him faithful service. Perhaps Hagar the Egyptian was bound to his service from some such consideration, and therefore was called a bond-woman. Indeed Abraham manifested so much benevolence in several instances, as might lead us to the conclusion that he was wholly indisposed to the practice of involuntary slavery. And his whole conduct towards his servants shows that he considered them to be merely subjects, and not slaves. Hence we find him bringing his eldest servant under solemn oath not to take a wife to Isaac of the daughters of the Canaanites. Gen. xxiv. 2, 3. This we might expect a prince to require of a subject, but not a master to require of a slave. This same servant had all his master's property in his hand; and even had authority over Isaac. Does this look like modern slavery? Thus a variety of circumstances make it evident to me that Abraham did not hold involuntary slaves. But again, if Abraham did practice involuntary slavery, still the argument adduced from his example must be inconclusive. He was an imperfect man, and therefore his example cannot be a standard of moral rectitude. He had two wives at one time; but who will argue from his example that polygamy is right. And it must be equally absurd to argue from his example that slavery is right. Such an argument evidences a bad cause.

JOHN G. WHITTIER
RENDERS A VIVID SLAVERY SCENE
AT THE NORTH

Between the years 1832 and 1865 Whittier poured out a constant stream of antislavery poetry. Some of it has retained a certain strength and impressiveness for readers a century away from the events that occasioned it; but most of it, written, as Whittier himself acknowledged, with little thought for literary merit and to fill an immediate need in the antislavery crusade, lacks polish and finish and appeals rather to the abolitionist enthusiast than to the careful literary student. Tear-jerking and tremulous as this poem on the Church's aid to the slavecatchers may be, however, it cannot hold a candle for corniness to the effusions of the myriad poetasters published in the antislavery press and in collections gotten up under such titles as the Liberty Bell *and the* Anti-Slavery Picknick.

Scarce had the solemn Sabbath bell ceased quivering in the steeple,
Scarce had the parson to his desk walked stately through his people,

When, down the summer-shaded street, a wasted female figure,
With dusky brow and naked feet, came rushing wild and eager.

She saw the white spire through the trees, she heard the sweet hymn swelling;
O! pitying Christ! a refuge give that poor one in thy dwelling.

Like a scared fawn before the hounds, right up the aisle she glided,
While close behind her, whip in hand, a lank-haired hunter strided.

John Greenleaf Whittier, "A Sabbath Scene," in **American Anti-Slavery Society**, *Platform of the American Anti-Slavery Society and its Auxiliaries* (New York: American Anti-Slavery Society, 1855), pp. 34–35.

She raised a keen and bitter cry, to Heaven and Earth
  appealing;
Were manhood's generous pulses dead? had woman's heart
  no feeling?

A score of stout hands rose between the hunter and the
  flying;
Age clenched his staff, and maiden eyes flashed tearful,
  yet defying.

"Who dares profane this house and day?" cried out the
  angry pastor;
"Why, bless your soul! the wench's a slave, and I'm
  her lord and master!

"I've law and Gospel on my side; and who shall dare
  refuse me?"
Down came the parson, bowing low, "My good sir, pray
  excuse me!

"Of course I know your right divine to own, and work, and
  whip her;
Quick, Deacon, throw that Polyglot before the wench,
  and trip her!"

Plump dropped the holy tome, and o'er its sacred pages
  stumbling,
Bound hand and foot, a slave once more the hopeless
  wretch lay trembling.

I saw the parson tie the knots, the while his flock
  addressing,
The Scriptural claims of slavery, with text on text
  impressing.

"Although," said he, "on Sabbath day, all secular
  occupations
Are deadly sins, we must fulfill our moral obligations;

"And this commends itself as one to every conscience
  tender;
As Paul sent back Onesimus, my Christian friends, we
  send her!"

Shriek rose on shriek; the Sabbath air her wild cries
  tore asunder;
I listened, with hushed breath, to hear God answering
  with his thunder!

All still!—the very altar-cloth had smothered down her
  shrieking,
And, dumb she turned from face to face, for human
  pity seeking!

I saw her dragged along the aisle, her shackles harshly
  clanking.
I heard the parson, over all, the Lord devoutly thanking!

My brain took fire: "Is this," I cried, "the end of
  prayer and preaching?
Then down with pulpit, down with priest, and give us
  Nature's teaching!

"Foul shame and scorn be on ye all, who turn the good
  to evil,
And steal the Bible from the Lord, to give it to the
  devil!

"Than garbled text or parchment law, I own a statute
  higher,

And God is true, though every book and every man's a
    liar!"

Just then, I felt the deacon's hand my coat-tail
    seize on,
I heard the priest cry "Infidel!" the lawyer mutter
    "Treason!"

I started up;—where now were church, slave, master,
    priest, and people?
I only heard the supper-bell, instead of clanging
    steeple.

I woke, and lo! the fitting cause of all my dream's
    vagaries—
Two bulky pamphlets,—Webster's text, with Stuart's
    commentaries!

But on the open window-sill, o'er which the white blooms
    drifted,
The pages of a good old Book the wind of summer lifted.

And flower and vine, like angel-wings around the Holy
    Mother,
Waved softly there, as if God's Truth and Mercy kissed
    each other.

And, freely, from the cherry-bough above the casement
    swinging,
With golden bosom to the sun, the oriole was singing.

As bird and flower made plain of old the lessons of
    the Teacher,
So now I heard the written Word interpreted by Nature;

For, to my ear, methought the breeze bore Freedom's
    blessed word on:—
Thus saith the Lord, BREAK EVERY YOKE, UNDO THE
    HEAVY BURDEN!

WILLIAM LLOYD GARRISON
DEFENDS ABOLITIONIST "INFIDELITY"

William Lloyd Garrison (1805–1879) was the leader, at least until 1850, of the New England abolitionists. A most pious man brought up in extreme Baptist orthodoxy, he won for himself and for his followers a reputation for "infidelity" because he attacked the churches for their support of slavery and because he supported such unacceptable causes as ending Sabbath observance and promoting John Humphrey Noyes' Perfectionism, associated in the public mind with plural marriage and anarchism. In the selection which follows, Garrison, late in his career, maintains the Christian orientation of antislavery leaders. Certainly he thought himself a far better Christian than those who stayed in the churches and called him infidel.

The vitality, the strength, the invulnerability of slavery are found in the prevailing religious sentiment and teaching of the people. While it has been pronounced an evil, a calamity, wrong in the abstract, as a system to be deplored, and grad-

---

From William Lloyd Garrison, *The "Infidelity" of Abolitionism* (Anti-Slavery Tracts, No. 10, New Series) (New York: American Anti-Slavery Society, 1860), pp. 6–11.

ually to be exterminated,—the act of individual and general slaveholding, the right to have property in man, has been universally recognized as compatible with Christian faith and fellowship, and sanctioned by the Holy Scriptures. More than half a million of slaves at the South are owned by ministers, office-bearers, and church members, who buy, sell, bequeath, inherit, mortgage, divide, and barter slave property, as they do any other portion of their personal or real estate. At the North, every sect, desirous of national extension, can secure it only by acknowledging slaveholders as brethren in Christ. All the great, controlling ecclesiastical bodies and religious denominations in the land,—constituting the American Church, comprehensively speaking,—are one in sentiment on the subject. All the leading Bishops, Doctors of Divinity, Theological Professors, ministers, and religious journalists, find ample justification for slaveholding at the South. . . .

Such, then, was the system,—so buttressed and defended,—to be assailed and conquered by the Abolitionists. And who were they? In point of numbers, as drops to the ocean, without station or influence; equally obscure and destitute of resources. Originally, they were generally members of the various religious bodies, tenacious of their theological views, full of veneration for the organized church and ministry, but ignorant of the position in which these stood to "the sum of all villanies." What would ultimately be required of them, by a faithful adherence to the cause of the slave, in their church relations, their political connections, their social ties, their worldly interest and reputation, they knew not. Instead of seeking a controversy with the pulpit and the church, they confidently looked to both for efficient aid to their cause. Instead of suddenly withdrawing from the pro-slavery religious and political organizations with which they were connected, they lingered long and labored hard to bring them to repentance. They were earnest, but well-balanced; intrepid, but circumspect; importunate, but long-suffering. Their controversy was neither personal nor sectional; their object, neither to arraign any sect nor to assail any party, primarily. They sought to liberate the slave, by every righteous instrumentality—and nothing more. But to their grief and amazement, they were gradually led to perceive, by the terrible revelations of the hour, that the religious forces on which they had relied were all arrayed on the side of the oppressor; that the North was as hostile to emancipation as the South; that the spirit of slavery was omnipresent, invading every sanctuary, infecting every pulpit, controlling every press, corrupting every household, and blinding every vision; that no other alternative was presented to them, except to wage war with "principalities, and powers, and spiritual wickedness in high places," and to separate themselves from every slaveholding alliance, or else to daub with untempered mortar, substitute compromise for principle, and thus betray the rights and liberties of the millions in thraldom, at a fearful cost to their own souls. If some of them faltered, and perished by the way; if others deserted the cause, and became its bitterest enemies; if others still withdrew from the ranks, their sectarian attachment overmastering their love of humanity, and leading them basely to misrepresent and revile their old associates; the main body proved fearless and incorruptible, and, through the American Anti-Slavery Society and its auxiliaries, have remained steadfast to the present hour. Either by way of distinction or of opprobrium, they are technically styled "Garrisonian Abolitionists." The Southern flesh-mongers brand them as an "infidel" party; the Northern pulpits and religious bodies join in the same outcry. Those who have treacherously seceded, but yet wear an anti-slavery mask, sedulously propagate the calumny; and they have resorted to every device that malice could suggest, or bigotry execute, at home and abroad, to cripple their resources, and destroy their influence. In England and Scotland, especially, extraordinary pains have been taken, in public and in private, by an artful appeal to sectarian narrowness, to hold up the American Anti-Slavery Society as unworthy of aid or countenance in any degree, on account of its "infidel" character. Contributions designed for its treasury have been withheld, or directed into hostile channels; and the most devoted advocates of the slave treated with coldness, suspicion, or contempt.

In all this, no strange thing has happened. It is an old device to divert attention from the true issue. It is a malicious fabrication—a "mad-dog" outcry to effect the death of the hated object.

Religion is, in every land, precisely and only what is popularly recognized as such. To pronounce it corrupt, spurious, oppressive, and especially to demonstrate it to be so, is ever a proof of "infidelity"—whether among Pagans or Mahommedans, Jews or Christians, Catholics or Protestants. In the United States, it is the bulwark of slavery—the untiring enemy of Abolitionism. How, then, has it been possible for the Abolitionists to establish a religious character, or to avoid the imputation of infidelity, while in necessary and direct conflict with such a religion? To say that they ought not to assail it, is to denounce them for refusing to go with the multitude to do evil, for being governed by the standard of eternal justice, for adhering to the Golden Rule.

To what, or to whom, have they been infidel? If to the cause of the enslaved, let it be shown. But this is not pretended; and yet this is the only test by which they are to be tried. They have but one bond of agreement—the inherent sinfulness of slavery, and, consequently, the duty of immediate emancipation. As *individuals*, they are of all theological and political opinions; having an undeniable right to advocate those opinions, and to make as many converts to them as possible. As an *organization*, they meet for a common object in which they are agreed, to endorse nothing but the right of the slave to himself as paramount to every other claim, and to apply no other principle as a rule whereby to measure sects, parties, institutions and men. No sectarian, no party exaction can be made, without destroying unity of spirit and general coöperation. The Episcopalian, the Presbyterian, the Baptist, the Methodist, the "Infidel," surrender not one jot or tittle of their right to be such, by uniting together for the abolition of slavery. No sectarian or party object can be sought, without a breach of good faith, and a perversion of the object ostensibly aimed at. No member can justly complain of any other member, or seek to weaken his testimony against slavery and its abettors, on account of any opinions held or promulgated by him on his individual responsibility.

Whence, then, this outcry of "infidelity" against the American Anti-Slavery Society? It has never proceeded from a manly spirit; it has never been raised by any one truly remembering the slave as bound with him; unless, indeed, it be true, that that Society has perfidiously turned aside from its original object, to accomplish some ulterior purpose, still assuming to be unchanged and undeviating. But it is not true:—though the charge has been repeated ten thousand times, at home and abroad, it is ten thousand times a calumny, uttered either through ignorance, sectarian enmity, personal jealousy, or pro-slavery malice. The Society has never arraigned or criticised any religious body, on account of its peculiar creed; it has never taken any action on theological matters; it has never discussed, never attempted to settle the question, whether the Bible is plenarily inspired, or whether the first day of the week is the Sabbath, or any other question foreign to its avowed purpose. Of the Sabbath it has declared, as Jesus did, that it is as lawful and obligatory to heal the sick, release the bound, and plead for the oppressed, on that day, as it is to succor cattle in distress. Of the Bible, as an anti-slavery instrumentality, it has made a constant and most powerful use against the pro-slavery interpretations of a time-serving clergy; though not deriving the rights of man from any book, but from his own nature. Of the true Church it has ever spoken with veneration, and vindicated it as animated and controlled by the spirit of impartial liberty, to the exclusion of all tyrants. Of the Gospel it has proclaimed, that in all its doctrines, teachings and examples, it is utterly at war with slavery, and for universal freedom. Of Jesus it has affirmed, that he is ever with the downtrodden and oppressed, whose case he has literally made his own, and that he has gloriously vindicated the brotherhood of the human race, to the confusion of all who desecrate the image of God. Its appeals have been unceasingly to the conscience and the heart; it has called to repentance a guilty nation, as the only condition of salvation; it has refused to compromise with sin.

If, therefore, it be an infidel Society, it is so only in the sense in which Jesus was a blasphemer, and the Apostles were "pestilent and seditious fellows, seeking to turn the world upside down." It is infidel to Satan, the enslaver; it is loyal to Christ, the redeemer. It is infidel to a Gospel which makes man the property of man; it is bound up with the Gospel which requires us to love our neighbors as ourselves, and to call no man master. It is infidel to a Church which receives to its communion the "traffickers in slaves and the souls of men;" it is loyal to the Church which is not stained with blood, nor polluted by oppression. It is infidel to the Bible as a pro-slavery interpreted volume; it is faithful to it as construed on the side of justice and humanity. It is infidel to the Sabbath, on which it is hypocritically pronounced unlawful to extricate the millions who lie bound and bleeding in the pit of slavery; it is true to the Sabbath, on which it is well-pleasing to God to bind up the brokenhearted, and to let the oppressed go free. It is infidel to all blood-stained compromises, sinful concessions, unholy compacts, respecting the system of slavery; it is devotedly attached to whatever is honest, straightforward, invincible for the right. No Society has ever erected a higher moral standard, or more disinterestedly pursued its object, or more unfalteringly walked by faith, or more confidingly trusted in the living God for succor in every extremity, and a glorious victory at last. At the jubilee, its vindication shall be triumphant and universal. . . .

. . . Genuine Abolitionism is not a hobby, got up for personal or associated aggrandizement; it is not a political ruse; it is not a spasm of sympathy, which lasts but for a moment, leaving the system weak and worn; it is not a fever of enthusiasm; it is not the fruit of fanaticism; it is not a spirit of faction. It is of heaven, not of men. It lives in the heart as a vital principle. It is an essential part of Christianity, and aside from it there can be no humanity. Its scope is not confined to the slave population of the United States, but embraces mankind. Opposition cannot weary it out, force cannot put it down, fire cannot consume it. It is the spirit of Jesus, who was sent "to bind up the broken-hearted, to proclaim liberty to the captives, and the opening of the prison to them that are bound; to proclaim the acceptable year of the Lord and the day of vengeance of our God."

STEPHEN S. FOSTER
DAMNS THE PRO-SLAVERY CHURCHES

Stephen Symonds Foster (1809–1881), a divinity student who deserted his studies for the cause of reform, was perhaps as radical and intemperate as any abolitionist in his denunciation of churches as pro-slavery organizations. With a small following he toured New England, attending, each Sunday, a different church. As the minister was about to start his sermon, Foster would stand up in his pew and launch a stirring condemnation of slavery. The not infrequent result was his bodily expulsion from the church by irate and none-too-gentle parish-

ioners. *The selection which follows is from his exposé of American churches, which grew out of his experiences with a mob on Nantucket where he had gone to preach his message to an antislavery convention.*

. . . Every assault which we have made upon the bloody slave system, as I shall hereafter show, has been promptly met and repelled by the church, which is herself the claimant of several hundred thousand slaves; and whenever we have attempted to expose the guilt and hypocrisy of the church, the *mob* has uniformly been first and foremost in her defense. But I rest not on presumptive evidence, however strong and conclusive, to sustain my allegations against the American church and clergy. The proof of their identity with Slavery, and of their consequent deep and unparalleled criminality, is positive and overwhelming; and is fully adequate to sustain the gravest charges, and to justify the most denunciatory language, that have ever fallen from the lips of their most inveterate opponents.

I said at your meeting, among other things, that the American church and clergy, as a body, were thieves, adulterers, man-stealers, pirates, and murderers—that the Methodist Episcopal Church was more corrupt and profligate than any house of ill fame in the city of New York—that the Southern ministers of that body were desirous of perpetuating Slavery for the purpose of supplying themselves with concubines from among its hapless victims—and that many of our clergymen were guilty of enormities that would disgrace an Algerine pirate!! These sentiments called forth a burst of holy indignation from the *pious* and *dutiful* advocates of the church and clergy, which overwhelmed the meeting with repeated showers of

From Stephen Symonds Foster, *The Brotherhood of Thieves, or A True Picture of the American Church and Clergy* (New London: William Bolles, 1843), pp. 7–13.

stones and rotten eggs, and eventually compelled me to leave your island, to prevent the shedding of human blood. But whence this violence and personal abuse, not only of the author of the obnoxious sentiments, but also of your own unoffending wives and daughters whose faces and dresses you will recollect, were covered with the most loathsome filth? It is reported of the ancient Pharisees and their adherents, that they stoned Stephen to death for preaching doctrines at war with the popular religion of their times, and charging them with the murder of the Son of God; but their successors of the modern church, it would seem, have discovered some new principle in Theology, by which it is made their duty not only to stone the heretic himself, but all those also who may at any time be found listening to his discourse without a *permit* from their *priest*. Truely, the church is becoming "Terrible as an army with banners."

This violence and outrage on the part of the church were, no doubt, committed to the glory of God and the honor of religion, although the connexion between rotten eggs and holiness of heart is not very obvious. It is, I suppose, one of the mysteries of religion which laymen cannot understand without the aid of the clergy; and I therefore suggest that the pulpit make it a subject of Sunday discourse. But are not the charges here alledged against the clergy strictly and literally true? I maintain that they are true to the letter—that the clergy and their adherents are literally, and beyond all controversy, a "brotherhood of thieves"—and in support of this opinion I submit the following considerations.

You will agree with me, I think, that slaveholding involves the commission of all the crimes specified in my first charge, viz: theft, adultery, man-stealing, piracy and murder. But should you have any doubts on this subject, they will be easily removed by analizing this atrocious outrage on the laws of God, and the rights and happiness of man, and examining separately, the elements of which it is composed. Wesley, the celebrated founder of the Methodists, once denounced it as the "sum of all villainies." Whether it be the sum of *all* villainies or not, I will not here express an opinion, but that it is the sum of at least *five*, and those by no means the least attrocious in the catalogue of human aberrations, will require but a small tax on your patience to prove.

1. Theft. To steal is to take that which belongs to another without his consent. Theft and robbery are, *morally*, the same act, differing only in form. Both are included under the command, "Thou shalt not Steal"—that is, thou shalt not take thy neighbor's property. Whoever, therefore, either secretly or by force, possesses himself of the property of another, is a thief. Now, no proposition is plainer than that every man owns his own industry. He who tills the soil, has a right to its products, and cannot be deprived of them but by an act of felony. This principle furnishes the only solid basis for the right of private or individual property, and he who denies it, either in theory or practice, denies that right also. But every slaveholder takes the entire industry of his slaves, from infancy to grey hairs. They dig the soil, but he receives its products. No matter how kind or humane the master may be, he lives by plunder. He is emphatically a freebooter, and, as such, he is as much more despicable a character than the common horse-thief, as his depredations are more extensive.

2. Adultery. This crime is disregard for the requisitions of marriage. The conjugal relation has its foundation deeply laid in man's nature, and its observance is essential to his happiness. Hence, Jesus Christ has thrown around it the sacred sanction of his written law, and expressly declared that the man who violates it, even by a lustful eye, is an adulterer. But does the slave-holder respect this sacred relation? Is he cautious never to tread upon forbidden ground? No! His very position makes him the minister of unbridled lust. By converting woman into a commodity, to be bought and sold, and used by her claimant as his avarice or lust may dictate, he totally annihi-

lates the marriage institution; and transforms the wife into what he very significantly terms a "BREEDER," and her children into "STOCK."

This change in woman's condition from a free moral agent to a chattel, places her domestic relations entirely beyond her own control, and makes her a mere instrument for the gratification of another's desires. The master claims her body as his property, and of course employs it for such purposes as best suit his inclinations—demanding free access to her bed; nor can she resist his demands, but at the peril of her life. Thus is her chastity left entirely unprotected, and she is made the lawful prey of every pale-faced libertine, who may choose to prostitute her!! To place woman in this situation, or to retain her in it, when placed there by another, is the highest insult that one could possibly offer to the dignity and purity of her nature; and the wretch who is guilty of it, deserves an epithet, compared with which adultery is spotless innocence. *Rape* is his crime!—death his desert, if death be ever due to criminals! . . . None but a moral monster ever consented to the enslavement of his own daughter, and none but fiends incarnate ever enslaved the daughter of another. Indeed, I think the demons in hell would be ashamed to do to their fellow demons, what many of our clergy do to their own church members.

3. Man-stealing. What is it to steal a man? Is it not to claim him as your property? To call him yours? God has given to every man an inalienable right to himself—a right of which no conceivable circumstance of birth, or forms of law, can divest him; and he who interferes with the free and unrestricted exercise of that right, who, not content with the proprietorship of his own body, claims the body of his neighbor, is a manstealer. The truth is self-evident. Every man, idiots and the insane only excepted, knows that he has no possible right to another's body; and he who persists, for a moment, in claiming it, incurs the guilt of manstealing. The plea of the slave claimant, that he has bought, or inherited his slaves, is of no avail. What

right had he, I ask, to purchase, or to inherit his neighbors? The purchase, or the inheritance of them as a legacy, was itself a crime of no less enormity than the original act of kidnapping. But every slaveholder, whatever his profession or standing in society may be, lays his felonious hands on the body and soul of his equal brother, robs him of himself, converts him into an article of merchandize, and leaves him a mere chattel personal in the hands of his claimant. Hence, he is a kidnapper or man thief.

4. Piracy. The American people, by an act of solemn legislation, have declared the enslaving of human beings, on the coast of Africa, to be piracy, and have affixed to this crime the penalty of death. And can the same act be piracy in Africa, and not be piracy in America? Does crime change its character by changing longitude? Is killing with malice aforethought no murder, where there is no human enactment against it? Or can it be less piratical and heaven-daring to enslave our own native countrymen, than to enslave the heathen sons of a foreign and barbarous realm? If there be any difference in the two crimes, the odds is in favor of the foreign enslaver. Slaveholding loses none of its enormity by a voyage across the Atlantic, nor by baptism into the Christian name. It is piracy in Africa—it is piracy in America—it is piracy the wide world over: and the American slaveholder, though he possess all the sanctity of the ancient Pharasees, and make prayers as numerous and long, is a *pirate* still, a base, profligate adulterer, and wicked contemner of the holy institution of marriage, identical in moral character with the African slavetrader, and guilty of a crime which, if committed on a foreign coast, he must expiate on the gallows.

5. Murder. Murder is an act of the mind, and not of the hand. "Whosoever hateth his brother is a murderer." A man may kill—that is, his hand may inflict a mortal blow, without committing murder. On the other hand, he may commit murder, without actually taking life. The intention constitutes the

crime. He who, with a pistol at my breast, demands my pocketbook or my life, is a murderer, whichever I may choose to part with. And is not he a murderer who, with the same deadly weapon, demands the surrender of what to me is of infinitely more value than my pocket book, nay, than life itself—my liberty—myself—my wife and children—all that I possess on earth, or can hope for in heaven? But this is the crime of which every slaveholder is guilty. He maintains his ascendency over his victims, extorting their unrequited labor, and sundering the dearest ties of kindred, only by the threat of extermination. With the slave, as every intelligent person knows, there is no alternative. It is submission or death, or, more frequently, protracted torture more horrible than death. Indeed, the South never sleeps, but on dirks, and pistols, and bowie knives, with a troop of blood-hounds standing sentry at every door! What, I ask, means this splendid enginery of death, which gilds the palace of the tyrant master? It tells the story of his guilt. The burnished steel which waits beneath his slumbering pillow, to drink the blood of outraged innocence, brands him as a murderer. It proves, beyond dispute, that the submission of his victims is the only reason why he has not already shed their blood.

By this brief analysis of slavery, we stamp upon the forehead of the slaveholder with a brand deeper than that which marks the victim of his wrongs, the infamy of theft, adultery, manstealing, piracy and murder. We demonstrate beyond the possibility of doubt, that he who enslaves another, that is, robs him of his right to himself, to his own hands, and head, and feet, and transforms him from a free moral agent into a mere *brute*, to obey, not the commands of God, but his claimant, is guilty of every one of these atrocious crimes. And in doing this, we have only demonstrated what, to every reflecting mind, is self-evident. Every man, if he would but make the case of the slave his own, would feel in his inmost soul the truth and justice of this charge. But these are the crimes which I have alledged against the American church and clergy. Hence, to sustain my charge against them, it only remains for me to show that they are slaveholders. That they are slaveholders—party to a conspiracy against the liberty of more than two millions of our countrymen, and, as such, are guilty of the crimes of which they stand accused—I affirm, and will now proceed to prove.

It may be necessary for me first, however, to show what constitutes slaveholding, as there seems to be no little confusion in the minds of many on this point. And here let me say, the word itself, if analized, will give an accurate description of the act. It is to *hold* one in slavery—to keep him in the condition of a chattel. But slaveholding, in all cases, is necessarily a social crime. A man may commit theft or murder alone, but no *solitary* individual can ever *enslave* another. It is only when several persons associate together, and combine their influence against the liberty of an individual, that he can be deprived of his freedom, and reduced to slavery. Hence, connection with an association, any part of whose object is to hold men in slavery, constitutes one a slaveholder. Nor is the nature or criminality of his offence altered or affected by the number of persons connected with him in such an association. If a million of people conspire together to enslave a solitary individual, each of them is a slaveholder, and no less guilty than if he were alone in the crime. It is no palliation of his offence to say, that he is opposed to slavery. The better feelings of every slaveholder are opposed to slavery. But if he be opposed to it, why, I ask, is he concerned in it? Why does he countenance, aid, or abet, the infernal system? The fact of his opposition to it, in feeling, instead of mitigating his guilt only enhances it, since it proves, conclusively, that he is not unconscious of the wrong he is doing.

It is a common but mistaken opinion, that to constitute one a slaveholder he must be the claimant of slaves. That title belongs alike to the slave claimant and all those who, by their countenance or otherwise, lend their influence to support the slave system. If I aid or countenance another in stealing, I am a thief, though he receive all the booty. . . . Hence, all who, through their political or ecclesiastical connexions, aid or countenance the master in his work of death, are slaveholders, and as such, are stained with all the moral turpitude which attaches to the man, who, by their sanction, wields the bloody lash over the heads of his trembling victims, and buries it deep in their quivering flesh. . . .

VI

Arguments from Economics

ELIAS HICKS
URGES PEOPLE NOT TO BUY
SLAVE-PRODUCED GOODS

The earliest attempts to oppose slavery on economic grounds were primarily those of the Quakers, who sought to boycott the products of slave labor. Their emphasis was essentially moral: to avoid the evil by refusing to consume its fruits. There was the attendant hope, however, that by making slavery unprofitable, such abstention would persuade slave traders and owners to emancipate their slaves. Elias Hicks (1748–1830), who became the leader of the liberal wing of the Friends in the late 1820's, both condemned slavery and sought to institute a "buy free" campaign. The excerpt which follows was first published in 1811.

From Elias Hicks, *Observations on the Slavery of the Africans and Their Descendants, and on the Use of the Produce of Their Labour* (Philadelphia: T. Ellwood Chapman, 1861), pp. 15–19.

Q. . . . By what class of the people is the slavery of the Africans and their descendants supported and encouraged?

A. Principally by the purchasers and consumers of the produce of the slaves' labour; as the profits arising from the produce of their labour, is the only stimulus or inducement for making slaves.

"The laws of our country may indeed prohibit us the sweets of the sugar cane,"[1] and other articles of the West-Indies and southern states, that are the produce of the slave's labour, "unless we will receive it through the medium of slavery; they may hold it to our lips, steeped in the blood of our fellow creatures, but they cannot compel us to accept the loathsome potion. With us it rests, either to receive it and be partners in the crime, or to exonerate ourselves from guilt, by spurning from us the temptation. For let us not think, that the crime rests alone with those who conduct the traffic, or the Legislature by which it is protected. If we purchase the commodity, we participate in the crime. The slave dealer, the slave holder, and the slave driver, are virtually the agents of the consumer, and may be considered as employed and hired by him, to procure the commodity. For, by holding out the temptation, he is the original cause, the first mover in the horrid process; and every distinction is done away by the moral maxim, *That whatever we do by another, we do ourselves.*

"Nor are we by any means warranted to consider our individual share in producing these evils in a trivial point of view: the consumption of sugar" and other articles of slavery "in this country is so immense, that the quantity commonly used by individuals will have an important effect."

Q. . . . What effect would it have on the slave holders and

---

[1] In the preface to the edition of the *Observations* from which the present excerpt is taken. Hicks noted that he had added passages which he thought further illuminated his points and which he had extracted from "an anonymous pamphlet, published some time since in England." (p. 7) He did not identify the source of the quoted passages beyond this single reference. [Eds.]

their slaves, should the people of the United States of America and the inhabitants of Great Britain, refuse to purchase or make use of any goods that are the produce of slavery?

A. It would doubtless have a particular effect on the slave holders, by circumscribing their avarice, and preventing their heaping up riches, and living in a state of luxury and excess on the gain of oppression: and it might have the salutary effect of convincing them of the unrighteousness and cruelty of holding their fellow creatures in bondage; and it would have a blessed and excellent effect on the poor afflicted slaves; as it would immediately meliorate their wretched condition and abate their cruel bondage; for I have been informed, and reason naturally dictates to every one who has made right observations on men and things, that the higher the price of such produce is, the harder they are driven at their work.

And should the people of the United States, and the inhabitants of Great Britain, withdraw from a commerce in, and the use of the produce of slavery, it would greatly lessen the price of those articles, and be a very great and immediate relief to the poor, injured and oppressed slaves, whose blood is continually crying from the ground for justice, as their lives are greatly shortened, and many of them do not live out half their days by reason of their cruel bondage.

"If we as individuals concerned in purchasing and consuming the produce of slavery, should imagine that our share in the transaction is so minute, that it cannot perceptibly increase the injury; let us recollect, that, though numbers partaking of a crime may diminish the shame, they cannot diminish its turpitude; can we suppose, that any injury of an enormous magnitude can take place, and the criminality be destroyed, merely by the criminals becoming so numerous as to render their particular shares indistinguishable? Were a hundred assassins to plunge their daggers into their victim, though each might plead, that without his assistance the crime would have been completed, and that his poniard neither occasioned nor accelerated the murder; yet, every one of them would be guilty of the entire crime. For, into how many parts soever a criminal action may be divided, the crime itself rests entire and complete on every perpetrator.

"But, waiving this latter consideration, and even supposing for a moment, that the evil has an existence from causes totally independent of us, yet it exists; and as we have it in our power jointly with others to remedy it, it is undoubtedly our duty to contribute our share, in hope that others will theirs; and to act that part from conscience, which we should from inclination in similar cases that interested our feelings:" for instance, let us suppose that the way for obtaining slaves from Africa was entirely intercepted, and no other place opened for obtaining any, except in the rivers Delaware and Hudson, in North America; that the slave traders were continually infesting the shores of those rivers, as the only places to be insulted with impunity; that they frequently kidnapped, and sometimes by force carried off numbers of the inhabitants to the West-Indies, and sold them as slaves, among whom were many of our fathers and brothers, with their wives and children. We now view them all hand-cuffed, two and two together, crowded down between the ship's decks, and so closely stowed, as to be almost suffocated; in consequence of which, a number sicken and die, which to them is a very happy release, when compared with the still more cruel sufferings that await the survivors. We next behold them in port, and the day of sale arrives, when they are taken from on ship-board, and driven like a herd of swine to market, but worse treated, being manacled together. They are here herded in a pen or yard, like the beasts of the field, exposed to public sale, and without regard to sex or age examined by those brutal men, who are to be their purchasers, as naked as they were born: and, when one is struck off to any bidder, a red hot iron is ready to brand the poor victim with the name of his tyrant purchaser. This leads to a scene still more grievous, still more deeply afflicting. All nature is forced to yield, when the husband is separated from a beloved wife, and a wife from a beloved husband, who had been for many years the joy of her life, and whom she had expected would have been the strength and comfort of her declining years; but now, alas! they are torn asunder, like bone from bone: a heart-rending separation takes place, without a small indulgence of taking a sympathetic farewell of each other, or the possibility of indulging the most distant hope of seeing each other again.

We behold the fond children, with ghastly look and frighted eyes, clinging to their beloved parents, not to be separated from them, but by the lash of their cruel drivers, who make the blood to start at every stroke on their mangled bodies. We next, with heavy hearts and minds overwhelmed with pity, follow them to their destined labour in the plantation field, and by the morning dawn, we hear them summoned to their daily task, by the clashing of cowskin scourges in the hands of their hard-hearted overseers. And should any of them, in consequence of fatigue and loss of strength, fall a little behind their fellow sufferers, they are immediately reminded of it by the lash of their cruel drivers. But here I must stop, as it is too much for nature to pursue farther the dreadfully degrading and cruel theme! And is it not enough to awaken and arouse to sympathy the hardest heart, and lead it to exclaim aloud with abhorrence against such brutal and unrighteous doings? Is it possible that there should be in the United States a man, or would he be worthy to bear the dignified name of man, were he so void of the feelings of humanity, as to purchase and make use of the labour of his fellow citizens, his kindred and his friends, produced in the horrid manner above stated? Would not every sympathetic heart, at the sight of a piece of sugar, or other article, that he believed to be the fruit of their labour, produced with agonizing hearts and trembling limbs, be filled with anguish and his eyes gush with tears? Would it not awaken in the feeling, unbiased mind, a sense of all the cruel sufferings above related? Would it not, instead of pleasing his palate, be deeply wounding to the heart? and, if rightly considered, cause cries to arise from the bottom of his soul, in moving accents of supplication to the righteous Judge of

Heaven and earth, that he would be graciously pleased to put a stop to such complicated misery and great distress of his creature man?

But some, who have not given the subject a full and impartial discussion, may object and say, the slaves in the West-Indies and southern states, are not our fellow citizens and friends. But it cannot be objected by the impartial and the just, who know, that although in a limited sense, as applied to a particular town or city, they may not be so, yet upon the general and universal scale of nature, they are our brethren and fellow creatures; all privileged by nature and nature's God, with liberty and free-agency, and with the blessings attendant thereon; of which they are not to be deprived, but by their own consent; and, therefore, have a right to demand of us the same justice and equity, as our fellow citizens and friends, in a more limited sense, as above stated, could have done; and to whom we are accountable for every act of injustice and omission of doing to them as we would they should do unto us, and for which we shall all have to answer ere long, at the dread tribunal bar, that we can neither awe nor bribe, but shall receive a just retribution for all our works, whether good or evil.

AMERICAN AND FOREIGN ANTI-SLAVERY SOCIETY ADDRESSES THE NON-SLAVEHOLDERS OF THE SOUTH

The antislavery societies were constantly perplexed by the problem of reaching those in the South whose action would be necessary to achieve emancipation. Those who should have been most ready to act against slavery, according to northern abolitionists and southern renegades, were the nonslaveholders of the South, whose labor was cheapened by competition with slaves and whose section was weakened by slavery's discouragement of manufacturing and immigration. The American and Foreign Anti-Slavery Society, the principal non-Garrisonian group, emphasized this argument in its 1843 address to the nonslaveholders of the South.

We all know that the sugar and cotton cultivation of the south is conducted, not like the agriculture of the north, on small farms and with few hands, but on vast plantations and with large gangs of negroes, technically called "the force." In the Breeding states,[1] men, women and children form the great staple for exportation; and like other stock, require capital on the part of those who follow the business of rearing them. It is also a matter of notoriety, that the price of slaves has been and still is such as to confine their possession almost exclusively to the rich. We might as well talk of poor men owning herds of cattle and studs of horses, as gangs of negroes. . . .

. . . At the north a farmer hires as many *men* as his work requires; at the south the laborers cannot be separated from the *women* and *children*. These are *property* and must be owned by somebody. Now when we take this last circumstance into consideration, and at the same time recollect that the very value of the slaves debars the poor from owning them; and connect these two facts with the character of the cultivation in which slave labor is employed, we must be ready to admit

---

From American and Foreign Anti-Slavery Society, *Address to the Non-Slaveholders of the South, on the Social and Political Evils of Slavery* (New York: S. W. Benedict, 1843), pp. 3–8, 24–26.

[1] The states of the Upper South turned their surplus of slaves into an asset by becoming the frequent suppliers of slaves to the cotton states in the Deep South. [Eds.]

that those who do employ this species of labor, cannot on an average hold less than *ten slaves,* including able bodied men, their wives and children. It appears by the census, that of the slave population, the two sexes are almost exactly equal in number; and that there are two children under 10 years of age, for every male slave over that age. Hence if a planter employs only three men, we may take it for granted that his slave family consists of at least 12 souls, viz.: 3 men, 3 women and 6 children. We of course estimate the number of children too low, since there will be some over two [*sic*] years of age. It thus appears that the average number of slaves we assign to each slaveholder is probably far below the truth, but we purposely avoid even the approach to exaggeration. Now the number of slaves in the United States (Am. Almanac for 1842,) is 2,487,113; of course according to our estimate of ten slaves to one master, there can be only 248,711 slave-holders.

The number of *white males over 20 years of age*
  in the slave states and territories is 1,016,307
Deduct slaveholders, viz. 248,711

And we have the number we are now addressing 767,596

We are not forgetful that our enumeration must embrace some who are the *sons* of slaveholders, and who are therefore interested in upholding the system,—but we are fully convinced that our estimate of the number of slaveholders is far beyond the truth, and that we may therefore safely throw out of account the very moderate number of slaveholders' sons above 20 years of age, and not themselves possessing slaves.

Here then, fellow citizens, you see your strength. You have a majority of 518,885 over the slaveholders; and now we repeat that with a numerical majority of more than half a million, slavery lives or dies at *your* behest. . . .

. . . It has been the policy of the slaveholders to keep entirely out of sight their own numerical inferiority, and to speak and act as if *their* interests were those of the whole community. They are the nobility of the south, and they find it expedient to forget that there are any commoners. Hence with them slavery is THE INSTITUTION of the SOUTH, while it is in fact the institution of only a portion of the people of the south. It is their craft to magnify and extol the importance and advantages of *their* institution; and hence we are told by Gov. McDuffie,[2] that slavery "is the CORNER STONE of our republican institutions." To defend this corner stone from the assaults of truth and reason, he audaciously proposed to the legislature that abolitionists should be punished "with death without benefit of clergy." This gentleman, like most demagogues, while professing great zeal for the PEOPLE whose interests were for the most part adverse to slavery, was in fact looking to his own aggrandizement. He was at the very time he uttered these absurd and murderous sentiments, a great planter, and his large "force" was said to have raised in 1836, no less than 122,500 lbs. of cotton. In the same spirit, and with the same design, the report of a committee of the South Carolina Legislature, made in 1842, speaks of slavery "as an ancient domestic institution *cherished in the hearts of the people at the south,* the eradication of which would demolish our whole system of policy, domestic, social and political."

The slaveholders form a powerful landed aristocracy, banded together for the preservation of their own privileges, and ever endeavoring, for obvious reasons, to identify their private interests with the public welfare. Thus have the landed proprietors of England declaimed loudly on the blessings of dear bread, because the corn laws keep up rents, and the price of land. The wealth and influence of your aristocracy, together

---

[2] George E. McDuffie (1790–1851) of South Carolina was a state and national Representative, Governor, and United States Senator. He was a nullificationist and was widely quoted for the sentiment expressed here. See, p. 237, James Forten, Jr., on the South Carolina legislature and its anti-abolitionist resolutions. [Eds.]

with your own poverty, have led you to look up to them with a reverence bordering on that which is paid to a feudal nobility by their hereditary dependents. Hence it is that, unconscious of your own power, you have permitted them to assume, as of right, the whole legislation and government of your respective states. We now propose to call your attention to the practical results of that control over *your* interests which by your sufferance, they have so long exercised. We ask you to join us in the inquiry how far you have been benefited by the care of your guardians, when compared with the people of the north, who have been left to govern themselves. We will pursue this inquiry in the following order, viz.:

1. INCREASE OF POPULATION.
2. STATE OF EDUCATION.
3. STATE OF INDUSTRY AND ENTERPRISE.
4. FEELING TOWARDS THE LABORING CLASSES.
5. STATE OF RELIGION.
6. STATE OF MORALS.
7. DISREGARD FOR HUMAN LIFE.
8. DISREGARD FOR CONSTITUTIONAL OBLIGATIONS.
9. LIBERTY OF SPEECH.
10. LIBERTY OF THE PRESS.
11. MILITARY WEAKNESS.

I. INCREASE OF POPULATION.

The ratio of increase of population, especially in this country, is one of the surest tests of public prosperity. Let us then again listen to the impartial testimony of the late census. From this we learn that the increase of population in the free states from 1830 to 1840, was at the rate of 38 per cent., while the increase of the *free* population in the slave states was only 23 per cent. Why this difference of 15 in the two ratios. No other cause can be assigned than slavery, which drives from your borders many of the virtuous and enterprising, and at the same time deters emigrants from other states and from foreign countries from settling among you.

The influence of slavery on population is strikingly illustrated by a comparison between Kentucky and Ohio. These two states are of nearly equal areas. Kentucky however having about 3000 square miles more than the other. They are separated only by a river and are both remarkable for the fertility of their soil, but one has, from the beginning, been cursed with slavery, and the other blessed with freedom. Now mark their respective careers. In 1792, Kentucky was erected into a state, and Ohio in 1802.

1790	Free population of Kentucky	61,227
	Ohio a wilderness.	
1800	Free population of Kentucky	180,612
	Free population of Ohio	45,365
1810	Free population of Kentucky	325,950
	Free population of Ohio	230,760
1820	Free population of Kentucky	437,585
	Free population of Ohio	581,434
1830	Free population of Kentucky	522,704
	Free population of Ohio	937,903
1840	Free population of Kentucky	597,570
	Free population of Ohio	1,519,467

The representation of the two states in Congress, has been as follows:

1802,	Kentucky	6,	Ohio	1
1812,	"	9,	"	6
1822,	"	12,	"	14
1832,	"	13,	"	19
1842,	"	10,	"	21

The value of land, other things being equal, is in proportion to the density of population. Now the population of Ohio is 38.8 to a square mile, while the free population of Kentucky is but 14.2 to a square mile,—and probably the price of land in the two states is much in the same proportion. You are told much of the wealth invested in negroes—yet it obviously is a wealth that impoverishes, and no stronger evidence of the truth of this assertion is needed, than the comparative price of land in the free and slave states. The two principal cities of Kentucky and Ohio are Louisville and Cincinnati; the former with a population of 21,210, the latter with a population of 46,338. Why this difference? The question is answered by the *Louisville Journal*. The editor, speaking of the two rival cities, remarks, "The most potent cause of the more rapid advancement of Cincinnati than Louisville is the ABSENCE OF SLAVERY. The same influences which made Ohio the young giant of the West, and is advancing Indiana to a grade higher than Kentucky, have operated in the *Queen* city. They have no *dead weight to carry*, and consequently have the advantage in the race." . . .

. . . We surely need not detain you with farther details on this head to convince you what an enormous sacrifice of happiness and prosperity you are offering on the altar of slavery. But of the character and extent of this sacrifice you have as yet had only a partial glimpse. Let us proceed to examine

II. THE STATE OF EDUCATION IN THE SLAVE STATES.

The maxim that "Knowledge is power," has ever more or less influenced the conduct of aristocracies. Education elevates the inferior classes of society, teaches them their rights, and points out the means of enforcing them. Of course, it tends to diminish the influence of wealth, birth, and rank. In 1671, Sir William Berkley, then Governor of Virginia, in his answer to the inquiries of the Committee of the Colonies, remarked, "I thank God, that there are no free schools nor printing presses, and I hope we shall not have them these hundred years." The spirit of Sir William seems still to preside in the councils of his own Virginia, and to actuate those of the other slave States.

The power of the slaveholders, as we have already showed you, depends on the acquiescence of the major part of the white inhabitants in their domination. It cannot be, therefore, the interest or the inclination of the sagacious and reflecting among them, to promote the intellectual improvement of the inferior class.

In the free States, on the contrary, where there is no caste answering to your slaveholders; where the *People* literally partake in the government, mighty efforts are made for general education; and in most instances, elementary instruction is, through the public liberality, brought within the reach of the children of the poor. You have lamentable experience, that such is not the case where slaveholders bear rule.

But you will receive with distrust whatever *we* may say as to the comparative ignorance of the free and slave States. Examine then for yourselves the returns of the late census on this point. This document gives us the number of white persons over twenty years of age in each State, who cannot read *and* write. It appears that these persons are to the *whole* white population in the several States as follows, viz.:

Connecticut,	1 to every	568	Louisiana,	1 to every	38½
Vermont,	1 "	473	Maryland	1 "	27
N. Hamp.	1 "	310	Mississippi,	1 "	20
Mass.	1 "	166	Delaware,	1 "	18
Maine,	1 "	108	S. Carolina,	1 "	17
Michigan,	1 "	97	Missouri.	1 "	16
R. Island,	1 "	67	Alabama,	1 "	15
New Jersey,	1 "	58	Kentucky,	1 "	13½
New York,	1 "	56	Georgia,	1 "	13
Penn.	1 "	50	Virginia,	1 "	12½
Ohio,	1 "	43	Arkansas	1 "	11½
Indiana,	1 "	18	Tennessee	1 "	11
Illinois,	1 "	17	N. Carolina,	1 "	7

It will be observed by looking at this table that Indiana and Illinois are the *only* free states, which in point of education are surpassed by *any* of the slave states: for this disgraceful circumstance three causes may be assigned, viz., their recent settlement, the influx of foreigners, and emigration from the slave states. The returns from New York, Rhode Island, New Jersey and Pennsylvania, are greatly affected by the vast number of foreigners congregated in their cities, and employed in their manufactories and on their public works. In Ohio also, there is a large foreign population, and it is well known that comparatively few emigrants from Europe seek a residence in the slave states, where there is little or no employment to invite them. But what a commentary on slavery and slaveholders is afforded by the gross ignorance prevailing in the old states of South Carolina, Virginia and North Carolina! . . .

. . . Whatever may be the leisure enjoyed by the slaveholders, they are careful not to afford the means of literary improvement to their fellow citizens who are too poor to possess slaves, and who are, by their very ignorance, rendered more fit instruments for doing the will, and guarding the human property of the wealthier class.

III. INDUSTRY AND ENTERPRISE.

In a community so unenlightened as yours, it is a matter of course, that the arts and sciences must languish; and the industry and enterprise of the country be oppressed by a general torpor. Hence multitudes will be without regular and profitable employment, and be condemned to poverty and numberless privations. The very advertisements in your newspapers, show that for a vast proportion of the comforts and conveniences of life, you are dependent on northern manufacturers and mechanics. You both know and feel that slavery has rendered labor disgraceful among you; and where this is the case, industry is necessarily discouraged. The great staple of the south is cotton; and we have no desire to undervalue its importance.

It, however, is worthy of remark, that its cultivation affords a livelihood to only a small proportion of the free inhabitants; and scarcely to any of those we are now addressing. Cotton is the product of slave labor, and its profits at home are confined almost exclusively to the slaveholders. Yet on account of this article, we hear frequent vaunts of the agricultural riches of the south. With the exception of cotton, it is difficult to distinguish your agricultural products arising from slave, and from free labor. But admitting, what we know is not the fact, that *all* the other productions of the soil are raised *exclusively* by free labor, we learn from the census that the agricultural products of the north exceed those of the south, cotton excepted, $226,219,714. Here then we have an appalling proof of the paralyzing influence of slavery on the industry of the whites.

In every community a large portion of the inhabitants are debarred from drawing their maintenance directly from the cultivation of the earth. Other and lucrative employments are reserved for them. If the slaveholders chiefly engross the soil, let us see how you are compensated by the encouragement afforded to mechanical skill and industry.

In 1839 the Secretary of the Treasury reported to Congress, that the tonnage of vessels built in the

United States was 120,988
Built in the Slave States and Territories 23,600

Or less than one fifth of the whole! But the difference is still more striking, when we take into consideration the comparative *value* of the shipping built in the two regions;

In the free states the value is $6,311,805
In the slave   " 704,291

It would be tedious and unprofitable to compare the results of the different branches of manufacture carried on at the north and the south. It is sufficient to state that according to the census the value of the manufactures

In the free States are $334,139,690
In the slave States .... 83,935,742...

In one species of manufacture the south apparently excels the north, but unfortunately, it is in appearance only. Of 9657 distilleries in the United States, no less than 7665 are found in the slave states and territories; but for want of skill and capital, these yield fewer gallons than the other 1992.

Where there is so much ignorance and idleness, we may well suppose that the inventive faculties will be but little exercised; and accordingly we find that of the 495 patents granted for new inventions in 1841, only 70 were received by citizens of the slave states. . . .

IV. FEELINGS OF THE SLAVEHOLDERS TOWARDS THE LABORING CLASSES.

Whenever the great mass of the laboring population of a country are reduced to beasts of burden, and toil under the lash, "bodily labor," as chancellor Harper[3] expresses it, must be disreputable, from the mere influence of association. Hence you know *white* laborers at the south are styled "mean whites." At the north, on the contrary, labor is regarded as the proper and commendable means of acquiring wealth; and our most influential men would in no degree suffer in public estimation, for holding the plough, or even repairing the highways. Hence no poor man is deterred from seeking a livelihood by honest labor from a dread of personal degradation. The different light in which labor is viewed at the north and the south is one cause of the depression of industry in the latter.

Another cause is the ever wakeful jealousy of your aristocracy. They fear the PEOPLE; they are alarmed at the very idea of power and influence being possessed by any portion of the

---

[3] William Harper (1790–1847), lawyer, Senator from South Carolina (1826), member of the South Carolina House; Chancellor of the state from 1834 until his death. [Eds.]

community not directly interested in slave property. Visions of emancipation, of agrarianism and of popular resistance to their authority, are ever floating in their distempered and excited imaginations. They know their own weakness, and are afraid you should know it also. Hence it is their policy to keep down the "mean whites." Hence their philippics against the lower classes. Hence their constant comparison of the laborers of the north, with their own slaves; and hence in no small degree the absence among you of those institutions which confer upon the poor that knowledge which is *power*. . . .

Prospects for the Future

If, fellow-citizens, with all the natural and political advantages we have enumerated, your progress is still downward, and has been so, compared with the other section of the country, since the first organization of the Government, what are the anticipations of the distant future, which sober reflection authorizes you to form? The causes which now retard the increase of your population must continue to operate, so long as slavery lasts. Emigrants from the north and from foreign countries, will, as at present, avoid your borders; within which no attractions will be found for virtue and industry. On the other hand, many of the young and enterprising among you will flee from the lassitude, the anarchy, the wretchedness engendered by slavery, and seek their fortunes in lands where law affords protection, and where labor is honored and rewarded.

In the meantime, especially in the cotton States, the slaves will continue to increase in a ratio far beyond the whites, and will at length acquire a fearful preponderance.

At the first census, in every slave State there was a very large majority of whites—now, the slaves outnumber the whites in South Carolina, Mississippi and Louisiana, and the next census will unquestionably add Florida and Alabama, and probably Georgia, to the number of negro States.

And think you that this is the country, and this the age, in which the republican maxim that the MAJORITY must govern, can be long and barbarously reversed. Think you that the majority of the PEOPLE in the cotton States, cheered and encouraged as they will be by the sympathy of the world, and the example of the West Indies, will for ever tamely submit to be beasts of burden for a few lordly planters? And remember, we pray you, that the number and physical strength of the negroes will increase in a much greater ratio than that of their masters.

In 1790 the whites in N. Carolina were to the slaves as 2.80 to 1, now as 1.97 to 1.

"	"	in S. Carolina,	"	1.31 to 1,	"	.79 to 1.
"	"	in Georgia,	"	1.76 to 1,	"	1.44 to 1.
"	"	Tennessee,	"	13.35 to 1,	"	3.49 to 1.
"	"	Kentucky,	"	5.16 to 1,	"	3.23 to 1.

Maryland and Virginia, the great breeding States, have reduced their stock within the last ten years, having been tempted by high prices, to ship off thousands and tens of thousands to the markets of Louisiana, Alabama, and Mississippi. But these markets are already glutted, and human flesh has fallen in value from 50 to 75 per cent. Nor is it probable that the great staple of Virginia and Maryland will hereafter afford a bounty on its production. In these States, slave labor is unprofitable, and the bondman is of but little value, save as an article of exportation. The cotton cultivation in the East Indies, by cheapening the article, will close the markets in the south, and thus it guarantees the abolition of slavery in the breeding States. When it shall be found no longer profitable to raise slaves for the market, the stock on hand will be driven south and sold for what it may fetch, and free labor substituted in its place. This process will be attended with results disastrous to the cotton States. To Virginia and Maryland, it will open a new era of industry, prosperity and wealth; and the industrious poor, the "mean whites" of the south, will remove within their borders, thus leaving the slaveholders more defenceless than ever. But while the white population of the south will be thus diminished, its number of slaves will be increased by the addition of the stock from the breeding States.

And what, fellow citizens, will be the condition of such of *you* as shall then remain in the slave States? The change to which we have referred will necessarily aggravate every present evil. Ignorance, vice, idleness, lawless violence, dread of insurrection, anarchy, and a haughty and vindictive aristocracy will all combine with augmented energy in crushing *you* to the earth. And from what quarter do you look for redemption? Think you your planting nobility will ever grant freedom to their serfs from sentiments of piety or patriotism? Remember that your clergy of all sects and ranks, many of them "Christian brokers in the trade of blood" unite in bestowing their benedictions on the system as *a Christian* institution, and teaching the slaveholders that they wield the whip as European monarchs the sceptre, "by the grace of God." Do you trust to their patriotism? Remember that the beautiful and affecting contrast between the prosperity of the north and the desolation of the south, already presented to you, was drawn by W. C. Preston, of *hanging* notoriety.[4] No, fellow citizens, your great slaveholders have no idea of surrendering the personal importance and the political influence they derive from their slaves. Your Calhouns, Clays, and Prestons, all go for everlasting slavery.

Unquestionably there are many of the smaller slaveholders who would embrace abolition sentiments, were they permitted

---

[4] William C. Preston, 1794–1860. South Carolina Senator, 1833–1842; President of the College of South Carolina, 1846–1851. He supported Calhoun's Nullification position while in the Senate. The reference to "hanging notoriety" is obscure. [Eds.]

to examine the subject; but at present they are kept in ignorance. If then the fetters of the slave are not to be broken by the master, by whom is he to be liberated? In the course of time a hostile army, invited by the weakness or the arrogance of the south, will land on your shores. Then, indeed, emancipation will be given, but the gift may be bathed in the blood of yourselves and of your children. Or the People, for they will be THE PEOPLE, may resolve to be free, and you and all you hold dear may be sacrificed in the contest.

Suffer us, fellow citizens, to show you "a more excellent way." We seek the welfare of all, the rich and the poor, the bond and the free. While we repudiate all acknowledgement of property in human beings, we rejoice in the honest, lawful prosperity of the planter. Let not, we beseech you, the freedom of the slave proceed from the armed invader of your soil, nor from his own torch and dagger—but from your own peaceful and constitutional interference in his behalf.

In breaking the chains which bind the slave, be assured you will be delivering yourselves from a grievous thraldom. . . .

Without your co-operation the slaveholders, much as they despise you, are powerless. To you they look for agents, and stewards, for overseers, and drivers, and patrols. To you they look for votes to elevate them to office, and to you they too often look for aid to enforce their Lynch laws. Feel then your own power; claim your rights, and exert them for the deliverence of the slave, and consequently for your own happiness and prosperity. . . .

. . . A glorious career opens before you. In the place of your present contempt, and degradation, and misery; honor, and wealth, and happiness, court your acceptance. By abolishing slavery, you will become the architects of your own fortune, and of your country's greatness. The times are propitious for the great achievement. You will be cheered by the approbation of your own consciences, and by the plaudits of mankind. The institution which oppresses you is suffering from the decrepitude of age, and is the scorn and loathing of the world. Out of the slave region, patriots and philanthropists, and Christians of every name and sect, abhor and execrate it. Do you pant for liberty and equality more substantial than such as is now found only in your obliterated and tattered bills of right—do you ask that your children may be rescued from the ignorance and irreligion to which they are now doomed, and that avenues may be opened for you and for them to honest and profitable employment? Then unite, we beseech you, with one heart and one mind for the legal constitutional abolition of slavery.

HINTON ROWAN HELPER
ADDRESSES THE NON-SLAVEHOLDERS
OF THE SOUTH

Not all antislavery arguments came from the North. Hinton Rowan Helper (1829–1909) was a North Carolinian who attacked slavery as an economic system highly detrimental to southern prosperity. Helper himself was not, like northern antislavery proponents, sympathetic to the Negro, whom he regarded as inferior to the white. Rather his position reflected that of the small upland farmer of the South doing battle with his economic antagonist, the large slaveholding plantation owner. His Impending Crisis, *setting forth his argument, was first published in 1857.*

From Hinton Rowan Helper, *The Impending Crisis of the South: How to Meet It* (New York: A. B. Burdick, 1860), pp. 123–131, 154–156.

Preliminary to our elucidation of what we conceive to be the most discreet, fair and feasible plan for the abolition of slavery, we propose to offer a few additional reasons why it should be abolished. Among the thousand and one arguments that present themselves in support of our position—which, before we part with the reader, we shall endeavor to define so clearly, that it shall be regarded as ultra only by those who imperfectly understand it—is the influence which slavery invariably exercises in depressing the value of real estate; and as this is a matter in which the non-slaveholders of the South, of the West, and of the Southwest, are most deeply interested, we shall discuss it in a sort of preamble of some length.

The oligarchs says we cannot abolish slavery without infringing on the right of property. Again we tell them we do not recognize property in man; but even if we did, and if we were to inventory the negroes at quadruple, the value of their last assessment, still, impelled by a sense of duty to others, and as a matter of simple justice to ourselves, we, the non-slaveholders of the South, would be fully warranted in emancipating all the slaves at once, and that, too, without any compensation whatever to those who claim to be their absolute masters and owners. We will explain. In 1850, the average value per acre, of land in the Northern States was $28,07; in the Northwestern $11,39; in the Southern $5,34; and in the Southwestern $6,26. Now, in consequence of numerous natural advantages, among which may be enumerated the greater mildness of climate, richness of soil, deposits of precious metals, abundance and spaciousness of harbors, and super-excellence of water-power, we contend that, had it not been for slavery, the average value of land in all the Southern and Southwestern States, would have been *at least* equal to the average value of the same in the Northern States. We conclude, therefore, and we think the conclusion is founded on principles of equity, that you, the slaveholders, are indebted to us, the non-slaveholders, in the sum of $22,73, which is the difference between

Arguments from Economics 165

$28,07 and $5,34, on every acre of Southern soil in our possession. This claim we bring against you, because slavery, which has inured exclusively to your own benefit, if, indeed, it has been beneficial at all, has shed a blighting influence over our lands, thereby keeping them out of market, and damaging every acre to the amount specified. Sirs! are you ready to settle the account? Let us see how much it is. There are in the fifteen slave States, 346,048 slaveholders, and 544,926,720 acres of land. Now the object is to ascertain how many acres are owned by slaveholders, and how many by non-slaveholders. Suppose we estimate five hundred acres as the average landed property of each slaveholder; will that be fair? We think it will, taking into consideration the fact that 174,503 of the whole number of slaveholders hold less than five slaves each—68,820 holding only one each. According to this hypothesis, the slaveholders own 173,024,000 acres, and the non-slaveholders the balance, with the exception of about 40,000,000 of acres, which belong to the General Government. The case may be stated thus:

Area of the Slave States 544,926,720 acres.

Estimates
{ Acres owned by slaveholders 173,024,000
Acres owned by government 40,000,000—213,024,000
Acres owned by non-slaveholders.........331,902,720

Now, chevaliers of the lash, and worshippers of slavery, the total value of three hundred and thirty-one million nine hundred and two thousand seven hundred and twenty acres, at twenty-two dollars and seventy-three cents per acre, is *seven billion five hundred and forty-four million one hundred and forty-eight thousand eight hundred and twenty-five dollars;* and this is our account against you on a single score. Considering how your villainous institution has retarded the development of our commercial and manufacturing interests, how it has stifled the aspirations of inventive genius; and, above all, how it has barred from us the heaven-born sweets of literature and religion—concernments too sacred to be estimated in a pecuniary point of view—might we not, with perfect justice and propriety, duplicate the amount, and still be accounted modest in our demands? Fully advised, however, of your indigent circumstances, we feel it would be utterly useless to call on you for the whole amount that is due us; we shall, therefore, in your behalf, make another draft on the fund of non-slaveholding generosity, and let the account, meagre as it is, stand as above. Though we have given you all the offices, and you have given us none of the benefits of legislation; though we have fought the battles of the South, while you were either lolling in your piazzas, or playing the tory, and endeavoring to filch from us our birthright of freedom; though you have absorbed the wealth of our communities in sending your own children to Northern seminaries and colleges, or in employing Yankee teachers to officiate exclusively in your own families, and have refused to us the limited privilege of common schools; though you have scorned to patronize our mechanics and industrial enterprises, and have passed to the North for every article of apparel, utility, and adornment; and though you have maltreated, outraged and defrauded us in every relation of life, civil, social, and political, yet we are willing to forgive and *forget* you, if you will but do us justice on a single count. Of you, the introducers, aiders and abettors of slavery, we demand indemnification for the damage our lands have sustained on account there of; the amount of that damage is $7,544,148,825; and now, Sirs, we are ready to receive the money, and if it is perfectly convenient to you, we would be glad to have you pay it in specie! It will not avail you, Sirs, to parley or prevaricate. We must have a settlement. Our claim is just and overdue. We have already indulged you too long. Your criminal extravagance has almost ruined us. We are determined that you shall no longer play the profligate, and fair sumptuously every day at our expense. How do you propose to settle? Do you offer us your negroes in part payment? We do not want your negroes. We would not have all of them, nor any number of them, even as a gift. We hold ourselves above the disreputable and iniquitous practices of buying, selling, and owning slaves. What we demand is damages in money, or other absolute property, as an equivalent for the pecuniary losses we have suffered at your hands. You value your negroes at sixteen hundred millions of dollars, and propose to sell them to us for that sum; we should consider ourselves badly cheated, and disgraced for all time, here and hereafter, if we were to take them off your hands at sixteen farthings! We tell you emphatically, we are firmly resolved never to degrade ourselves by becoming the mercenary purchasers or proprietors of human beings. Except for the purpose of liberating them, we would not give a handkerchief or a tooth-pick for all the slaves in the world. But, in order to show how brazenly absurd are the howls and groans which you invariably set up for compensation, whenever we speak of the abolition of slavery, we will suppose your negroes are worth all you ask for them, and that we are bound to secure to you every cent of the sum before they can become free—in which case, our accounts would stand thus:

Non-slaveholder's account against Slaveholders.... $7,544,148,825
Slaveholder's account against Non-Slaveholders.... 1,600,000,000

Balance due Non-slaveholders............... $5,944,148,825

Now, Sirs, we ask you in all seriousness, Is it not true that you have filched from us nearly five times the amount of the assessed value of your slaves? Why, then do you still clamor for more? Is it your purpose to make the game perpetual? Think you that we will ever continue to bow at the wave of your wand, that we will bring humanity into everlasting disgrace by licking the hand that smites us, and that with us there is no point beyond which forbearance ceases to be a virtue? Sirs, if these be your thoughts, you are laboring under a most fatal delusion. You can goad us no further; you shall oppress us no longer; heretofore, earnestly but submissively, we have asked you to redress the more atrocious outrages which you have perpetrated against us; but what has been the invariable fate of our petitions? With scarcely a perusal, with a degree of contempt that added insult to injury, you have laid them on the table, and from thence they have been swept into the furnance of oblivion. Henceforth, Sirs, we are demandants, not suppliants. We demand our rights, nothing more, nothing less. It is for you to decide whether we are to have justice peaceably or by violence, for whatever consequences may follow, we are determined to have it one way or the other. Do you aspire to become the victims of white non-slaveholding vengeance by day, and of barbarous massacre by the negroes at night? Would you be instrumental in bringing upon yourselves, your wives, and your children, a fate too horrible to contemplate? shall history cease to cite, as an instance of unexampled cruelty, the Massacre of St. Bartholomew, because the world—the South—shall have furnished a more direful scene of atrocity and carnage? Sirs, we would not wantonly pluck a single hair from your heads; but we have endured long, we have endured much; slaves only of the most despicable class would endure more. An enumeration or classification of all the abuses, insults, wrongs, injuries, usurpations, and oppressions, to which you have subjected us, would fill a larger volume than this; it is our purpose, therefore, to speak only of those that affect us most deeply. Out of our effects your have long since overpaid yourselves for your negroes; and now, Sirs, you *must* emancipate them—speedily emancipate them, or we will emancipate them for you! Every non-slaveholder in the South is, or ought to be, and will be, against you. You yourselves ought to join us at once in our laudable crusade against "the mother of harlots." Slavery has polluted and impoverished your lands; freedom will restore them to their virgin purity, and add from twenty to thirty dollars to the value of every acre. Correctly speaking, emancipation will cost you nothing; the moment you abolish slavery, that very moment will the putative value of the slave become actual value in the soil. Though there are ten millions of people in the South, and though you, the slaveholders, are only three hundred and forty-seven thousand in number, you have within a fraction of one-third of all the territory belonging to the fifteen slave States. You have a landed estate of 173,024,000 acres, the present average market valve of which is only $5,34 per acre; emancipate your slaves on Wednesday morning, and on the Thursday following the value of your lands, and ours too, will have increased to an average of at least $28,07 per acre. Let us see, therefore, even in this one particular, whether the abolition of slavery will not be a real pecuniary advantage to you. The present total market value of all your landed property, at $5,34 per acre, is only $923,248,160! With the beauty and sunlight of freedom beaming on the same estate, it would be worth, at $28,07 per acre, $4,856,873,680. The former sum, deducted from the latter, leaves a balance of $3,933,535,520, and to the full extent of this amount will *your* lands be increased in value whenever you abolish slavery; that is, provided you abolish it before it completely "dries up all the organs of increase." Here is a more manifest and distinct statement of the case:—

Estimated value of slaveholders' lands after slavery
  shall have been abolished...................$4,856,783,680
Present value of slaveholders' lands..............   923,248,160

Probable aggregate enhancement of value........$3,933,535,520

Now, Sirs, this last sum is considerably more than twice as great as the estimated value of your negroes; and those of you, if any there be, who are yet heirs to sane minds and honest hearts, must, it seems to us, admit that the bright prospect which freedom presents for a wonderful increase in the value of real estate, ours as well as yours, to say nothing of the thousand other kindred considerations, ought to be quite sufficient to induce all the Southern States, in their sovereign capacities, to abolish slavery at the earliest practical period. You yourselves, instead of losing anything by the emancipation of your negroes—even though we suppose them to be worth every dime of $1,600,000,000—would, in this one particular, the increased value of land, realize a *net profit* of over *twenty three hundred millions of dollars!* Here are the exact figures:—

Net increment of value which it is estimated will accrue to slaveholders' lands in consequence of the abolition of slavery.	$3,933,535,520
Putative value of the slaves.	1,600,000,000
Slaveholders' estimated net landed profits of eman.	$2,333,535,520

What is the import of these figures? They are full of meaning. They proclaim themselves the financial intercessors for freedom, and, with that open-hearted liberality which is so characteristic of the sacred cause in whose behalf they plead, they propose to pay you upward of three thousand nine hundred millions of dollars for the very "property" which you, in all the reckless extravagance of your inhuman avarice, could not find a heart to price at more than one thousand six hundred millions. In other words, your own lands, groaning and languishing under the monstrous burden of slavery, announce their willingness to pay you all you ask for the negroes, and offer you, besides, a bonus of more than twenty-three hundred millions of dollars, if you will but convert those lands into free soil! *Our* lands, also, cry aloud to be spared from the further pollutions and desolations of slavery; and now, Sirs, we want to know explicitly whether, or not, it is your intention to heed these lamentations of the ground? We want to know whether you are men or devils—whether you are entirely selfish and cruelly dishonest, or whether you have any respect for the rights of others. We, the non-slaveholders of the South, have many very important interests at stake—interests which, heretofore, you have steadily despised and trampled under foot, but which, henceforth, we shall foster and defend in utter defiance of all the unhallowed influences which it is possible for you, or any other class of slaveholders or slavebreeders to bring against us. Not the least among these interests is our landed property, which, to command a decent price, only needs to be disencumbered of slavery. . . .

. . . That our plan for the abolition of slavery, is the best that can be devised, we have not the vanity to contend; but that it is a good one, and will do to act upon until a better shall have been suggested, we do firmly and conscientiously believe. . . .

Inscribed on the banner, which we herewith unfurl to the world, with the full and fixed determination to stand by it or die by it, unless one of more virtuous efficacy shall be presented, are the mottoes which, in substance, embody the principles, as we conceive, that should govern us in our patriotic warfare against the most subtle and insidious foe that ever menaced the inalienable rights and liberties and dearest interests of America:

1st. Thorough Organization and Independent Political Action on the part of the Non-Slaveholding whites of the South.
2nd. Ineligibility of Slaveholders—Never another vote to the Trafficker in Human Flesh.
3rd. No Co-operation with Slaveholders in Politics—No Fellowship with them in Religion—No Affiliation with them in Society.
4th. No Patronage to Slaveholding Merchants—No Guestship in Slave-waiting Hotels—No Fees to Slaveholding Lawyers—No Employment of Slaveholding Physicians—No Audience to Slaveholding Parsons.
5th. No Recognition of Pro-Slavery Men, except as Ruffians, Outlaws, and Criminals.
6th. Abrupt Discontinuance of Subscription to Pro-slavery Newspapers.
7th. The Greatest Possible Encouragement to Free White Labor.

8. No more Hiring of Slaves by Non-slaveholders.

9th. Immediate Death to Slavery, or if not immediate, unqualified Proscription of its Advocates during the Period of its Existence.

10th. A Tax of Sixty Dollars on every Slaveholder for each and every Negro in his Possession at the present time, or at any intermediate time between now and the 4th of July, 1863—said Money to be Applied to the transportation of the Blacks to Liberia, to their Colonization in Central or South America, or to their Comfortable Settlement within the Boundaries of the United States.

11th. An additional Tax of Forty Dollars per annum to be levied annually, on every Slaveholder for each and every Negro found in his possession after the 4th of July, 1863—said Money to be paid into the hands of the Negroes so held in Slavery, or, in cases of death, to their next of kin, and to be used by them at their own option.

CHARLES CALISTUS BURLEIGH

EMPHASIZES ECONOMIC ADVANTAGE

FOR THE NORTH

Northern labor was frequently suspicious of the abolitionists' plans to free the slaves, who, they feared, would rush to the North and compete unfairly with white labor. Similarly, northerners in general feared inundation by an overwhelming black tide. Slavery's opponents, therefore, tried to play down the possibility of Negro migration northward and to play up the vast market that would be created by a free Negro farm labor force in the South, which, suddenly enriched, would clamor for northern industrial produce. Charles Calistus Burleigh (1810–1878), whose opposition to shaving and cutting his hair gained him fame as one of the more eccentric antislavery lecturers, wrote the argument for such expediency which appears below in 1855.

. . . To emancipate . . . is not to outlaw, or cut loose from society or any of its natural relations or real duties; but it is to cease from holding men as property, and begin to treat them as men; enabling them to claim and receive the earnings of their toil; giving them a voice in the choosing of their work, their employers, their associates, abodes, and manner of life; respecting their domestic ties and rights and duties; allowing them to improve their minds with knowledge and their hearts with moral culture; and leaving them free to worship God when, where and how their consciences require.

WHO CAN OBJECT?

To what, in all this, can any one reasonably object? The master cannot justly complain of a loss of property, for what he loses was never his; but so much as the change takes from him, so much has he been wrongfully withholding from the real owner, to whom—long due—it is at last restored. Nay, if either loses, it is still the slave; for his past toils and wrongs are unrequited. He is merely to be robbed no longer;—not to have back what has been plundered from him. The state or country cannot complain of loss, for, to it, the slave was only worth what work could be forced out of him, and that is less than he

---

From Charles Calistus Burleigh, *Slavery and the North* (Anti-Slavery Tract No. 10) (New York: American Anti-Slavery Society, [1855]), pp. 2–3, 8–10.

will do unforced, when free. The change takes nothing from his strength or skill, but adds much to his willingness to use them. When laboring, of his own accord, with the prospect of receiving what he earns, he has a motive to be diligent and faithful, which he never had while toiling reluctantly for another's gain. Even as a mere working-tool, therefore, he is worth more for being free. And then, too, freedom makes him infinitely more than a mere working-tool. He is now a man, with all the priceless treasures of mind and soul, with all the growing powers and upward aspirations which belong to manhood; with ever-widening scope for his unfolding faculties, and nothing to forbid his progress toward any height, however lofty, of human excellence. As much as brain and muscle are worth more than muscle only; as much as moral joined to mental power is a better wealth than mere brute force; in a word, as much as *men* with human skill, contrivance and invention, with reason, affection and the sense of right, are of more account than cattle yoked, and horses trained to harness; so much will the emancipation of a nation's slaves enrich the nation. Why, then, should not our slaves go free? . . .

. . . One sign of the much improved outward condition of the laboring class—no longer slaves—is the great increase of imports of such articles as they use. For instance, in Jamaica, since slavery was abolished, the yearly average importation of flour, rice, corn, and bread has considerably more than doubled; of corn-meal, butter, lard and soap, almost doubled; of pork, about trebled; of candles, and of lumber, has increased nearly one half; and of cattle, more than four-fold. If exports have lessened, one reason is, a greater home-consumption. The planter sends away less, for the laborer uses more, thus having not only more comforts from abroad, but also more of those produced at home. Many of the freedmen have become small landholders, and live in easy independence on their little properties. Women, to a great extent, have left field-labor, and now attend to household duties and the care of their children, formerly, of necessity, so much neglected. Self-respect and manly bearing, have, in a good degree, taken the place of that cringing servility which generally marks the slave. Thus facts refute the falsehood that negroes are fit only to be slaves; and neither wish for freedom, nor would be bettered by it.

OVERRUN THE NORTH.

But if freed, it is said, they will overrun the North. Ah! Wouldn't leave their masters if they could; so if allowed to do as they please, they will all run off! Sound logic, truly! And as sound morality, is the inference that therefore they must still be enslaved! If they *would* come north, to hinder is to wrong them. As rightfully might the West shut out the eastern emigrant, as the North shut out the southern. But there is no danger of their coming. Free them, and the motive which brings them here is gone. When they come now, it is for freedom. Let them have it at home, and they will stay there. The climate of the South suits them better than ours, they are used to its employments, their habits are formed by and fitted to a southern life, there are all their attachments and associations, there the strong home-feeling binds them. There too they are needed. They do the hard work of the South, and could not be spared from its fields and shops. To employ them there at liberal wages would cost much less than to put other laborers in their places. Hence it would be for the employers' interest to keep them, and for theirs to stay. Moreover they do stay there now, when freed; although oppressive laws—which would be repealed when the abolition of slavery had removed their cause—are now in force there against free blacks.

Of the whole South, about one man in thirty-six is free colored. And more than two-thirds of these are in the northern border slave States, whence, of course, they could most easily "come north." In Virginia, they are one in twenty-five of all the people; in Maryland, nearly one in ten; in Delaware, more than one in five. Yet hardly ever does one of them remove into a free State, though slaves come often—sometimes hundreds in a year.

EFFECT ON NORTHERN LABOR.

This reasoning also proves the notion false, that emancipation at the South will lower the price of labour at the North. For, instead of sending up the southern blacks to compete with the working classes here, it would both keep them at home and draw back many who were driven hither by slavery, but would gladly return when they could do so and be free. Besides, it would much enlarge the market at the South, for the fruits of northern industry and enterprise. The southern laborers, when free and paid, would buy of us many comforts and conveniences not allowed them now;—cloths, hats, shoes, furniture, household utensils, improved working-tools, a countless variety of northern manufactures, and of foreign wares, imported through the North;—the demand for which would give new activity to our shops and mills and shipping, and steadier employment, and, most likely, higher wages, to all kinds of labor here. Three million new consumers of the wares we make and sell, would add greatly to the income of the North. New shops and factories, built to meet their wants, would grow to villages and towns; and, employing many busy hands in every useful calling, create home markets for the farmers' produce; increase the worth of lands and houses; put life into every branch of business; and spread the benefits of the change among all classes, over the whole country. Slavery keeps from us all these benefits, and thus, in robbing southern labor, robs also northern. Yet worse; it degrades labor; coupling it, at the South, with the lowest social debasement, and thereby lessening its respectability at the North, till now it has become, in the esteem of many, a positive disgrace, and the honest sons of toil are shut out of self-styled "good society," by reason solely of their useful occupations. Hence, doubtless, is it that our hopeful youth so often flee from field or shop, into some over-crowded "profession," and suffer in proud poverty through life, or are corrupted and depraved by the manifold temptations of their unwisely chosen lot. Hence, too, the laborer, failing of the respect which is his due from others, too often loses somewhat of his *self*-respect, grows careless of his character and conduct, makes little or no earnest effort to increase in worth and rise in social standing, and perhaps *becomes* at length, in many instances, as low as he is *rated*. Thus the enslavement of labor at the South, is by no means least among the causes which keep down labor at the North, and, of course, emancipation there would be no detriment, but a great advantage, to the working classes here.

WILLIAM HENRY SEWARD WARNS OF AN IRREPRESSIBLE ECONOMIC CONFLICT

Occasionally economic arguments were introduced into the northern politics of antislavery in an attempt to gain Democratic votes of those who feared collaboration between "the lords of the loom" and "the lords of the lash." William Henry Seward (1801–1872), in his famed "Irrepressible Conflict" campaign speech of 1858, appealed to northern labor to avoid the inevitable enslavement which, he assured them, would ensue if the slave labor system won in the irrepressible conflict between it and the free labor system.

From William Henry Seward, "The Irrepressible Conflict" in *The Works of William H. Seward*, ed., George E. Baker, new edition, IV (Boston: Houghton, Mifflin and Company, 1884), 289–292.

Our country is a theatre, which exhibits, in full operation, two radically different political systems; the one resting on the basis of servile or slave labor, the other on the basis of voluntary labor of freemen.

The laborers who are enslaved are all negroes, or persons more or less purely of African derivation. But this is only accidental. The principle of the system is, that labor in every society, by whomsoever performed, is necessarily unintellectual, groveling and base; and that the laborer, equally for his own good and for the welfare of the state, ought to be enslaved. The white laboring man, whether native or foreigner, is not enslaved, only because he cannot, as yet, be reduced to bondage.

You need not be told now that the slave system is the older of the two, and that once it was universal.

The emancipation of our own ancestors, Caucasians and Europeans as they were, hardly dates beyond a period of five hundred years. The great melioration of human society which modern times exhibit, is mainly due to the incomplete substitution of the system of voluntary labor for the old one of servile labor, which has already taken place. This African slave system is one which, in its origin and in its growth, has been altogether foreign from the habits of the races which colonized these states, and established civilization here. It was introduced on this new continent as an engine of conquest, and for the establishment of monarchical power, by the Portuguese and the Spaniards, and was rapidly extended by them all over South America, Central America, Louisiana and Mexico. Its legitimate fruits are seen in the poverty, imbecility, and anarchy, which now pervade all Portuguese and Spanish America. The free-labor system is of German extraction, and it was established in our country by emigrants from Sweden, Holland, Germany, Great Britain and Ireland.

We justly ascribe to its influences the strength, wealth, greatness, intelligence, and freedom, which the whole American people now enjoy. One of the chief elements of the value of human life is freedom in the pursuit of happiness. The slave system is not only intolerable, unjust, and inhuman, towards the laborer, whom, only because he is a laborer, it loads down with chains and converts into merchandise, but is scarcely less severe upon the freeman, to whom, only because he is a laborer from necessity, it denies facilities for employment, and whom it expels from the community because it cannot enslave and convert him into merchandise also. It is necessarily improvident and ruinous, because, as a general truth, communities prosper and flourish or droop and decline in just the degree that they practise or neglect to practise the primary duties of justice and humanity. The free-labor system conforms to the divine law of equality, which is written in the hearts and consciences of man, and therefore is always and everywhere beneficent.

The slave system is one of constant danger, distrust, suspicion, and watchfulness. It debases those whose toil alone can produce wealth and resources for defense, to the lowest degree of which human nature is capable, to guard against mutiny and insurrection, and thus wastes energies which otherwise might be employed in national development and aggrandizement.

The free-labor system educates all alike, and by opening all the fields of industrial employment, and all the departments of authority, to the unchecked and equal rivalry of all classes of men, at once secures universal contentment, and brings into the highest possible activity all the physical, moral and social energies of the whole state. In states where the slave system prevails, the masters, directly or indirectly, secure all political power, and constitute a ruling aristocracy. In states where the free-labor system prevails, universal suffrage necessarily obtains, and the state inevitably becomes, sooner or later, a republic or democracy.

Russia yet maintains slavery, and is a despotism. Most of the other European states have abolished slavery, and adopted the system of free labor. It was the antagonistic political tendencies of the two systems which the first Napoleon was contemplating when he predicted that Europe would ultimately be either all Cossack or all republican. Never did human sagacity utter a more pregnant truth. The two systems are at once perceived to be incongruous. But they are more than incongruous—they are incompatible. They never have permanently existed together in one country, and they never can. It would be easy to demonstrate this impossibility, from the irreconcilable contrast between their great principles and characteristics. But the experience of mankind has conclusively established it. Slavery, as I have already intimated, existed in every state in Europe. Free labor has supplanted it everywhere except in Russia and Turkey. State necessities developed in modern times, are now obliging even those two nations to encourage and employ free labor; and already, despotic as they are, we find them engaged in abolishing slavery. In the United States, slavery came into collision with free labor at the close of the last century, and fell before it in New England, New York, New Jersey and Pennsylvania, but triumphed over if effectually, and excluded it for a period yet undetermined, from Virginia, the Carolinas and Georgia. Indeed, so incompatible are the two systems, that every new state which is organized within our ever extending domain makes its first political act a choice of the one and the exclusion of the other, even at the cost of civil war, if necessary. The slave states, without law, at the last national election, successfully forbade, within their own limits, even the casting of votes for a candidate for president of the United States supposed to be favorable to the establishment of the free-labor system in new states.

Hitherto, the two systems have existed in different states, but side by side within the American Union. This has happened because the Union is a confederation of states. But in another aspect the United States constitute only one nation. Increase of population, which is filling the states out to their very borders, together with a new and extended net-work of railroads and other avenues, and an internal commerce which daily becomes more intimate, is rapidly bringing the states into a higher and more perfect social unity or consolidation. Thus, these antagonistic systems are continually coming into closer contact, and collision results.

Shall I tell you what this collision means? They who think that it is accidental, unnecessary, the work of interested or fanatical agitators, and therefore ephemeral, mistake the case altogether. It is an irrepressible conflict between opposing and enduring forces, and it means that the United States must and will, sooner or later, become either entirely a slaveholding nation, or entirely a free-labor nation. Either the cotton and rice-fields of South Carolina and the sugar plantations of Louisiana will ultimately be tilled by free labor, and Charleston and New Orleans become marts for legitimate merchandise alone, or else the rye-fields and wheat-fields of Massachusetts and New York must again be surrendered by their farmers to slave culture and to the production of slaves, and Boston and New York become once more markets for trade in the bodies and souls of men. It is the failure to apprehend this great truth that induces so many unsuccessful attempts at final compromise between the slave and free states, and it is the existence of this great fact that renders all such pretended compromises, when made, vain and ephemeral. Startling as this saying may appear to you, fellow citizens, it is by no means an original or even a moderate one. Our forefathers knew it to be true, and unanimously acted upon it when they framed the constitution of the United States. They regarded the existence of the servile system in so many of the states with sorrow and shame, which they openly confessed, and they looked upon the collision between them, which was then just revealing itself, and which we are now accustomed to deplore, with favor and hope. They knew that either the one or the other system must exclusively prevail.

VII

Argument for Direct Action

BERIAH GREEN
COUNSELS NORTHERN MEN
ABOUT WHAT TO DO

Antislavery people throughout the country were concerned not only with the arguments for antislavery but also with what they might do to implement their ideals. Beriah Green (1795–1874), former professor at Western Reserve College in Ohio and constant enthusiast for manual labor schools as well as an ardent abolitionist, sermonized his fellow white citizens on the things which northern men should do to promote the antislavery crusade. In a particularly vigorous and vivid discourse delivered from his home base at the Oneida Manual Labor Institute, Whitesboro', New York, in 1836, he made a plea for what, more and more, became the standard modes of direct action among the antislavery people.

From Beriah Green, *Things for Northern Men to Do: A Discourse Delivered Lord's Day Evening, July 17, 1836, in the Presbyterian Church, Whitesboro', N.Y.* (New York: Published by Request, 1836), pp. 5-20.

Argument for Direct Action 183

The North has much to do with American slavery. It has deeply involved her in guilt. It is exposing her, every day, and at a thousand points, to the most mortifying insults, and to the deadliest injuries. In what dreams do we indulge? Can the South be rent with earthquakes, scathed with thunderbolts for crimes, *clearly national*,[1] while the North looks on with the airs of an unconcerned spectator? No, no. If the ship, to change the figure, strikes on the rocks, which "dead ahead" lift up their horrid forms, must we not go down together—swallowed up by the same waves?

But what can *we do?* exclaim a thousand northern voices. I answer, you can,

I. *Thoroughly examine and freely discuss the whole subject of American slavery.* That the subject is one of the first *importance*, every one is ready to admit. Its bearings on the interests of both bond and free are direct and vital . . . .

---

[1] 1. The prejudice against the complexion of the Africo-American, while it is with the people of this country a *national* sentiment, had its origin in slaveholding, and powerfully supports it.

2. The nation, *as such*, is responsible for the existence and continuance of slavery in the District of Columbia. There, on ground belonging to the nation, a market for the sale of human beings is kept open; there, in the prison belonging to the nation, human beings are confined on suspicion of being goods and chattels; there, into the treasury belonging to the nation, the "price of blood" is admitted.

3. It is the general sentiment, that the nation is bound by the terms of "the union" to aid in restoring the fugitive to his oppressor; and, under the protection of this sentiment, the most savage usages and horrid outrages are prevalent even in the city of New York. Unoffending men, women, and children are seized in open day, and in the public streets, with tiger-like ferocity, and thrust into the narrow cells of a most abominable jail, to be *legally* given over by the *legalized* man-trapper to the *legalized* man-holder!

4. An extensive conspiracy has been formed, embracing a great number of the appointed guardians of the public welfare, both civil and ecclesiastical, to support *American* slavery by the sacrifice of *American* freedom! To subserve the foul and execrable ends of this conspiracy, nothing in church or state has been found too sacred to be prostituted. Witness the attacks upon the United States' mail; upon the freedom of the press and of speech; and upon the rights of private property.

Can any thing, then, exceed the *importance* of the subject of slavery? It is important, vitally so, to every man, woman, and child in our republic. No matter what may be his color, character, or standing, to him it is important. As it has a powerful bearing on every department of life, to every department of life it is important.

American slavery is, moreover, admitted to be a subject difficult to dispose of. This is the testimony of grave divines and profound statesmen; of shrewd politicians and acute philosophers. It is the complaint of the inexperienced and unlettered. Go where you will, and urge on whom you may the evils of slavery, and how generally will you not be reminded, that you have touched upon a delicate and difficult subject! Slavery is almost universally admitted to be wrong and hurtful; but the wisest heads and the best hearts among us, we are told, are sadly puzzled with the problem, how can we get rid of what has well nigh identified itself with our very existence. Will not the nation bleed "to death," if the cancer is extracted?

Here, then, we have a matter to dispose of as difficult as it is important. The monster, fattening on the blood of our countrymen, has already acquired the size and strength of a giant. Every hour adds something to its ferocity and greediness. If let alone, it will swallow up the nation. Something must be done. But what? That is the question. How shall we obtain the right answer? By shutting up our eyes? and closing our ears? and holding our tongues? By refusing to read? to reflect? to inquire? **to discuss? Is this the way to escape from such perplexities and embarrassments?** No. If we sit still, we must die. Where great difficulties are to be encountered, and formidable obstacles to be removed, it is our wisdom and our duty to summon and employ the collected powers of the nation. Every body should be encouraged to read, and think, and inquire, and discuss; and all in good earnest. The whole mass of mind among us should be aroused. Let all who will, present their expedients, propose their plans, bring forward their methods. Every thing should be thoroughly scrutinized, with the fixed determination of making "full proof" of the best methods. Thus, in any other case where we had so much at stake, we should be sure to conduct. Is this the course, my brethren, which you have recommended and pursued? Have you opened your eyes on the various bearings and tendencies of American slavery? Have you diligently collected facts, and thoroughly examined them, and done your best, with skill and judgment, to arrange them, and made them the occasion of laying hold on great elemental principles, in the light of which you might shape your plans and expend your powers? Have you studied the recorded experience of philanthropists abroad, especially in Great Britain? And have you made yourselves familiar with the history of emancipation, wherever the enslaved have been enfranchised? And have you done all this in good faith and sober earnest? resolved to turn every thing to the highest practical account? If not, it is well for you to ask, what can the North attempt for the abolition of American slavery? And so to put this question, as if nothing could be done?

II. *You can regard the enslaved as the children of our common Father, Saviour, and Sanctifier.* Thus regarding them, you cannot help presenting them at the throne of His grace. With what unwearied importunity will you not pour out prayers, that the Former of their bodies and the Father of their spirits would graciously look upon the wrongs, which they can neither endure nor escape. As their wise and merciful Creator, you will entreat Him to open His eyes upon His own image, on His handiwork, now marred, broken, trampled in the dust. As their Redeemer, you will beseech Him to behold the purchase of His blood, thrown away as mere refuse amidst worthless rubbish. As their Sanctifier, you will entreat Him to pity those, who are entitled to His heavenly gifts, who are driven as if they were cattle from His gracious presence. To the God of truth and righteousness, you will humbly carry these, His outraged and insulted children, for protection and redress. You will seek for them every blessing which His mercy has bestowed on you. Kneeling at His feet, you will long, as His almoner, to dispense among them the gifts of His heavenly grace. You will earnestly inquire how, as His servant, you may best subserve their welfare. In selecting the modes in which you may try to do them good, you will seek the guidance of His hand. . . .

. . . But we ought to know what we may easily and certainly perceive, that the interests of the slave are identified with ours. To leave him to perish is to cut our own throats! American slavery makes the creatures who support it, more and more eager, insolent, and outrageous in their claims on all around them for homage and subserviency. These petty tyrants are by no means satisfied with domineering over the helpless slave. Their despotic spirit overleaps the limits of their plantations. It lifts its head among the freemen of the North, threatening to strangle in its snaky folds every one who may dare to resist its claims or oppose its progress. Can we stand by in safety and see it crush and swallow our enslaved brethren? Surely not. The fangs which are now dripping in their blood, must ere long be fastened in our shrinking flesh. . . .

You can, then, promptly and generously mingle in the great conflict for human freedom, in which your own highest interests are vitally involved. You can act as if you felt that you were bound with those who are in bonds; as if their cause was all your own; as if every blow that cuts their flesh, lacerated yours. You can plead their cause with the earnestness, and zeal, and decision, which self-defence demands. You can hazard all for holy freedom; and maintain with steadfast perseverance the noble resolution to sink or rise with the victims of oppression. All this you *can do*. All this have you done? If not, how can you inquire, what, living at the North, you can attempt in the cause of the oppressed?

III. *The people of the North can avail themselves of the light, which the history of emancipation sheds upon the claims of the enslaved.* How many among us speak as if the subject of abolition had never been discussed and disposed of! They tremble at the thought of making what they regard [?] as an untried experiment. As an abstract matter, they find no difficulty in seeing and saying, that the slave is robbed of inalienable rights; and that he is fairly entitled to the immediate enjoyment of those privileges, which have been wrested from him by remorseless tyranny. But they are afraid to act on abstract principles, though legibly written on the very foundations of their nature! Those first truths which are wrought into the very texture of their hearts; which they cannot deny without stifling the voice of reason, they dare not reduce to practice! Convictions inherent in the simplest elements of humanity, they hesitate to embody in their conduct! They loudly call for *facts;* as if it were possible, that these, whenever and wherever found, could be at variance with the principles of their own nature! And these, they imagine, have not yet occurred!

If such facts have occurred, why have they not been urged on the attention of the American community? Why have we, to so wide an extent, been left in ignorance of some of the most interesting and important events in the history of man? Let the conductors of our periodical presses give an answer. What defence can they set up of the mean and treacherous silence they have selfishly maintained, when they ought to have spoken in tones of thunder? Why have they not kept their readers familiar with the history of emancipation; especially as given in the records of the British Legislature? Were they afraid to let the light of truth shine upon us? Afraid of what? To see us give up our foolish prejudices and groundless fears? Afraid to assist us in escaping from the scorn and abhorrence of the civilized world, by ceasing to utter in defence of slavery, such silly words as would disgrace the lips of an idiot? No. These mercenary creatures were afraid that their subscription list would be reduced, if they should give offense to the chivalry of the South! Let them take home to their hearts the solemn warning, that the chivalry of the South will fail to protect them from the frown of insulted humanity! The hour of retribution is coming on apace. They have no time to lose. Let them make haste and repent. . . .

. . . *The history of emancipation teaches us to ply the South with strong argumentation, earnest entreaty, pointed rebuke.* The pretended friends and apologists of the South, have at different times and on various occasions, tried to dissuade us from attempting any thing to convince the slave-holder of his guilt and danger, on the ground, that his known character must render all such attempts for ever fruitless. He has been likened to a "mad bull," who, if you should attempt to reason with him, would be sure to bellow and toss his horns! If we would escape being gored to death, we have been warned to keep our distance and hold our tongues! . . .

. . . But we have abundant evidence that he retains enough of the elements of humanity to feel the force of truth. He is not entirely dead to the light of reason, or the impulses of compassion, or the dictates of self-love. He cannot refuse to be wrought upon by the power of moral suasion. So far from this, that a glimpse of his own features, even when obscurely reflected on his eye, tortures him. . . . If the friends of Human Freedom should find access to the ears and hearts of those who live amidst the monuments of slavery, they might even there raise up friends and coadjutors. Even there the standard of immediate and universal emancipation might be erected, and thousands eagerly flock around it. Thus Southern tyranny would be exposed and denounced by Southern philanthropy! The oppressor cannot bear the thought of having his own neighbors—his intimate acquaintance point at him, as feasting on the unrequited labor of the helpless poor.

From how many statesmen at the South has not the confession been extorted—extorted by the remorse and fear which they could neither dissipate nor conceal—that the infamy with which they were already branded by all the philanthropists of Christendom, was fast becoming insupportable! The plunder of our goods we do not dread, they exclaim; but what is more to be deprecated, *the loss of character.* What can our goods be worth, while we are constrained to bear the scorn and execration of the civilized world, as a nest of pirates? So sensitive, and irritable, and apprehensive has the South become, that she fears to admit a newspaper, pamphlet, nay, a page of fiction into her presence, till assured they contain no exposure or reproof of her favorite sin! She is trying to establish a censorship of the press so rigid and extensive, as to exclude every ray of light from the knot of snakes she is nestling in her bosom! Is this the people whom you say we cannot reach by moral suasion? Who cannot be wrought upon by warning, expostulations, and appeals? Who cannot be moved by admonition, or rebuke, or entreaty? How shallow and superficial must that thinker be, who, for a moment can admit such a supposition! And so we must not expect to awaken in the slaveholder a sense of his guilt and danger, because a single word of expostulation so annoys and distresses him! And because his inward pains make him rave and foam, we are to run away, disheartened and affrighted! How silly and how wicked that would be! Let him writhe and rave. Let him flout and foam; kick, and strike, and bite. He cannot escape from the fires which surround him. The sooner he spits out his venom and exhausts his fury the better. He must not be permitted to escape. He must not have a moment's respite. Wherever he may turn, truth's searching rays must be kept upon him. After rending and tearing him a little longer, the demon, which has so long had possession of him will retire, and leave him in his right mind to appropriate wholesome instruction. Every one of you, my hearers, might contribute something to hasten this result. What have you done?

Your hold, as an American citizen, upon the District of Columbia, you may turn to high account in the cause of human freedom.—Along with myriads of the friends of man, you can put your name to a petition to the national legislature for the abolition of slavery at the centre of the republic. Less than this you cannot do, without involving yourself, personally, in the guilt of slavery. Harbor not the thought for a moment, that such efforts must be useless. Useless they cannot be. Their various bearings cannot but be powerful and happy. It will *do you* good, good unspeakable, thus to "remember those who are in bonds." It will keep you alive to their condition, claims, and prospects. It will give you a deeper interest and greater power, at the throne of mercy. Never fear, morever, that you will pour your petitions on deaf ears and palsied arms. Tyrants there may have "bound themselves by a great curse," that your voice shall not be heard. But these poor creatures are as weak as they are insolent. They cannot dispose of your petitions without attending directly or indirectly to your claims. Your petitions must be read. The facts you state; the arguments you employ; your earnest remonstrances, your strong appeals, your loud warnings, your fervent entreaties, will force their way into ears, which a thousand artifices may have been employed in vain to stop. And those ears will tingle. Tongues, which a thousand artifices had been employed in vain to tie, will be set in motion. Tyrants may roar, and stamp, and curse. But what then? Surely, the noise and tumult in which they may give vent to their windy rage, will but ill promote the cause of *silence.* By the very act of swearing that a word shall not be spoken, their own oath they will violate! Their hot blood and rash tongues will drive them headlong into fiery debate. The discussion of the matter may be furious; but discussion will arise. The agitation of the subject may be fierce; but agitation cannot be avoided. Come it will, whoever may object. *Nay, nothing can more certainly and effectually introduce it than objections!* Urge your petitions, then. Let them fly by thousands on the wings of every breeze. Laden with the names of all who love their country, let them speak "the words of truth and soberness" to every trembling Felix, who has a place in the national legislature. . .

. . . *Our ecclesiastical connexions with churches which toler-*

ate in their members the sin of slaveholding, we ought at once to dissolve. Till we do this, we can never reach the vitals of the evil, with which we are bound to contend. Could either of the principal religious denominations at the South be brought in the spirit of true repentance to renounce the crime of oppressing the poor, the monster, which is now fattening on the blood of innocence, must fall beneath the fatal blow. The enormous guilt of stealing men could not fail to attract universal attention. Every man's mind and mouth would be full of the matter. . . .

The church must be aroused to her guilt in this matter, or she is undone. The blighting curse of God will waste and wither her. Nothing but repentance can hold her back from the grave of infamy, which is even now yawning, impatient to swallow its prey! Nor can she perish alone. The republic must rot with her in the same dishonored tomb!

THE AMERICAN ANTI-SLAVERY SOCIETY ADMONISHES THE NEGROES HOW TO ACT

Much of the effectiveness of the antislavery movement depended, day by day, upon the progress which could be made in the North in assimilating free Negroes to the white community in which they found themselves. This was an issue whose solution hinged not only on the activities of the white community but on those of the Negroes as well. In the early 1830's

> the American Anti-Slavery Society issued an address to the Negroes of New York in which it admonished them how to act and sermonized them on what they should do to raise themselves to a level of equality with the rest of the community.

If we would be good, we must strive for that character. If we would acquire knowledge, we must apply ourselves to study, as often as our circumstances permit. If we would secure all our civil privileges, we must take the steps prescribed by law; and if we would acquire property, we must put ourselves diligently to business, with reference to that end. The efforts which many of you have made, and are now making to support religious worship, to improve your minds, to educate your children, and to acquire property and all your civil rights, are worthy of high commendation.

The prejudices of society against your complexion, which sometimes is evidenced by persecution, are often checked or surmounted by you. It cannot be denied that a vast amount of ignorance, vice and misery, exists in this city; and although we are not of the number who underrate the virtues of the colored people, and magnify their faults, but on the contrary would repel the constant slanders brought against them, it would be folly in us to deny that there are numbers of colored persons, who are helping to swell the amount of degradation, infamy and ruin, which so fearfully abounds in this great city. It is no part of real friendship, to hide the causes of human wretchedness, but to point them out and also their remedies.

Intemperance has certainly found as few practical advocates amongst the colored people, according to their comparative number, as among the whites. We perceive however, with

---

From American Anti-Slavery Society, *Address to the People of Color, in the City of New York. By Members of The Executive Committee of the American Anti-Slavery Society* (New York: S. W. Benedict & Co., 1834), pp. 4–7.

great pain, several Porter Houses and dram shops, not a few of which are open on the Sabbath, and are kept by colored persons, which are resorted to by many of the youth and other persons of color. The number of these places appears to increase with the population of the city. The awful consequences attending such establishments, to youth, to families, and to the community, cannot be described. It is lamentable that any persons who profess any respect for themselves, should enter these gates of destruction.

We have noticed with sorrow, that some of the colored people are purchasers of lottery tickets, and confess ourselves shocked to learn that some persons, who are situated to do much good, and whose example might be most salutary, engage in games of chance for money and for strong drink. A moment's thought will show the folly, as well as wickedness of their course. Gambling strikes at the very vitals of society, and surely the laboring but rising classes of the community, have no time to waste, nor money foolishly to hazard. All persons of color who are keepers of places for dram drinking, gambling, lewdness and other infamy, should be faithfully remonstrated with; and continuing their practices should be regarded as the most injurious of all your enemies. It is in vain for any man to pretend in this age to be worthy of respect, who is engaged in any of these ruinous practices. No excuse can justify wrong doing—To labor is honorable, but to resort to dram selling, and other iniquity for support, can no better be justified than common robbery or man-stealing. To rob our neighbor of property, cannot, certainly, be more heinous, than to rob him of reputation, health, and life, by tempting him to the indulgence of ruinous passions and appetites. It is said that many well disposed, industrious laborers, cannot find employment in the city. We think such instances are rare,—and if it be true that the city is over stocked with laborers, the country is large, and there are multitudes of farmers, and others all over the land, who will give employment to the industrious of any complexion. There are considerable numbers of colored persons in this state, who are respectable farmers and mechanics; of the latter class, we are happy to find several in this city who are superior in their several departments. A little effort and enterprize, might secure for persons not sufficiently employed and for their children, real advantages, whilst by resorting to petty and dishonorable traficking, and other injurious pursuits, all may be ruined. We cannot too strongly urge the importance of securing for your children the knowledge of some mechanic art, and if there are difficulties in the way, make great efforts to overcome them.

When the providence of God plainly indicates that the time for the improvement, and the moral and civil advancement of the colored people is come—when white and colored persons of benevolence, are acting with new energy to promote these important objects,—is it not a crime of great magnitude, for any one to oppose, by vice or by alluring others into vice, so excellent a design? We would urge you to union as a people, to fellow-feeling and Christian benevolence; but you will be doing injustice to yourselves and your families to give currency to evil persons, however well they may appear, by treating them as persons entitled to confidence and esteem, but who like the spider with her subtle web, live by the life blood of their unsuspecting victims. The boldness of impiety is manifest, where individuals appropriate the Lord's Day to such labors of destruction.

From these men and their snares turn away; and on the Sabbath be present with your families in the house of the Lord.—God's judgments rest upon Sabbath breakers.

It is scarcely less certain, that he who neglects Divine worship and profanes the Sabbath, will eventually be degraded and without respect in a Christian community, than that he will lose his soul, and be covered with contempt in eternity.

Children brought up by Sabbath breakers, and who are not encouraged to go to church, and to Sabbath School, are almost certain to be disobedient, "reprobate children," and a curse to society.

The age in which we live, is one of hope to the world. All persons may hope except they be vicious. With all the obstacles in the way of the people of color in times past, many have acquired moderate property by their industry, economy and skill. Do you say it requires more virtue and effort, for a colored person to succeed, on account of the prejudices of this country against them? This is true; but is it not blessed to be excellent, and industrious, and even to make extraordinary efforts to attain so important an end?

In most of the free states, colored men may secure the privilege of voting for rulers, and in some instances have been elected to town and state offices. In several of the states, colored men become voters on the same terms as white men; property not always being necessary. This is the case in the state of Maine; their vote is of much consequence in the city of Portland, and they are from this and other circumstances, treated as worthy of much consideration. Two of their number were recently invited to attend a Convention at Augusta, the capital of the state, for the nomination of the Governor, and other important business.

They were received, deliberated with the Convention, and dined at the same table with other delegates, on terms of perfect equality. And on board the steam boat, going and returning, were treated with the same respect as other delegates.

In this state and city, considerable numbers of colored citizens, by acquiring a moderate property in real estate, have become voters. $250 worth of property in real estate is necessary for a colored man to become a voter. It is for the respectability of your whole people, that you should secure this privilege. You will yet be admitted as voters in this state, no doubt, on the same conditions as white citizens. No one should be disheartened who will be virtuous, and useful to his country. By means of education, industry, and piety, with a due sense of your individual and collective responsibility, you will attain at an early day, every desirable object for yourselves and your posterity. You will exert a most happy influence upon the emancipation of your and our enslaved brethren—cause the hearts of your friends to rejoice, and be amply rewarded in your own peace and prosperity. God will smile upon all the work of your hands and make you and your children blessed.

WILLIAM KING PLANS A NEGRO SETTLEMENT

Although African Colonization never attracted a substantial number of Negroes, there were many slaves who, following the so-called Underground Railroad, finished their journey in Canada. Many free Negroes also, particularly after the passage of the Fugitive Slave Bill in 1850, sought haven there. William King (1812–1895), who had been a Louisiana slaveholder, also went to Canada where he tried, in a specially organized Negro community, to prepare these Negroes for life in a predominantly white America. The selection which follows is the draft of his plan for the Elgin settlement, as it was called. Interestingly, this community was one of the very few which was at all successful, and it had more than twenty years of highly effective operation between 1849 and 1873, when it formally dissolved.

From William King, "Scheme for improving the Coloured People of Canada [1848]" (MS. in the Public Archives of Canada, Ottawa). Printed with permission of the Public Archives of Canada.

... British America is the only place on this side of the Atlantic where a Coloured man can enjoy freedom; The free states of the Union do not afford this privilege. relieved from slavery as a system, they do not wish to be burdened with its fruit, and accordingly all those states have passed laws depriving the coloured man of a portion of his civil rights, they permit him to remain, but do not give him the privileges of free citizens; Privileges which every man is morally bound, by lawful means to secure to himself and posterity whenever in the Providence of God it is practicable. . . .

With the view of enjoying the equity of our law, and securing the privileges which it confers to his children, he [the coloured man] is induced to settle among us. But his hopes have been disappointed, his expectations have not been realized. The law is good, but owing to the prejudice which exists against coloured persons they do not enjoy its benefits. Without waiting to enquire whether this prejudice is well or ill founded, I state the fact that it does exist, and operates powerfully against their moral improvement. This prejudice will remain as long as they continue in ignorance. . . . We need not think it strange that persons who have long been held in bondage, when delivered from the fear of punishment, will commit many excesses, and, if permitted to live in the degraded state in which slavery has left them, will become a dangerous and troublesome society. From what I know of the negro character, I am convinced that if we permit them to remain in ignorance, and retain them among us, with the full privileges of free citizens, [it] would be a calamity that would induce every white man who could escape to move from a society so constituted. . . .

The good of the state, and the welfare of the community requires that they should be educated. But we have a stronger motive why we should educate them. They are fellow beings, possessed with immortal souls, it is our duty as Christians to educate them not only for time, but for eternity. Several benevolent individuals from the U. States have attempted to improve their condition, but their efforts have not been very successful. The want of success may be attributed to various causes, such as a want of adequate support, incompetency of the persons employed, and an ignorance of the negro character. . . .

. . . The scheme which I propose consists of two parts the one secular, and the other educational, the former is necessary in order to carry out the latter.

With the wish of carrying out both parts, I propose to purchase a block of land in the Township of Raleigh, in the Western District, settle the block with coloured persons, selling to each family a farm of fifty acres, the purchase money to be paid in annual installments—Provide the adult population with the means of grace, and the youth with a Christian education. There is the scheme in a few words, now for the practical way in which I would carry it out.

To secure the land for the settlement I propose forming a lay association, composed of men of all denominations, with a capital, equal in amount, to the sum necessary to purchase the land, the stock to be taken up in shares of £ 20 each, one tenth to be paid in hand and the balance in nine equal annual installments with interest. The association to be incorporated by act of Parliament, and its affairs managed by a President, Vice-President, Directors, Treasurer and Secretary, to be appointed annually by the stock holders. The property would be held in the name of the society, and by them deeded to actual settlers, they paying the purchase money at the time and manner prescribed by the company. The capital of the association would be invested in real estate, that would be increasing annually in value and would be perfectly secure. . . .

. . . But as the object of the Society is one of pure benevolence undertaken solely with the view of improving the social condition of the coloured people: It is not contemplated that it shall continue longer than the time necessary to settle the lands. At the end of ten years the affairs of the Society would be wound up, the money advanced by the share holders returned, with the profits arising from the advanced sale of the land.

This is the secular part of the scheme, the association is simply to protect the land for coloured settlers, where they can be collected together, and enjoy a permanent residence, with the view of improving their moral condition.

The second part of the scheme is educational, and refers to their spiritual improvement. As the whole scheme is catholic in its spirit, having only one object in view, the moral improvement of the coloured people of Canada, the field will be open to all denominations who wish to occupy it. And I would rejoice to cooperate with any of the sister churches in the work.

The block of land contains nearly 9000 acres, and will settle about 180 families, these will form four school districts sufficently large for educational purposes.

I propose to purchase Lot 12, 11th Con[cession] containing 200 acres, convert it into a model farm, and on it erect the necessary buildings for the mission. A temporary school house, and dwelling would only be required at first; as the settlers would increase we could enlarge the buildings. The farm would in a great measure supply the boarding establishment with provisions. On it adults, who wished it, could work several hours in the day for their board and education.

Besides keeping the farm in a high state of cultivation, as a model for the rest of the settlers, the person occupying it would act as agent for the company, attend to the settling of the land, and collecting the annual payments as they fell due. In this way a whol[e]some vigilence would be exercised over the whole settlement that would stimulate the idle, encourage the industrious, and promote the social improvement of all. The farm would be selfsupporting. The funds required to purchase it, and erect the necessary buildings, I would raise by voluntary contributions during the winter and spring.

While on the collecting tour and bringing the claims of the coloured mission before the people of Canada, I would look out among the coloured settlements for youth of promising talents and piety (some of whom I have seen already) induce the parents to send them to the seminary, that in connection with the youth of the settlement they might receive a Christian education. The spiritual object which we have in view would thus be advanced; and the young men would be trained up as teachers and preachers. We could look forward with certainty to a day not far distant, trusting in God to bless our united efforts, when a band of native missionaries, would be prepared to go forth with the gospel to their brethren in Africa. The gospel planted on the shores, would raise a moral barrier, that would put an end to the inhuman traffic that is still carried on along her coast.

The whole scheme aims at the extension of Christ's Kingdom, and we have the sure promise that he will bless our efforts. The door is now open for this Christian enterprize the sympathies of the people are awakened in behalf of the coloured man he is willing to cooperate with us in the movement, and it only requires prayerful, united, vigorous, and persevering effort on our part to accomplish the object.

ELIHU BURRITT PROPOSES COMPENSATED EMANCIPATION

One of the more interesting of the Middle Period reformers was Elihu Burritt (1810–1879). By trade a blacksmith, he taught himself many languages and became an active participant in the peace movement, temperance reform, and the antislavery crusade. Unlike the majority of antislavery people, Burritt's remedy for slavery rested on a quid pro quo. He proposed, therefore, in the middle 1850's, a program of compensated emancipation based upon the proceeds from the sale of public land.

Possessing all these present and prospective elements of power, it is natural and inevitable, that the American citizen, at home and abroad, should feel that the time has come when his country can do a great thing before the nations, should it put forth all the strength of its Samson sinews. The Governments and people of Europe perceive and admit this capacity of the American Union, and frequently call it the mighty Republic of the Western World. In a word, there seems to be an expectation prevalent throughout Christendom that our nation will soon do some great thing; that it will show all the giant strength of its young manhood in some vast undertaking. It has stood quietly by and seen the foremost Powers of Europe put forth their strength in a tremendous war,[1] in which at least 700,000 human beings were sacrificed, and $1,500,000,000 lavished upon the work of human destruction. England has expended $500,000,000 in the vague and fruitless struggle; France as much more; and Russia an almost equal sum. It is now the turn of this great continental family of States to do something large—something to enhance its estimation in the eyes of the world; to increase its political power at home and abroad, and to strengthen and perpetuate its bonds of union. What shall it do to secure these objects? Shall it go to war with a coalition of European Powers? A victorious conflict with a world in arms would not be so glorious in the estimation of the other nations of Christendom, as the extirpation of that great domestic foe, which is arraying one section of

---

From Elihu Burritt, *A Plan of Brotherly Copartnership of the North and South, for the Peaceful Extinction of Slavery* (New York: Dayton and Burdick, 1856), pp. 11–18, 30–33.

[1] The Crimean War. [Eds.]

the Republic in the bitterest antagonism to the other, and filling it with the malignant breathings of malice and mutiny. . . .

. . . The utter extirpation of Slavery from American soil, should be achieved in a way and in a spirit that should attach all the members of the confederacy to each other by stronger bonds than had ever existed between them; which should bequeath to their numerous posterity of States a rich legacy of precious memories, deepening and perpetuating their sense of relationship, as co-heirs of the noblest chapters of American history. There is a magnanimous and glorious way by which this terrible evil in our midst may be removed, so as to produce these happy associations and results. That is, by a fraternal union and co-operation of all the States of our Republic in emancipating it fully and forever from this distructive system, at whatever cost it may be peacefully and honorably effected. In the first place, such a copartnership is indispensable to the work, for its achievement will require the concentrated energies of the mightiest nation ever erected on the face of the globe. When we come to the final tug of an undertaking, the like of which no nation on earth ever accomplished, no State, town or village, from California to Canada, can be spared. Every praying heart and willing hand will be needed for the grand effort.

There is but one way by which the whole nation can take upon its shoulders the total extinction of slavery. That is, by compensating the slave holders, out of the public treasury or the public domain, for the act of manumission.

Let us face the cost of this vast pecuniary transaction at the outset. Would the undertaking devolve a burden upon the nation which would exceed its financial ability, and prove onerous to its population? Taking all the slaves in the Union, young and old, sick and disabled, $250 per head must be admitted as an equitable average price. Three millions and a half, at this valuation, would amount to $875,000,000; a much smaller sum than England and France expended in the recent war with Russia. Even suppose, what could hardly be possible, that all the Southern States would accept this pecuniary consideration, and emancipate their slaves simultaneously and at once, the annual interest of the whole amount would be $52,500,000 at 6 per cent. This interest would not be half the sum appropriated every year by Great Britain to her army and navy in time of peace. If the population and wealth of the nation continue to increase at the ratio of the last ten years, its ordinary revenue must reach $100,000,000, in 1860, and advance by several millions annually after that date. Thus, if emancipation took effect in 1860, the natural income of the nation would yield about $50,000,000 for the current expenses of the Government, besides the interest of the debt contracted for freeing the country from slavery. With due economy, the people would be burdened with no more taxation than at the present moment. . . .

. . . National indemnification would not be a mere compromise, but an earnest and brotherly partnership between the North and South, in working out a glorious consummation, which would bless equally both sections of the Republic. The extinction of slavery, at every stage of this process, instead of dissevering, would unite the States by affinities and relationships that have never existed between them. A new spirit would be generated in the heart of the nation, and cover it like an atmosphere of fraternal amity. Such a spirit would be worth to the country twice the value of all the slaves in its borders. Without this spirit pervading the Union, the wrongs of the slaves can never be righted. Nothing but slavery itself, of the most atrocious stamp, could be worse for them than emancipation in the midst of a tempest of malignant passions, of fierce and fiery hate. Fearful and almost hopeless would be their condition, if the fetters of their physical bondage should be rent asunder in a thunder-burst of burning wrath. Of all parties to this great moral struggle, their well-being will be most dependent upon the prevalence of benevolent sentiments and fraternal sympathies throughout the nation at the time of their manumission.

The means at the command of the nation for the extinction of slavery by the mode proposed, are ample. There is one source of revenue alone, not needed for the current expenses of the Government, which would be sufficient to emancipate all the slaves in the Union. This is the Public Domain of the United States. This landed estate of the nation, according to official estimate, contains, exclusive of the lands acquired from Mexico by the treaty of 1853, 1,600,000,000 of acres. At the average of 75 cents per acre, they would yield $1,200,000,000. Admitting $250 per head for the whole slave population to be a fair average price, taking infant and aged, sick and infirm, the 3,500,000 in the United States would amount to $875,000,-000. Thus, the public lands would not only defray the expense of emancipating all these slaves, but would also yield a large surplus for their education and moral improvement.

Did any nation ever have such an extent of territory as a free gift from Providence? How could we more appropriately recognize this gift, than by consecrating it to freedom? than by making it the ransom-price from slavery of all the chattelized human beings in the Union? Wherein and how could they contribute more to the true dignity, harmony and well-being of the nation? If not thus appropriated in advance, they will be alienated from the Federal Government altogether. They will be frittered away in sectional bribes, or sources of Executive patronage, and thus become capital for political corruption—the pension money for partisan warfare. This is the very moment to arrest this squandering process, and to appropriate what remains of this public domain to some great object connected with the peace and prosperity of the whole nation. The act, or even the certainty of emancipation, would greatly enhance the value of the public lands in all the Slave States; thus producing the revenue necessary to accomplish the magnificent enterprise.

The only action which it would be necessary to ask Congress to take in this matter at the outset, would be—

To make a provision by law, that whenever any State of the Union, in which slavery now exists, shall decree the emancipation of all slaves, and the abolition of involuntary servitude, except for crime, within its borders, an exact enumeration shall be made, and for each and every slave thus emancipated, there shall be paid from the National Treasury to such State, for equitable distribution among the slaveholders, a certain sum of money, to be ascertained as Congress may direct; and that the net revenue from all the future sales of the public lands, shall be appropriated exclusively to the emancipation of all the slaves in the United States in this manner.

The prerogative of each individual State to retain or abolish slavery, remains untouched by the Congressional enactment proposed. Not the slightest form or aspect of Federal compulsion is assumed towards its sovereignty. The Central Government only makes a generous offer to each and every Southern State simultaneously. It leaves that State in the freest exercise of its sovereign will to accept or reject that offer. If it accepts, then the stipulated sum of money is paid to its appointed agent by the Government. That money is distributed by the State receiving it in its own way.

MARIA WESTON CHAPMAN URGES SUPPORT OF THE AMERICAN ANTI-SLAVERY SOCIETY

How can I help abolish slavery? asked Maria Weston Chapman (1806–1885), leader of the female abolitionists of Boston and a principal and steady cohort of Garrison. Her *answer reflected the very best of the Garrisonian position and pointed dramatically to one of the great weaknesses of that position. Having systematically attacked virtually every other plan then in practice Mrs. Chapman concluded that the really effective way to promote antislavery was to support the American Anti-Slavery Society in its own insistence upon immediate emancipation. Her answer summarized the extreme: do it all at once and deny, in the same breath, the utility of any specific program of direct and practical action.*

Yes, my friend, I can resolve your question. Twenty years of actual experience qualify one to reply. I have stood, as you now stand, on the threshold of this grandest undertaking of any age—this effort to elevate a whole people in the scale of moral being—with my head full of plans, and my heart of devotedness, asking the same question. I really longed for this coming of millennial glory, and therefore soon found the road on which to go forth to meet it. My disgust was unutterable, as yours, too, will be, if you desire the abolition of slavery more than the temporary triumph of sect or party, at the stupid schemes by which selfish men were then, as now, trying to make capital for themselves out of the sacred cause of human rights—seeking to sell the gift of the Holy Ghost for money. Hear them clamorously and meanly taking advantage of ignorance, for the promotion of self-interest.

First, hear the agents of slavery presenting the colonization scheme as the instrument of abolition.

"Aid the Colonization Society." Yes; to make slavery stronger by exalting prejudice as an ordination of divine Providence; to make slavery safer by eliminating that dangerous element, the free black; to make its term longer by stultifying national

From Maria Weston Chapman, *"How Can I Help to Abolish Slavery?" or, Counsels to the Newly Converted* (Anti-Slavery Tract, No. 14) (New York: American Anti-Slavery Society, [1855]), pp. 1–6.

conscience. See that society making the laws of slave States more cruel, the men of the free States more obdurate, the situation of the free men of color more difficult and insupportable, as a part of its plan. It could not, if it would, transport three millions of souls to Africa; the navies and revenues of the world would be insufficient. It would not, if it could; for slavery has no intention of parting with its three millions of victims; unless induced to free them out of generosity, it will keep them on speculation. Its forty years of colonization labor, and its million of gold and silver, have exiled fewer to Liberia than have escaped into Canada in spite of it—less in that period than the monthly increase of the slaves! It can do nothing for Christianizing Africa, for it sends a slaveholding gospel, which is anti-Christ. Be not deceived, then, by a tyrannical mockery like this, working to perpetuate slavery, and not to abolish it. Aid the American Anti-Slavery Society, which deals with the heart and conscience of this slaveholding nation, demanding immediate, unconditional emancipation, without expatriation; the abolition of slavery by the spirit of repentance, in conformity with all your own principles and traditions, whether religious or political.

Hear another cry, (coming, not like the first, from the enemies of abolition, but from friends, generally those of more pretension than devotedness:) "Form a political party, free soil or other, to vote down slavery."

Yes, don't *kill* the growing monster—call to him to stop growing; merge immediatism, which always succeeds, in gradualism, which never does. Substitute a secondary object for the primary one. Strive in the first place not to abolish slavery, but to get one set of men out of office and another in, to learn by the event that the last are as incapable to turn back the whirlpool that masters the government as the first were. Make an appeal to force of numbers in a case where you know it is against you; in a case, too, where, having sworn assistance, you must lose influence by such an appeal. Spend your time and money, not in making new abolitionists, but in counting the old ones, that at every count diminish. Politics, in the common, small sense of the term, merely takes the circumstances it finds, and does its best with them. But the present circumstances are unfavorable. THEN CREATE NEW ONES. This is true politics, in the enlarged, real meaning of the word. Here is a building to be erected, and no sufficient materials. A *little* untempered mortar, a *few* unbaked bricks—that is all. Go to the deep quarries of the human heart, and make of your sons and daughters polished stones to build the temple of the Lord. It is this cleaving into the living rock the AMERICAN ANTI-SLAVERY SOCIETY girds itself to do. Under its operations men become better and better abolitionists. Under the labors of political partisanship they necessarily grow worse and worse. They must ever ask themselves how *little* anti-slavery feeling and principle they can make serve the temporary turn; because the less of either, the greater the chance. They must always be sacrificing the end to the means. Call them to the witness box in their capacity of philosophical observers, and out of their little circumventing political characters, and themselves will tell you that the effect of electioneering on anti-slavery is most unfavorable, adding to the existing opposition to right the fury of party antagonism, throwing away the balance of power, lowering the tone of moral and religious feeling and action, and thus letting a sacred enterprise degenerate into a scramble for office. But labor with the AMERICAN ANTI-SLAVERY SOCIETY *directly* to the great end, and even Franklin Pierce and Co., pro-slavery as they are, will grovel to do your bidding. The administration now *on* the throne is as good for your bidding as any other. In a republican land the power behind the throne is *the* power. Save yourself the trouble of calling caucuses, printing party journals, distributing ballots, and the like. Let men who are fit for nothing of more consequence do this little work, which is best done by mere nobodies. *More* than enough of them are always ready for it. You, who are smitten by the sacred beauty of the great cause, should serve it greatly. Don't drag the engine, like an ignoramus, but bring wood and water and flame, like an engineer. The AMERICAN ANTI-SLAVERY SOCIETY has laid the track.

"Buy slaves and set them free." Yes; lop the branches and strengthen the root; make the destruction of the system more difficult by practising upon it; create a demand for the slave breeder to supply; compromise with crime; raise the market price, when you ought to stop the market; put a philanthropic mark upon the slave trade; spend money enough in buying one man to free fifty gratis, and convert a thousand. But there is a *wholesale* way, cries one. "Sell the public lands, and set every means in motion, from the merely mercantile donation of a million to the infant cent society,[1] and thus raise two thousand millions of dollars, and beg the slaveholders to take it, (not as compensation, but as a token of good will,) and let their bondmen go." I marvel at this insufficient notion of the heart of a slaveholder. I wonder exceedingly at such a want of imagination. "Not as compensation" is well put; for what sum can compensate a monarch for his throne? This system of slavery makes the south the parent of long lines of princes. It gives to her diabolical dominions

"Kingdoms, and sway, and strength, and length of days."

I am strangely divided in sympathy. I feel at once the generosity of the proposal, and have the feeling of contempt with which its insufficient inappropriateness is received.

"Organize vigilance committees, and establish underground railroads." Yes; hide from tyranny, instead of defying it; *whisper* a testimony; form a bad habit of mind in regard to despotism; try to keep out the sea with a mop, when you ought to

---

[1] Cent societies were really a way of raising money for benevolent purposes by the adherents' banding together and agreeing to save one cent per day for the particular cause in question. [Eds.]

build a dike; flatter your sense of compassion by taking private retail measures to have suffering ameliorated, when you might, with the AMERICAN ANTI-SLAVERY SOCIETY, be taking public wholesale measures to have *wrong* (the cause of suffering) *righted*. You may safely leave with the half and quarter converted, with the slaveholders, nay, even with the Curtises,[2] the charge of all these things, which without the American Anti-Slavery Society are but as hydrogen and nitrogen without oxygen, however good with it, as the natural fruits of its labors. What I would discourage is, not mercy and compassion in an individual case, but a disgraceful mistake in the economy of well doing; spending in salving a sore finger what would buy the elixir vitae; preferring the less, which *e*xcludes the greater, to the greater, which *i*ncludes the less. Slavery can only be abolished by raising the character of the people who compose the nation; and *that* can be done only by showing them a higher one. Now, there is *one* thing that can't be done in *secret;* you can't *set a good example under a bushel*.

"But instruction! instruction! found schools and churches for the blacks, and thus *prepare* for the abolition of slavery." O, shallow and shortsighted! the *demand* is the *preparation;* nothing can supply the place of *that*. And *exclusive* instruction, teaching for *blacks,* a school founded on color, a church in which men are herded ignominiously apart from the refining influence of association with the more highly educated and accomplished,—what are they? A direct way of fitting white men for tyrants, and black men for slaves. No; if you would teach and Christianize the nation, strengthen the AMERICAN ANTI-SLAVERY SOCIETY, the *only* American institution founded on the Christian and republican idea of the equal brotherhood of man, and in opposition to a church and state which deny

---

[2] George T. Curtis, United States Commissioner in Boston under the Fugitive Slave Act of 1850. It was he who was responsible for the fugitives Shadrach (Frederick Wilkins) and Thomas Sims. [Eds.]

human brotherhood by sanctioning slavery, and pull down Christ to their own level. The American Anti-Slavery Society is church and university, high school and common school to all who need real instruction and true religion. Of it what a throng of authors, editors, lawyers, orators, and accomplished gentlemen of color have taken their degree! It has equally implanted hopes and aspirations, noble thoughts and sublime purposes in the hearts of both races. It has prepared the white man for the freedom of the black man, and it has made the black man scorn the thought of enslavement, as does a white man, as far as its influence has extended. *Strengthen that noble influence.* Before its organization, the country only saw here and there in slavery some "faithful Cudjoe or Dinah," whose strong natures blossomed even in bondage, like a fine plant beneath a heavy stone. Now, under the elevating and cherishing influence of the American Anti-Slavery Society, the colored race, like the white, furnishes Corinthian capitals for the noblest temples. Aroused by the American Anti-Slavery Society, the very white men who had forgotten and denied the claim of the black man to the rights of humanity now thunder that claim at every gate, from cottage to capitol, from school house to university, from the railroad carriage to the house of God. He has a place at their firesides, a place in their hearts—the man whom they once cruelly hated for his color. So feeling, they *cannot* send him to Coventry with a hornbook in his hand, and call it *instruction!* They inspire him to climb to their side by a visible acted gospel of freedom. Thus, instead of bowing to prejudice, they conquer it.

"Establish free-labor warehouses." Indeed! is that a good business calculation that leads to expend in search of the products of free labor the time and money that would make all labor free? While wrong exists in the world, you cannot (short of suicide) but draw your every life breath in involuntary connection with it; nor is conscience to be satisfied with any thing short of a complete devotion to the anti-slavery cause of the life that is sustained by slavery. We *may* draw good out of evil: we *must not* do evil, that good may come. Yet I counsel you to honor those who eat no sugar, as *you* ask no questions for conscience's sake; while you despise those who thrust forward such a call upon conscience, *impossible,* in the nature of things, to be obeyed, and therefore not binding, as if it were the end of the law for righteousness, in order to injure Garrison, the great and good founder of the American Anti-Slavery Society. I have seen men stand drawing bills of exchange between England and the United States, while uttering maledictions against the American Anti-Slavery Society, because it does not, as such, occupy itself with the free produce question. This I brand as pro-slavery in disguise—sheer hypocrisy.

You see, my friend, that I have replied to your question in the conviction that you desire the abolition of slavery above all other things in this world; as one assured that it is the great work of Christianity in our age and country, as the conflict with idolatry was in other times and climes. Thus you see the salvation of the souls, the maintenance of the rights, the fulfilment of the duties, and the preservation of the free institutions of Americans, to depend upon the extirpation of this accursed and disgraceful disease which is destroying them.

THE NEW ENGLAND ANTI-SLAVERY CONVENTION EXHORTS THE SLAVES TO DIRECT ACTION

In 1843 the New England Anti-Slavery Convention published a pamphlet which stands virtually unique among antislavery documents, pointing out a type of direct action almost without precedent in the antislavery crusade. The Address to the Slaves, here reproduced in its entirety, was directed specifically at the slaves themselves, and it urged upon them the arguments that, under God, they were meant to be free; that people in the North were working for their freedom; that they should try to escape to the North; that should disunion come the slaves would obviously rebel and put an end to slavery.

BRETHREN AND FELLOW COUNTRYMEN:

ASSEMBLED in Convention, from all parts of New-England, in Faneuil Hall, the OLD CRADLE OF LIBERTY, in the city of Boston, we, the friends of universal emancipation—the enemies of slavery, whether at home or abroad—your advocates and defenders—would improve this opportunity to address to you words of sympathy, of consolation, of encouragement and hope.

We wish you to know who you are—by whom and for what purpose you were created—who are your oppressors, and what they profess to receive as self-evident truths, in regard to the rights of man—who are your friends, and in what manner they stand ready to aid you—what has been effected in your cause, within the last ten years, in the United States—and what is the prospect of your emancipation from chains and servitude.

In the first place, then, you are men—created in the same divine image as all other men—as good, as noble, as free, by birth and destiny, as your masters—as much entitled to 'life, liberty, and the pursuit of happiness,' as those who cruelly enslave you—made but a little lower than the angels of heaven, and destined to an immortal state of existence—equal members of the great human family. These truths you must believe and

---

From New England Anti-Slavery Convention, *Address of the New England Anti-Slavery Convention to the Slaves of the United States with an Address to President Tyler, Faneuil Hall, May 31, 1843* (Boston: O. Johnson, 1843), pp. 3–13.

understand, if you desire to have your chains broken, and your oppression come to a speedy end.

Know this, also, that God never made a slave master, nor a slave. He abhors cruelty and injustice in every form, and his judgments have been poured out on those nations that have refused to let the oppressed go free. He pities all who are sighing in bondage, and will work out their redemption, at whatever cost to those who are crushing them in the dust. He 'has made of one blood all nations of men, to dwell on all the face of the earth'—not to war with each other—not to defraud, degrade, torment, persecute, or oppress each other—but to enjoy equal rights and perfect liberty, to love and do good to each other, to dwell together in unity. He is no respecter of persons, but has given to all the stamp of his divinity, and his tender mercies are over all the works of his hands. 'Thus saith the Lord, Execute judgment and righteousness, and deliver the spoiled out of the hand of the oppressor; and do no wrong, do no violence to the stranger, the fatherless, nor the widow, neither shed innocent blood.' Such is your Creator, Father, and God.

Your masters say that you are an inferior race; that you were born to be slaves; that it is by the will and direction of God, that you are held in captivity. Your religious teachers declare that the Bible (which they call the word of God) sanctions slavery, and requires you to submit to it as of righ[t]ful authority. Believe them not! They all speak falsely, and the truth is not in them. They libel the character of God, and pervert the teachings of the Bible in the most awful manner. They combine to take from you all your hard earnings; they cover your bodies with stripes; they will not allow you to obtain light and knowledge; they call you their property, and sell you and your children at auction, as they do their cattle and swine. If they will steal, will they not lie? Listen not to what they tell you. They are the enemies of God and man. Their religion is of Beelzebub, the prince of devils; not of Jesus, the Son of

God. As long as they keep you in slavery, they defy Jehovah, reject Christ, and grieve the Holy Spirit.

God made you to be free—free as the birds that cleave the air, or sing on the branches—free as the sunshine that gladdens the earth—free as the winds that sweep over sea and land; —free at your birth, free during your whole life, free to-day, this hour, this moment! He has given you faculties to be improved, and souls to live forever. He has made you to glorify him in your bodies and spirits, to be happy here and hereafter, and not to be a degraded and miserable race. Your masters have no more right to enslave you, than you have to enslave them—to sell your children, and lacerate your bodies, and take your lives, than you have to inflict these outrages on them and theirs. The complexion of your masters is no better than yours —a black skin is as good as a white one. It is for you to say when, or where, or for whom you will work; where you will go, or in what part of the country or the world you will reside. If your masters prevent you from doing as you wish, they rob you of an inalienable right, and your blood will be required at their hands. If you submit unresistingly to their commands, do it for Christ's sake, (who died the just for the injust,) and not because they claim a rightful authority over you—for they have no such authority.

Your masters tell us that you do not wish to be free; that you are contented and happy as slaves; that you are much attached to their persons, and ready to lay down your lives to save them from harm; that you have an abundance of good clothes, good food, and all that you need to make your situation comfortable; that your tasks are light, and easily performed; and that you are much better off than such of your number as have been liberated from bondage. We do not believe one word that they say. We know, from the natural desire for liberty that burns in the bosom of every human being—from the horribly unjust code of laws by which you are governed— from the attempts of slaves, in all countries, to obtain their freedom by insurrection and massacre—from the vigilance with which all your movements are watched, as though you only waited for an opportunity to strike an effectual blow for your rights—from the testimony of thousands of slaves, who have escaped to the North and to Canada—from the numerous advertisements, in southern newspapers, of runaways from the plantations—that your masters are trying to deceive us. We are sure that your situation is a dreadful one, and that there is nothing in the world you desire so much as liberty.

We know that you are driven to the field like beasts, under the lash of cruel overseers or drivers, and there compelled to toil from earliest dawn till late at night; that you do not have sufficient clothing or food; that you have no laws to protect you from the most terrible punishment your masters may choose to inflict on your persons; that many of your bodies are covered with scars, and branded with red hot irons; that you are constantly liable to receive wounds and bruises, stripes, mutilations, insults and outrages innumerable; that your groans are borne to us on every southern breeze, your tears are falling thick and fast, your blood is flowing continually; that you are regarded as four-footed beasts and creeping things, and bought and sold with farming utensils and household furniture. We know all these things, and a great deal more, in regard to your condition.

Who, O unhappy countrymen, are your oppressors? They are the descendants of those, who, in 1776, threw off the British yoke, and for seven years waged war against a despotic power, until at length they secured their independence. In a certain Declaration which they published to the world, at that period, and which is now read and subscribed to on the fourth of July annually, they said—'We hold these truths to be self-evident—that all men are created equal; that they are endowed by their Creator with certain inalienable rights; that among these are life, liberty, and the pursuit of happiness:—That, to secure these rights, governments are instituted among men, deriving their just powers *from the consent of the governed;* that whenever any form of government becomes destructive of these ends, it is the right of the people to alter or abolish it, and to institute a new government, laying its foundation on such principles, and organizing its powers in such form, as to them shall seem most likely to effect their safety and happiness. . . . When a long train of abuses and usurpations, pursuing invariably the same object, evinces a design to reduce them under absolute despotism, it is *their right,* it is THEIR DUTY, to THROW OFF SUCH GOVERNMENT, and to provide new guards for their future security.'

In acknowledging the truths set forth in this Declaration to be self-evident, your masters, in reducing you to slavery, are condemned as hypocrites and liars, out of their own mouths. By precept and example, they declare that it is both your right and your duty to wage war against them, and to wade through their blood, if necessary, to secure your own freedom. They glory in the revolutionary war, and greatly honor the names of those heroes who took up arms to destroy their oppressors. One of those heroes—Patrick Henry, of Virginia—exclaimed, 'Give me liberty, or give me death!' Another—Joseph Warren, of Massachusetts—said, 'My sons, scorn to be slaves!' Their cry was,

> 'Hereditary bondsmen! know ye not,
> Who would be free, themselves must strike the blow?'

When, a few years since, the Poles rose in insurrection against the Russian power—and the Greeks rushed to the strife of blood against their Turkish oppressors—and the South Americans broke in pieces the Spanish yoke, and made themselves free and independent—your masters, in common with all the people of the North, cheered them on to the conflict, and sent them banners and arms to enable them to triumph in the cause of liberty—exclaiming,

> 'O, where's the slave, so lowly,
> Condemned to chains unholy,
> Who, could he burst his bonds at first,
> Would pine beneath them slowly?'

Yet, should you attempt to regain your freedom in the same manner, you would be branded as murderers and monsters, and slaughtered without mercy! But the celebrated Thomas Jefferson, of Virginia, has truly said that, in such a contest, the Almighty has no attribute which can take side with your oppressors; and, though a slaveholder himself, he was forced many years ago to exclaim, in view of your enslavement,—'I tremble for my country when I reflect that God is just; that his justice cannot sleep forever; that considering numbers, nature, and natural means only, a revolution of the wheel of fortune, an exchange of situation, is among possible events; that it may become probable by supernatural inte[r]ference!' And he concluded by expressing the hope that the way was 'preparing, under the auspices of Heaven, for a total emancipation, and that this was disposed, in the order of events, to be with the consent of the masters, rather than by their extirpation.'

Thomas Jefferson wrote in this manner more than sixty years since. At that period, your number was a little more than half a million; now it is more than two millions and a half. Sad and dreary has been your existence up to the present hour; and, doubtless, you have almost given up all hope of ever celebrating the day of jubilee—your own emancipation—on this side of the grave.

Take courage! Be filled with hope and comfort!—Your redemption draws nigh, for the Lord is mightily at work in your behalf. Is it not frequently the darkest before day-break? The word has gone forth that you shall be delivered from your chains, and it has not been spoken in vain.

Although you have many enemies, yet you have also many friends—warm, faithful, sympathizing, devoted friends—who will never abandon your cause; who are pledged to do all in their power to break your chains; who are laboring to effect your emancipation without delay, in a peaceable manner, without the shedding of blood; who regard you as brethren and countrymen, and fear not the frowns or threats of your masters.—They call themselves abolitionists. They have already suffered much, in various parts of the country, for rebuking those who keep you in slavery—for demanding your immediate liberation—for revealing to the people the horrors of your situation—for boldly opposing a corrupt public sentiment, by which you are kept in the great southern prison-house of bondage. Some of them have been beaten with stripes; others have been stripped, and covered with tar and feathers; others have had their property taken from them, and burnt in the streets; others have had large rewards offered by your masters for their seizure; others have been cast into jails and penitentiaries; others have been mobbed and lynched with great violence; others have lost their reputation, and been ruined in their business; others have lost their lives. All these, and many other outrages of an equally grievous kind, they have suffered for your sakes, and because they are your friends. They cannot go to the South, to see and converse with you, face to face; for, so ferocious and bloody-minded are your taskmasters, they would be put to an ignominious death as soon as discovered. Besides, it is not necessary that they should incur this peril; for it is solely by the aid of the people of the North, that you are held in bondage, and, therefore, they find enough to do at home, to make the people here your friends, and to break up all connexion with the slave system. They have proved themselves to be truly courageous, insensible to danger, superior to adversity, strong in principle, invincible in argument, animated by the spirit of impartial benevolence, unwearied in devising ways and means for your deliverance, the best friends of the whole country, the noblest champions of the human race. Ten years ago, they were so few and feeble as only to excite universal contempt; now they number in their ranks, hundreds of thousands of the people. Then, they had scarcely a single anti-slavery society in operation; now they have thousands. Then, they had only one or two presses to plead your cause; now they have multitudes.— They are scattering all over the land their newspapers, books, pamphlets, tracts, and other publications, to hold up to infamy the conduct of your oppressors, and to awaken sympathy in your behalf. They are continually holding anti-slavery meetings in all parts of the free States, to tell the people the story of your wrongs.—Wonderful has been the change effected in public feeling, under God, through their instrumentality. Do not fear that they will grow weary in your service. They are confident of success, in the end. They know that the Lord Almighty is with them—that truth, justice, right, are with them—that you are with them. They know, too, that your masters are cowardly and weak, through conscious wrongdoing, and already begin to falter in their course. Lift up your heads, O ye despairing slaves! Yet a little while, and your chains shall snap asunder, and you shall be tortured and plundered no more! Then, fathers and mothers, your children shall be yours, to bring them up in the nurture and admonition of the Lord. Then, husbands and wives, now torn from each other's arms, you shall be reunited in the flesh, and man then shall no longer dare to put asunder those whom God hath joined together. Then, brothers and sisters, you shall be sold to the remorseless slave speculator no more, but dwell together in unity. 'God hasten that joyful day!' is now the daily prayer of millions.

The weapons with which the abolitionists seek to effect your deliverance are not bowie knives, pistols, swords, guns, or any other deadly implements. They consist of appeals, warnings, rebukes, arguments and facts, addressed to the understandings, consciences and hearts of the people. Many of your friends believe that not even those who are oppressed, whether their skins are white or black, can shed the blood of their oppressors in accordance with the will of God; while many others believe that it is right for the oppressed to rise and take their liberty by violence, if they can secure it in no other manner; but they, in common with all your friends, believe that every attempt at insurrection would be attended with disaster and defeat, on your part, because you are not strong enough to contend with the military power of the nation; consequently, their advice to you is, to be patient, long-suffering, and submissive, yet awhile longer—trusting that, by the blessing of the Most High on their labors, you will yet be emancipated without shedding a drop of your masters' blood, or losing a drop of your own.

The abolitionists of the North are the only true and unyielding friends on whom you can rely. They will never receive nor betray you. They have made your cause their own, and they mean to be true to themselves and to you, whatever may be the consequence. They are continually increasing in number, in influence, in enterprise and determination; and, judging from the success which has already attended their measures, they anticipate that, in a comparatively short period, the entire North will receive you with open arms, and give you shelter and protection, as fast as you escape from the South. We, who now address you, are united with them in spirit and design. We glory in the name of abolitionists, for it signifies friendship for all who are pining in servitude. We advise you to seize every opportunity to escape from your masters, and, fixing your eyes on the North star, travel on until you reach a land of liberty. You are not the property of your masters. God never made one human being to be owned by another. Your right to be free, at any moment, is undeniable; and it is your duty, whenever you can, peaceably to escape from the plantations on which you are confined, and assert your manhood.

Already, within a few years, twenty thousand of your number have successfully run away, many of whom are now residing at the North, but a very large proportion of whom are living in Canada, enjoying safety and freedom under the British flag. To that country, the slave-hunters dare not go; nor will they much longer dare to come to the North, in pursuit of fugitive slaves. But, while we thus invite and encourage you to transform yourselves from things into men by flight, we would counsel you to use the utmost caution in attempting to escape; for many dangers yet lurk in the path of every fugitive, and should any of you be caught, you know that your fate would be a terrible one. Still, we assure you that there are now thousands in the free States to succor you, where, a few years since, scarcely an individual could be found to hide the outcast. If you come to us, and are hungry, we will feed you; if thirsty, we will give you drink; if naked, we will clothe you; if sick, we will administer to your necessities; if in prison, we will visit you; if you need a hiding-place from the face of the pursuer, we will provide one that even blood-hounds cannot scent out. This is the pledge we sacredly give to you.

We are not in favor of sending you to Africa, for we regard you as fellow-countrymen, and, with few exceptions, you have a right to claim this as your native land, for you were born on its soil. We do not, therefore, make your removal out of the country a condition of freedom, but demand for you all that we claim for ourselves—liberty, equal rights, equal privileges.

Your masters threaten that, if we do not stop pleading your cause, and assailing their slave system, they will dissolve the Union. Such a dissolution has for us no terrors; for we regard it as far preferable to a perpetuity of slavery. Such a dissolution you would have no occasion to lament; for it would enable you to obtain your freedom and independence in a single day.—Your masters are only two hundred and fifty thousand in number; you are nearly three millions; and what could they do, if they should be abandoned to their fate by the North? If it were not now for the compact existing between the free and the slave States, by which the whole military power of the nation is pledged to supress all insurrections, you would have long ere this been free. Your blood is the cement which binds the American Union together; your bodies are crushed beneath the massy weight of this Union; and its repeal or dissolution would ensure the downfall of slavery.—We tell your masters that we shall not be intimidated by their threats, but shall continue to expose their guilt, to rebuke their oppression, to agitate the public mind, to demand your release, until there shall be none to help them, and they be separated from all political and religious connexion with the people of the North —or (what we most earnestly desire as a matter of choice) until liberty be proclaimed throughout all the land unto all the inhabitants thereof, with the hearty consent of the whole people.

Done in Faneuil Hall, May 31, 1843.
EDMUND QUINCY, *President.*

VIII

Argument from Natural Rights and Natural Law

CHARLES FOLLEN LINKS EQUALITY WITH NATURAL RIGHTS

The antislavery crusaders were ever alert to the argument based on natural rights to further their cause. Particularly well equipped to elaborate the argument that the eighteenth century idea of the rights of man applied, not only to free white men but to all men, was Charles Follen (1796–1840), a refugee from the 1820 revolutions in Germany. Because of his outspoken antislavery views Follen lost his professorship at Harvard. Thereafter he was a Unitarian clergyman and antislavery crusader until his death.

Charles Theodore Christian Follen, "Speech before the Anti-Slavery Society. At the Annual Meeting of the Massachusetts Anti-Slavery Society, January 20th, 1836," in *Works, With a Memoir of His Life*, I (Boston: Hilliard, Gray and Company, 1841), 627–633.

At the Annual Meeting of the Massachusetts Anti-slavery Society, January 20th, 1836, Rev. Professor Follen offered the following resolution:

Resolved, that we consider the Anti-slavery cause as the cause of philanthropy, with regard to which all human beings, white men and colored men, citizens and foreigners, men and women, have the same duties and the same rights.

Philanthropy means the love of man; and the love of man is the true and only foundation of the Anti-slavery cause. Our whole creed is summed up in this single position, that the slave is a man, created by God in his own image, and, therefore, by divine right, a freeman. The slave is a man, and we are men; this is the only needful and all-sufficient title, from which every Anti-slavery society, and every Abolitionist, derive their duties and their rights. Every human being, whether colored or white, foreigner or citizen, man or woman, is, in virtue of a common nature, a rightful and responsible defender of the natural rights of all. These are the sentiments of every Abolitionist: these the principles of the Declaration of Independence, which was intended to make this whole nation one great Anti-slavery Society.

Professor Follen observed, that these self-evident truths had been opposed in full by the consistent enemies of human freedom, and obstructed in detail by its inconsistent friends.

In the first place, we have been advised, if we really wish to benefit the slave and the colored race generally, not unnecessarily to shock the feelings, though they be but prejudices, of the white people, by admitting colored persons to our anti-slavery meetings and societies. We have been told, that many, who would otherwise act in union with us, are kept away by our disregard of the feelings of the community in this respect.

Grant the fact, that this piece of bad policy in us keeps away many who would otherwise be with us at this time, in this hall, or in some other more spacious room, which their personal influence might open to our holy cause, which still has to go begging from the door of one Christian church to another, without finding admission. But what, I would ask, is the great, the single object of all our meetings and societies? Have we any other object, than to impress upon the community this one principle, that *the colored man is a* MAN? And, on the other hand, is not the prejudice, which would have us exclude colored people from our meetings and societies here, the same which, in the Southern States, dooms them to perpetual bondage? It needs no long argument, then, to prove, that, by excluding the colored people from our anti-slavery proceedings, we should not only deprive ourselves of many faithful fellow-laborers, but, by complying with that inhuman prejudice, we should sanction and support the first principles of slavery, as well as give the lie to our own most solemn professions. In his private intercourse, in his personal and domestic relations, let every one choose his company according to his own principles, or his own whims. But, as for any meetings and associations designed for the establishment of *human rights,*—how can we have the effrontery to expect the white slave-holder of the South to live on terms of civil equality with his colored slave, if we, the white Abolitionists of the North, will not admit colored freemen as members of our anti-slavery societies?

This may be sufficient to vindicate the first part of my resolution, claiming for colored men and white men that essential equality of rights and duties with regard to the Anti-slavery cause, which should lead to united action.

In the second place, I assert, that, with regard to this cause, foreigners and citizens have the same duties and the same rights.

Professor Follen observed, that, in defending this clause in his resolution, he felt, or rather he had been made to feel, as if he were, in part, speaking in self-defence. For, though he had come to this country for no other reason that to live under a government of equal laws, which was not to be found in Europe; and though for eleven years he had sustained the duties, and during five years possessed all the rights, of the citizens of this Republic, his devotion to the anti-slavery cause had been condemned, both in private and in public, on the grave and undeniable charge of his having been born in a foreign land. His active interest in this cause had become more extensively known by the "Address to the People of the United States," which he, as the chairman of a committee appointed for this purpose by the New England Anti-slavery Convention of 1834, had been called upon to draw up, and which, according to a vote of the Board of Managers, had been sent to every member of Congress. A copy of this address had been returned to him by an unknown hand, with the words, "A foreigner should recollect the protection afforded him by the institutions of this country, when he undertakes to cast a firebrand among the people, by which they may be destroyed." Similar ingenious substitutes for argument, being rendered more striking by studied vulgarity, had appeared in some of our newspapers. For himself, he had nothing to offer to the distinguished few, who had, notwithstanding his rightful citizenship, insisted upon treating him as a foreigner, unless it were the plea, which had been entered for him by a generous friend, "that, though not a son of the Pilgrims, he was himself a Pilgrim."

I should have passed over, in silence, these petty vexations, as solitary exceptions to the uniform experience of generous confidence and kindness, which I have never ceased to enjoy in this community, if it were not for the great principle involved in these disagreeable trifles.

Our cause is the cause of man; therefore our watchword from the beginning has been, "Our country is the world,—our countrymen are all mankind." We reverence patriotism as a virtue, so far as it is philanthropy applied to our own country, while we look down upon it as a vice, so far as it would sacrifice the rights of man,—the moral to the selfish interests of our nation. The anti-slavery cause, then, being the cause of man, knows no difference between natives and foreigners. Nay, more, we have here amongst us large numbers of natives of this country, deprived, without a shadow of right, of the fruits of their labor, stripped of the sacred rights of husbands and wives, parents and children, citizens and Christians; we see them daily driven out to merciless toil, sold like beasts, imprisoned, lacerated, and degraded without redress. Now when we see many millions of our countrymen, yea, the priests and the rulers of the people, going on in their own course of prosperity, and, without pity, passing by an innocent brother, stripped of every thing, and wounded in soul and body; and perchance there should be journeying this way a foreigner, who should have compassion on him, and try to lift him up, and pour into his wounds the oil of consolation and the wine of hope, or, from the rich treasury of his heart, should pour out the pure gold of sterling truth to redeem him from bondage,—which of these, I ask, would be a neighbour to him who had been robbed and wounded? And shall we, the favored citizens, on beholding such signal kindness, cry out with the Jews of old, "He is a Samaritan, and has a devil!"—or with our modern, national bigots,—"He is a foreigner; an English emissary; mob him! tar and feather him!"

We look upon the foreigner, who holds up before us the law of liberty, proclaimed in our Declaration of Independence, in opposition to the law of servitude, imposed and enforced by our free institutions upon one sixth of our population, as a true friend; and we see, in his open rebuke, the surest pledge of confidence in our love of truth and sense of justice. On the other hand, the violent attempts at preventing the free expression of sentiment on this great moral subject, by strangers or citizens,—the lawless, shameless, and merciless proceedings against all who are convicted or suspected of nothing worse than a consistent adherence to the first principles of the Declaration of Independence, seem to us more criminal when perpetrated or tolerated in this country than in any other, simply because we have "pledged our lives, our fortunes, and our sacred honor," to the support of the equal rights of all. Our

Constitution has secured a government of law, freedom of conscience, the liberty of speaking and printing, to every citizen, nay, to every stranger sojourning amongst us. As citizens of the world, as members of the human family, as Christians, we look upon every one as a fellow-citizen, as a neighbour, who defends the rights, and respects the feelings, of all men; while he who does not see in every human being an equal and a brother, whether he be born here or elsewhere, he alone is regarded by us as a stranger and an enemy.

And now, Mr. President, I come to the last topic of my resolution. I maintain, that, with regard to the anti-slavery cause, *men* and *women* have the same duties and the same rights. The ground I take on this point is very plain. I wish to spare you, I wish to spare myself, the worthless and disgusting task of replying, in detail, to all the coarse attacks and flattering sophisms by which men have endeavoured to entice or to drive women from this and from many other spheres of moral action. "Go home and spin!" is the well-meaning advice of the domestic tyrant of the old school. "Conquer by personal charms and fashionable attractions!" is the brilliant career marked out for her by the idols and the idolaters of fashion. "Never step out of the bounds of decorum and the *customary* ways of doing good," is the sage advice of maternal caution. "Rule by obedience, by submission sway!" is the golden saying of the moralist poet, sanctioning female servitude, and pointing out a resort and compensation in female cunning. What with the fear of the insolent remarks about women, in which those of the dominant sex, whose bravery is the generous offspring of conscious impunity, are particularly apt to indulge, and with the still stronger fear of being thought unfeminine,—it is, indeed, a proof of uncommon moral courage, or of an overpowering sense of religious duty and sympathy with the oppressed, that a woman is induced to embrace the unpopular, unfashionable, obnoxious principles of the Abolitionists. Popular opinion, the habits of society, are all calculated to lead women to consider the place, the privileges, and the duties, which etiquette has assigned to them as their peculiar portion, as more important than those which nature has given them in common with men. Men have at all times been inclined to allow to women peculiar privileges, while withholding from them essential rights. In the progress of civilization and Christianity, one right after another has been conceded, one occupation after another has been placed within the reach of women. Still are we far from a practical acknowledgment of the simple truth, that the rational and moral nature of man is the foundation of all rights and duties, and that women as well as men are rational and moral beings. It is on this account that I look upon the formation of Ladies' anti-slavery societies as an event of the highest interest, not only for its direct beneficial bearing on the cause of emancipation, but still more as an indication of the moral growth of society. Women begin to feel, that the place which men have marked out for them is but a small part of what society owes to them, and what they themselves owe to society, to the whole human family, and to that Power to whom each and all are indebted and accountable for the use of the powers intrusted to them. It is, indeed, a consoling thought, that such is the providential adaptation of all things, that the toil and the sufferings of the slave, however unprofitable to himself, and however hopeless, are not wholly thrown away and vain;— that the master who has deprived him of the fruits of his industry, of every motive and opportunity for exercising his highest faculties, has not been able to prevent his exercising, unconsciously, a moral and spiritual influence all over the world, breaking down every unnatural restraint, and calling forth the simplest and deepest of all human emotions, the feeling of man for his fellow-man, and bringing out the strongest intellectual and moral powers to his rescue. It is, indeed, natural, that the cry of misery, the call for help, that is now spreading far and wide, and penetrating the inmost recesses of society, should thrill, with peculiar power, through the heart of woman. For it is woman, injured, insulted woman, that exhibits the most baneful and hateful influences of slavery. But I cannot speak of what the free woman ought and must feel for her enslaved sister,—because I am overwhelmed by the thought of what we men, we, who have mothers, and wives, and daughters, should not only feel, but do, and dare, and sacrifice, to drain the marshes whose exhalations infect the moral atmosphere of society.

The remarks I have made in support of my resolution may be summed up in a few words. The only object of the anti-slavery societies is, to restore the slave to his natural rights. To promote this object, all human beings, white men and colored men, citizens and foreigners, men and women, have the same moral calling, simply because, in virtue of a common rational and moral nature, all human beings are in duty bound, and divinely authorized, to defend their own and each other's *natural rights.*

Our rights, our duties, with regard to the oppressed, require and authorize the use of all lawful and moral means, to accomplish the great object of deliverance. As members of this Union, we are debarred all direct political influence with regard to the legal existence of slavery in other States. But slavery in the District of Columbia and in the Territories, as well as the internal slave-trade, are evils within the reach of our Federal Legislature, and, consequently, within the control and responsibility of every citizen of the Union.

The guilt of the existence of slavery within the bounds of the Federal legislation, rests upon every citizen who is not exerting himself to the utmost, by free discussion and petitions to Congress, that this cruel and disgraceful inconsistency may be removed. But the sphere of moral action is not confined within the limits of our political rights. The North is connected with the South by numerous relations, which may be made so many channels of influence on the minds and consciences of the slave-holders. There are family connexions, commercial relations, political and religious interests, by which individuals of different States are brought in contact, and a continual intercourse is thus kept up between the free North and the slaveholding South. With all these means of private intercourse within our reach, we require no alteration in the Constitution, we demand no especial aid from Congress or from any State Legislature, to induce the slave-holders, by moral motives and by considerations of enlightened self-interest, to rid themselves of this great evil. We require of government nothing but to be protected in the exercise of one undoubted constitutional right, a right, which, as Gerrit Smith justly observes, has a deeper foundation than the Constitution which solemnly secures it, being grounded on the nature of man and the sovereign decree of his Creator. Let us dismiss all controversy concerning the exciting question, whether, or how far, the Constitution sanctions slavery; but let us assert and defend the freedom of communication by speaking, writing, and printing, which is the first requisite of the freeman, and the last hope of the slave. Slavery and free discussion, Sir, it is well known, cannot live together. They will quarrel until one of them quits the neighbourhood.

We claim freedom of communication with the slave-holder of the South, as well as with the advocates of slavery, and those who think themselves justified in their neutrality at the North. We contend with a national prejudice; we aim at a national reform. Every individual, who is free from the long-cherished and deep-rooted prejudice, which prevents the white men of the North, as well as those of the South, from looking upon the colored man as a man and a brother, is in duty bound to become a fellow-laborer in this work of reform. For this reason, our societies are founded, not on the exclusive principle of election, but on the broad, philanthropic ground of free admission; we elect no one, but cordially receive every one who may elect himself. Our audiences do not consist of select companies; but as the Report, which you have accepted, eloquently sets forth, in humble imitation of Jesus and the Apostles, we address all who have ears to hear and will hear.

We are told, we must not agitate this subject;—let it alone, and it will remedy itself. This is not the course of Providence. Such reformations are never accomplished without human means. God will not indulge us in our indolence, and do the work without our instrumentality.

The Declaration of Independence, so far as those in bonds are concerned, is a dead letter; and we must not rest from our labors until it is raised from the dead.

JAMES FORTEN, JR., PLEADS FOR NEGRO RIGHTS

Son of the outstanding early antislavery spokesman, the Philadelphia sailmaker, James Forten, James Forten, Jr., (fl. 1835) was also an active abolitionist. In the selection which follows, Forten pleads the rights of the Negro—both slave and free. Poignant as the plea itself is, it has added significance because of the way in which Forten, himself a Negro, related the issue to the broader context of American citizenship.

I will now claim your indulgence for a few moments while I make some remarks on the subject of natural rights. It certainly is one of great magnitude. I will not, however, enter into an extensive discussion of its various branches; but would

From James Forten, Jr., *An Address Delivered before the Ladies' Anti-Slavery Society of Philadelphia, On the Evening of the 14th of April, 1836* (Philadelphia: Merrihew and Gunn, 1836), pp. 6–12.

earnestly suggest it for the future consideration of our friends. Of what incalculable value must these rights be to those who possess them unrestricted? And yet they were intended for all —high and low—rich and poor—of whatever clime or complexion. They were spoke into existence along with the world; and although the establishment of legal authority was unknown to us, and there "subsisted not a vestige of civil government any where, still they would belong to man." Or, if we who form this present assembly were, by some sudden and unknown cause, thrown upon a desolate spot in the remotest corner of the Globe, we would, from the very first moment, be entitled to these rights—the right to the produce of our own labour, to our limbs, life, liberty and property—perfect rights, not human institutions, but Divine ordinations. Now, with these facts before you, the question should arise, whether all your fellow creatures are in the full enjoyment of these rights. If you look to the South, you will see how they are violated—how outrage, oppression and wrong has blighted them—how man, (corrupted worm of the earth) forgetting his accountability to God, suffering passion and avarice to dethrone reason, has torn them from his fellow man. Yes, the poor slave is deprived of these rights —these great essentials to man's happiness—these bountiful gifts of nature—he does not possess even as much freedom "as the beasts that perish." My friends, reflect for a moment upon what constitutes natural rights; analyze them, search deep into their component parts, and then ask yourselves if slavery recognizes any of them? Why, every rational being who has bestowed one thought upon the inhuman traffic must come to the conclusion that it does not. Again, look on the other side of the picture—turn your eyes to your own city, and behold that class of American citizens with whom I am identified; see them borne down by the weight of innumerable persecutions, their situation but little better than the millions of their brethren now suffering under the galling yoke of servitude; they are nearly stripped of their rights. The remorseless hand of prejudice—the despoiler of our rights—our inveterate foe, whose birth place is the nethermost pit—year after year wages an ignoble warfare against us. If we are arrested on suspicion of having stolen our own bodies, and run away with them, so few are the advocates we have at the Bar of Justice, that the pleadings of humanity are silenced, and we too frequently consigned to hopeless bondage. If our property be destroyed by a cowardly and ruffian mob, our persons maltreated and our limbs broken, the hand of charity is scarcely extended to the sufferer; seldom do we find that redress shown to us which would be fully bestowed upon any other class of people similarly situated. The omnipotent Being said, "Let there be light." Is it permitted to shine brightly around our path? No. Where is that all-powerful light of knowledge? Where are the academies thrown open for our reception, that we may come in and quench our parched lips at the fountain of Literature? With but few exceptions there are none; even the doors of the sanctuary, devoted to all that is sacred, are closed against us. And is this fair—is it noble—is it generous—is it patriotic—is it consistent with the professions of our republican principles? Was it ever intended that man should lift his rebel hand against the natural rights of his brother, and try to uproot them from his breast? That he should thus tamper with the works of nature?—should thus presumptuously exercise his own will in defiance of the benevolent and comprehensive wisdom of Providence? My friends, ought not the united efforts of every Christian to be aimed at the destruction of this persecution, which, like a universal pall, overspreads our prospects? Is not the call imperative? What have we done to merit this abuse? Have we usurped the authorities of the land? No. Are we outlaws—cut-throats? No. Are we not men, in common with other men; fully capable of appreciating the inestimable worth of these rights, which are our own? True, we are told by our enemies that we are inferior to them in intellect—our mental faculties being of the lowest order—that we stand but one degree above the brute creation; these are assertions without a shadow of proof; they tie our feet and seal our mouths, and then exclaim, "see how superior we are to these people!" They have no authority for crushing us to the ground, therefore we will not cease to urge our case, calmly and dispassionately. We are stimulated to act thus by the instinct of our natures. There is nothing that our enemies can bring against us but the colour of our skin; and is this not a mean, pitiful objection to the elevation of any one? Oh! what a shameful prejudice. If this is to be our judge, if the uncertain and wavering shades of colour are to decide whether we shall be entitled to rights in common with our fellow citizens, (which is all we ask,) if mercy and compassion is to be disregarded, and beneficence utterly annihilated, no longer to strengthen, guide and ennoble the hearts of men, then has our country's grandeur fallen—then has she sunk into a state which would have disgraced the dark ages, when civilization was unknown, and man had not yet begun to do homage to the potency of mind. We claim our rights, then, not as a mere boon, for that would be doing violence to that honest pride which is always found pervading the breast and flowing through every vein of conscious innocence, but we claim then as rights guaranteed by the living God—natural, indefeasible rights.

There is another point to which I would draw your notice. The recent scenes in Congress are a specimen of the evil times we live in, the corrupted atmosphere we breathe. There, behold the Constitution of the United States—our national compact, the great organ of national sentiment, perjured, immolated upon the altar of expediency there; the right to petition, the right of free discussion, the freedom of speech, the freedom of the press—rights which should be the pride and boast of a republic, are trampled under foot, scoffed at by statesmen and senators, and the gag and Lynch law held up as a model of the glorious march of *Virtue, Liberty* and *Independence;* as the dearest gift that a noble and dignified people could transfer to posterity; why posterity would spurn such a legacy as coming from heathens, and not from their Christian forefathers. The demands of the South are growing every day more extravagant, insolent and imperative. As an evidence of this, I have only to refer you to the report and resolutions adopted in the Legislature of South Carolina, published in the 9th number of the Liberator. I allude to the report of the Joint Committee of Federal Relations, on so much of Gov. M'Duffie's message as relates to the institution of domestic slavery, and the proceedings of the Abolitionists in the non-slaveholding states.[1] It ought to be extensively read, for I think it would be the means of arousing many to a sense of the danger which threatens their own liberties. I will read a few of the resolutions offered by Mr. Hamilton, chairman of that most grave and reverend committee.

"*Resolved*, That the formation of Abolition Societies, and the acts and doings of certain fanatics calling themselves Abolitionists, in the non-slaveholding states of this confederacy, are in direct violation of the obligations of the compact of Union, dissocial and incendiary in the extreme.

"*Resolved*, That the Legislature of South Carolina, having every confidence in the justice and friendship of the non-slaveholding states, announces to her co-states her confident expectations, and she earnestly requests that the governments of these states will promptly and effectually suppress all those associations within their respective limits, purporting to be Abolition Societies; and that they will make it highly penal, to

---

[1] For Governor McDuffie, see p. 151, footnote 2. The message itself was delivered to the South Carolina legislature and was printed in the *Liberator*, December 12, 1835. Among other things he defended slavery on Biblical, rational, economic, political, and humanitarian grounds; and called for harsh laws to deal with those who incited slaves against their masters to be enacted not only by South Carolina but also by northern states. In the latter case the laws would be directed against the abolitionists. The ninth number of the *Liberator* refers to the issue of February 27, 1836.

print, publish and distribute newspapers, pamphlets, tracts, and pictorial representations, calculated and having an obvious tendency to excite the slaves of the southern states to insurrection and revolt.

"*Resolved*, In order that a salutary negative may be put on the mischievous and unfounded assumption of some of the Abolitionists—the non-slaveholding states are requested to disclaim, by legislative declaration, all right, either on the part of themselves or the government of the United States, to interfere in any manner with domestic slavery, either in the states or in the territories where it exists."

Was ever a request so modest? There never was a request more unreasonable, more abominable—evincing in its tone the greatest insult that could be offered to a free and independent people. But what do the majority of the citizens in the North about the matter? Why, I regret to have it in my power to say, that, with few exceptions, they are yielding to this daring presumption of the South; tamely acquiescing without venturing even as much as a word in reply. They ask of them to relinquish the sacred and legitimate right to think and act as they please. Freemen are, in one sense, threatened with slavery; the chains are shaken in their faces, and yet they appear unwilling to resist them as becomes freemen. Such votaries are they at the shrine of mammon that they have not courage enough to join the standard of patriotism which their fathers reared, and with the dignity of a free and unshackled people, repel with scorn, this unheard of infringement upon their dearest rights—this death-blow to their own liberties. My friends, do you ask why I thus speak? It is because I love America; it is my native land; because I feel as one should feel who sees destruction, like a corroding cancer, eating into the very heart of his country, and would make one struggle to save her;—because I love the stars and stripes, emblems of our National Flag—and long to see the day when not a slave shall be found resting under its shadow; when it shall play with the winds pure and unstained by the blood of "captive millions."

Again, the South most earnestly and respectfully solicits the North to let the question of Slavery alone, and leave it to their bountiful honesty and humanity to settle. Why, honesty, I fear, has fled from the South, long ago; sincerity has fallen asleep there; pity has hidden herself; justice cannot find the way; helper is not at home; charity lies dangerously ill; benevolence is under arrest; faith is nearly extinguished; truth has long since been buried, and conscience is nailed on the wall. Now, do you think it would be better to leave it to the bountiful honesty and humanity of the South to settle? No, no. Only yield to them in this one particular and they will find you vulnerable in every other. I can tell you, my hearers, if the North once sinks into profound silence on this momentous subject, you may then bid farewell to peace, order and reform; then the condition of your fellow creatures in the southern section of our country will never be ameliorated; then may the poor slave look upon his weighty chains, and exclaim, in the agony of his heart, "To these am I immutably doomed; the glimmering rays of hope are lost to me for ever; robbed of all that is dear to man, I stand a monument of my country's ingratitude. A *husband,* yet separated from the dearest tie which binds me to this earth. A *father,* yet compelled to stifle the feelings of a father, and witness a helpless offspring torn by a savage hand from its mother's fond embrace, no longer to call her by that endearing title. A wretched slave, I look upon the departing brightness of the setting sun, and when her glorious light revists the morn, these clanking irons tell me I am that slave still; still am I to linger out a life of ignominious servitude, till death shall unloose these heavy bars—unfetter my body and soul."

Will not the wrath of offended Heaven visit my guilty brethren? My friends, this is no chimera of the imagination, but it is the reality; and I beseech you to consider it as such. Cease not to do as you are now doing, notwithstanding the invidious frowns that may be cast upon your efforts; regard not these—for bear in mind that the future prosperity of the nation rests upon the successful labours of the Abolitionists; this is as certain as that there is a God above. Recollect you have this distinction—you have brought down upon your heads the anger of many foes for that good which you seek to do your country; you are insulted and sneered at because you feel for the proscribed, the defenceless, the down-trodden; you are despised because you would raise them in the scale of beings; you are charged as coming out to the world with the Bible in one hand and a firebrand in the other. May you never be ashamed of that firebrand. It is a holy fire, kindled from every page of that sacred chronicle.

WILLIAM ELLERY CHANNING DEFINES THE USE OF THE HIGHER LAW

Channing, although he came fairly late in his career to espouse the antislavery cause with real vigor, nevertheless brought the rational analysis of his Unitarian training to bear on the slavery issue. Shortly before his death he moved rapidly into an open antislavery position—stimulated, at least in part, by the destruction of Birney's press in 1836. In the selection which follows, Channing specifically deals with natural rights and their bearing on the issue of fugitive slaves.

The grand principle to be laid down is, that it is infinitely more important to preserve a free citizen from being made a slave, than to send back a fugitive slave to his chain. This idea is to rule over and determine all the legislation on this subject.

From William Ellery Channing, *The Duty of the Free States. Second Part* (Boston: William Crosby & Co., 1842), pp. 10–14, 41–43.

Let the fugitive be delivered up, but by such processes as will prevent a freeman from being delivered up also. For this end full provision must be made. On this point the Constitution, and a still higher law, that of nature and God, speak the same language; and we must insist that these high authorities shall be revered.

The Constitution opens with these memorable words: "We, the people of the United States, in order to form a more perfect union, establish justice, insure domestic tranquility, provide for the common defence, promote the general welfare, and secure *the blessings of liberty* to ourselves and our posterity, do ordain and establish this Constitution for the United States of America." It is understood and conceded, that this preamble does not confer on the national government any powers but such as are specified in the subsequent articles of the instrument; but it teaches and was designed to teach the spirit in which these powers are to be interpreted and brought into action. "To secure the blessings of liberty," is enumerated among the purposes of the national compact; and whoever knows the history of the Constitution, knows that this was the grand purpose for which the powers of the Constitution were conferred. That the liberty of each man, of the obscurest man, should be inviolate; this was the master-thought in the authors of this immortal charter. According to these views, we have a right to demand of Congress, as their highest constitutional duty, to carry into the enactment of every law a reverence for the freedom of each and all. A law palpably exposing the freeman to be made a slave, and even rendering his subjection to this cruel doom nearly sure, is one of the most unconstitutional acts, if the spirit of the Constitution be regarded, which the national legislature can commit. The Constitution is violated, not only by the assumption of powers not conceded, but equally by using conceded powers to the frustration of the end for which they were conferred. In the law regulating the delivery of supposed fugitives, the great end of the national charter is sacrificed to an accidental provision. This Constitution was not established to send back slaves to chains. The article requiring this act of the Free States was forced on them by the circumstances of the times, and submitted to as a hard necessity. It did not enter into the essence of the instrument; whilst the security of freedom was its great, living, all-pervading idea. We see the tendency of slavery to warp the Constitution to its purposes, in the law for restoring the flying bondman. Under this not a few, having not only the same natural but legal rights with ourselves, have been subjected to the lash of the overseer.

But a higher law than the Constitution protests against the act of Congress on this point. According to the law of nature, no greater crime against a human being can be committed, than to make him a slave. This is to strike a blow at the very heart and centre of all his rights as a man; to put him beneath his race. On the ground of the immutable law of nature, our government has pronounced the act of making a man a slave on the coast of Africa, to be piracy, a capital crime. And shall the same government enact or sustain a law which exposes the freeman here to be reduced to slavery, which gives facilities to the unprincipled for accomplishing this infinite wrong? And what is the end for which the freeman is so exposed? It is that a man flying from an unjust yoke may be forced back to bondage, an end against which natural and divine justice protests; so that to confirm and perpetuate one violation of the moral law, another still greater is left open and made easy to the kidnapper. . . .

. . . To condemn a man to perpetual slavery is as solemn a sentence as to condemn him to death. Before being thus doomed, he has a right to all the means of defence which are granted to a man who is tried for his life. All the rules, forms, solemnities, by which innocence is secured from being confounded with guilt, he has a right to demand. In the present case, the principle is eminently applicable, that many guilty should escape, rather than that one innocent man should suffer; because the guilt of running away from an "owner," is of too faint a color to be seen by some of the best eyes, whilst that of enslaving the free is of the darkest hue.

The Constitution provides that no man shall "be deprived of life, liberty, or property, without due process of law." A man delivered up as a slave is deprived of all property, all liberty, and placed in a condition where life and limb are held at another's pleasure. Does he enjoy the benefits of "a due process of law," when a common justice of peace, selected by the master, and receiving the master as a witness, passes sentence on him without jury and without appeal? . . .

. . . A trial by jury ought to be granted to the suspected fugitive, as being the most effectual provision for innocence known to our laws. It is said, that under such a process, the slave will not be restored to his master. Undoubtedly the jury is an imperfect tribunal, and may often fail of a wise and just administration of the laws. But, as we have seen, the first question to be asked is, How shall the free man be preserved from being sentenced to slavery? This is an infinitely greater evil than the escape of the fugitive; and to avert this, a trial by jury should be granted, unless some other process as safe and effectual can be devised. . . .

. . . Earnestly as I oppose slavery, I deprecate all interference with the slave within the jurisdiction of the Slaveholding States. I will plead his cause with whatever strength God has given me. But I can do no more. God forbid that I should work out his deliverance by force and blood.

These remarks are the more important, because there seem to be growing up among us looser ideas than formerly prevailed on the subject of inciting the slaves to vindicate their rights. The common language leads to error. We are told, and told truly, that the slave-holder has no property in the man whom he oppresses; that the slave has a right to immediate freedom; and the inference, which some make, is, that the slave is authorized to use, without regard to consequences, the means of emancipation. The next inference is, that he is to be urged and aided to break his chain. But these views are too sweeping, and need important modifications.

The slave has a right to liberty; but a right does not imply that it may be asserted by any and every means. There is a great law of humanity to which all are subject, the bond as well as the free, and which we must never lose sight of in redressing wrongs, or in claiming and insisting on our due. The slave cannot innocently adopt any and every expedient for vindicating his liberty. He is bound to waive his right, if in maintaining it he is to violate the law of humanity, and to spread general ruin. Were I confined unjustly to a house, I should have no right to free myself by setting it on fire, if thereby a family should be destroyed. An impressed seaman cannot innocently withhold his service in a storm, and would be bound to work even in ordinary weather, if this were needed to save the ship from foundering. We owe a debt of humanity even to him who wrongs us, and especially to those who are linked with him, and who must suffer, perhaps perish with him, if we seek to redress our wrong.

The slave is not property. He owes nothing as a slave to his master. On the contrary, the debt is on his master's side. But though owing nothing as a slave, he owes much as a man. He must not, for the sake of his own liberty, involve a household in destruction. He must not combine with fellow slaves, and expose a community of men, women, children, to brutal outrage and massacre. When the chain can only be broken by inhumanity, he has no right to break it. A higher duty than that of asserting personal rights is laid on him. He is bound by divine authority, by the Christian law, by enlightened conscience, to submit to his hard fate.

The slave's right to liberty then is a qualified one; qualified not in the slightest degree by any right of property in his master, but solely by the great law of humanity. He is a man under all the obligations of a member of the human family, and, therefore, bound at all times to unite a regard for others with a regard to himself. His master, indeed, denies his humanity, and treats him as a brute; and were he what his master deems him, he might innocently at any moment cut the throats of his master and master's wife and child. But his human nature, though trampled on, endures, and lays on him obligation to refrain from cruelty. From these views we learn that the right of the slave to free himself is not to be urged on him without reserve.

In these remarks I do not mean to say, that I should blame the slave for rising at any moment against his master. In so doing, he would incur no guilt; for in his ignorance he cannot comprehend why he should forbear. He would vindicate an undoubted right. His rude conscience would acquit him, and far be it from me to condemn. But we, who are more enlightened, who know the consequences of revolt, should beware of rousing that wild mass of degraded men to the assertion of their rights. Such consequences humanity commands us to respect. Were it not for these, I would summon that mass as loudly as any to escape. Could I by my words so awaken and guide the millions of slaves, that without violence and bloodshed they could reach safely a land of freedom and order, I would shout in thunder-tones, Fly, Fly! But it is not given us thus to act in human affairs. It is not given us to enter and revolutionize a state, to subvert old institutions and plant new, without carrying with us strife, tumult, bloodshed, horrible crimes. The law of humanity then restrains us from this direct agency on other states. It restrains us from abandoning ourselves to our zeal for the oppressed. It restrains us from kindling the passions of the slave. It commands us to teach him patience and love.

THEODORE PARKER WARNS OF THE DANGERS WHICH THREATEN THE RIGHTS OF MAN

Theodore Parker (1810–1860), the leading Unitarian clergyman of the 1850's, was not only a radical abolitionist but was particularly concerned with the natural rights argument. Preaching to his large Boston congregation in the middle 1850's, he examined the role of government in relation to the Higher Law and predicted that liberty would be destroyed if slavery was not. Parker's prediction of bloody vengeance in the South and his implicit appeal to action later bore fruit in his aid to John Brown in planning the Harper's Ferry raid.

II. The next hypothesis is, Freedom may triumph over Slavery.[1] That was the expectation once, at the time of the Declaration of Independence; nay, at the formation of the Constitution. But only two national steps have been taken against Slavery since then—one the Ordinance of 1787, the other the abolition of the African Slave-Trade; really that was done in 1788, formally twenty years after. In the individual States, the white man's freedom enlarges every year; but the Federal

---

From Theodore Parker, "A Sermon of the Dangers which Threaten the Rights of Man in America. Preached at the Music Hall, on Sunday, July 2, 1854," in *Additional Speeches, Addresses, and Occasional Sermons. In Two Volumes*, II (Boston: Horace B. Fuller, 1867), 266–271, 274–275, 283–293.

[1] The first hypothesis was that the United States might split into two nations, one free, the other slave—"a Despotism with the Idea of Slavery, [and] a Democracy with the Idea of Freedom." [Eds.]

Government becomes more and more addicted to Slavery. This hypothesis does not seem very likely to be adopted.

III. Shall Slavery destroy Freedom? It looks very much like it. Here are nine great steps, openly taken since '87, in favor of Slavery. First, America put Slavery into the Constitution. Second, out of old soil she made four new Slave States. Third, America, in 1793, adopted Slavery as a Federal institution, and guaranteed her protection for that kind of property as for no other. Fourth, America bought the Louisiana territory in 1803, and put Slavery into it. Fifth, she thence made Louisiana, Missouri, and then Arkansas Slave States. Sixth, she made Slavery perpetual in Florida. Seventh, she annexed Texas. Eighth, she fought the Mexican War, and plundered a feeble sister republic of California, Utah, and New Mexico, to get more Slave Soil. Ninth, America gave ten millions of money to Texas to support Slavery, passed the Fugitive Slave Bill, and has since kidnapped men in New England, New York, New Jersey, Pennsylvania, Ohio, Michigan, Wisconsin, Illinois, Indiana, in all the East, in all the West, in all the Middle States. All the great cities have kidnapped their own citizens. Professional Slave-hunters are members of New England Churches; kidnappers sit down at the Lord's table in the city of Cotton, Chauncey, and Mayhew. In this very year, before it is half through, America has taken two more steps for the destruction of freedom. The repeal of the Missouri Compromise and the enslavement of Nebraska: that is the tenth step. Here is the eleventh: The Mexican Treaty, giving away ten millions of dollars and buying a little strip of worthless land, solely that it may serve the cause of Slavery.

Here are eleven great steps openly taken towards the ruin of Liberty in America. Are these the worst? Very far from it! Yet more dangerous things have been done in secret.

I. Slavery has corrupted the Mercantile Class. Almost all the leading merchants of the North are Pro-Slavery men. They hate freedom, hate your freedom and mine! This is the only

Christian country in which commerce is hostile to freedom.

II. See the corruption of the Political Class. There are forty thousand officers of the Federal Government. Look at them in Boston,—their character is as well known as this Hall. Read their journals in this city,—do you catch a whisper of freedom in them? Slavery has sought its menial servants,—men basely born and basely bred: it has corrupted them still further, and put them in office. America, like Russia, is the country for mean men to thrive in. Give him time and mire enough, a worm can crawl as high as an eagle flies. State rights are sacrificed at the North; centralization goes on with rapid strides; State laws are trodden underfoot. The Northern President is all for Slavery. The Northern Members of the Cabinet are for Slavery; in the Senate, fourteen Northern Democrats were for the enslavement of Nebraska; in the House of Representatives, forty-four Northern Democrats voted for the bill,—fourteen in the Senate, forty-four in the House; fifty-eight Northern men voted against the conscience of the North and the Law of God. Only eight men out of all the South could be found friendly to justice and false to their own local idea of injustice. The present administration, with its supple tools of tyranny, came into office while the cry of "No Higher Law" was echoing through the land!

III. Slavery has debauched the Press. How many leading journals of commerce and politics in the great cities do you know that are friendly to Freedom and opposed to Slavery? Out of the five large daily commercial papers in Boston, Whig or Democratic, I know of only one that has spoken a word for freedom this great while. The American newspapers are poor defenders of American liberty. Listen to one of them, speaking of the last kidnapping in Boston: "We shall need to employ the same measures of coercion as are necessary in monarchical countries." There is always some one ready to do the basest deeds. Yet there are some noble journals—political and commercial; such as the New York Tribune and Evening Post.

IV. Then our Colleges and Schools are corrupted by Slavery. I do not know of five colleges in all the North which publicly appear on the side of freedom. What the hearts of the presidents and professors are, God knows, not I. The great crime against humanity, practical atheism, found ready support in Northern colleges, in 1850 and 1851. Once, the common reading books of our schools were full of noble words. Read the schoolbooks now made by Yankee peddlers of literature, and what liberal ideas do you find there? They are meant for the Southern market. Slavery must not be offended!

V. Slavery has corrupted the Churches! There are twenty-eight thousand Protestant clergymen in the United States. There are noble hearts, true and just men among them, who have fearlessly borne witness to the truth. I need not mention their names. Alas! they are not very numerous; I should not have to go over my fingers many times to count them all. I honor these exceptional men. Some of them are old, far older than I am; older than my father need have been; some of them are far younger than I; nay, some of them younger than my children might be:—and I honor these men for the fearless testimony which they have borne—the old, the middle-aged, and the young. But they are very exceptional men. Is there a minister in the South who preaches against Slavery? How few in all the North! . . .

. . . VI. Slavery corrupts the Judicial Class. In America, especially in New England, no class of men has been so much respected as the judges; and for this reason: we have had wise, learned, excellent men for our judges; men who reverenced the Higher Law of God, and sought by human statutes to execute Justice. You all know their venerable names, and how reverentially we have looked up to them. Many of them are dead; some are still living, and their hoary hairs are a crown of glory on a judicial life, without judicial blot. But of late Slavery has put a different class of men on the benches of the Federal Courts—mere tools of the government; creatures which get their appointment as pay for past political service, and as pay in advance for iniquity not yet accomplished. You see the consequences. Note the zeal of the Federal Judges to execute iniquity by statute and destroy Liberty. See how ready they are to support the Fugitive Slave Bill, which tramples on the spirit of the Constitution, and its letter too; which outrages Justice and violates the most sacred principles and precepts of Christianity. Not a United States Judge, Circuit or District, has uttered one word against that "bill of abominations." Nay, how greedy they are to get victims under it! No wolf loves better to rend a lamb into fragments than these judges to kidnap a Fugitive Slave, and punish any man who dares to speak against it. You know what has happened in Fugitive Slave Bill Courts. You remember the "miraculous" rescue of Shadrach: the peaceable snatching of a man from the hands of a cowardly kidnapper was "high treason;" it was "levying war." You remember the "trial" of the rescuers! Judge Sprague's charge to the Grand Jury that if they thought the question was which they ought to obey, the law of man or the Law of God, then they must "Obey both!" serve God and Mammon, Christ and the Devil, in the same act! You remember the "trial," the "ruling" of the Bench, the swearing on the stand, the witness coming back to alter and "enlarge his testimony" and have another gird at the prisoner! You have not forgotten the trials before Judge Kane at Philadelphia, and Judge Grier at Christiana and Wilkesbarre.[2]

These are natural results of causes well known. You cannot escape a Principle. Enslave a negro, will you?—you doom to bondage your own sons and daughters, by your own act. . . .

. . . Thus has Slavery debauched the Federal Courts.

VII. Alas me! Slavery has not ended yet its long career of

---

[2] The events referred to here were all well-known cases of the rescue of fugitives and the trial of the rescuers for violation of the Fugitive Slave Act of 1850. [Eds.]

sin. Its corruption is seven-fold. It debauches the elected officers of our City, and even our State. In the Sims time of 1851, the laws of Massachusetts were violated nine days running, and the Free Soil Governor sat in the State House as idle as a feather in his chair. In the wicked week of 1854, the Whig Governor sat in the seat of his predecessor; Massachusetts was one of the inferior counties of Virginia, and a Slave-hunter had eminent domain over the birthplace of Franklin and the burial-place of Hancock! Nay, against our own laws the Free Soil Mayor put the neck of Boston in the hands of a "train-band captain"—the people "wondering much to see how he did ride!" Boston was a suburb of Alexandria; the Mayor a a Slave-catcher for our masters at the South! You and I were only fellow Slaves![3]

All this looks as if Slavery was to triumph over Freedom. But even this is not the end. Slavery has privately emptied her seven vials of wrath upon the nation—committing seven debaucheries of human safeguards of our Natural Rights. That is not enough—there are other seven to come. This Apocalyptic Dragon, grown black with long-continued deeds of shame and death, now meditates five further steps of crime. Here is the programme of the next attempt—a new political Tragedy in five acts.

I.—The acquisition of Dominica—and then all Hayti—as new Slave Territory.

II.—The acquisition of Cuba, by purchase, or else by private fillibustering and public war,—as new Slave Territory.

III.—The reëstablishment of Slavery in all the Free States, by Judicial "decision" or legislative enactment. Then the Master of the North may "sit down with his Slaves at the foot of Bunker Hill Monument!"

IV.—The restoration of the African Slave-Trade, which is

---

[3] For the events referred to here, see the Introduction, pp. lxxix–lxxxi. [Eds.]

already seriously proposed and defended in the Southern Journals. Nay, the Senate Committee on Foreign Relations recommend the first steps towards it—the withdrawal of our fleet from the coast of Africa. You cannot escape the consequence of your first principle: if Slavery is right, then the Slave-trade is right; the traffic between Guinea and New Orleans is no worse than between Virginia and New Orleans; it is no worse to kidnap in Timbuctoo than in Boston.

V.—A yet further quarrel must be sought with Mexico, and more Slave Territory be stolen from her.

Who shall oppose this five-fold wickedness? The Fugitive Slave Bill Party;—the Nebraska Enslavement Party? Northern servility has hitherto been ready to grant more than Southern arrogance dared to demand!

All this looks as if the third hypothesis would be fulfilled, and Slavery triumph over Freedom; as if the nation would expunge the Declaration of Independence from the scroll of time, and instead of honoring Hancock and the Adamses and Washington, do homage to Kane and Grier and Curtis and Hallett and Loring.[4] Then the preamble to our Constitution might read—"to establish injustice, insure domestic strife, hinder the common defence, disturb the general welfare, and inflict the curse of bondage on ourselves and our posterity." Then we shall honor the Puritans no more, but their Prelatical tormentors; nor reverence the great Reformers, only the Inquisitors of Rome. Yea, we may tear the name of Jesus out of the American Bible; yes, God's name; worship the Devil at our Lord's table, Iscariot for Redeemer!

See the steady triumph of Despotism! Ten years more like the ten years past, and it will be all over with the liberties of America. Every thing must go down, and the heel of the tyrant will be on our neck. It will be all over with the Rights of Man

---

[4] Judges or Commissioners notorious for their actions in various fugitive rescue cases in upholding the enforcement of the Fugitive Slave Act against the antislavery people. [Eds.]

in America, and you and I must go to Austria, to Italy, or to Siberia for our freedom; or perish with the liberty which our fathers fought for and secured to themselves,—not to their faithless sons! Shall America thus miserably perish? Such is the aspect of things to-day! . . .

. . . Well, is this to be the end? Was it for this the Pilgrims came over the sea? Does Forefathers' Rock assent to it? Was it for this that the New England clergy prayed, and their prayers became the law of the land for a hundred years? Was it for this that Cotton planted in Boston a little branch of the Lord's vine, and Roger Williams and Higginson—he still lives in an undegenerate son—did the same in the city which they called of Peace, Salem? Was it for this that Eliot carried the Gospel to the Indians? that Chauncey, and Edwards, and Hopkins, and Mayhew, and Channing, and Ware labored and prayed? for this that our fathers fought—the Adamses, Washington, Hancock? for this that there was an eight years' war, and a thousand battle fields? for this the little monuments at Acton, Concord, Lexington, West Cambridge, Danvers, and the great one over there on the spot which our fathers' blood made so red? Shall America become Asia Minor? New England, Italy? Boston such as Athens—dead and rotten? Yes,! if we do not mend, and speedily mend. Ten years more, and the Liberty of America is all gone. We shall fall—the laugh, the byword, the proverb, the scorn, the mock of the nations, who shall cry against us. Hell from beneath shall be moved to meet us at our coming, and in derision shall it welcome us;—

"The Heir of all the ages, and the youngest born of time!"

We shall lie down with the unrepentant prodigals of old time, damned to everlasting infamy and shame.
Would you have it so? Shall it be?
To-day, America is a debauched young man, of good blood,

fortune, and family, but the companion of gamesters and brawlers; reeking with wine; wasting his substance in riotous living; in the lap of harlots squandering the life which his mother gave him. Shall he return? Shall he perish? One day may determine.

Shall America thus die? I look to the past,—Asia, Africa, Europe, and they answer, "Yes!" Where is the Hebrew Commonwealth; the Roman Republic; where is liberal Greece,—Athens, and many a far-famed Ionian town; where are the Commonwealths of Mediæval Italy; the Teutonic free cities—German, Dutch, or Swiss? They have all perished. Not one of them is left. Parian Statues of Liberty, sorely mutilated, still remain; but the Parian rock whence Liberty once hewed her sculptures out—it is all gone. Shall America thus perish? Greece and Italy both answer, "Yes!" I question the last fifty years of American history, and it says, "Yes." I look to the American pulpit, I ask the five million Sunday School scholars, and they say, "Yes." I ask the Federal Court, the Democratic Party, and the Whig, and the answer is still the same.

But I close my eyes on the eleven past missteps we have taken for Slavery; on that sevenfold clandestine corruption; I forget the Whig party; I forget the present Administration; I forget the Judges of the Courts;—I remember the few noblest men that there are in society, Church and State; I remember the grave of my father, the lessons of my mother's life; I look to the Spirit of this Age—it is the nineteenth century, not the ninth;—I look to the history of the Anglo-Saxons in America, and the history of Mankind; I remember the story and the song of Italian and German Patriots; I recall the dear words of those great-minded Greeks—Ionian, Dorian, Ætolian; I remember the Romans who spoke, and sang, and fought for truth and right; I recollect those old Hebrew Prophets, earth's nobler sons, Poets and Saints; I call to mind the greatest, noblest, purest soul that ever blossomed in this dusty world;—and I say, "No!" Truth shall triumph, Justice shall be law! And if America fail, though she is one fortieth of God's family, and it is a great loss, there are other nations behind us; our Truth shall not perish, even if we go down.

But we shall not fail! I look into your eyes—young men and women, thousands of you, and men and women far enough from young! I look into the eyes of fifty thousand other men and women, whom, in the last eight months, I have spoken to, face to face, and they say, "No! America shall not fail!"

I remember the women, who were never found faithless when a sacrifice was to be offered to great principles; I look up to my God, and I look into my own heart, and I say, We shall not fail! We shall not fail!

This, at my side, it is the willow;[5] it is the symbol of weeping:—but its leaves are deciduous; the autumn wind will strew them on the ground; and beneath, here is a perennial plant; it is green all the year through. When this willow branch is leafless, the other is green with hope, and its buds are in its bosom; its buds will blossom. So it is with America.

Did our fathers live? are we dead? Even in our ashes live their holy fires! Boston only sleeps; one day she will wake! Massachusetts will stir again! New England will rise and walk! the vanished North be found once more, queenly and majestic! Then it will be seen that Slavery is weak and powerless in itself, only a phantom of the night.

Slavery is a "Finality," is it? There shall be no "Agitation,"—not the least,—shall there? There is a Hispaniola in the South, and the South knows it. She sits on a powder magazine, and then plays with fire, while Humanity shoots rockets all round the world. To mutilate, to torture, to burn to death revolted Africans whom outrage has stung to crime—that is only to light the torches of San Domingo. This Black Bondage will be Red Freedom one day; nay, Lust, Vengeance, redder yet. I would not wait till that Flood comes and devours all.

---

[5] Referring to the floral ornaments that day on the desk.

When the North stands up, manfully, united, we can tear down Slavery in a single twelve-month; and when we do unite, it must be not only to destroy Slavery in the territories, but to uproot every weed of Slavery throughout this whole wide land. Then leanness will depart from our souls; then the blessing of God will come upon us; we shall have a Commonwealth based on righteousness, which is the strength of any people, and shall stand longer than Ægypt,—National Fidelity to God our age-outlasting Pyramid!

How feeble seems a single nation; how powerless a solitary man! But one of a family of forty, we can do much. How much is Italy, Rome, Greece, Palestine, Ægypt to the world? The solitary man—a Luther, a Paul, a Jesus—he outweighs millions of coward souls! Each one of you take heed that the Republic receive no harm!

IX

Argument from Civil Liberties

GERRIT SMITH DEFENDS FREE SPEECH AS A GOD-GIVEN RIGHT

One of the early responses to antislavery activity was mob violence. Meetings were disrupted, conventions broken up, speakers liberally showered with eggs and more lethal weaponry, and the participants as a whole generally terrified. Such tactics not infrequently boomeranged, as men incensed at the gross violations of the rights of free speech, of free assembly, and of civil liberties as a whole, found themselves therefore ranged alongside the abolitionists. When, in 1835, the New York antislavery convention at Utica was scattered by the mob, the wealthy upstate landowner, Gerrit Smith (1797–1874) still a staunch colonizationist, invited the convention to adjourn to his home at Peterboro. Thereafter he enlisted his talents, his wide contacts among philanthropists and reformers, and his sizable fortune in the antislavery crusade.

From Gerrit Smith, "Speech of Mr. Gerrit Smith," in New York Anti-Slavery Convention, *Proceedings of the . . . Convention, Held at Utica, October 21, and New York Anti-Slavery State Society, Held at Peterboro', October 22, 1835* (Utica: Standard & Democrat Office, 1835), pp. 20–22.

There is one class of men, whom it especially behooves to be tenacious of the right of free discussion. I mean the poor. The rich and the honorable, if divested of this right, have still their wealth and their honors to repose on, and to solace them. But, when the poor are stripped of this right, they are poor indeed. . . . Let the poor man count as his enemy, and his worst enemy, every invader of the right of free discussion.

We are threatened with legislative restraints on this right. Let us tell our legislators in advance, that this is a right, restraints on which, we will not, cannot bear; and that every attempt to restrain it is a palpable wrong on God and man. Submitting to these restraints, we could not be what God made us to be; we could not perform the service, to which He has appointed us; we could not be *men*. Laws to gag a man—to congeal the gushing fountains of his heart's sympathy—and to shrivel up his soul by extinguishing its ardor and generosity— are laws not to assist him in carrying out God's high and holy purposes in calling him into being; but they are laws to throw him a passive, mindless, worthless being at the feet of despotism.

And to what end is it that we are called on to hold our tongues, and throw down our pens, and give up our influence? Were it for a good object, and could we conceive that such a sacrifice would promote it, there would be a color of fitness in asking us to do so. But, this is a sacrifice, which righteousness and humanity never invoke. Truth and mercy require the *exertion*—never the *suppression*, of man's noble rights and powers. We are called on to degrade and unman ourselves, and to withhold from others that influence, which we are bound to exert upon them, to the end that the victim of oppression may lie more quietly beneath the foot of his oppressor; to the end, that one sixth of our countrymen, plundered of their dearest rights—of their bodies, and minds, and souls—may never know of those rights; to the end, that TWO MILLIONS AND A HALF of our fellow men, crushed in the iron folds of slavery, may remain in all their suffering and debasement and despair. It is for such an object—an object so wicked and inexpressibly mean—that we are called on to lie down beneath the slaveholders' blustering and menace, like whipped and trembling spaniels. We reply, that our Republican spirit cannot thus succumb; and, what is infinitely more, that God did not make us—that Jesus did not redeem us, for such sinful and vile uses.

We knew before, that slavery could not endure, could not survive free discussion; that the minds of men could not remain firm and their consciences quiet under the continued appeals of truth, and justice, and mercy: but the demand, which slaveholders now make on us to surrender the right of free discussion, together with their avowed reasons for this demand, involves their own full concession, that free discussion is incompatible with slavery. The South now admits by her own showing, that slavery cannot live, unless the North be tongue-tied. But we have two objections to being thus tongue-tied. One is, that we desire and purpose to exert all our powers and influence—lawfully, temperately, kindly—to persuade the slaveholders of the south to deliver our colored brethren from their bonds; nor shall we give rest to our lips or pens, until this righteous object is accomplished: and the other is, that we are not willing to be slaves ourselves. The enormous and insolent demands of the South, sustained, I am deeply ashamed to say, by craven and mercenary spirits at the North, manifest, beyond all dispute, that the question now is, not merely, nor mainly, whether the blacks at the south shall remain slaves—but whether the whites at the North shall become slaves also. And thus, whilst we are endeavoring to break the yokes, which are on other's necks, we are to see to it, that yokes are not imposed on our own.

Is it said that the South will not molest our freedom, if we will not disturb their slavery—if we will not insist on the liberty to speak and write about this abomination? Our reply is, that God gave us the freedom for which we contend—that it is not a freedom bestowed by man;—not an *ex gratia* freedom, which we have received at the hands of the South;—not a freedom, which stands, on the one hand, in the surrender of our dearest rights, and, on the other, in the conceded perpetuity of the body and mind and soul-crushing system of American slavery. We ask not, we accept not, we scornfully reject, the conditional and worthless freedom, which the South proffers us.

It is not to be disguised, that a war has broken out between the North and the South. Political and commercial men are industriously striving to restore peace: but the peace which they would effect, is superficial, false, and temporary. True, permanent peace can never be restored, until slavery, the occasion of the war, has ceased. The sword, which is now drawn, will never be returned to its scabbard, until victory, entire, decisive victory is ours or theirs; not, until that broad and deep and damning stain on our country's escutcheon is clean washed out—that plague spot on our country's honor gone forever; or, until slavery has riveted anew her present chains, and brought our heads also to bow beneath her withering power. It is idle—it is criminal, to hope for the restoration of peace, on any other condition.

JOHN QUINCY ADAMS DEFENDS THE RIGHT OF PETITION

As part of the campaign to end slavery in the District of Columbia and elsewhere petitions poured in on Congress. The response in the House of Representatives was the "Gag Rule" (1836), which provided for the tabling of all petitions on the subject of slavery. Here, in the minds of many who had not yet espoused the cause of abolition, was a further erosion of civil liberties in an effort to restrain an unpopular minority. John Quincy Adams (1767–1848), former President and later a Representative from Massachusetts, who refused to endorse the program of the abolitionists, made himself their hero and Congressional leader by his extended campaign on the floor of the House to repeal the "Gag Rule." Once again civil liberties had become inextricably entangled with antislavery.

I beg leave to explain my views of the argument on the right of petition. One of my colleagues (Mr. Cushing)[1] has justly said, that the right of petition is not a right derived from the the Constitution, but a preëxisting right of man, secured by a direct prohibition in the Constitution to Congress to pass any law to impair or abridge it. Sir, the framers of the Constitution would have repudiated the idea that they were giving to the people the right of petition. No, sir. That right God gave to the whole human race, when he made them *men*,—the right of prayer, by asking a favor of another. My doctrine is, that this right belongs to humanity,—that the right of petition is the right of prayer, not depending on the condition of the petitioner; and I say, if you attempt to fix any limit to it, you lay the foundation for restriction to any extent that the madness of party spirit may carry it. This is my belief, and if the House

---

From John Quincy Adams, *Letters of John Quincy Adams to his Constituents of the Twelfth Congressional District in Massachusetts to which is added his Speech in Congress delivered February 9, 1837* (Boston: Isaac Knapp, 1837), pp. 48–51, 56–57, 62–63.

[1] Caleb Cushing (1800–1879), Representative from Massachusetts, 1835–1843. Whig and later a Democrat, Cushing was also active in the diplomatic service and in Massachusetts politics. He had been a source of intellectual stimulation to the young Garrison, although the two had a later falling out. Antislavery in his personal views, Cushing was not an active participant in the antislavery crusade. [Eds.]

decide that the paper I have described comes within the resolution, I will present it, and, in so doing, shall feel that I am performing a solemn duty.

What, sir! place the right of petition on the character and condition of the petitioner, or base it upon a mere political privilege! Such a decision would present this country to all the civilized world as more despotic than the worst of barbarian nations. The sultan of Turkey cannot walk the streets of Constantinople and refuse to receive a petition from the vilest slave, who stands to meet him as he passes by. The right of petition contests no power; it admits the power. It is supplication; it is prayer; it is the cry of distress, asking for relief; and, sir, sad will be the day when it is entered on the Journals of this House, that we will, under no circumstances, receive the petition of slaves. When you begin to limit the right, where shall it stop? The gentleman on my left (Mr. Patton, of Virginia)[2] objected to another petition, which I did present, from women of Fredericksburg, because it came from free colored people. That was giving *color to an idea* with a vengeance![3] But the gentleman went further, and made the objection that I had presented a petition from women of infamous character —prostitutes, I think he called them.

[Mr. FULTON[4] rose to explain. It was not so. When the gentleman presented that petition, which I knew came from mulattoes in a slave state, I meant to confine my objection to petitions of mulattoes or free negroes in the Southern States.

---

[2] John Mercer Patton (1796–1858), Representative from Virginia (1830–1839). Democrat. [Eds.]

[3] One of the resolutions proposed to censure Mr. Adams for having attempted to *give color to the idea* that slaves had a right to petition!

[4] This is undoubtedly a misprint for Mr. Patton. There was no Fulton in the House at this time. A John H. Fulton of Virginia had served in the prior Congress. The brackets which occur throughout this excerpt appear in the original. [Eds.]

I meant to rescue the ladies of Fredericksburg from the stigma of having signed such a petition. Sir, no lady in Fredericksburg would sign such a petition.]

Mr. ADAMS. With respect to the question what female is entitled to the character of a lady, and what not, I should be sorry to enter into a discussion here. I have never made it a condition of my presenting a petition here, from females, that they should all be ladies, though, sir, I have presented petitions for the abolition of slavery in this District, from ladies as eminently entitled to be called such, as the highest aristocrats in the land. When I have presented these petitions, I have usually said they were from *women,* and that, to my heart, is a dearer appellation than *ladies.*

But, sir, I recur to my first position—that when you establish the doctrine that a slave shall not petition because he is a slave, that he shall not be permitted to raise the cry for mercy, you let in a principle subversive of every foundation of liberty, and you cannot tell where it will stop. The next step will be that the character, and not the claims, of petitioners will be the matter to be discussed on this floor; and whenever, as in the case of the gentleman from Virginia, (Mr. Patton,) any member finds a name on a petition which belongs to a person whom he says he knows to be of bad character, a motion will be made not to receive the petition, or to return it to the member who offered it. The gentleman from Virginia (Mr. Patton) says he knows these women, and that they are infamous. *How* does the gentleman know it? [A laugh.]

[Mr. PATTON. I did not say that I knew the women, personally. I knew from others that the character of one of them was notoriously bad.]

Mr. ADAMS. I am glad the gentleman now says he does not know these women, for if he had not disclaimed that knowledge, I might have asked *who* it was that made these women infamous,—whether it was those of their own color or their masters. I have understood that there are those among the colored population of slaveholding states, who bear the image of their masters. [Great sensation.]

Mr. GLASCOCK,[5] of Georgia, here went across the hall to the seat of Mr. Adams, and, amidst cries of "Order," held up to him the petition of the women of Fredericksburg, and said, "Is not that your hand-writing, endorsed 'From ladies of Fredericksburg'?"

Mr. ADAMS. Mr. Speaker, I did not designate them as ladies when I presented the petition. That is my handwriting; but when I endorsed it, and sent it to the table, I did not know or suspect that the petitioners were colored people.

Here, then, is another limitation to the right of petition. First, it is denied to slaves, then to free persons of color, and then to persons of notoriously bad character. Now, sir, if you begin by limiting this right as to slaves, you next limit it as to all persons of color, and then you go into inquiries as to the character of petitioners before you will receive petitions. There is but one step more, and that is to inquire into the political faith of petitioners. Each side will represent their opponents as being infamous; and what becomes of the right of petition? Where and how will the right of petition exist at all, if you put it on these grounds?

A gentleman from Virginia, (Mr. Robertson,)[6] to whose candor and generosity on this occasion I offer my tribute of thanks, as it contrasts with the treatment I experience from others,—though disapproving, in the strongest terms, the pertinacity of zeal which I have so often manifested in behalf of this right of petition,—is unwilling to pass a vote of formal censure upon me, because he sees how manifestly incompatible that would be with *any* freedom of speech in this House. He

---

[5] Thomas Glascock (?–1841), Representative from Georgia, 1835–1839. Democrat. [Eds.]

[6] John Robertson (1787–1873), Representative from Virginia, 1834–1839. Whig. [Eds.]

says—and he is a distinguished lawyer—that there can be no right to petition, where there is no power to grant the prayer. This is ingenious and plausible; but that gentleman, even whose disapprobation is more painful to me than would be the formal censure of others, might excuse me, if I cannot assent to the correctness of his argument. The want of power to grant the prayer of a petition is a very sufficient reason for rejecting that prayer, but it cannot impair the right of the petitioner to pray.

The question of power applies to the authority to grant the petition, but not to the right of the petitioner to present his petition. The power to grant it is often one of the most mooted questions in the world. In relation to this very matter of slavery, the power to grant the prayer of those who ask for its abolition in the District of Columbia, is the question that divides this House. Ask the gentlemen from slaveholding states, in this House, whether Congress has that power. Not one of them will say they have. . . .

. . . There, sir, stands the sentiment—there is the printed language, in which the gentleman[7] threatened me with indictment by a grand jury of the District, as a felon and an incendiary, *for words spoken in this House!* The gentleman has again avowed it, and declares that, if the petition had been for abolition, and I had presented it, he would not only have brought me to the bar to be censured by this House, or have voted to expel me, but he would have invoked upon my head the vengeance of the grand jury of this District! Yes, sir, he would make a member of this House, for words spoken in this House, amenable to the grand and petit juries of the District of Columbia! Sir, the only answer I make to such a threat from that

---

[7] Waddy Thompson (1798–1868), Representative from South Carolina, 1835–1841. He had earlier remarked, during this debate over a petition from slaves, that he thought it "an incendiary act, the presenting of such a petition; and any person. . . is amenable to the laws, who will present a petition from slaves for the abolition of slavery." (p. 56) [Eds.]

gentleman, is to invite him, when he returns home to his constituents, to *study a little the first principles of civil liberty!* That gentleman appears here the representative of slaveholders; and I should like to be informed, how many there are of such representatives on this floor, who endorse that sentiment. ["I do not," exclaimed Mr. UNDERWOOD,[8] of Kentucky. "I do not," was heard from several other voices.] Is it to be tolerated, that, for any thing a member says on this floor, though it were blasphemy or treason, he is to be held accountable and punished by a grand and petit jury of the District, and not by this House? If that is the doctrine of the slaveholding representatives on this floor, let it, in God's name, go forth, and let us see what the people of this nation think of such a sentiment, and of those who make such an avowal. . . .

. . . And this brings me to the resolutions before the House.[9] I object to the first resolution (offered by Mr. Patton, of Virginia) because it does not meet and answer my question. Let the question be put by yeas and nays, and I am willing to record my *yea* that it is the duty of the House to receive petitions from slaves; and I shall regard it as of high import to free institutions, if, on full deliberation, the House *refuse* to say

---

[8] Joseph Rogers Underwood (1791–1876), Representative from Kentucky, 1835–1843. Whig. [Eds.]

[9] The resolutions were as follows:—

"*Resolved*, That the right of petition does not belong to slaves of this Union; that no petition from them can be presented to this House, without derogating from the rights of the slaveholding states, and endangering the integrity of the Union.

"*Resolved*, That every member, who shall hereafter present any such petitions to this House, ought to be considered as regardless of the feelings of this House, the rights of the South, and as enemy to the Union.

"*Resolved*, That, the Hon. John Quincy Adams having solemnly disclaimed a design of doing any thing disrespectful to the House, in the inquiry he made of the Speaker, as to the right of petition purporting to be from slaves, and having avowed his intention not to offer to present the petition, if the House was of opinion that it ought not to be presented,—therefore all further proceedings as to his conduct now cease."

that they will receive petitions from slaves. The resolution does not say whether they will or not. That question, and the only question really before the House, is not met. We do not know whether it is proper or not to present such petitions. But suppose it is *not* proper. Can there be any offence, before the House have settled or considered that question, for a member respectfully to ask whether it be proper? Now, sir, this question is not met, and that is my objection to the first resolution.

The second resolution touches neither my question nor me, but pounces on an ideal man. It says, "Every member who shall *hereafter* present such petition ought to be considered an enemy to the Union," &c. What is that, sir, but the same threat, indirectly made, which the member from South Carolina (Mr. Waddy Thompson) directly made, of sending the man who should present such a petition, to the grand jury of the District of Columbia? This resolution declares that the member who shall hereafter make an attempt to present any such petition, shall be held *infamous.* Is this another maxim of the slaveholding representatives, touching the freedom of speech in this House? Sir, if that resolution passes, I will submit to it so far as not to present any petitions of slaves, but I shall consider it as a resolution most disgraceful and dishonorable to this House. What, sir! is any member of this House to be pronounced infamous for offering to aid human misery so far as to present its cry for mercy and relief to this House?

But, sir, not only would such a resolution dishonor this body in the eyes of the whole civilized world, it would also limit the rights and the liberties of members of this House, so as, in fact, to surrender them all. If, sir, you can get a vote to pronounce a member infamous who shall hereafter present a petition from slaves, you have but one step further to take, and that will be easy in the rage of the spirit of party; you will declare that every man shall be held infamous if he proposes any thing displeasing to the majority.

EDWARD BEECHER EXAMINES THE ALTON AFFAIR

The confiscation of antislavery tracts by the Post Office and the destruction of the antislavery presses of James G. Birney in Cincinnati (1836) and of Elijah Lovejoy in Alton, Illinois (1837) —in the latter case Lovejoy lost his third press to the mobs and his life as well—roused those who feared for freedom of the press. Edward Beecher (1803–1895), President of Illinois College, was incensed by the occurrences at Alton. Subsequently he helped found the first Illinois antislavery society. The selection which follows is from his account of the Alton Affair.

Resolved,[1] 1. That the free communication of thoughts and opinions is one of the invaluable rights of man; and that every citizen may freely speak, write and print on any subject, being responsible for, the abuse of that liberty.

2. That the abuse of this right is the only legal ground for restraining its use.

From Edward Beecher, *Narrative of Riots at Alton: In Connection with the Death of Rev. Elijah P. Lovejoy* (Alton: George Holton, 1838), pp. 53–54, 74–78.

[1] Beecher had drawn up a series of resolutions, stemming out of public hostility to Lovejoy, and presented them as here given to a citizens' committee. The committee studied them and then, in its report, rejected them. What follows the resolutions in this excerpt is Beecher's commentary on the resolutions and on the committee's position. [Eds.]

3. That the question of abuse must be decided solely by a regular civil court, and in accordance with the law, and not by an irresponsible and unorganized portion of the community, be it great or small.

4. For restraining what the law will not reach, we are to depend solely on argument and moral means, aided by the controlling influences of the Spirit of God; and that these means, appropriately used, furnish an ample defense against all ultimate prevalence of false principles and unhealthy excitement.

5. That when discussion is free and unrestrained, and proper means are used, the triumph of truth is certain—and that with the triumph of truth, the return of peace is sure; but that all attempts to check or prohibit discussion, will cause a daily increase of excitement until such checks or prohibitions are removed.

6. That our maintenance of these principles should be independent of all regard to persons or sentiments.

7. That we are more especially called on to maintain them in case of unpopular sentiments or persons, as in no other case will any effort to maintain them be needed.

8. That these principles demand the protection of the editor and of the press of the Alton Observer, on grounds of principle solely, and altogether disconnected with approbation of his sentiments, personal character or course as editor of the paper.

9. That on these grounds alone, and irrespective of all political, moral, or religious differences, but solely as American citizens, from a sacred regard to the great principles of civil society, to the welfare of our country, to the reputation and honor of our city, to our own dearest rights and privileges, and those of our children, we will protect the press, the property and the editor of the Alton Observer, and maintain him in the free exercise of his rights, to print and publish whatever he pleases, in obedience to the supreme laws of the land, and under the guidance and directions of the constituted civil au-

thorities, he being responsible for the abuse of this liberty only to the laws of the land. . . .

. . . The great object of [these] resolutions . . . was, to secure the defense of a citizen in the exercise of his inalienable rights against the violence of a mob. "As a whole" they consisted of two parts: a statement of principles; and a resolution to act according to them. To these it seems the committee gave a "deliberate and candid examination;" and what is the result? They approve their general spirit, but do not consider them as a whole suited to the exigency which had called them together. "The justice of the principles of the first three resolutions they fully and freely recognize;" of course the only thing to which they object is, the rest of the resolutions—designed to put them in practice.

The committee then admit that Mr. Lovejoy has the right to print what he pleases; and to be deprived of this right only for abusing it; and that the question of abuse is to be settled by law, and not by a mob. They fully and freely recognize the justice of these principles. Then why not recommend that they be enforced? Why not speak out in tones of manly indignation, and rebuke the violators of law, and call on all who love their country to rally to its defense? If the first three resolutions are true, why are not the last six suited to the exigency? Are they false? Do the committee mean to say that, in opposing erroneous views, such as the law will not reach, we are *not* to depend solely on argument and moral means aided by the Spirit of God? and that these means are *not* an ample defense against error and excitement? Do they hold that, in addition to these, mobs are sometimes needed? Do they believe that when discussion is free and proper means are used the triumph of the truth is *not* certain? and that the triumph of the truth will *not* produce peace? And do they mean to say that all attempts to check discussion will *not* produce excitement? And do they mean to advocate and justify the suppression of discussion by force? Do they believe that we ought not to maintain these principles without respect to parties or persons? Do they mean that the right of speech is to be protected only in the case of popular opinions, where it needs no protection, and to be left defenseless in case of unpopular opinions, where protection is needed? Did they mean to say to the citizens of Alton, You are under no obligation to defend Mr. Lovejoy or his paper on the ground of principle, and that a sacred regard to the principles of society do not require it? Are the committee willing before the civilized world to avow sentiments like these? If not: if the resolutions are true, why not recommend them?

But we are told they are not adapted to the emergency which had called them together. And what is this emergency? A mob had attempted to silence a press, and expel an editor from Alton. The resolutions recommended that this attempt should be resisted and the liberty of the press maintained; and gave reasons for so doing. Now, why are not these resolutions adapted to the emergency? Is it possible that the committee did not see what must be the influence of such a report on the mob? We approve of the principles of the laws, but a resolution to maintain them is not adapted to the present crisis! Is it possible that they did not see that if they had proposed a resolution to violate them, its influence could not have been more deadly?

The reasons assigned for refusing to recommend the resolutions are truly surprising. They are in brief that two parties were now organizing for a conflict, which may terminate in a train of mournful consequences unless some compromise is made.

It is indeed true that two parties did exist as it regards the truth or falsehood of the opinions of the abolitionists; and as it regards the expediency of forming a state society; and as it regards the time and mode of carrying on the discussions. But on these points the abolitionists had never refused to compromise. They had offered to do all in their power to unite good men and avert division; and all their efforts had been vain; and a plan was adopted to vote down all discussion. It was not *moderate* discussion which their opponents demanded, but *no* discussion. Not that Mr. Lovejoy should print his opinions moderately but that he should not print them at all.

Now, at the moment this claim was made, it ceased to be a party question. It assumed a new ground and changed its nature entirely. It was now the question, Shall a citizen, guilty of no crime and without judicial process, be stripped of all his rights? And whoever undertakes to do this is no longer a party but a mob. And this was the precise attitude of affairs at this time. It was not a question between abolitionists and anti-abolitionists; but between the friends of law and a mob; and are these the parties intended by the committee?

The committee further say that excitements between these parties have led to excesses *on both sides,* deeply to be deplored. Is it so? Of the mob the assertion is true. But what had the friends of law and order done? Nothing but strive to sustain the law. And is this an excess deeply to be deplored?

Again, they say, too much crimination and recrimination have been indulged: and specify charges mutually made by the parties. That the abolitionists have thus been charged is true. I heard these and numerous other false charges publicly made against them in Alton. But abolitionists did not render railing for railing. Nothing of the kind specified was said or hinted at in the convention. Nor did Mr. Lovejoy or his friends ever load their opponents with opprobrious epithets, as pirates, manstealers, &c. Indeed he was always very cautious not to use such language: and so far as I know, all the proceedings of the abolitionists at Alton were, at all times, gentlemanly and decorous.

The simple fact is, and no sophistry can hide it, that Mr. Lovejoy's rights, and those of all his subscribers had been assailed by a mob: and nothing was needed to restore quiet but that the mob should let them alone. But the mob would not; and for this reason the friends of law armed themselves to repel illegal violence.

COLORED MEN OF AMERICA DEMAND EQUAL RIGHTS AS AMERICANS

Increasingly in the 1850's, the free Negroes of the North met in conventions and concerned themselves about the civil liberties and civil rights denied their fellow Negroes. Their unequal treatment as citizens was reflected in discriminatory restrictions in regard to voting, schools, treatment in court, as well as in those restrictions on civil liberties from which abolitionists generally suffered. In 1853 the Colored National Convention, addressing the people of the United States, asserted their demand for full and equal citizenship.

As an apology for addressing you, fellow-citizens! we cannot announce the discovery of any new principle adapted to ameliorate the condition of mankind. The great truths of moral and political science, upon which we rely and which we press upon your consideration, have been evolved and ennunciated by you. We point to your principles, your wisdom, and to your great example as the full justification of our course this day. That "ALL MEN ARE CREATED EQUAL: that "LIFE, LIBERTY, AND THE PURSUIT OF HAPPINESS" ARE THE RIGHT OF ALL; that "TAXATION AND REPRESENTATION" SHOULD GO TOGETHER; that GOVERNMENTS ARE TO PROTECT, NOT TO DESTROY, THE RIGHTS OF MANKIND; that THE CONSTITUTION OF THE UNITED STATES WAS FORMED TO ESTABLISH JUSTICE, PROMOTE THE GENERAL WELFARE, AND SECURE THE BLESSING OF LIBERTY TO ALL THE PEOPLE OF

From Colored [Men of America], *Proceedings of the Colored National Convention, Held in Rochester, July 6th, 7th and 8th, 1853* (Rochester: Frederick Douglass, 1853), pp. 8–10, 16–18.

THIS COUNTRY; that RESISTANCE TO TYRANTS IS OBEDIENCE TO GOD—are American principles and maxims, and together they form and constitute the constructive elements of the American government. From this elevated platform, provided by the Republic for us, and for all the children of men, we address you. In doing so, we would have our spirit properly discerned. On this point we would gladly free ourselves and our cause from all misconception. We shall affect no especial timidity, nor can we pretend to any great boldness. We know our poverty and weakness, and your wealth and greatness. Yet we will not attempt to repress the spirit of liberty within us, or to conceal, in any wise, our sense of the justice and the dignity of our cause.

We are Americans, and as Americans, we would speak to Americans. We address you not as aliens nor as exiles, humbly asking to be permitted to dwell among you in peace; but we address you as American citizens asserting their rights on their own native soil. Neither do we address you as enemies, (although the recipients of innumerable wrongs;) but in the spirit of patriotic good will. In assembling together as we have done, our object is not to excite pity for ourselves, but to command respect for our cause, and to obtain justice for our people. We are not malefactors imploring mercy; but we trust we are honest men, honestly appealing for righteous judgment, and ready to stand or fall by that judgment. We do not solicit unusual favor, but will be content with roughhanded "fair play." We are neither lame or blind, that we should seek to throw off the responsibility of our own existence, or to cast ourselves upon public charity for support. We would not lay our burdens upon other men's shoulders; but we do ask, in the name of all that is just and magnanimous among men, to be freed from all the unnatural burdens and impediments with which American customs and American legislation have hindered our progress and improvement. We ask to be disencumbered of the load of popular reproach heaped upon us—for no better cause than that we wear the complexion given us by our God and our Creator.

We ask that in our native land, we shall not be treated as strangers, and worse than strangers.

We ask that, being friends of America, we should not be treated as enemies of America.

We ask that, speaking the same language and being of the same religion, worshipping the same God, owing our redemption to the same Savior, and learning our duties from the same Bible, we shall not be treated as barbarians.

We ask that, having the same physical, moral, mental, and spiritual wants, common to other members of the human family, we shall also have the same means which are granted and secured to others, to supply those wants.

We ask that the doors of the school-house, the work-shop, the church, the college, shall be thrown open as freely to our children as to the children of other members of the community.

We ask that the American government shall be so administered as that beneath the broad shield of the Constitution, the colored American seaman, shall be secure in his life, liberty and property, in every State in the Union.

We ask that as justice knows no rich, no poor, no black, no white, but, like the government of God, renders alike to every man reward or punishment, according as his works shall be—the white and black man may stand upon an equal footing before the laws of the land.

We ask that (since the right of trial by jury is a safeguard to liberty, against the encroachments of power, only as it is a trial by impartial men, drawn indiscriminately from the country) colored men shall not, in every instance, be tried by white persons; and that colored men shall not be either by custom or enactment excluded from the jury-box.

We ask that (inasmuch as we are, in common with other American citizens, supporters of the State, subject to its laws, interested in its welfare liable to be called upon to defend it in time of war, contributors to its wealth in time of peace) the complete and unrestricted right of suffrage, which is essential to the dignity even of the white man, be extended to the Free Colored man also.

Whereas the colored people of the United States have too long been retarded and impeded in the development and improvement of their natural faculties and powers, ever to become dangerous rivals to white men, in the honorable pursuits of life, liberty and happiness; and whereas, the proud Anglo-Saxon can need no arbitrary protection from open and equal competition with any variety of the human family; and whereas, laws have been en[a]cted limiting the aspirations of colored men, as against white men—we respectfully submit that such laws are flagrantly unjust to the man of color, and plainly discreditable to white men; and for these and other reasons, such laws ought to be repealed.

We especially urge that all laws and usages which preclude the enrollment of colored men in the militia, and prohibit their bearing arms in the navy, disallow their rising, agreeable to their merits and attainments—are unconstitutional—the constitution knowing no color—are anti-Democratic, since Democracy respects men as equals—are unmagnanimous, since such laws are made by the many, against the few, and by the strong against the weak.

We ask that all those cruel and oppressive laws, whether enacted at the South or the North, which aim at the expatriation of the free people of color, shall be stamped with national reprobation, denounced as contrary to the humanity of the American people, and as an outrage upon the Christianity and civilization of the nineteenth century.

We ask that the right of pre-emption, enjoyed by all white settlers upon the public lands, shall also be enjoyed by colored settlers; and that the word *"white"* be struck from the pre-emption act. We ask that no appropriations whatever, state or national, shall be granted to the colonization scheme; and we would have our right to leave or to remain in the United States placed above legislative interference.

We ask that the Fugitive Slave Law of 1850, that legislative monster of modern times, by whose atrocious provisions the writ of *"habeas corpus,"* the "right of trial by jury," have been virtually abolished, shall be repealed.

We ask, that the law of 1793 be so construed as to apply only to apprentices, and others really owing service or labor; and not to slaves, who can *owe* nothing. Finally, we ask that slavery in the United States shall be immediately, unconditionally, and forever abolished.

To accomplish these just and reasonable ends, we solemnly pledge ourselves to God, to each other, to our country, and to the world, to use all and every means consistent with the just rights of our fellow men, and with the precepts of Christianity.

We shall speak, write and publish, organize and combine to accomplish them.

We shall invoke the aid of the pulpit and the press to gain them.

We shall appeal to the church and to the government to gain them.

We shall vote, and expend our money to gain them.

We shall send eloquent men of our own condition to plead our cause before the people.

We shall invite the co-operation of good men in this country and throughout the world—and above all, we shall look to God, the Father and Creator of all men, for wisdom to direct us and strength to support us in the holy cause to which we this day solemnly pledge ourselves. . . .

. . . Fellow-citizens, we have had, and still have, great wrongs of which to complain. A heavy and cruel hand has been laid upon us.

As a people, we feel ourselves to be not only deeply injured, but grossly misunderstood. Our white fellow-countrymen do not know us. They are strangers to our character, ignorant of our capacity, oblivious of our history and progress, and are misinformed as to the principles and ideas that control and guide us as a people. The great mass of American citizens estimate us as being a characterless and purposeless people; and hence we hold up our heads, if at all, against the withering influence of a nation's scorn and contempt.

It will not be su[r]prising that we are so misunderstood and misused when the motives for misrepresenting us and for degrading us are duly considered. Indeed, it will seem strange, upon such consideration, (and in view of the ten thousand channels through which malign feelings find utterance and influence,) that we have not even fallen lower in public estimation than we have done. For, with the single exception of the Jews, under the whole heavens, there is not to be found a people pursued with a more relentless prejudice and persecution, than are the Free Colored people of the United States.

Without pretending to have exerted ourselves as we ought, in view of an intelligent understanding of our interest, to avert from us the unfavorable opinions and unfriendly action of the American people, we feel that the imputations cast upon us, for our want of intelligence, morality and exalted character, may be mainly accounted for by the injustice we have received at your hands. What stone has been left unturned to degrade us? What hand has refused to fan the flame of popular prejudice against us? What American artist has not caricatured us? What wit has not laughed at us in our wretchedness? What songster has not made merry over our depressed spirits? What press has not ridiculed and contemned us? What pulpit has withheld from our devoted heads its angry lightning, or its sanctimonious hate? Few, few, very few; and that we have borne up with it all—that we have tried to be wise, though denounced by all to be fools—that we have tried to be upright, when all around us have esteemed us as knaves—that we have striven to be gentlemen, although all around us have been teaching us its impossibility—that we have remained here, when all our neighbors have advised us to leave, proves that we possess qualities of head and heart, such as cannot but be commended by impartial men. It is believed that no other nation on the globe could have made more progress in the midst of such an universal and stringent disparagement. It would humble the proudest, crush the energies of the strongest, and retard the progress of the swiftest. In view of our circumstances, we can, without boasting, thank God, and take courage, having placed ourselves where we may fairly challenge comparison with more highly favored men.

Among the colored people, we can point, with pride and hope, to men of education and refinement, who have become such, despite of the most unfavorable influences; we can point to mechanics, farmers, merchants, teachers, ministers, doctors, lawyers, editors, and authors, against whose progress the concentrated energies of American prejudice have proved quite unavailing.—Now, what is the motive for ignoring and discouraging our improvement in this country? The answer is ready. The intelligent and upright free man of color is an unanswerable argument in favor of liberty, and a killing condemnation of American slavery. It is easily seen that, in proportion to the progress of the free man of color, in knowledge, temperance, industry, and righteousness, in just that proportion will he endanger the stability of slavery; hence, all the powers of slavery are exerted to prevent the elevation of the free people of color.

The force of fifteen hundred million dollars is arrayed against us; hence, the *press*, the pulpit, and the platform, against all the natural promptings of uncontaminated manhood, point their deadly missiles of ridicule, scorn and contempt at us; and bid us, on pain of being pierced through and through, to remain in our degradation.

Let the same amount of money be employed against the interest of any other class of persons, however favored by nature they may be, the result could scarcely be different from that seen in our own case. Such a people would be regarded with aversion; the money-ruled multitude would heap contumely upon them, and money-ruled institutions would proscribe them. Besides this money consideration, fellow-citizens, an explanation of the erroneous opinions prevalent concerning us is furnished in the fact, less creditable to human nature, that men are apt to hate most those whom they have injured most.—Having despised us, it is not strange that Americans should seek to render us despicable; having enslaved us, it is natural that they should strive to prove us unfit for freedom; having denounced us as indolent, it is not strange that they should cripple our enterprise; having assumed our inferiority, it would be extraordinary if they sought to surround us with circumstances which would serve to make us direct contradictions to their assumption.

In conclusion, fellow-citizens, while conscious of the immense disadvantages which beset our pathway, and fully appreciating our own weakness, we are encouraged to persevere in efforts adapted to our improvement, by a firm reliance upon God, and a settled conviction, as immovable as the everlasting hills, that all the truths in the whole universe of God are allied to our cause.

CHARLES SUMNER ARGUES FOR SCHOOL DESEGREGATION

Segregation in public education had been one of the early and long-standing manifestations of inequality against Negroes living in the northern states. By the 1840's, however, its continuance was being increasingly challenged by parents and sympathizers who petitioned school boards to allow Negroes to attend the schools nearest their homes—which, unlike a similar situation more than a century later, tended to be all-white schools. Particularly in Boston the issue was agitated; and, finally, in 1849, a colored citizen named Roberts took the case of his daughter, Sarah, to court. He obtained the legal services of Charles Sumner (1811-1874). Sumner, Boston lawyer and a United States Senator from 1851 until his death, presented his case. His argument that separate educational facilities were by definition unequal was ignored, and the case itself was lost.

The way is now prepared to consider the nature of Equality, as secured by the Constitution of Massachusetts. The Declaration of Independence, which followed the French Encyclopedia and the political writings of Rousseau, announces among self-evident truths, *"that all men are created equal; that they are endowed by their Creator with certain unalienable rights; that among these are life, liberty, and the pursuit of happiness."* The Constitution of Massachusetts repeats the same truth in a different form, saying, in its first article: *"All men are born free and equal, and have certain natural essential, and unalienable rights, among which may be reckoned the right of enjoying and defending their lives and liberties."* . . .

These declarations, though in point of time before the ampler declarations of France, may be construed in the light of the latter. Evidently, they seek to declare the same principle. They are declarations of *Rights;* and the language employed, though general in character, is obviously limited to those matters with-

---

From Charles Sumner, "Equality before the Law: Unconstitutionality of Separate Colored Schools in Massachusetts. Argument before the Supreme Court of Massachusetts, in the Case of Sarah C. Roberts *v.* The City of Boston, December 4, 1849," in *The Works of Charles Sumner,* II (Boston: Lee and Shepard, 1872), 340–372.

in the design of a declaration of *Rights*. And permit me to say, it is a childish sophism to adduce any physical or mental inequality in argument against Equality of Rights.

Obviously, men are not born equal in physical strength or in mental capacity, in beauty of form or health of body. Diversity or inequality in these respects is the law of creation. From this difference springs divine harmony. But this inequality is in no particular inconsistent with complete civil and political equality.

The equality declared by our fathers in 1776, and made the fundamental law of Massachusetts in 1780, was *Equality before the Law*. Its object was to efface all political or civil distinctions, and to abolish all institutions founded upon *birth*. "All men are *created* equal," says the Declaration of Independence. "All men are *born* free and equal," says the Massachusetts Bill of Rights. These are not vain words. Within the sphere of their influence, no person can be *created*, no person can be *born*, with civil or political privileges not enjoyed equally by all his fellow-citizens; nor can any institution be established, recognizing distinction of birth. Here is the Great Charter of every human being drawing vital breath upon this soil, whatever may be his condition, and whoever may be his parents. He may be poor, weak, humble, or black,—he may be of Caucasian, Jewish, Indian, or Ethiopian race,—he may be of French, German, English, or Irish extraction; but before the Constitution of Massachusetts all these distinctions disappear. He is not poor, weak, humble, or black; nor is he Caucasian, Jew, Indian, or Ethiopian; nor is he French, German, English, or Irish; he is a MAN, the equal of all his fellow-men. He is one of the children of the State, which, like an impartial parent, regards all its offspring with an equal care. To some it may justly allot higher duties, according to higher capacities; but it welcomes all to its equal hospitable board. The State, imitating the divine justice, is no respecter of persons. . . .

. . . The Legislature of Massachusetts, in entire harmony

with the Constitution, has made no discrimination of race or color in the establishment of Common Schools.

Any such discrimination by the Laws would be unconstitutional and void. But the Legislature has been too just and generous, too mindful of the Bill of Rights, to establish any such privilege of *birth*. The language of the statutes is general, and applies equally to all children, of whatever race or color.

The provisions of the Law are entitled, *Of the Public Schools*, meaning our Common Schools. To these we must look to ascertain what constitutes a Public School. Only those established in conformity with the Law can be legally such. They may, in fact, be more or less public; yet, if they do not come within the terms of the Law, they do not form part of the beautiful system of our Public Schools,—they are not Public Schools, or, as I prefer to call them, Common Schools. The two terms are used as identical; but the latter is that by which they were earliest known, while it is most suggestive of their comprehensive character. A "common" in law is defined to be *"open ground equally used* by many persons"; and the same word, when used as an adjective, is defined by lexicographers as "belonging equally to many or to the public," thus asserting Equality.

If we examine the text of this statute, we shall find nothing to sustain the rule of exclusion which has been set up. . . .

. . . There is but one Public School in Massachusetts. This is the Common School, equally free to all the inhabitants. There is nothing establishing an exclusive or separate school for any particular class, rich or poor, Catholic or Protestant, white or black. In the eye of the law there is but *one class*, where all interests, opinions, conditions, and colors commingle in harmony,—excluding none, therefore comprehending all.

EQUALITY UNDER JUDICIAL DECISIONS.

The Courts of Massachusetts, in harmony with the Constitution and the Laws, have never recognized any discrimination founded on race or color, in the administration of the Common Schools, but have constantly declared the equal rights of all the inhabitants.

There are only a few decisions bearing on this subject, but they breathe one spirit. The sentiment of Equality animates them all. In the case of *The Commonwealth* v. *Dedham,* (16 Mass. R., 146,) while declaring the equal rights of all the inhabitants, in both Grammar and District Schools, the Court said:—

"The schools required by the statute are to be maintained for the benefit of the whole town, *as it is the wise policy of the law to give all the inhabitants equal privileges for the education of their children in the Public Schools.* Nor is it in the power of the majority to deprive the minority of this *privilege.* . . . . Every inhabitant of the town has a right to participate in the benefits of both descriptions of schools; and it is not competent for a town to establish a grammar school for the benefit of one part of the town to the exclusion of the other, although the money raised for the support of schools may be in other respects fairly apportioned."

Here is Equality from beginning to end.

In the case of *Withington* v. *Eveleth,* (7 Pick. R., 106,) the Court say they "are all satisfied that the power given to towns to determine and define the limits of school districts can be executed only by a geographical division of the town for that purpose." A limitation of the district merely *personal* was held invalid. This same principle was again recognized in *Perry* v. *Dover,* (12 Pick. R., 213,) where the Court say, "Towns, in executing the power to form school districts, are bound so to do it as to include *every inhabitant* in some of the districts. They cannot lawfully omit any, and thus deprive them of *the benefits of our invaluable system of free schools.*" Thus at every point the Court has guarded the Equal Rights of all.

The Constitution, the Legislation, and the Judicial Decisions of Massachusetts have now been passed in review. We have seen what is contemplated by the Equality secured by the Constitution,—also what is contemplated by the system of Common Schools, as established by the laws of the Commonwealth and illustrated by decisions of the Supreme Court. The way is now prepared to consider the peculiarities in the present case, and to apply the principle thus recognized in Constitution, Laws, and Judicial Decisions.

SEPARATE SCHOOLS INCONSISTENT WITH EQUALITY.

It is easy to see that the exclusion of colored children from the Public Schools is a constant inconvenience to them and their parents, which white children and white parents are not obliged to bear. Here the facts are plain and unanswerable, showing a palpable violation of Equality. *The black and white are not equal before the law.* I am at a loss to understand how anybody can assert that they are.

Among the regulations of the Primary School Committee is one to this effect. "Scholars to go to the school nearest their residences. Applicants for admission to our schools (with the exception and provision referred to in the preceding rule) are especially entitled to enter the schools nearest to their places of residence." The exception here is "of those for whom special provision has been made" in separate schools,—that is, colored children.

In this rule—without the unfortunate exception—is part of the beauty so conspicuous in our Common Schools. It is the boast of England, that, through the multitude of courts, justice is brought to every man's door. It may also be the boast of our Common Schools, that, through the multitude of schools, education in Boston is brought to every *white* man's door. But it is not brought to every *black* man's door. He is obliged to go for it, to travel for it, to walk for it,—often a great distance. The facts in the present case are not so strong as those of other cases within my knowledge. But here the little child, only five years old, is compelled, if attending the nearest African School, to go a distance of two thousand one hundred feet from her home, while the nearest Primary School is only nine hundred feet, and, in doing this, she passes by no less than five different Primary Schools, forming part of our Common Schools, and open to white children, all of which are closed to her. Surely this is not *Equality before the Law*. . . .

. . . Looking beyond the facts of this case, it is apparent that the inconvenience from the exclusion of colored children is such as to affect seriously the comfort and condition of the African race in Boston. The two Primary Schools open to them are in Belknap Street and Sun Court. I need not add that the whole city is dotted with schools open to white children. Colored parents, anxious for the education of their children, are compelled to live in the neighborhood of the schools, to gather about them,—as in Eastern countries people gather near a fountain or a well. The liberty which belongs to the white man, of choosing his home, is not theirs. Inclination or business or economy may call them to another part of the city; but they are restrained for their children's sake. There is no such restraint upon the white man; for he knows, that, wherever in the city inclination or business or economy may call him, there will be a school open to his children near his door. Surely this is not *Equality before the Law.*

If a colored person, yielding to the necessities of position, removes to a distant part of the city, his children may be compelled daily, at an inconvenience which will not be called trivial, to walk a long distance for the advantages of the school. In our severe winters this cannot be disregarded, in the case of children so tender in years as those of the Primary Schools. There is a peculiar instance of hardship which has come to my knowledge. A respectable colored parent became some time since a resident of East Boston, separated from the mainland by water. Of course there are Common Schools at East Boston, but none open to colored children. This parent was obliged to send his children, three in number, daily across the ferry to the distant African School. The tolls amounted to a sum which formed a severe tax upon a poor man, while the long way to travel was a daily tax upon the time and strength of his children. Every toll paid by this parent, as every step taken by the children, testifies to that inequality which I now arraign.

This is the conduct of a colored parent. He is well deserving of honor for his generous efforts to secure the education of his children. As they grow in knowledge they will rise and call him blessed; but at the same time they will brand as accursed that arbitrary discrimination of color in the Common Schools of Boston which rendered it necessary for their father, out of small means, to make such sacrifices for their education. . . .

. . . We abjure nobility of all kinds; but here is a nobility of the skin. We abjure all hereditary distinctions; but here is an hereditary distinction, founded, not on the merit of the ancestor, but on his color. We abjure all privileges of birth; but here is a privilege which depends solely on the accident whether an ancestor is black or white. We abjure all inequality before the law; but here is an inequality which touches not an individual, but a race. We revolt at the relation of Caste; but here is a Caste which is established under a Constitution declaring that all men are born equal.

Condemning Caste and inequality before the law, the way is prepared to consider more particularly the powers of the School Committee. Here it will be necessary to enter into details.

SCHOOL COMMITTEE HAVE NO POWER TO DISCRIMINATE
ON ACCOUNT OF COLOR.

The Committee charged with the superintendence of the Common Schools of Boston have no *power* to make any discrimination on account of race or color.

It has been seen already that this power is inconsistent with the Declaration of Independence, with the Constitution and

Laws of Massachusetts, and with adjudications of the Supreme Court. The stream cannot rise higher than the fountain-head; and if there be nothing in these elevated sources from which this power can spring, it must be considered a nullity. Having seen that there is nothing, I might here stop; but I wish to show the shallow origin of this pretension.

Its advocates, unable to find it among express powers conferred upon the School Committee, and forgetful of the Constitution, where "either it must live or bear no life," place it among implied or incidental powers. The Revised Statutes provide for a School Committee "who shall have *the general charge and superintendence* of all the Public Schools" in their respective towns.[1] Another section provides that "the School Committee shall determine the number and qualifications of the scholars to be admitted into the school kept for the use of the whole town."[2] These are all the clauses conferring powers on the Committee.

From them no person will imply a power to defeat a cardinal principle of the Constitution. It is absurd to suppose that the Committee in general charge and superintendence of schools, and in determining the number and qualifications of scholars, may engraft upon the schools a principle of inequality, not only unknown to the Constitution and Laws, but in defiance of their letter and spirit. In the exercise of these powers they cannot put colored children to personal inconvenience greater than that of white children. Still further, they cannot brand a whole race with the stigma of inferiority and degradation, constituting them a Caste. They cannot in any way violate that fundamental right of all citizens, Equality before the Law. To suppose that they can do this would place the Committee above the Constitution. It would enable them, in the exercise of a brief and local authority, to draw a fatal circle, within which

---

[1] Chap. 23, sec. 10.
[2] Chap. 23, sec. 15.

the Constitution cannot enter,—nay, where the very Bill of Rights becomes a dead letter.

In entire harmony with the Constitution, the law says expressly what the Committee shall do. Besides the general charge and superintendence, they shall "determine the *number* and *qualifications* of the scholars to be admitted into the school,"—thus, according to a familiar rule of interpretation, excluding other powers: *Mentio unius est exclusio alterius.*[3] The power to determine the "number" is easily executed, and admits of no question. The power to determine the "qualifications," though less simple, must be restricted to age, sex, and fitness, moral and intellectual. The fact that a child is black, or that he is white, cannot of itself be a qualification or a disqualification. Not to the skin can we look for the criterion of fitness.

It is sometimes pretended, that the Committee, in the exercise of their power, are intrusted with a discretion, under which they may distribute, assign, and classify all children belonging to the schools *according to their best judgment,* making, if they think proper, a discrimination of race or color. Without questioning that they are intrusted with a discretion, it is outrageous to suppose that their discretion can go to this extent. The Committee can have no discretion which is not in harmony with the Constitution and Laws. Surely they cannot, in any mere discretion, nullify a sacred and dear-bought principle of Human Rights expressly guaranteed by the Constitution.

REGULATIONS OF COMMITTEE MUST BE REASONABLE.

Still further,—and here I approach a more technical view of the subject,—it is an admitted principle, that the regulations and by-laws of municipal corporations must be *reasonable,* or they are inoperative and void. This has been recognized by

---

[3] The mention of the one excludes the other. [Eds.]

the Supreme Court in two different cases,—*Commonwealth* v. *Worcester,* (3 Pick. R., 462,) and in Vandine's case (6 Pick. R., 187). In another case, *City of Boston* v. *Shaw,* (1 Met. R., 130,) it was decided that a by-law of Boston, prescribing a particular form of contribution toward the expenses of making the common sewers, was void for inequality and unreasonableness.

Assuming that this principle is applicable to the School Committee, their regulations and by-laws must be *reasonable.* Their discretion must be exercised in a reasonable manner. And this is not what the Committee or any other body of men think reasonable, but what is reasonable in the eye of the Law. It must be *legally reasonable.* It must be approved by the *reason* of the Law.

Here we are brought once more, in another form, to the question of the discrimination on account of color. Is this *legally reasonable?* Is it reasonable, in the exercise of a just discretion, to separate descendants of the African race from white children merely in consequence of descent? Passing over those principles of the Constitution and those provisions of Law which of themselves decide the question, constituting as they do *the highest reason,* but which have been already amply considered, look for a moment at the educational system of Massachusetts, and it will be seen that practically no discrimination of color is made by Law in any part of it. A descendant of the African race may be Governor of the Commonwealth, and as such, with the advice and consent of the Council, may select the Board of Education. As Lieutenant-Governor, he may be *ex officio* a member of the Board. He may be Secretary of the Board, with the duty imposed on him by law of seeing "that *all* children in this Commonwealth, who depend upon Common Schools for instruction, may have the best education which those schools can be made to impart."[4] He may be member of any School Committee, or teacher in any Common School of

---

[4] General Laws of Massachusetts, 1837, Ch. 241, sec. 2.

the State. As legal voter, he can vote in the selection of any School Committee.

Thus, in every department connected with our Common Schools, throughout the whole hierarchy of their government, from the very head of the system down to the humblest usher in the humblest Primary School, and to the humblest voter, there is no distinction of color known to the law. It is when we reach the last stage of all, the children themselves, that the beautiful character of the system is changed to the deformity of Caste, as, in the picture of the ancient poet, what above was a lovely woman terminated below in a vile, unsightly fish. And all this is done by the School Committee, with more than necromantic power, in the exercise of a mere discretion.

It is clear that the Committee may classify scholars according to age and sex, for the obvious reasons that these distinctions are inoffensive, and that they are especially recognized as *legal* in the law relating to schools.[5] They may also classify scholars according to moral and intellectual qualifications, because such a power is necessary to the government of schools. But the Committee cannot assume, *a priori,* and without individual examination, that all of an *entire race* are so deficient in proper moral and intellectual qualifications as to justify their universal degradation to a class by themselves. Such an exercise of discretion must be unreasonable, and therefore illegal.

SEPARATE SCHOOL NOT AN EQUIVALENT FOR COMMON SCHOOL.

But it is said that the School Committee, in thus classifying the children, have not violated any principle of Equality, inasmuch as they provide a school with competent instructors for colored children, where they have advantages equal to those provided for white children. It is argued, that, in excluding

---

[5] Revised Statutes, Ch. 23, sec. 63.

colored children from Common Schools open to white children, the Committee furnish an *equivalent.*

Here there are several answers. I shall touch them briefly, as they are included in what has been already said.

1. The separate school for colored children is not one of the schools established by the law relating to Public Schools.[6] It is not a Common School. As such it has no legal existence, and therefore cannot be a *legal equivalent.* In addition to what has been already said, bearing on this head, I call attention to one other aspect. It has been decided that a town can execute its power to form School Districts only by geographical divisions of its territory, that there cannot be what I would call a *personal* limitation of a district, and that *certain individuals* cannot be selected and set off by *themselves* into a district.[7] The admitted effect of this decision is to render a separate school for colored children illegal and impossible in towns divided into districts. They are so regarded in Salem, Nantucket, New Bedford, and in other towns of this Commonwealth. . . .

But there cannot be one law for the country and another for Boston. It is true that Boston is not divided strictly into geographical districts. In this respect its position is anomalous. But if separate colored schools are illegal and impossible in the country, they must be illegal and impossible in Boston. It is absurd to suppose that this city, failing to establish School Districts, and treating all its territory as a single district, should be able to legalize a Caste school, which otherwise it could not do. Boston cannot do indirectly what other towns cannot do directly. This is the first answer to the allegation of equivalents.

2. The second is that in point of fact the separate school is not an equivalent. We have already seen that it is the occasion of inconvenience to colored children, which would not arise, if they had access to the nearest Common School, besides com-

---

[6] Revised Statutes, Ch. 23.
[7] Perry *v.* Dover, 12 Pick. R., 213.

pelling parents to pay an additional tax, and inflicting upon child and parent the stigma of Caste. Still further,—and this consideration cannot be neglected,—the matters taught in the two schools may be precisely the same, but a school exclusively devoted to one class must differ essentially in spirit and character from that Common School known to the law, where all classes meet together in Equality. It is a mockery to call it an equivalent.

3. But there is yet another answer. Admitting that it is an equivalent, still the colored children cannot be compelled to take it. Their rights are found in Equality before the Law; nor can they be called to renounce one jot of this. They have an equal right with white children to the Common Schools. A separate school, though well endowed, would not secure to them that precise Equality which they would enjoy in the Common Schools. The Jews in Rome are confined to a particular district called the Ghetto, and in Frankfort to a district known as the Jewish Quarter. It is possible that their accommodations are as good as they would be able to occupy, if left free to choose throughout Rome and Frankfort; but this compulsory segregation from the mass of citizens is of itself an *inequality* which we condemn. It is a vestige of ancient intolerance directed against a despised people. It is of the same character with the separate schools in Boston.

Thus much for the doctrine of Equivalents as a substitute for Equality.

DISASTROUS CONSEQUENCES OF POWER TO MAKE SEPARATE SCHOOLS.

In determining that the School Committee have no *power* to make this discrimination we are strengthened by another consideration. If the power exists in the present case, it cannot be restricted to this. The Committee may distribute all the children into classes, according to mere discretion. They may establish a separate school for Irish or Germans, where each may nurse an exclusive nationality alien to our institutions. They may separate Catholics from Protestants, or, pursuing their discretion still further, may separate different sects of Protestants, and establish one school for Unitarians, another for Presbyterians, another for Baptists, and another for Methodists. They may establish a separate school for the rich, that the delicate taste of this favored class may not be offended by the humble garments of the poor. They may exclude the children of mechanics, and send them to separate schools. All this, and much more, can be done in the exercise of that highhanded power which makes a discrimination on account of race or color. The grand fabric of our Common Schools, the pride of Massachusetts,—where, at the feet of the teacher, innocent childhood should come, unconscious of all distinctions of birth,—where the Equality of the Constitution and of Christianity should be inculcated by constant precept and example,—will be converted into a heathen system of proscription and Caste. We shall then have many different schools, representatives of as many different classes, opinions, and prejudices; but we shall look in vain for the true Common School of Massachusetts. Let it not be said that there is little danger that any Committee will exercise a discretion to this extent. They must not be intrusted with the power. Here is the only safety worthy of a free people. . . .

. . . But it is said that these separate schools are for the benefit of both colors, and of the Public Schools. In similar spirit Slavery is sometimes said to be for the benefit of master and slave, and of the country where it exists. There is a mistake in the one case as great as in the other. This is clear. Nothing unjust, nothing ungenerous, can be for the benefit of any person or any thing. From some seeming selfish superiority, or from the gratified vanity of class, short-sighted mortals may hope to draw permanent good; but even-handed justice rebukes

Argument from Civil Liberties 295

these efforts and redresses the wrong. The whites themselves are injured by the separation. Who can doubt this? With the Law as their monitor, they are taught to regard a portion of the human family, children of God, created in his image, co-equals in his love, as a separate and degraded class; they are taught practically to deny that grand revelation of Christianity, the Brotherhood of Man. Hearts, while yet tender with childhood, are hardened, and ever afterward testify to this legalized uncharitableness. Nursed in the sentiments of Caste, receiving it with the earliest food of knowledge, they are unable to eradicate it from their natures, and then weakly and impiously charge upon our Heavenly Father the prejudice derived from an unchristian school. Their characters are debased, and they become less fit for the duties of citizenship. . . .

. . . A child should be taught to shun wickedness, and, as he is yet plastic under impressions, to shun wicked men. Horace was right, when, speaking of a person morally wrong, false, and unjust, he calls him black, and warns against him. . . . The Boston Committee adopt the warning, but apply it not to the black in heart, but the black in skin. They forget the admonition addressed to the prophet: "The Lord said unto Samuel, *Look not on his countenance:* . . . . for the Lord seeth not as man seeth; for man looketh on the outward appearance, *but the Lord looketh on the heart.*"[8] The Committee look on the outward appearance, without looking on the heart, and thus fancy that they are doing right!

Who can say that this does not injure the blacks? Theirs, in its best estate, is an unhappy lot. A despised class, blasted by prejudice and shut out from various opportunities, they feel this proscription from the Common Schools as a peculiar brand. Beyond this, it deprives them of those healthful, animating influences which would come from participation in the studies of their white brethren. It adds to their discouragements. It

---

[8] 1 Samuel, xvi. 7.

widens their separation from the community, and postpones that great day of reconciliation which is yet to come.

The whole system of Common Schools suffers also. It is a narrow perception of their high aim which teaches that they are merely to furnish an equal amount of knowledge to all, and therefore, provided all be taught, it is of little consequence where and in what company. The law contemplates not only that all shall be taught, but that *all* shall be taught *together*. They are not only to receive equal quantities of knowledge, but all are to receive it in the same way. All are to approach the same common fountain together; nor can there be any exclusive source for individual or class. The school is the little world where the child is trained for the larger world of life. It is the microcosm preparatory to the macrocosm, and therefore it must cherish and develop the virtues and the sympathies needed in the larger world. And since, according to our institutions, all classes, without distinction of color, meet in the performance of civil duties, so should they all, without distinction of color, meet in the school, beginning there those relations of Equality which the Constitution and Laws promise to all.

As the State derives strength from the unity and solidarity of its citizens without distinction of class, so the school derives strength from the unity and solidarity of all classes beneath its roof. In this way the poor, the humble, and the neglected not only share the companionship of the more favored, but enjoy also the protection of their presence, which draws toward the school a more watchful superintendence. A degraded or neglected class, if left to themselves, will become more degraded or neglected. "If any man have ears to hear, let him hear. . . . . For he that hath, to him shall be given; and he that hath not, from him shall be taken even that which he hath."[9] The world, perverting the true sense of these words, takes from the outcast that which God gave him capacity to enjoy. Hap-

---

[9] Mark, iv. 23, 25.

pily, our educational system, by the blending of all classes, draws upon the whole school that attention which is too generally accorded only to the favored few, and thus secures to the poor their portion of the fruitful sunshine. But the colored children, placed apart in separate schools, are deprived of this peculiar advantage. Nothing is more clear than that the welfare of classes, as well as of individuals, is promoted by mutual acquaintance. Prejudice is the child of ignorance. It is sure to prevail, where people do not know each other. Society and intercourse are means established by Providence for human improvement. They remove antipathies, promote mutual adaptation and conciliation, and establish relations of reciprocal regard. Whoso sets up barriers to these thwarts the ways of Providence, crosses the tendencies of human nature, and directly interferes with the laws of God.

X

Argument for Racial Equality

DAVID WALKER PROPOSES
ACTIVISM AND REVOLUTION

The calm assumptions that emancipation or slavery was in the hands of white men to determine were severely challenged from time to time by Negroes—slave or free—who undertook to settle the issue by preaching or actually using violence. To those who read David Walker's (1785–1830) Appeal . . . to the Coloured Citizens of the World, his call for violence if all else failed seemed, in the North, shocking; in the South, downright vicious. Walker, a free Negro originally from North Carolina, who disappeared mysteriously in 1830, was preaching from the doctrine of the equality of men of the various races and appealing to the Negroes to achieve and enforce this equality. He came much closer to proposing revolution than the later radical abolitionists, such as Stephen S. Foster, who used the term revolution much more freely.

From David Walker, *Walker's Appeal, in Four Articles; Together with a Preamble, to the Coloured Citizens of the World, But in Particular, and Very Expressly, to Those of the United States of America, Written in Boston, State of Massachusetts, September 28, 1829* (Boston: David Walker, 1830), pp. 3–5, 15–21, 70–80.

Having travelled over a considerable portion of these United States, and having, in the course of my travels, taken the most accurate observations of things as they exist—the result of my observations has warranted the full and unshaken conviction, that we, (coloured people of these United States,) are the most degraded, wretched, and abject set of beings that ever lived since the world began; and I pray God that none like us ever may live again until time shall be no more. . . .

. . . I am fully aware, in making this appeal to my much afflicted and suffering brethren, that I shall not only be assailed by those whose greatest earthly desires are, to keep us in abject ignorance and wretchedness, and who are of the firm conviction that Heaven has designed us and our children to be slaves and *beasts of burden* to them and their children. I say, I do not only expect to be held up to the public as an ignorant, impudent and restless disturber of the public peace, by such avaricious creatures, as well as a mover of insubordination—and perhaps put in prison or to death, for giving a superficial exposition of our miseries, and exposing tyrants. But I am persuaded, that many of my brethren, particularly those who are ignorantly in league with slave-holders or tyrants, who acquire their daily bread by the blood and sweat of their more ignorant brethren—and not a few of those too, who are too ignorant to see an inch beyond their noses, will rise up and call me cursed —Yea, the jealous ones among us will perhaps use more abject subtlety, by affirming that this work is not worth perusing, that we are well situated, and there is no use in trying to better our condition, for we cannot. I will ask one question here.—Can our condition be any worse?—Can it be more mean and abject? If there are any changes, will they not be for the better, though they may appear for the worst at first? Can they get us any lower? Where can they get us? They are afraid to treat us worse, for they know well, the day they do it they are gone. But against all accusations which may or can be preferred against me, I appeal to Heaven for my motive in writing—

who knows that my object is, if possible, to awaken in the breasts of my afflicted, degraded and slumbering brethren, a spirit of inquiry and investigation respecting our miseries and wretchedness in this *Republican Land of Liberty!* ! ! ! ! ! . . .

. . . The sufferings of the Helots among the Spartans, were somewhat severe, it is true, but to say that theirs, were as severe as ours among the Americans, I do most strenuously deny—for instance, can any man show me an article on a page of ancient history which specifies, that, the Spartans chained, and hand-cuffed the Helots, and dragged them from their wives and children, children from their parents, mothers from their suckling babes, wives from their husbands, driving them from one end of the country to the other? Notice the Spartans were heathens, who lived long before our Divine Master made his appearance in the flesh. Can Christian Americans deny these barbarous cruelties? Have you not, Americans, having subjected us under you, added to these miseries, by insulting us in telling us to our face, because we are helpless, that we are not of the human family? I ask you, O! Americans, I ask you, in the name of the Lord, can you deny these charges? Some perhaps may deny, by saying, that they never thought or said that we were not men. But do not actions speak louder than words?—have they not made provisions for the Greeks, and Irish? Nations who have never done the least thing for them, while *we*, who have enriched their country with our blood and tears—have dug up gold and silver for them and their children, from generation to generation, and are in more miseries than any other people under heaven, are not seen, but by comparatively, a handful of the American people? There are indeed, more ways to kill a dog, besides choking it to death with butter. Further—The Spartans or Lacedemonians, had some frivolous pretext, for enslaving the Helots, for they (Helots) while being free inhabitants of Sparta, stirred up an intestine commotion, and were, by the Spartans subdued, and made prisoners of war. Consequently they and their children were condemned to perpetual slavery.

I have been for years troubling the pages of historians, to find out what our fathers have done to the *white Christians of America*, to merit such condign punishment as they have inflicted on them, and do continue to inflict on us their children. But I must aver, that my researches have hitherto been to no effect. I have therefore, come to the immoveable conclusion, that they (Americans) have, and do continue to punish us for nothing else, but for enriching them and their country. For I cannot conceive of any thing else. Nor will I ever believe otherwise, until the Lord shall convince me.

The world knows, that slavery as it existed among the Romans, (which was the primary cause of their destruction) was, comparatively speaking, no more than a *cypher,* when compared with ours under the Americans. Indeed I should not have noticed the Roman slaves, had not the very learned and penetrating Mr. Jefferson said, "when a master was murdered, all his slaves in the same house, or within hearing, were condemned to death."[1]—Here let me ask Mr. Jefferson, (but he is gone to answer at the bar of God, for the deeds done in his body while living,) I therefore ask the whole American people, had I not rather die, or be put to death, than to be a slave to any tyrant, who takes not only my own, but my wife and children's lives by the inches? Yea, would I meet death with avidity far! far!! in preference to such *servile submission* to the murderous hands of tyrants. Mr. Jefferson's very severe remarks on us have been so extensively argued upon by men whose attainments in literature, I shall never be able to reach, that I would not have meddled with it, were it not to solicit each of my brethren, who has the spirit of a man, to buy a copy of Mr. Jefferson's "Notes on Virginia," and put it in the hand of his son. For let no one of us suppose that the refutations which have been written by our white friends are enough —they are *whites*—we are *blacks*. We, and the world wish to see the charges of Mr. Jefferson refuted by the blacks *them-*

---

[1] See his Notes on Virginia, page 210.

selves, according to their chance; for we must remember that what the whites have written respecting this subject, is other men's labours, and did not emanate from the blacks. I know well, that there are some talents and learning among the coloured people of this country, which we have not a chance to develope, in consequence of oppression; but our oppression ought not to hinder us from acquiring all we can. For we will have a chance to develope them by and by. God will not suffer us, always to be oppressed. Our sufferings will come to an *end,* in spite of all the Americans this side of *eternity.* Then we will want all the learning and talents among ourselves, and perhaps more, to govern ourselves.—"Every dog must have its day," the American's is coming to an end.

But let us review Mr. Jefferson's remarks respecting us some further. Comparing our miserable fathers, with the learned philosophers of Greece, he says: "Yet notwithstanding these and "other discouraging circumstances among the Romans, their "slaves were often their rarest artists. They excelled too, in "science, insomuch as to be usually employed as tutors to their "master's children; Epictetus, Terence and Phædrus, were "slaves,—but they were of the race of whites. It is not their "*condition* then, but *nature,* which has produced the distinc-"tion."[2] See this, my brethren!! Do you believe that this assertion is swallowed by millions of the whites? Do you know that Mr. Jefferson was one of as great characters as ever lived among the whites? See his writings for the world, and public labours for the United States of America. Do you believe that the assertions of such a man, will pass away into oblivion unobserved by this people and the world? If you do you are much mistaken—See how the American people treat us—have we souls in our bodies? Are we men who have any spirits at all? I know that there are many *swell-bellied* fellows among us, whose greatest object is to fill their stomachs. Such I do not mean—I

---

[2] See his Notes on Virginia, page 211.

am after those who know and feel, that we are MEN, as well as other people; to them, I say, that unless we try to refute Mr. Jefferson's arguments respecting us, we will only establish them.

But the slaves among the Romans. Every body who has read history, knows, that as soon as a slave among the Romans obtained his freedom, he could rise to the greatest eminence in the State, and there was no law instituted to hinder a slave from buying his freedom. Have not the Americans instituted laws to hinder us from obtaining our freedom? Do any deny this charge? Read the laws of Virginia, North Carolina, &c. Further: have not the Americans instituted laws to prohibit a man of colour from obtaining and holding any office whatever, under the government of the United States of America? Now, Mr. Jefferson tells us, that our condition is not so hard, as the slaves were under the Romans! ! ! ! ! ! . . .

. . . Are we MEN!!—I ask you, O my brethren! are we MEN? Did our Creator make us to be slaves to dust and ashes like ourselves? Are they not dying worms as well as we? Have they not to make their appearance before the tribunal of Heaven, to answer for the deeds done in the body, as well as we? Have we any other Master but Jesus Christ alone? Is he not their Master as well as ours?—What right then, have we to obey and call any other Master, but Himself? How we could be so *submissive* to a gang of men, whom we cannot tell whether they are *as good* as ourselves or not, I never could conceive. However, this is shut up with the Lord, and we cannot precisely tell—but I declare, we judge men by their works.

The whites have always been an unjust, jealous, unmerciful, avaricious and blood-thirsty set of beings, always seeking after power and authority.—We view them all over the confederacy of Greece, where they were first known to be any thing, (in consequence of education) we see them there, cutting each other's throats—trying to subject each other to wretchedness and misery—to effect which, they used all kinds of deceitful, unfair, and unmerciful means. We view them next in Rome, where the spirit of tyranny and deceit raged still higher. We view them in Gaul, Spain, and in Britain.—In fine, we view them all over Europe, together with what were scattered about in Asia and Africa, as heathens, and we see them acting more like devils than accountable men. But some may ask, did not the blacks of Africa, and the mulattoes of Asia, go on in the same way as did the whites of Europe. I answer, no—they never were half so avaricious, deceitful and unmerciful as the whites, according to their knowledge.

But we will leave the whites or Europeans as heathens, and take a view of them as Christians, in which capacity we see them as cruel, if not more so than ever. In fact, take them as a body, they are ten times more cruel, avaricious and unmerciful than ever they were; for while they were heathens, they were bad enough it is true, but it is positively a fact that they were not quite so audacious as to go and take vessel loads of men, women and children, and in cold blood, and through devilishness, throw them into the sea, and murder them in all kind of ways. While they were heathens, they were too ignorant for such barbarity. But being Christians, enlightened and sensible, they are completely prepared for such hellish cruelties. Now suppose God were to give them more sense, what would they do? If it were possible, would they not *dethrone* Jehovah and seat themselves upon his throne? I therefore, in the name and fear of the Lord God of Heaven and of earth, divested of prejudice either on the side of my colour or that of the whites, advance my suspicion of them, whether they are *as good by nature* as we are or not. Their actions, since they were known as a people, have been the reverse, I do indeed suspect them, but this, as I before observed, is shut up with the Lord, we cannot exactly tell, it will be proved in succeeding generations.—The whites have had the essence of the gospel as it was preached by my master and his apostles—the Ethiopians have not, who are to have it in its meridian splendor—the Lord will give it to them to their satisfaction. I hope and pray my God, that they will make good use of it, that it may be well with them. . . .

. . . They keep us miserable now, and call us their property, but some of them will have enough of us by and by—their stomachs shall run over with us; they want us for their slaves, and shall have us to their fill. (We are all in the world together!!—I said above, because we cannot help ourselves, (viz. we cannot help the whites murdering our mothers and our wives) but this statement is incorrect—for we can help ourselves; for, if we lay aside abject servility, and be determined to act like men, and not brutes—the murder[er]s among the whites would be afraid to show their cruel heads. But O, my God!—in sorrow I must say it, that my colour, all over the world, have a mean, servile spirit. They yield in a moment to the whites, let them be right or wrong—the reason they are able to keep their feet on our throats. Oh! my coloured brethren, all over the world, when shall we arise from this death-like apathy?—And be men!! You will notice, if ever we become men, I mean *respectable* men, such as other people are,) we must exert ourselves to the full. For remember, that it is the greatest desire and object of the greater part of the whites, to keep us ignorant, and make us work to support them and their families.—Here now, in the Southern and Western sections of this country, there are at least three coloured persons for one white, why is it, that those few weak, good-for-nothing whites, are able to keep so many able men, one of whom, can put to flight a dozen whites, in wretchedness and misery? It shows at once, what the blacks are, we are ignorant, abject, servile and mean—and the whites know it—they know that we are too servile to assert our rights as men—or they would not fool with us as they do. Would they fool with any other people as they do with us? No, they know too well, that they would get themselves ruined. Why do they not bring the inhabitants of Asia to be body servants to them? They know they would get their bodies rent and torn from head to foot. Why do they not get the Aborigines of this country to be slaves to them and their children, to work their farms and dig their mines? They know well that the Aborigines of this country, or (Indians) would tear them from the earth. The Indians would not rest day or night, they would be up all times of night, cutting their cruel throats. But my colour, (some, not all,) are willing to stand still and be murdered by the cruel whites. In some of the West-India Islands, and over a large part of South America, there are six or eight coloured persons for one white. Why do they not take possession of those places? Who hinders them? It is not the avaricious whites—for they are too busily engaged in laying up money—derived from the blood and tears of the blacks. The fact is, they are too servile, they love to have Masters too well!! Some of our brethren, too, who seeking more after self aggrandisement, than the glory of God, and the welfare of their brethren, join in with our oppressors, to ridicule and say all manner of evils falsely against our Bishop.[3] They think, that they are doing great things, when they can get in company with the whites, to ridicule and make sport of those who are labouring for their good. Poor ignorant creatures, they do not know that the sole aim and object of the whites, are only to make fools and slaves of them, and put the whip to them, and make them work to support them and their families. But I do say, that no man, can well be a despiser of Bishop Allen, for his public labours among us, unless he is a despiser of God and of Righteousness. Thus, we see, my brethren, the two very opposite positions of those great men, who have written respecting this "Colonizing Plan." (Mr. Clay and his slaveholding party,) men who are resolved to keep us in eternal wretchedness, are also bent upon sending us to Liberia. While

---

[3] Richard Allen (1760–1831), free Negro preacher and circuit rider; one of the founders of the African Methodist Episcopal Church and its first bishop (1816). Early colonizationist and later abolitionist. [Eds.]

the Reverend Bishop Allen, and his party, [are] men who have the fear of God, and the wellfare of their brethren at heart. The Bishop, in particular, whose labours for the salvation of his brethren, are well known to a large part of those, who dwell in the United States, are completely opposed to the plan —and advise us to stay where we are. Now we have to determine whose advice we will take respecting this all important matter, whether we will adhere to Mr. Clay and his slave holding party, who have always been our oppressors and murderers, and who are for colonizing us, more through apprehension than humanity, or to this godly man who has done so much for our benefit, together with the advice of all the good and wise among us and the whites. Will any of us leave our homes and go to Africa? I hope not. Let them commence their attack upon us as they did on our brethren in Ohio, driving and beating us from our country, and my soul for theirs, they will have enough of it.[4] Let no man of us budge one step, and let slave-holders come to beat us from our country. America is more our country, than it is the whites—we have enriched it with our *blood and tears.* The greatest riches in all America have arisen from our blood and tears:—and will they drive us from our property and homes, which we have earned with our *blood?* They must look sharp or this very thing will bring swift destruction upon them. The Americans have got so fat on our blood and groans, that they have almost forgotten the God of armies. But let them go on. . . .

. . . How cunning slave-holders think they are! ! !—How much like the king of Egypt who, after he saw plainly that God was determined to bring out his people, in spite of him and his, as powerful as they were. He was willing that Moses,

---

[4] The enforcement of Ohio's Black Code in the late 1820's caused many Negroes to flee the state. Particularly they left Cincinnati between 1829–1830 and settled, many of them, in Canada at Wilberforce, Western Ontario. The Cincinnati migration was being organized at the very time Walker was writing the *Appeal.* [Eds.]

Aaron and the Elders of Israel, but not all the people should go and serve the Lord. But God deceived him as he will Christian Americans, unless they are very cautious how they move. What would have become of the United States of America, was it not for those among the whites, who not in words barely, but in truth and in deed, love and fear the Lord?—Our Lord and Master said:—[5] "Whoso shall offend one of these little "ones which believe in me, it were better for him that a mill-"stone were hanged about his neck, and that he were drowned "in the depth of the sea." But the Americans with this very threatening of the Lord's, not only beat his little ones among the Africans, but many of them they put to death or murder. Now the avaricious Americans, think that the Lord Jesus Christ will let them off, because his words are no more than the words of a man! ! ! In fact, many of them are so avaricious and ignorant, that do not believe in our Lord and Saviour Jesus Christ. Tyrants may think they are so skillful in State affairs is the reason that the government is preserved. But I tell you, that this country would have been given up long ago, was it not for the lovers of the Lord. They are indeed, the salt of the earth. Remove the people of God among the whites, from this land of blood, and it will stand until they cleverly get out of the way. . . .

. . . Americans! notwithstanding you have and do continue to treat us more cruel than any heathen nation ever did a people it had subjected to the same condition that you have us. Now let us reason—I mean you of the United States, whom I believe God designs to save from destruction, if you will hear. For I declare to you, whether you believe it or not, that there are some on the continent of America, who will never be able to repent. God will surely destroy them, to show you his disapprobation of the murders they and you have inflicted on us. I say, let us reason; had you not better take our body, while

---

[5] See St. Matthew's Gospel, chap. xviii. 6.

Argument for Racial Equality 309

you have it in your power, and while we are yet ignorant and wretched, not knowing but a little, give us education, and teach us the pure religion of our Lord and Master, which is calculated to make the lion lay down in peace with the lamb, and which millions of you have beaten us nearly to death for trying to obtain since we have been among you, and thus at once, gain our affection while we are ignorant? Remember Americans, that we must and shall be free and enlightened as you are, will you wait until we shall, under God, obtain our liberty by the crushing arm of power? Will it not be dreadful for you? I speak Americans for your good. We must and shall be free I say, in spite of you. You may do your best to keep us in wretchedness and misery, to enrich you and your children, but God will deliver us from under you. And wo, wo, will be to you if we have to obtain our freedom by fighting. Throw away your fears and prejudices then, and enlighten us and treat us like men, and we will like you more than we do now hate you, and tell us now no more about colonization, for America is as much our country, as it is yours.—Treat us like men, and there is no danger but we will all live in peace and happiness together. For we are not like you, hard hearted, unmerciful, and unforgiving. What a happy country this will be, if the whites will listen. What nation under heaven, will be able to do any thing with us, unless God gives us up into its hand? But Americans, I declare to you, while you keep us and our children in bondage, and treat us like brutes, to make us support you and your families, we cannot be your friends. You do not look for it, do you? Treat us then like men, and we will be your friends. And there is not a doubt in my mind, but that the whole of the past will be sunk into oblivion, and we yet, under God, will become a united and happy people. The whites may say it is impossible, but remember that nothing is impossible with God.

The Americans may say or do as they please, but they have to raise us from the condition of brutes to that of respectable men, and to make a national acknowledgement to us for the wrongs they have inflicted on us. As unexpected, strange, and wild as these propositions may to some appear, it is no less a fact, that unless they are complied with, the Americans of the United States, though they may for a little while escape, God will yet weigh them in a balance, and if they are not superior to other men, as they have represented themselves to be, he will give them wretchedness to their very heart's content.

JAMES RUSSELL LOWELL CONDEMNS THE PREJUDICE OF COLOR

James Russell Lowell (1819–1891), like Whittier, devoted his talent both as poet and journalist to the cause of antislavery. His dialect Bigelow Papers *were directed against the Mexican War and had considerable impact as a series and later as a book. The selection which follows comes from the* Pennsylvania Freeman, *which he edited for a few months, and it contains many of the arguments used by those antislavery men who preached against racial discrimination.*

There is nothing more sadly and pitiably ludicrous in the motley face of our social system than the prejudice of color. As if no arrangement of society could be perfect in which there

---

James Russell Lowell, "The Prejudice of Color," reprinted from *The Pennsylvania Freeman,* February 13, 1845, in *The Anti-Slavery Papers of James Russell Lowell,* I (Boston: Houghton, Mifflin and Company, 1902), 16–22.

was not some arbitrary distinction of rank, we Democrats, after abolishing all other artificial claims of superiority, cling with the despair of persons just drowning, in the dreadful ocean of equality, to one more absurd and more wicked than all the rest. An aristocracy of intellect may claim some leniency of judgment from the reason, and there are certain physiological arguments to bolster up an aristocracy of birth; but a patent of nobility founded on no better distinction than an accidental difference in the secreting vessels of the skin would seem ridiculous even to a German count who had earned his title by the more valid consideration of thirty-six dollars. Or is it in some assumed superiority of intellect that the white man finds his claim to enslave his colored brother? In that case the most exclusive of this chromatic *noblesse* would stand in imminent peril of the lash of the overseer at the South, or of the editor (who occupies the position and discharges the duties of that distinguished member of our democratic system) at the North. For we assume it as a primary step in our argument that, when the moral vision of a man becomes perverted enough to persuade him that he is superior to his fellow, he is in reality looking up at him from an immeasurable distance beneath.

Regarding the American people as a professedly Christian people, their anti-Christian prejudices are at first sight astonishing enough. Were this the place, the greater part of them might be traced to the timidity and unfaithfulness of the Church, which to most men supplies the place of a conscience, and whose sacredness, instead of being founded immutably upon a living inward principle, rises and falls with the popular lukewarmness or zeal. Claiming to be of divine origin and appointment, its main occupation would nevertheless seem to be to prove by its subservience to popular fallacies that it is merely a mechanical contrivance of man's ingenuity—a labor-saving national conscience. Our people go once or twice in a week to hear the praises of meekness, humanity, and forbearance, so curiously intertwined with theological dogmas that the latter seem equally sacred with the former, and then go home to practise the very reverse of these virtues without the slightest perception of their inconsistency. For example, the black men, having endured unparalleled hardships and oppressions with resignation and patience, are despised as wanting in spirit and capacity, while the red men, having returned blow for blow,—having displayed, perhaps, more hideous qualities than any other savages,—become the theme of novels and romances, are made the subject of rhymes almost as atrocious as one of their own war songs, and furnish even our children's books with pernicious examples of utterly barbarous and pagan virtues. This proves that we give only a theoretical assent to the doctrines of Christ, and that, like Louis the Eleventh of France, though we wear the badges of our religion most conspicuously, we contrive adroitly to hide them away whenever it suits our convenience to break any of its commandments.

Meanwhile, as a prophecy is sometimes known to bring about its own fulfilment, the national prejudice against the colored race is fast producing a plentiful crop of statistical facts on which to base an argument in its own favor. The colored people of the so-called free states are still held in slavery by something stronger than a constitution, more terrible than the cannon and the bayonet,—the force of a depraved and unchristian public opinion. We shut them rigidly out from every path of emulation or ambition, and then deny to them the possession of ordinary faculties. No talent will show itself till there is a demand for its exercise, and then it leaps spontaneously and irresistibly into vigorous action. The proportion of degraded whites in this country is to the full as great as that of the colored population; it is infinitely greater if we consider the respective opportunities of the two races.

The oppressor has always endeavored to justify his sin by casting reproach upon the moral or intellectual qualities of the oppressed. The Romans held their miserable victims in contempt, until Spartacus displayed a military genius and a heroism which their ablest generals were unable to make head against until his little army was divided against itself. Yet these very slaves were among the ancestors of two nations now the most distinguished in Europe, the one for philanthropy and profound scholarship, the other for science. The Norman barons (a race of savages, strong chiefly in their intense and selfish acquisitiveness, to whom our Southern brethren are fond of comparing themselves) looked upon their Saxon serfs as mere cattle, and indeed reduced them as nearly as might be to that degraded level by their cruelty. Yet these very serfs were part and parcel of that famous Anglo-Saxon race, concerning whom we have seen so much claptrap in the newspapers for a few years past, especially since the project of extending the area of freedom has been discussed and glorified. A still more prominent example may be found in the case of the Jews, who by a series of enormous tyrannies were reduced to the condition of the most abject degradation among nations to whom they had given a religious system, and who borrowed from them their choicest examples of eloquence and pathos and sublime genius. Here was and is a people remarkable above almost all others for the possession of the highest and clearest intellect, and yet absolutely dwarfed and contracted in mind by being sternly debarred from any but the very lowest exercise of mental capacity. But they had the advantage of a less palpable outward distinguishment from the nations among whom they underwent their latest and worst captivity, and a few of them have been enabled to raise themselves to power and distinction—but never *as Jews*.

With us the color is made the most prominent feature. The newspapers can never say simply man or woman in speaking of the African race; they must always prefix the badge of inferiority, and in the same way that they say the *Honorable* Member of Congress or the *Reverend* Doctor of Divinity to excite our favorable sympathies, they say a *colored* man or woman to indicate that there is no need of our troubling our sympathies at all. Nor is this the worst. Though it is a part of the religious faith of our Northern editors, and a part (apparently) of their constitutional compact of fealty to the South, to consider the colored race as incapable of high civilization, as incapable indeed, even of manhood, yet, so surely as a colored man commits any offence, a paragraph runs the rounds of our newspapers, religious and all, headed *"a black ruffian,"* as if his color were an aggravation of his offence, instead of being, according to their own standard, a palliation of it.

It has always seemed to us that abolitionists could in no way more usefully serve their holy cause than by seeking to elevate the condition of the colored race in the free states, and to break down every barrier of invidious distinction between them and their privileged brothers. We know that a great deal has been done, but we think that it has not been made sufficiently a primary object. A few such men as Douglass and Remond[1] are the strongest anti-slavery arguments. The very look and bearing of Douglass are eloquent, and are full of an irresistible logic against the oppression of his race.

We have never had any doubt that the African race was intended to introduce a new element of civilization, and that the Caucasian would be benefited greatly by an infusion of its gentler and less selfish qualities. The Caucasian mind, which seeks always to govern, at whatever cost, can never come to so beautiful or Christian a height of civilization, as with a mixture of those seemingly humbler, but truly more noble, qualities which teach it to obey. While our moral atmosphere is so dense and heavy with prejudice, it will be impossible for the colored man to stand erect or to breathe freely. Even if he make the attempt, he can never attain that quiet unconsciousness so necessary to a full and harmonious development, while

---

[1] Frederick Douglass and Charles Lenox Remond. For selections from their writings see pp. 348 and 452 and 335 respectively [Eds.]

he is continually forced to resist the terrible pressure from without. It is for us to endeavor to reduce this atmosphere to the true natural weight, and so struggle as manfully and earnestly and as constantly also against the slave system of the North as against that of the South. Had we room we might easily prove by historical examples that no race has ever so rapidly improved by being brought into contact with a higher civilization (even under the most terrible disadvantages) as the one of which we have been speaking.

NATHANIEL P. ROGERS RIDICULES THE BLUE COLLAPSE STAGE OF PREJUDICE

Nathaniel P. Rogers (1794–1846), editor of the New Hampshire Herald of Freedom, *was an eccentric even within the antislavery movement. He espoused a variety of reforms so ardently that he was constantly subject to criticism from every side. Ultimately he lost an effective voice in antislavery as the result of a battle for control of his paper. He attempted to start another paper by the same name, but eventually devoted most of his efforts to speaking tours, accompanied by the indefatigable antislavery singers, the Hutchinson family. Equally unusual in the company of earnest reformers was his use of wit.*

Nathaniel Peabody Rogers, "Color-Phobia," reprinted from *Herald of Freedom,* November 10, 1838, in *A Collection from the Newspaper Writings of Nathaniel Peabody Rogers* (Concord, N.H.: J. R. French, 1847), pp. 44–47.

Our people have got it. They have got it in the blue, collapse stage. Many of them have got it so bad, they can't get well. They will die of it. It will be a mercy, if the nation does not. What a dignified, philosophic malady! Dread of complexion. They don't know they have got it—or think, rather, they took it the natural way. But they were inoculated. It was injected into their veins and *incided* into their systems, by old Doctor Slavery, the great doctor that the famous Dr. Wayland[1] studied with. There is a kind of varioloid type, called *colonization*. They generally go together, or all that have one are more apt to catch the other. Inoculate for one, (no matter which,) and they will have both, before they get over it. The remedy and the preventive, if taken early, is a kine-pock sort of matter, by the name of *anti-slavery*. It is a safe preventive and a certain cure. None that *have it, genuine,* ever catch slavery or colonization or the color-phobia. You can't inoculate either into them. It somehow changes and redeems the constitution, so that it is unsusceptible of them. An abolitionist can sleep safely all night in a close room, where there has been a colonization meeting the day before. He might sleep with R. R. Gurley[2] and old Dr. Proudfit,[3] three in a bed, and not catch it. The remedy was discovered by Dr. William Lloyd Jenner-Garrison.[4]

This color-phobia is making terrible havoc among our communities. Anti-slavery *drives it out*, and after a while cures

---

[1] Francis Wayland (1796–1865). Baptist clergyman, president of Brown University (1827–1855). Active in reform causes, notably prison reform. Considered himself antislavery, but by the abolitionists was held suspect as an equivocator and as a southern sympathizer. [Eds.]

[2] Ralph Randolph Gurley (1797–1872). Agent of the American Colonization Society and, after 1825, Secretary. Though a controversial figure, his identification with the fortunes of the Society lasted more than fifty years. He acted also as a colonization lecturer in America and in England, and was editor of the *African Repository*. [Eds.]

[3] Probably Dr. Proudfit is the Reverend Mr. Alexander Proudfit, a well-known clergyman of Washington County, New York, and active in the formation of the national lyceum movement. [Eds.]

[4] The reference is to Edward Jenner (1749–1823), English physician and developer of the inoculation technique against smallpox. [Eds.]

it. But it is a base, low, vulgar ailment. It is meaner, in fact, than the itch. It is worse to get rid of than the "seven years' itch." It is fouler than Old Testament leprosy. It seems to set the dragon into a man, and make him treat poor, dark-skinned folks like a tiger. It goes hardest with *dark-complect* white people. They have it longer and harder than light-skinned people. It makes them sing out "Nigger—nigger," sometimes in their sleep. Sometimes they make a noise like this, "Darkey—darkey—darkey." Sometimes, "Wully—wully—wully." They will turn up their noses, when they see colored people, especially if they are of a pretty rank, savory habit of person, themselves. They are generally apt to turn up their noses, as though there was some "bad smell" in the neighborhood, when they have it bad, and are naturally pretty odoriferous. It is a tasty disorder—a beautiful ailment; very genteel, and apt to go in "first families." We should like to have Hogarth take a sketch of a community that had it—of ours, for instance, when the St. Vitus' fit was on. We have read somewhere of a painter, who made so droll a picture, that he died a-laughing at the sight of it. Hogarth might not laugh at this picture. It would be a sight to cry at, rather than laugh, especially if he could see the poor objects of our frenzy, when the fit is on—which indeed is all the time, for it is an unintermittent. Our attitude would be most ridiculous and ludicrous, if it were not too mortifying and humiliating and cruel. Our Hogarth would be apt to die of something else than laughter, at sight of his sketch.

The courtly malady is the secret of all our anti-abolition, and all our mobocracy. It shuts up all the consecrated meeting-houses—and all the *temples of justice*, the court-houses, against the friends of negro liberty. It is all alive with fidgets about *desecrating the Sabbath* with anti-slavery lectures. It thinks anti-slavery pew-owners can't go into them, or use their pulpit, when it is empty, without leave of the minister whom they employ to preach in it. It will forcibly shut people out of their own houses and off their own land,—not with the respectful violence of enemies and trespassers, but the contemptuous unceremoniousness of the plantation overseer—mingled moreover with the slavish irascibility of the poor negro, when he holds down his fellow-slave for a flogging. It sneers at human rights through the *free* press. It handed John B. Mahan over to the alligators of Kentucky. It shot Elijah P. Lovejoy at Alton. It dragged away the free school, at Canaan. It set Pennsylvania Hall a-fire. It broke Miss Crandall's school windows, and threw filth into her well. It stormed the female prayer meeting in Boston, with a "property and standing" forlorn hope. It passed the popish resolution at Littleton, in Grafton county. It shut up the meeting-house at Meredith Bridge, against minister and all,—and the homely court-house there, and howled like bedlam around the little, remote district school-house, and broke the windows at night.[5] It excludes consideration and prayer in regard to the forlorn and christian-made heathenism of the American colored man, from county conferences and clerical associations. It broods over the mousings of the New York Observer, and gives *keenness* to the edge and point of its New Hampshire name-sake. It votes anti-slavery lectures out of the New Hampshire state house, and gives it *public hearing* on petitions, in a seven by nine committee room. It answers the most insulting mandate of southern governors, calling for violations of the state constitution and bill of rights, by legislative report and resolves that the paramount rights of slavery are safe enough in New Hampshire, without these violations. It sneers and scowls at woman's speaking *in company,* unless to simper, when she is flattered by a fool of the masculine or neuter gender. It won't sign an anti-slavery petition, for fear

---

[5] John B. Mahan, Ohio Underground Railroad Operator, was convicted in Kentucky in 1838, for aiding fugitive slaves. For the Alton affair, see p. xli. For Prudence Crandall and the Pennsylvania Hall incidents, see pp. lxxii and xliii respectively. The Noyes Academy at Canaan, New Hampshire, which had accepted Negro students, was bodily moved into a swamp in 1835. In 1835 the female antislavery society meetings in Boston were attacked by the mob and Garrison was nearly lynched. The Littleton reference and presumably the Meredith Bridge reference are to local New Hampshire events. [Eds.]

it will put back emancipation half a century. It votes in favor of communing with slaveholders, and throwing the pulpit wide open to men-stealers, to keep peace in the churches, and prevent disunion. It will stifle and strangle sympathy for the slave and "remembrance of those in bonds," to prevent disturbance of religious revivals. It will sell the American slave to buy Bibles, or hire negro-hating and negro-buying missionaries for foreign heathen of all quarters but christian-wasted Africa. It prefers *American* lecturers on slavery, to having that foreign emissary, George Thompson,[6] come over here, to interfere with American rights and prejudices. It abhors "church action" and "meddling with politics." In short, it abhors slavery in the abstract—wishes it might be done away, but denies the right of any body or any thing to devise its overthrow, but slavery itself and slaveholders. It prays for the poor slave, that he might be elevated, while it stands both feet on his breast to keep him down. It prays God might open a way in his own time for the deliverance of the slave, while it stands, with arms akimbo, right across the way he has already opened. Time would fail us to tell of its extent and depth in this free country, or the deeds it has done. Anti-slavery must cure it, or it must die out like the incurable drunkards.

MARTIN DELANY EXHORTS THE NEGRO TO STRAIGHTEN HIS SHOULDERS AND RAISE HIS EYES

Evidences of prejudice and discrimination existed within the antislavery fold, ranging from overt opposition to Negroes' joining antislavery societies to a more pervasive paternalistic

---

[6] George Thompson (1804–1878), prominent British antislavery leader. He toured the United States in the middle 1830's lecturing on antislavery. [Eds.]

condescension. Martin Delany (1812–1885), a physician, journalist, and prominent Negro leader, rejected all such discriminatory treatment. He preached economic self-sufficiency, and, ultimately, migration to Africa as the only answer to the plight of the colored man in a predominantly white America.

It is true, that the Anti-Slavery, like all good causes, has produced some recreants, but the cause itself is no more to be blamed for that, than Christianity is for the malconduct of any professing hypocrite, nor the society of Friends, for the conduct of a broad-brimmed hat and shad-belly coated horse-thief, because he spoke *thee* and *thou* before stealing the horse. But what is our condition even amidst our Anti-Slavery friends? And here, as our sole intention is to contribute to the elevation of our people, we must be permitted to express our opinion freely, without being thought uncharitable.

In the first place, we should look at the objects for which the Anti-Slavery cause was commenced, and the promises or inducements it held out at the commencement. It should be borne in mind, that Anti-Slavery took its rise among *colored men,* just at the time they were introducing their greatest projects for their own elevation, and that our Anti-Slavery brethren were converts of the colored men, in behalf of their elevation. Of course, it would be expected that being baptized into the new doctrines, their faith would induce them to embrace the principles therein contained, with the strictest possible adherence.

The cause of dissatisfaction with our former condition, was, that we were proscribed, debarred, and shut out from every respectable position, occupying the places of inferiors and menials.

From Martin Robinson Delany, *The Condition, Elevation, Emigration, and Destiny of the Colored People of the United States Politically Considered* (Philadelphia: The Author, 1852), pp. 25–29, 41–48, 197–201.

It was expected that Anti-Slavery, according to its professions, would extend to colored persons, as far as in the power of its adherents, those advantages nowhere else to be obtained among white men. That colored boys would get situations in their shops and stores, and every other advantage tending to elevate them as far as possible, would be extended to them. At least, it was expected, that in Anti-Slavery establishments, colored men would have the preference. Because, there was no other ostensible object in view, in the commencement of the Anti-Slavery enterprise, than the *elevation* of the *colored man*, by facilitating his efforts in attaining to equality with the white man. It was urged, and it was true, that the colored people were susceptible of all that the whites were, and all that was required was to give them a fair opportunity, and they would prove their capacity. That it was unjust, wicked, and cruel, the result of an unnatural prejudice, that debarred them from places of respectability, and that public opinion could and should be corrected upon this subject. That it was only necessary to make a sacrifice of feeling, and an innovation on the customs of society, to establish a different order of things,—that as Anti-Slavery men, they were willing to make these sacrifices, and determined to take the colored man by the hand, making common cause with him in affliction, and bear a part of the odium heaped upon him. That his cause was the cause of God—that "In as much as ye did it not unto the least of these my little ones, ye did it not unto me," and that as Anti-Slavery men, they would "do right if the heavens fell." Thus, was the cause espoused, and thus did we expect much. But in all this, we were doomed to disappointment, sad, sad disappointment. Instead of realising what we had hoped for, we find ourselves occupying the very same position in relation to our Anti-Slavery friends, as we do in relation to the pro-slavery part of the community—a mere secondary, underling position, in all our relations to them, and any thing more than this, is not a matter of course affair—it comes not by established antislavery custom or right, but like that which emanates from the proslavery portion of the community, by mere sufferance.

It is true, that the "Liberator" office, in Boston, has got Elijah Smith, a colored youth, at the cases—the "Standard," in New York, a young colored man, and the "Freeman," in Philadelphia, William Still,[1] another, in the publication office, as "packing clerk;" yet these are but three out of the hosts that fill these offices in their various departments, all occupying places that could have been, and as we once thought, would have been, easily enough, occupied by colored men. Indeed, we can have no other idea about anti-slavery in this country, than that the legitimate persons to fill any and every position about an anti-slavery establishment are colored persons. Nor will it do to argue in extenuation, that white men are as justly entitled to them as colored men; because white men do not from *necessity* become anti-slavery men in order to get situations; they being white men, may occupy any position they are capable of filling—in a word, their chances are endless, every avenue in the country being opened to them. They do not therefore become abolitionists, for the sake of employment—at least, it is not the song that anti-slavery sung, in the first love of the new faith, proclaimed by its disciples.

And if it be urged that colored men are incapable as yet to fill these positions, all that we have to say is, that the cause has fallen far short; almost equivalent to a failure, of a tithe, of what it promised to do in half the period of its existence, to this time, if it have not as yet, now a period of twenty years, raised up colored men enough, to fill the offices within its patronage. We think it is not unkind to say, if it had been half as faithful to itself, as it should have been—its professed principles we mean; it could have reared and tutored from childhood, colored men enough by this time, for its own especial

---

[1] William Still went on to write one of the early accounts of the activities of the Underground Railroad, originally published in 1872. [Eds.]

purpose. These we know could have been easily obtained, because colored people in general, are favorable to the anti-slavery cause, and wherever there is an adverse manifestation, it arises from sheer ignorance; and we have now but comparatively few such among us. There is one thing certain, that no colored person, except such as would reject education altogether, would be adverse to putting their child with an anti-slavery person, for educational advantages. This then, could have been done. But it has not been done, and let the cause of it be whatever it may, and let whoever may be to blame, we are willing to let all that pass, and extend to our anti-slavery brethren the right-hand of fellowship, bidding them God-speed in the propagation of good and wholesome sentiments—for whether they are practically carried out or not, the professions are in themselves all right and good. Like Christianity, the principles are holy and of divine origin. And we believe, if ever a man started right, with pure and holy motives, Mr. Garrison did; and that, had he the power of making the cause what it should be, it would be all right, and there never would have been any cause for the remarks we have made, though in kindness, and with the purest of motives. We are nevertheless, still occupying a miserable position in the community, wherever we live; . . .

. . . Moral theories have long been resorted to by us, as a means of effecting the redemption of our brethren in bonds, and the elevation of the free colored people in this country. Experience has taught us, that speculations are not enough; that the *practical* application of principles adduced, the thing carried out, is the only true and proper course to pursue.

. . . By the regulations of society, there is no equality of persons, where there is not an equality of attainments. By this, we do not wish to be understood as advocating the actual equal attainments of every individual; but we mean to say, that if these attainments be necessary for the elevation of the white man, they are necessary for the elevation of the colored man. That some colored men and women, in a like proportion to the whites, should be qualified in all the attainments possessed by them. It is one of the regulations of society the world over, and we shall have to conform to it, or be discarded as unworthy of the associations of our fellows.

Cast our eyes about us and reflect for a moment, and what do we behold! every thing that presents to view gives evidence of the skill of the white man. Should we purchase a pound of groceries, a yard of linen, a vessel of crockeryware, a piece of furniture, the very provisions that we eat,—all, all are the products of the white man, purchased by us from the white man, consequently, our earnings and means, are all given to the white man.

Pass along the avenues of any city or town, in which you live—behold the trading shops—the manufactories—see the operations of the various machinery—see the stage-coaches coming in, bringing the mails of intelligence—look at the railroads interlining every section, bearing upon them their mighty trains, flying with the velocity of the swallow, ushering in the hundreds of industrious, enterprising travellers. Cast again your eyes widespread over the ocean—see the vessels in every direction with their white sheets spread to the winds of heaven, freighted with the commerce, merchandise and wealth of many nations. Look as you pass along through the cities, at the great and massive buildings—the beautiful and extensive structures of architecture—behold the ten thousand cupolas, with their spires all reared up towards heaven, intersecting the territory of the clouds—all standing as mighty living monuments, of the industry, enterprise, and intelligence of the white man. And yet, with all these living truths, rebuking us with scorn, we strut about, place our hands akimbo, straighten up ourselves to our greatest height, and talk loudly about being "as good as any body." How do we compare with them? Our fathers are their coachmen, our brothers their cookmen, and ourselves their waiting-men. Our mothers their nurse-women, our sisters their scrub-women, our daughters their maid-women, and our wives their washer-women. Until colored men, attain to a position above permitting their mothers, sisters, wives, and daughters, to do the drudgery and menial offices of other men's wives and daughters; it is useless, it is nonsense, it is pitiable mockery, to talk about equality and elevation in society. The world is looking upon us, with feelings of commisseration, sorrow, and contempt. We scarcely deserve sympathy, if we peremptorily refuse advice, bearing upon our elevation. . . .

. . . White men are producers—we are consumers. They build houses, and we rent them. They raise produce, and we consume it. They manufacture clothes and wares, and we garnish ourselves with them. They build coaches, vessels, cars, hotels, saloons, and other vehicles and places of accommodation, and we deliberately wait until they have got them in readiness, then walk in, and contend with as much assurance for a "right," as though the whole thing was bought by, paid for, and belonged to us. By their literary attainments, they are the contributors to, authors and teachers of, literature, science, religion, law, medicine, and all other useful attainments that the world now makes use of. . . .

These are the means by which God intended man to succeed: and this discloses the secret of the white man's success with all of his wickedness, over the head of the colored man, with all of his religion. . . . Until we are determined to change the condition of things, and raise ourselves above the position in which we are now prostrated, we must hang our heads in sorrow, and hide our faces in shame. It is enough to know that these things are so; the causes we care little about. Those we have been examining, complaining about, and moralising over, all our life time. This we are weary of. What we desire to learn now is, how to effect a *remedy;* this we have endeavored to point out. Our elevation must be the result of *self-efforts,* and work of our *own hands*. No other human power can accomplish it. If we but determine it shall be so, it will be so. Let each one make the case his own, and endeavor to rival his neighbor, in honorable competition.

These are the proper and only means of elevating ourselves and attaining equality in this country or any other, and it is useless, utterly futile, to think about going any where, except we are determined to use these as the necessary means of developing our manhood. The means are at hand, within our reach. Are we willing to try them? Are we willing to raise ourselves superior to the condition of slaves, or continue the meanest underlings, subject to the beck and call of every creature bearing a pale complexion? If we are, we had as well remained in the South, as to have come to the North in search of more freedom. What was the object of our parents in leaving the south, if it were not for the purpose of attaining equality in common with others of their fellow citizens, by giving their children access to all the advantages enjoyed by others? Surely this was their object. They heard of liberty and equality here, and they hastened on to enjoy it, and no people are more astonished and disappointed than they, who for the first time, on beholding the position we occupy here in the free north—what is called, and what they expect to find, the free States. They at once tell us, that they have as much liberty in the south as we have in the north—that there as free people, they are protected in their rights—that we have nothing more—that in other respects they have the same opportunity, indeed the preferred opportunity, of being their maids, servants, cooks, waiters, and menials in general, there, as we have here—that had they known for a moment, before leaving, that such was to be the only position they occupied here, they would have remained where they were, and never left. Indeed, such is the disappointment in many cases, that they immediately return back again, completely insulted at the idea, of having us here at the north, assume ourselves to be their superiors. Indeed, if our superior advantages of the free States, do not induce and stimulate us to the higher attainments in life, what in the name of degraded humanity will do it? Nothing, surely nothing. If, in fine, the advantages of free schools in Massachusetts, New York, Pennsylvania, Ohio, Michigan, and wherever else we may have them, do not give us advantages and pursuits superior to our slave brethren, then are the unjust assertions of . . . the host of our oppressors, slave-holders and others, true, that we are insusceptible and incapable of elevation to the more respectable, honorable, and higher attainments among white men. But this we do not believe—neither do you, although our whole life and course of policy in this country are such, that it would seem to prove otherwise. The degradation of the slave parent has been entailed upon the child, induced by the subtle policy of the oppressor, in regular succession handed down from father to son—a system of regular submission and servitude, menialism and dependence, until it has become almost a physiological function of our system, an actual condition of our nature. Let this no longer be so, but let us determine to equal the whites among whom we live, not by declarations and unexpressed self-opinion, for we have always had enough of that, but by actual proof in acting, doing, and carrying out practically, the measures of equality. Here is our nativity, and here have we the natural right to abide and be elevated through the measures of our own efforts.

We have said much to our young men and women, about their vocation and calling; we have dwelt much upon the menial position of our people in this country. Upon this point we cannot say too much, because there is a seeming satisfaction and seeking after such positions manifested on their part, unknown to any other people. There appears to be, a want of a sense of propriety or *self-respect,* altogether inexplicable; because young men and women among us, many of whom have good trades and homes, adequate to their support, voluntarily leave them, and seek positions, such as servants, waiting maids, coachmen, nurses, cooks in gentlemens' kitchen, or such like occupations, when they can gain a livelihood at something more respectable, or elevating in character. And the worse part of the whole matter is, that they have become so accustomed to it, it has become so "fashionable," that it seems to have become second nature, and they really become offended, when it is spoken against.

Among the German, Irish, and other European peasantry who come to this country, it matters not what they were employed at before and after they come; just so soon as they can better their condition by keeping shops, cultivating the soil, the young men and women going to night-schools, qualifying themselves for usefulness, and learning trades—they do so. Their first and last care, object and aim is, to better their condition by raising themselves above the condition that necessity places them in. We do not say too much, when we say, as an evidence of the deep degradation of our race, in the United States, that there are those among us, the wives and daughters, some of the *first ladies,* (and who dare say they are not the "first," because they belong to the "first class" and associate where any body among us can?) whose husbands are industrious, able and willing to support them, who voluntarily leave home, and become chamber-maids, and stewardesses, upon vessels and steamboats, in all probability, to enable them to obtain some more fine or costly article of dress or furniture.

We have nothing to say against those whom *necessity* compels to do these things, those who can do no better; we have only to do with those who can, and will not, or do not do better. The whites are always in the advance, and we either standing still or retrograding; as that which does not go forward, must either stand in one place or go back. The father in all probability is a farmer, mechanic, or man of some independent business; and the wife, sons and daughters, are chamber-maids, on vessels, nurses and waiting-maids, or coachmen and cooks in families. This is retrogradation. The wife, sons, and daughters should be elevated above this condition as a necessary consequence.

If we did not love our race superior to others, we would not concern ourself about their degradation; for the greatest desire of our heart is, to see them stand on a level with the most elevated of mankind. No people are ever elevated above the condition of their *females;* hence, the condition of the *mother* determines the condition of the child. To know the position of a people, it is only necessary to know the *condition* of their *females;* and despite themselves, they cannot rise above their level. Then what is our condition? Our *best ladies* being washerwomen, chamber-maids, children's traveling nurses, and common house servants, and menials, we are all a degraded, miserable people, inferior to any other people as a whole, on the face of the globe.

These great truths, however unpleasant, must be brought before the minds of our people in its true and proper light, as we have been too delicate about them, and too long concealed them for fear of giving offence. It would have been infinitely better for our race, if these facts had been presented before us half a century ago—we would have been now proportionably benefitted by it.

As an evidence of the degradation to which we have been reduced, we dare premise, that this chapter will give offence to many, very many, and why? Because they may say, "He dared to say that the occupation of a *servant* is a degradation." It is not necessarily degrading; it would not be, to one or a few people of a kind; but a *whole race of servants* are a degradation to that people.

Efforts made by men of qualifications for the toiling and degraded millions among the whites, neither gives offence to that class, nor is it taken unkindly by them; but received with manifestations of gratitude; to know that they are thought to be, equally worthy of, and entitled to stand on a level with the elevated classes; and they have only got to be informed of the way to raise themselves, to make the effort and do so as far as they can. But how different with us. Speak of our position in society, and it at once gives insult. Though we are servants; among ourselves we claim to be *ladies* and *gentlemen*, equal in standing, and as the popular expression goes, "Just as good as any body"—and so believing, we make no efforts to raise above the common level of menials; because the *best* being in that capacity, all are content with the position. We cannot at the same time, be domestic and lady; servant and gentleman. We must be the one or the other.

HOSEA EASTON CONDEMNS
COLOR PREJUDICE AGAINST THE NEGROES

In 1837 Hosea Easton, an obscure Negro minister, about whom little is known, published a pamphlet over Garrison's Boston imprint in which he heartily condemned prejudice against the Negro which rested on a presumed color distinction. In the selection which follows, Easton also emphasizes the sad lot of the Negro compared to that of other minority groups, and exhorts Americans to cease their discriminatory practices against the Negroes.

From Hosea Easton, A *Treatise on the Intellectual Character, and Civil and Political Conditions of the Colored People of the U. States, and the Prejudice Exercised Towards Them: With a Sermon on the Duty of the Church to Them* (Boston: I. Knapp, 1837), pp. 36–37, 49–50, 52–53.

Prejudice seems to possess a nature peculiar to itself. It never possesses any vitiating qualities, except when it is exercised by one who has done, or intends to do, another an injury. And its malignity is heightened in proportion as its victim in any way recovers, or has a manifest prospect of recovering the injury; or if there is apparently a door open by which a superior power to that which he possesses, may bring him to an account for the wrong done to his neighbor, all have a direct tendency to heighten the malignity of prejudice in the heart of its possessor.

The colored population are the injured party. And the prejudice of the whites against them is in exact proportion to the injury the colored people have sustained. There is a prejudice in this country against the Irish, who are flocking here by thousands. Still there is nothing malignant in the nature and exercise of that prejudice, either national or personal. It grows out of the mere circumstance of their different manners and religion. The moment an Irishman adopts the maxims and prevailing religion of the country, he is no longer regarded an Irishman, other than by birth. It is to be remembered, also, that the Irish are not an injured, but a benefited party; therefore, it is not possible that the bestower of benefits could be at the same time malignantly exercising prejudice towards those he is benefiting.

There exists, therefore, no injurious prejudice against the Irish. There exists a prejudice against the Indians, but it is almost entirely national, and for the very reason that the injury they have sustained is essentially national. The jealous eye of this nation is fixed upon them as a nation, and has ever exercised the rigor of its prejudice towards them, in proportion as they attempted to recover their rightful possessions; or, in other words, just in proportion as the physical powers of the Indians, have dwindled to inefficiency, prejudice against them has become lax and passive. It revives only as they shows signs of national life.

The injury sustained by the colored people, is both national and personal; indeed, it is national in a twofold sense. In the first place, they are lineally stolen from their native country, and detained for centuries, in a strange land, as hewers of wood and drawers of water. In this situation, their blood, habits, minds, and bodies, have undergone such a change, as to cause them to lose all legal or natural relations to their mother country. They are no longer her children; therefore, they sustain the great injury of losing their country, their birthright, and are made aliens and illegitimates. Again, they sustain a national injury by being adopted subjects and citizens, and then be denied their citizenship, and the benefits derivable therefrom —accounted as aliens and outcasts, hence, are identified as belonging to no country—denied birthright in one, and had it stolen from them in another—and, I had like to have said, they had lost title to both worlds; for certainly they are denied all title in this, and almost all advantages to prepare for the next. In this light of the subject, they belong to no people, race, or nation; subjects of no government—citizens of no country—scattered surplus remnants of two races, and of different nations—severed into individuality—rendered a mass of broken fragments, thrown to and fro, by the boisterous passions of this and other ungodly nations. Such, in part, are the national injuries sustained by this miserable people. . . .

. . . The colored people being constitutionally Americans, they are depending on American climate, American aliment, American government, and American manners, to sustain their American bodies and minds; a withholding of the enjoyment of any American principle from an American man, either governmental, ecclesiastical, civil, social or alimental, is in effect taking away his means of subsistence; and consequently, taking away his life. Every ecclesiastical body which denies an American the privilege of participating in its benefits, becomes his murderer. Every state which denies an American a citizenship with all its benefits, denies him his life. Every community which denies an American the privilege of public conveyances, in common with all others, murders him by piece-meal. Every community which withholds social intercourse with an American, by which he may enjoy current information, becomes his murderer of the worst kind. The claims the colored people set up, therefore, are the claims of an American.

They ask priests and people to withhold no longer their inalienable rights to seek happiness in the sanctuary of God, at the same time and place that other Americans seek happiness. They ask statesmen to open the way whereby they, in common with other Americans, may aspire to honor and worth as statesmen—to place their names with other Americans—subject to a draft as jurymen and other functionary appointments, according to their ability. They ask their white American brethren to think of them and treat them as American citizens, and neighbors, and as members of the same American family. They urge their claims in full assurance of their being founded in immutable justice. They urge them from a sense of patriotism, from an interest they feel in the well being of their common country. And lastly, they urge them from the conviction that God, the judge of all men, will avenge them of their wrongs, unless their claims are speedily granted.

There are some objections urged against these claims. One is, that the greater part of the colored people are held as property, and if these claims are granted, their owners would be subject to great loss. In answer to this objection, I would remark, that were I to accede to the right of the master to his property in man, still I should conceive the objection groundless, for it is a well known fact that a far greater portion of the colored people who are free, purchased their freedom, and the freedom of their families. Many of them have purchased themselves several times over. Thousands of dollars have been paid over to masters annually, which was the proceeds of extra labor, in consideration of their expected freedom. My colored acquaintances are numerous who have thus done, some of whom were under the necessity of running away to obtain their freedom after all.

I am sufficiently acquainted with the sentiments and views of the slave population of every slave state in the union, to warrant me in the conclusion, that if the despotic power of the master was wrested from him, and the slaves placed under a law of ever so rigid a nature, with the privilege of paying for themselves by their extra labor, there would be comparatively few slaves in the country in less than seven years. The most of them would pay the round price of their bodies, and come out freemen.

Another objection is, that the slaves, if freed at once, would not be capable of enjoying suffrages.

This objection has less foundation than the former, for the several state legislatures of the slave states are continually assisting the masters to keep them in ignorance, and why not legislate in favor of their being informed?

Some contend that they are not now fit for freedom, but ought to be prepared and then freed.

Such a calculation is preposterous. We might as well talk about educating a water machine to run against its propelling power, as to talk about educating a slave for a free man. . . .

. . . Let the country, then, no longer act the part of the thief. Let the free states no longer act the part of them who passed by on the other side, and leaving the colored people half dead, especially when they were beaten by their own hands, and so call it emancipation—raising a wonderment why the half dead people do not heal themselves. Let them rather act the part of the good Samaritan. That only will open an effectual door through which sympathies can flow, and by which a reciprocity of sentiment and interest can take place—a proper knowledge acquired by the benefactor relative to his duty, and reciprocated on the part of the benefited.

This state of things would possess redeeming power. Every collateral means would be marshaled under the heaven-born principle, that requires all men to do unto others as they would that others should do unto them. It would kindle anew the innate principles of moral, civil and social manhood, in the downtrodden colored Americans; bidding them arise as from the dead, and speed their way back to the height from whence they have fallen. Nor would the call be in vain. A corresponding action on their part would respond to the cheering voice. The countenance which has been cast down, hitherto, would brighten up with joy. Their narrow foreheads, which have hitherto been contracted for the want of mental exercise, would begin to broaden. Their eye balls, hitherto strained out to prominence by a frenzy excited by the flourish of the whip, would fall back under a thick foliage of curly eyebrows, indicative of deep penetrating thought. Those muscles, which have hitherto been distended by grief and weeping, would become contracted to an acuteness, corresponding to that acuteness of perception with which business men are blessed. That interior region, the dwelling place of the soul, would be lighted up with the fires of love and gratitude to their benefactors on earth, and to their great Benefactor above, driving back those clouds of slavery and of prejudice which have hitherto darkened and destroyed its vision. And thus their whole man would be redeemed, rendering them fit for the associates of their fellow men in this life, and for the associates of angels in the world to come.

CHARLES REMOND

CONDEMNS DISCRIMINATION IN

PUBLIC TRANSPORTATION

Concerned with the practice of segregation and discrimination in public transportation, Charles Lenox Remond (1810–1873), agent for the American Anti-Slavery Society and con-

stant supporter of abolitionist causes at home and in England, where he lectured for two years, appeared before "the Legislative Committee in the [Massachusetts] House of Representatives, respecting the rights of colored citizens in travelling, &c." In his remarks he spoke out against the "wrongs inflicted and injuries received" when such discrimination was practiced against himself and other Negroes.

Mr. Chairman, and Gentlemen of the Committee:

In rising at this time, and on this occasion, being the first person of color who has ever addressed either of the bodies assembling in this building, I should, perhaps, in the first place, observe that, in consequence of the many misconstructions of the principles and measures of which I am the humble advocate, I may in like manner be subject to similar misconceptions from the moment I open my lips in behalf of the prayer of the petitioners for whom I appear, and therefore feel I have the right at least to ask, at the hands of this intelligent Committee, an impartial hearing; and that whatever prejudices they may have imbibed, be eradicated from their minds, if such exist. I have, however, too much confidence in their intelligence, and too much faith in their determination to do their duty as the representatives of this Commonwealth, to presume they can be actuated by partial motives. Trusting, as I do, that the day is not distant, when, on all questions touching the rights of the citizens of this State, men shall be considered *great* only as they are *good*—and not that it shall be told, and painfully experienced, that, in this country, this State, ay, this city, the Athens of America, the rights, privileges and immunities of its citizens are measured by complexion, or any other physical

---

From Charles Lenox Remond, "Remarks . . . before the Legislative Committee in the [Massachusetts] House of Representatives, respecting the rights of colored citizens in traveling, &c.," in the *Liberator*, February 25, 1842.

peculiarity or conformation, especially such as over which no man has any control. Complexion can in no sense be construed into crime, much less be rightfully made the criterion of rights. Should the people of color, through a revolution of Providence, become a majority, to the last I would oppose it upon the same principle; for, in either case, it would be equally reprehensible and unjustifiable—alike to be condemned and repudiated. It is JUSTICE I stand here to claim, and not FAVOR for either complexion. . . .

. . . Our right to citizenship in this State has been acknowledged and secured by the allowance of the elective franchise and consequent taxation; and I know of no good reason, if admitted in this instance, why it should be denied in any other.

With reference to the wrongs inflicted and injuries received on rail-roads, by persons of color, I need not say they do not end with the termination of the route, but, in effect, tend to discourage, disparage and depress this class of citizens. All hope of reward for upright conduct is cut off. Vice in them becomes a virtue. No distinction is made by the community in which we live. The most vicious is treated as well as the most respectable, both in public and private.

But it is said, we all look alike. If this is true, it is not true that we all behave alike. There is a marked difference; and we claim a recognition of this difference.

In the present state of things, they find God's provisions interfered with in such a way, by these and kindred regulations, that virtue may not claim her divinely appointed rewards. Color is made to obscure the brightest endowments, to degrade the fairest character, and to check the highest and most praiseworthy aspirations. If the colored man is vicious, it makes but little difference; if besotted, it matters not; if vulgar, it is quite as well; and he finds himself as well treated, and received as readily into society, as those of an opposite character. Nay, the higher our aspirations, the loftier our purposes and pursuits, does this iniquitous principle of prejudice fasten upon us, and especial pains are taken to irritate, obstruct and injure. No reward of merit, no remuneration for services, no equivalent is rendered the deserving. And I submit, whether this unkind and unchristian policy is not well calculated to make every man disregardful of his conduct, and every woman unmindful of her reputation.

The grievances of which we complain, be assured, sir, are not imaginary, but real—not local, but universal—not occasional, but continual, every day matter of fact things—and have become, to the disgrace of our common country, matter of history.

Mr. Chairman, the treatment to which colored Americans are exposed in their own country finds a counterpart in no other; and I am free to declare, that, in the course of nineteen months' travelling in England, Ireland and Scotland,[1] I was received, treated and recognised, in public and private society, without any regard to my complexion. From the moment I left the American packet ship in Liverpool, up to the moment I came in contact with it again, I was never reminded of my complexion; and all that know any thing of my usage in the American ship, will testify that it was unfit for a brute, and none but one could inflict it. But how unlike that afforded in the British steamer Columbia! Owing to my limited resources, I took a steerage passage. On the first day out, the second officer came to inquire after my health; and finding me the only passenger in that part of the ship, ordered the steward to give me a berth in the second cabin; and from that hour until my stepping on shore at Boston, every politeness was shown me by the officers, and every kindness and attention by the stewards; and I feel under deep and lasting obligations to them, individually and collectively.

In no instance was I insulted, or treated in any way distinct

---

[1] Remond stayed in England after the World Antislavery Convention of 1840 for nearly two years. [Eds.]

or dissimilar from other passengers or travellers, either in coaches, rail-roads, steampackets, or hotels; and if the feeling was entertained, in no case did I discover its existence.

I may with propriety here relate an incident, illustrative of the subject now under consideration. I took a passage ticket at the steam packet office in Glasgow, for Dublin; and on going into the cabin to retire, I found the berth I had engaged occupied by an Irish gentleman and merchant. I enquired if he had not mistaken the number of his berth? He thought not. On comparing tickets, we saw that the clerk had given two tickets of the same number; and it appeared I had received mine first. The gentleman at once offered to vacate the berth, against which I remonstrated, and took my berth in an opposite stateroom. Here, sir, we discover treatment just, impartial, reasonable; and we ask nothing beside.

There is a marked difference between social and civil rights. It has been well and justly marked, by my friend Mr. Phillips,[2] that we all claim the privilege of selecting our society and associations; but, in civil rights, one man has not the prerogative to define rights for another. For instance, sir, in public conveyances, for the rich man to usurp the privileges to himself, to the injury of the poor man, would be submitted to in no well regulated society. And such is the position suffered by persons of color. On my arrival home from England, I went to the railway station, to go to Salem, being anxious to see my parents and sisters as soon as possible—asked for a ticket—paid 50 cents for it, and was pointed to the American designation car. Having previously received information of the regulations, I took my seat peaceably, believing it better to suffer wrong than do wrong. I felt then, as I felt on many occasions prior to leaving home, unwilling to descend so low as to bandy words with the superintendents, or contest my rights with conductors, or any others in the capacity of servants of any stage

---

[2] Wendell Phillips, see pp. 459–479. [Eds.]

or steamboat company, or rail-road corporation; although I never, by any means, gave evidence that, by my submission, I intended to sanction usages which would derogate from uncivilized, much less long and loud professing and high pretending America.

Bear with me, while I relate an additional occurrence. On the morning after my return home, I was obliged to go to Boston again, and on going to the Salem station, I met two friends, who enquired if I had any objection to their taking seats with me. I answered, I should be most happy. They took their seats accordingly, and soon afterwards one of them remarked to me—'Charles, I don't know if they will allow us to ride with you.' It was some time before I could understand what they meant, and, on doing so, I laughed—feeling it to be a climax to every absurdity I had heard attributed to Americans. To say nothing of the wrong done those friends, and the insult and indignity offered me by the appearance of the conductor, who ordered the friends from the car in a somewhat harsh manner—they immediately left the carriage.

On returning to Salem some few evenings afterwards, Mr. Chase, the superintendent on this road, made himself known to me by recalling by-gone days and scenes, and then enquired if I was not glad to get home, after so long an absence in Europe. I told him I was glad to see my parents and family again, and this was the only object I could have, unless he thought I should be glad to take a hermit's life in the great pasture; inasmuch as I never felt to loathe my American name so much as since my arrival. He wished to know my reasons for the remark. I immediately gave them, and wished to know of him, if, in the event of his having a brother with red hair, he should find himself separated while travelling because of this difference, he should deem it just. He could make no reply. I then wished to know if the principle was not the same; and if so, there was an insult implied by his question. In conclusion, I challenged him, as the instrument inflicting the manifold injuries upon all not colored like himself, to the presentation of an instance in any other christian or unchristian country, tolerating usages at once so disgraceful, unjust and inhuman. What if some few of the West or East India planters and merchants should visit our liberty-loving country, with their colored wives—how would he manage? Or, if R. M. Johnson, the gentleman who has been elevated to the second office in the gift of the people, should be travelling from Boston to Salem, if he was prepared to separate him from his wife or daughters. (Involuntary burst of applause, instantly restrained.)

Sir, it happens to be my lot to have a sister a few shades lighter than myself; and who knows, if this state of things is encouraged, whether I may not on some future occasion be mobbed in Washington street, on the supposition of walking with a white young lady! (Suppressed indications of sympathy and applause.)

Gentlemen of the Committee, these distinctions react in all their wickedness—to say nothing of their concocted and systematised odiousness and absurdity—upon those who instituted them; and particularly so upon those who are illiberal and mean enough to practise them.

Mr. Chairman, if colored people have abused any rights granted them, or failed to exhibit due appreciation of favors bestowed, or shrunk from dangers or responsibility, let it be made to appear. Or if our country contains a population to compare with them in loyalty and patriotism, circumstances duly considered, I have it yet to learn. The history of our country must ever testify in their behalf. In view of these and many additional considerations, I unhesitatingly assert their claim, on the naked principle of merit, to every advantage set forth in the Constitution of this Commonwealth.

Finally, Mr. Chairman, there is in this and other States a large and growing colored population, whose residence in your midst has not been from choice, (let this be understood and reflected upon,) but by the force of circumstances, over which they never had control. Upon the heads of their oppressors and calumniators be the censure and responsibility. If to ask at your hands redress for injuries, and protection in our rights and immunities, as citizens, is reasonable, and dictated alike by justice, humanity and religion, you will not reject, I trust, the prayer of your petitioners.

XI

Arguments on the Constitution

WILLIAM I. BOWDITCH CONDEMNS THE CONSTITUTION AS PROSLAVERY

William Ingersoll Bowditch (1819–1909), lawyer and one of the Boston group of abolitionists, represented the Garrisonian view that the Constitution was a proslavery document. He adduces in his extended work, Slavery and the Constitution, *the standard arguments and references which he and others used widely to justify Garrison's assertion that the Constitution was "a covenant with death and an agreement with hell."*

From William Ingersoll Bowditch, *Slavery and the Constitution* (Boston: Robert F. Wallcutt, 1849), pp. 120–126.

At the time of the adoption of the Constitution, slavery existed in all the States except Massachusetts. How far, if at all, does this instrument support or countenance the institution?

Art. 1, sec. 2: "Representatives and direct taxes shall be apportioned among the several States which may be included within this union, according to their respective numbers, which shall be determined by adding to the whole number of free persons, including those bound to service for a term of years, and excluding Indians not taxed, three-fifths of all other persons."

By this section, persons are divided into those who are free and those who are slaves; for to the whole number of *free* persons are to be added three-fifths of *all other* persons, that is, persons not free, or *slaves*. If we adopt the plain, obvious, and common meaning of the words as their true meaning, this conclusion is incontrovertible.

It is sometimes urged, that by "free person" is meant "citizen." But the expression cannot be taken in any such technical sense. Under the expression "free persons" are included those bound to service for a term of years, and therefore from it are excluded those bound to service for life, or slaves.

This article, therefore, recognizes slavery as explicitly as if the word *slave* itself had been used, and gives to the free persons in a Slave State, solely because they are slaveholders, a large representation, and consequently greater political power, than the same number of free persons in a Free State. A BOUNTY ON SLAVEHOLDING!

Art. 1, sec. 9: "The *migration or importation* of such persons as any of the States now existing shall think proper to admit, shall not be prohibited by the Congress prior to the year one thousand eight hundred and eight; but a tax or duty may be imposed on such *importation*, not exceeding ten dollars for each person."

It is clear that this section recognizes a difference between the meaning of *migration* and *importation*, since, if both words mean the same thing, no reason whatever can be assigned why a tax is not permitted in both cases. This difference, whatever it is, must afford a good reason why persons imported may be taxed, and persons migrating not. The true meaning of the section seems obvious. A person who migrates does so of his own accord: he cannot be said to be migrated by any other person. He is wholly a free agent. A person who is imported does not import himself, but is imported by some other person. He is passive. The importer is the free agent; the person imported is not a free agent. Thus the slave-laws of Virginia of 1748 and 1753 begin—"All *persons* who have been or shall be *imported*," &c. &c. *"shall be* accounted and be *slaves."* Whenever we hear an importation spoken of, we instantly infer an importer, an *owner*, and *property* imported. This distinction between the meaning of the two words is, then, real. It affords a good reason for the restriction on the right to tax. Therefore, we say, it is the true distinction. On our construction, Congress had power to lay a tax on persons imported as property or slaves, but had no right to tax free persons migrating.

By this clause, therefore, Congress was prevented, during twenty years, from prohibiting the foreign slave-trade with any State that pleased to allow it. But, by Art. 1, sec. 8, Congress had the general power "to regulate commerce with foreign nations." Consequently, *the slave-trade was excepted from the operation of the general power, with a view to place the slave-trade, during twenty years, solely under the control of the Slave States.* It could not be wholly stopped, so long as one State wished to continue it. It is a clear compromise in favor of slavery. True, the compromise was a temporary one; but it will be noticed, that Congress, even after 1808, was not obliged to prohibit the trade; and, in point of fact, until 1819 the laws of Congress authorized the States to sell into slavery, for their own benefit, negroes imported contrary to the laws of the United States! . . .

Art. 4, sec. 2: "No person held to service or labor in one State, under the laws thereof, escaping into another, shall, in consequence of any law or regulation therein, be discharged from such service or labor; but shall be delivered up, on claim of the party to whom such service or labor may be due."

The time of holding not being limited, the expression here used must include not only persons held to service or labor for a term of years, but also those held to service or labor for life. Consequently, it includes those who are free persons within the meaning of Art. 1, sec. 2, and slaves or persons held to service or labor for life.

That the expression "person held to service or labor" was a correct definition of the condition of a slave, at the time the Constitution was adopted, is evident. The sixth article of the North-western ordinance reads thus: "There shall be neither slavery nor involuntary servitude in the said territory, otherwise than in the punishment of crimes, whereof the party shall have been duly convicted; provided always, that, any person escaping into the same, from whom labor or service is lawfully claimed in any one of the original States, such fugitive may be lawfully reclaimed, and conveyed to the person claiming his or her labor or service as aforesaid." In other words, the expression "a person from whom labor or service is lawfully claimed" so correctly described the condition of a slave, that Congress deemed it necessary to except such persons from the operation of an article relating only to slaves. In less than three months after the passage of this ordinance, this clause in the Constitution was drafted. It needs no argument to show, that the expression in the Constitution means the same as that in the ordinance. "A person from whom labor or service is lawfully claimed in any one of the original States" means the same as "a person held to service or labor in one State under the laws thereof." If the former correctly described the condition of a slave, the latter did also. . . .

. . . By this section, therefore, it is provided that no person held as a slave in one State under the laws thereof, escaping into another, shall, in consequence of any law or regulation therein, be discharged from his slavery, but shall be delivered up on claim of his owner. The laws of one State, whether they support slavery or any other institution, have no power in another State. Consequently, if a slave escapes into a Free State, he becomes free. This is the general rule of law. In virtue of it, thousands of slaves are now free on the soil of Canada. In virtue of it, a fugitive slave from South Carolina would be free in this State, were it not for this section in the Constitution. But this section declares that he shall not thereby become free, but shall be delivered up. Again, *the Constitution makes an exception from a general rule of law in favor of slavery.* It gives to slaveholders, and slave-laws, a power which the general rule of law does not give. It enables a South Carolina slaveholder to drag from the soil of Massachusetts a person whom the general rule of law pronounces free, solely because South Carolina laws declare the contrary. It makes the whole Union a vast hunting-ground for slaves! There is not a single spot from the Atlantic to the Pacific, from the St. John's to the Rio del Norte, or "wheresoe'er may be the fleeting boundary of this republic," on which a fugitive slave may rest, and his owner may not, in virtue of this clause, claim and retake him as his slave!

Art. 1, sec. 8: "Congress shall have power. . . . to provide for calling forth the militia . . . . to *suppress insurrections.*"[1]

Art. 4, sec. 4: "The United States shall guarantee to every State in this Union a republican form of government, and shall protect each of them against invasion; and, on application of the legislature

---

[1] The ellipses occur in the original. [Eds.]

or of the executive (when the legislature cannot be convened), against *domestic violence.*"

All insurrections and *all* cases of domestic violence are here provided for. To constitute an insurrection within the meaning of the Constitution, there must be a rising against those laws which are recognized as such by the Constitution; and, to make out a case of domestic violence, the violence must be exerted against that right or power which is recognized by the Constitution as lawful. But, by Art. 4, sec. 2, the Constitution admits that some persons are legally slaves; else the clause itself must be entirely inoperative. Consequently, if these persons rise in rebellion, or commit acts of violence contrary to the laws which hold them in slavery, their rising constitutes an insurrection; such acts are acts of violence within the meaning of the Constitution, and consequently must be suppressed by the national power. And what insurrections were more likely to happen and more to be dreaded than slave-insurrections, and therefore more likely to have been provided for?

Slave-owners are not the only slaveholders. All persons who voluntarily assist or pledge themselves to assist in holding persons in slavery are slaveholders. *In sober truth, then, we are a nation of slaveholders!* for we have bound our whole national strength to the slave-owners, to aid them, if necessary, in holding their slaves in subjection!

FREDERICK DOUGLASS ASSERTS THAT THE CONSTITUTION IS ANTISLAVERY

Frederick Douglass (ca. 1817–1895) was, as an ex-slave, far more eager than most Garrisonians to use every means available to end slavery. He broke in the late 1840's with Garrison over the issue of establishing his own paper (The North Star, later called Frederick Douglass' Paper). *Later he became an active exponent of political antislavery. Here, in his defence of the Constitution as an antislavery document, he shows his underlying concern to use the governmental structure as it was to end slavery as speedily as possible rather than to delay acting until the government was wholly reformed or revolutionized.*

Here then are the several provisions of the Constitution to which reference has been made. I read them word for word just as they stand in the paper, called the United States Constitution, Art. 1, sec. 2. "Representatives and direct taxes shall be apportioned among the several States which may be included in this Union, according to their respective numbers, which shall be determined by adding to the whole number of free persons, including those bound to service for a term of years, and excluding Indians not taxed, three-fifths of all other persons; Art. 1, sec. 9. The migration or importation of such persons as any of the States now existing shall think fit to admit, shall not be prohibited by the Congress prior to the year one thousand eight hundred and eight, but a tax or duty may be imposed on such importation, not exceeding ten dollars for each person; Art. 4, sec. 2. No person held to service or labour in one State, under the laws thereof, escaping into another shall, in consequence of any law or regulation therein, be discharged from such service or labour; but shall be delivered up on claim of the party to whom such service or labour may be due; Art. 1, sec. 8. To provide for calling forth the militia to execute the laws of the Union, suppress insurrections, and repel invasions." Here, then, are those provisions of the Constitution, which the most extravagant defenders of slavery can claim to

---

From Frederick Douglass, *The Constitution of the United States: Is It Pro-Slavery or Anti-Slavery?* (Halifax: T. & W. Birtwhistle, [1860]), pp. 8–16.

guarantee a right of property in man. These are the provisions which have been pressed into the service of the human flesh-mongers of America. Let us look at them just as they stand, one by one. Let us grant, for sake of the argument, that the first of these provisions, referring to the basis of representation and taxation, does refer to slaves. We are not compelled to make that admission, for it might fairly apply to aliens—persons living in the country, but not naturalized. But giving the provisions the very worst construction, what does it amount to? I answer—It is a downright disability laid upon the slaveholding States; one which deprives those States of two-fifths of their natural basis of representation. A black man in a free State is worth just two-fifths more than a black man in a slave State, as a basis of political power under the Constitution. Therefore, instead of encouraging slavery, the Constitution encourages freedom by giving an increase of "two-fifths" of political power to free over slave States. So much for the three-fifths clause; taking it at its worst, it still leans to freedom, not to slavery; for, be it remembered that the Constitution nowhere forbids a coloured man to vote. I come to the next, that which it is said guaranteed the continuance of the African slave trade for twenty years. I will also take that for just what my opponent alleges it to have been, although the Constitution does not warrant any such conclusion. But, to be liberal, let us suppose it did, and what follows? why, this—that this part of the Constitution, so far as the slave trade is concerned, became a dead letter more than 50 years ago, and now binds no man's conscience for the continuance of any slave trade whatever. Mr. Thompson[1] is just 52 years too late in dissolving the Union on account of this clause. He might as well dissolve the British Government, because Queen Elizabeth granted to Sir John Hawkins to import Africans into the West Indies 300 years ago! But there is still more to be said about this abolition of the

---

[1] George Thompson; see p. 319. [Eds.]

slave trade. Men, at that time, both in England and in America, looked upon the slave trade as the life of slavery. The abolition of the slave trade was supposed to be the certain death of slavery. Cut off the stream, and the pond will dry up, was the common notion at that time. Wilberforce and Clarkson,[2] clear-sighted as they were, took this view; and the American statesmen, in providing for the abolition of the slave trade, thought they were providing for the abolition of slavery. This view is quite consistent with the history of the times. All regarded slavery as an expiring and doomed system, destined to speedily disappear from the country. But, again, it should be remembered that this very provision, if made to refer to the African slave trade at all, makes the Constitution anti-slavery rather than for slavery, for it says to the slave States, the price you will have to pay for coming into the American Union is, that the slave trade, which you would carry on indefinitely out of the Union, shall be put an end to in twenty years if you come into the Union. Secondly, if it does apply, it expired by its own limitation more than fifty years ago. Thirdly, it is anti-slavery, because it looked to the abolition of slavery rather than to its perpetuity. Fourthly, it showed that the intentions of the framers of the Constitution were good, not bad. I think this is quite enough for this point. I go to the "slave insurrection" clause, though, in truth, there is no such clause. The one which is called so has nothing whatever to do with slaves or slaveholders any more than your laws for the suppression of popular outbreaks has to do with making slaves of you and your children. It is only a law for suppression of riots or insurrections. But I will be generous here, as well as elsewhere, and grant that it applies to slave insurrections. Let us suppose that an anti-slavery man is President of the United States (and

---

[2] William Wilberforce (1759–1833) and Thomas Clarkson (1760–1846) were British reformers and antislavery enthusiasts. Together they are credited with the principal efforts leading ultimately to the abolition, in 1833, of slavery throughout the British Empire. [Eds.]

the day that shall see this the case is not distant) and this very power of suppressing slave insurrection would put an end to slavery. The right to put down an insurrection carries with it the right to determine the means by which it shall be put down. If it should turn out that slavery is a source of insurrection, that there is no security from insurrections while slavery lasts, why, the Constitution would be best obeyed by putting an end to slavery, and an anti-slavery Congress would do that very thing. Thus, you see, the so-called slave-holding provisions of the American Constitution, which a little while ago looked so formidable, are, after all, no defence or guarantee for slavery whatever. But there is one other provision. This is called the "Fugitive Slave Provision." It is called so by those who wish to make it subserve the interest of slavery in America, and the same by those who wish to uphold the views of a party in this country. It is put thus in the speech at the City Hall:[3]— "Let us go back to 1787, and enter Liberty Hall, Philadelphia, where sat in convention the illustrious men who framed the Constitution—with George Washington in the chair. On the 27th of September, Mr. Butler and Mr. Pinckney, two delegates from the State of South Carolina, moved that the Constitution should require that fugitive slaves and servants should be delivered up like criminals, and after a discussion on the subject, the clause, as it stands in the Constitution, was adopted. After this, in the conventions held in the several States to ratify the Constitution, the same meaning was attached to the words. For example, Mr. Madison (afterwards President), when recommending the Constitution to his constituents, told them that the clause would secure them their property in slaves." I must ask you to look well to this statement. Upon its face, it would seem a full and fair statement of the history of the transaction it professes to describe and yet I declare unto you, knowing as I

---

[3] The speech referred to here was one delivered on February 28, 1860, in the City Hall of Glasgow, attacking Douglass. [Eds.]

do the facts in the case, my utter amazement at the downright untruth conveyed under the fair seeming words now quoted. The man who could make such a statement may have all the craftiness of a lawyer, but who can accord to him the candour of an honest debater? What could more completely destroy all confidence in his statements? Mark you, the orator had not allowed his audience to hear read the provision of the Constitution to which he referred. He merely characterized it as one to "deliver up fugitive slaves and servants like criminals," and tells you that that provision was adopted as it stands in the Constitution. He tells you that this was done "after discussion." But he took good care not to tell you what was the nature of that discussion. He would have spoiled the whole effect of his statement had he told you the whole truth. Now, what are the facts connected with this provision of the Constitution? You shall have them. It seems to take two men to tell the truth. It is quite true that Mr. Butler and Mr. Pinckney introduced a provision expressly with a view to the recapture of fugitive slaves: it is quite true also that there was some discussion on the subject—and just here the truth shall come out. These illustrious kidnappers were told promptly in that discussion that no such idea as property in man should be admitted into the Constitution. The speaker in question might have told you, and he would have told you but the simple truth, if he had told you that the proposition of Mr. Butler and Mr. Pinckney—which he leads you to infer was adopted by the convention that framed the Constitution—was, in fact, promptly and indignantly rejected by that convention. He might have told you, had it suited his purpose to do so, that the words employed in the first draft of the fugitive clause were such as applied to the condition of slaves, and expressly declared that persons held to "servitude" should be given up; but that the word "servitude" was struck from the provision, for the very reason that it applied to slaves. He might have told you that that same Mr. Madison declared that that word was struck out because the convention would not consent that the idea of property in men should be admitted into the Constitution. The fact that Mr. Madison can be cited on both sides of this question is another evidence of the folly and absurdity of making the secret intentions of the framers the criterion by which the Constitution is to be construed. But it may be asked—if this clause does not apply to slaves, to whom does it apply? I answer, that when adopted, it applied to a very large class of persons—namely, redemptioners—persons who had come to America from Holland, from Ireland, and other quarters of the globe—like the Coolies to the West Indies—and had, for a consideration duly paid, become bound to "serve and labour" for the parties to whom their service and labour was due. It applies to indentured apprentices and others who had become bound for a consideration, under contract duly made, to serve and labour. To such persons this provision applies, and only to such persons. The plain reading of this provision shows that it applies, and that it can only properly and legally apply, to persons "bound to service." Its object plainly is, to secure the fulfilment of contracts for "service and labour." It applies to indentured apprentices, and any other persons from whom service and labour may be due. The legal condition of the slave puts him beyond the operation of this provision. He is not described in it. He is a simple article of property. He does not owe and cannot owe service. He cannot even make a contract. It is impossible for him to do so. He can no more make such a contract than a horse or an ox can make one. This provision, then, only respects persons who owe service, and they only can owe service who can receive an equivalent and make a bargain. The slave cannot do that, and is therefore exempted from the operation of this fugitive provision. In all matters where laws are taught to be made the means of oppression, cruelty, and wickedness, I am for strict construction. I will concede nothing. It must be shown that it is so nominated in the bond. The pound of flesh, but not one drop of blood. The very nature of law is opposed to all such wickedness, and makes it difficult to accomplish such objects under the forms of law. Law is not merely an arbitrary enactment with regard to justice, reason, or humanity. Blackstone defines it to be a rule prescribed by the supreme power of the State commanding what is right and forbidding what is wrong. The speaker at the City Hall laid down some rules of legal interpretation. These rules send us to the history of the law for its meaning. I have no objection to such a course in ordinary cases of doubt. But where human liberty and justice are at stake, the case falls under an entirely different class of rules. There must be something more than history—something more than tradition. The Supreme Court of the United States lays down this rule, and it meets the case exactly—"Where rights are infringed—where the fundamental principles of the law are overthrown—where the general system of the law is departed from, the legislative intention must be expressed with irresistible clearness." The same court says that the language of the law must be construed strictly in favour of justice and liberty. Again, there is another rule of law. It is—Where a law is susceptible of two meanings, the one making it accomplish an innocent purpose, and the other making it accomplish a wicked purpose, we must in all cases adopt that which makes it accomplish an innocent purpose. Again, the details of a law are to be interpreted in the light of the declared objects sought by the law. I set these rules down against those employed at the City Hall. To me they seem just and rational. I only ask you to look at the American Constitution in the light of them, and you will see with me that no man is guaranteed a right of property in man, under the provisions of that instrument. If there are two ideas more distinct in their character and essence than another, those ideas are "persons" and "property," "men" and "things." Now, when it is proposed to transform persons into "property" and men into beasts of burden, I demand that the law that contemplates such a purpose shall be expressed with irresistible clearness. The thing must not be left to inference, but must be done in plain English. I know how this view of the subject is treated by the class represented at the City Hall. They are in the habit of treating the negro as an exception to general rules. When their own liberty is in question they will avail themselves of all rules of law which protect and defend their freedom; but when the black man's rights are in question they concede everything, admit everything for slavery, and put liberty to the proof. They reverse the common law usage, and presume the negro a slave unless he can prove himself free. I, on the other hand, presume him free unless he is proved to be otherwise. Let us look at the objects for which the Constitution was framed and adopted, and see if slavery is one of them. Here are its own objects as set forth by itself:—"We, the people of these United States, in order to form a more perfect union, establish justice, ensure domestic tranquillity, provide for the common defence, promote the general welfare, and secure the blessings of liberty to ourselves and our prosperity [sic], do ordain and establish this Constitution for the United States of America." The objects here set forth are six in number: union, defence, welfare, tranquillity, justice, and liberty. These are all good objects, and slavery, so far from being among them, is a foe of them all. But it has been said that negroes are not included within the benefits sought under this declaration. This is said by the slaveholders in America—it is said by the City Hall orator—but it is not said by the Constitution itself. Its language is "we the people;" not we the white people, not even we the citizens, not we the privileged class, not we the high, not we the low, but we the people; not we the horses, sheep, and swine, and wheel-barrows, but we the people, we the human inhabitants; and, if negroes are people, they are included in the benefits for which the Constitution of America was ordained and established. But how dare any man who pretends to be a friend to the negro thus gratuitously concede away what the negro has a right to claim under the Constitution? Why should such friends invent new arguments to increase the hopelessness of his bondage? This, I undertake to say, as the conclusion of the whole matter, that the constitutionality of slavery can be made out only by disregarding the plain and common-sense reading of the Constitution itself; by discrediting and casting away as worthless the most beneficent rules of legal interpretation; by ruling the negro outside of these beneficent rules; by claiming everything for slavery; by denying everything for freedom; by assuming that the Constitution does not mean what it says, and that it says what it does not mean; by disregarding the written Constitution, and interpreting it in the light of a secret understanding. It is in this mean, contemptible, and underhand method that the American Constitution is pressed into the service of slavery. They go everywhere else for proof that the Constitution is pro-slavery but to the Constitution itself. The Constitution declares that no person shall be deprived of life, liberty, or property without due process of law; it secures to every man the right of trial by jury, the privilege of the writ of habeas corpus—that great writ that put an end to slavery and slave-hunting in England— it secures to every State a republican form of government. Any one of these provisions, in the hands of abolition statesmen, and backed up by a right moral sentiment, would put an end to slavery in America. The Constitution forbids the passing of a bill of attainder: that is, a law entailing upon the child the disabilities and hardships imposed upon the parent. Every slave law in America might be repealed on this very ground. The slave is made a slave because his mother is a slave. But to all this it is said that the practice of the American people is against my view. I admit it. They have given the Constitution a slaveholding interpretation. I admit it. They have committed innumerable wrongs against the negro in the name of the Constitution. Yes, I admit it all; and I go with him who goes farthest in denouncing these wrongs. But it does not follow that the Constitution is in favour of these wrongs because the slaveholders have given it that interpretation. To be consistent in his logic, the City Hall speaker must follow the example of some of his brothers in America—he must not only fling away the Constitution, but the Bible. The Bible must follow the Constitution, for that, too, has been interpreted for slavery by American divines. Nay, more, he must not stop with the Constitution of America, but make war upon the British Constitution, for, if I mistake not, that gentleman is opposed to the union of Church and State. In America he called himself a Republican. Yet he does not go for breaking down the British Constitution, although you have a Queen on the throne, and bishops in the House of Lords. My argument against the dissolution of the American Union is this: It would place the slave system more exclusively under the control of the slaveholding States, and withdraw it from the power in the Northern States which is opposed to slavery. Slavery is essentially barbarous in its character. It, above all things else, dreads the presence of an advanced civilisation. It flourishes best where it meets no reproving frowns, and hears no condemning voices. While in the Union it will meet with both. Its hope of life, in the last resort, is to get out of the Union. I am, therefore, for drawing the bond of the Union more closely, and bringing the Slave States more completely under the power of the Free States. What they most dread, that I most desire. I have much confidence in the instincts of the slaveholders. They see that the Constitution will afford slavery no protection when it shall cease to be administered by slaveholders. They see, moreover, that if there is once a will in the people of America to abolish slavery, there is no word, no syllable in the Constitution to forbid that result. They see that the Constitution has not saved slavery in Rhode Island, in Connecticut, in New York, or Pennsylvania; that the Free States have increased from one up to eighteen in number, while the Slave States have only added three to their original number. There were twelve Slave States at the beginning of the Government: there are fifteen now. There was one Free State at the beginning of the Government: there are eighteen now. The dissolution of the Union would not give the North a single advantage over slavery, but would take from it many. Within the Union we have a firm basis of opposition to slavery. It is opposed to all the great objects of the Constitution. The dissolution of the Union is not only an unwise but a cowardly measure—15 millions running away from three hundred and fifty thousand slaveholders. Mr. Garrison and his friends tell us that while in the Union we are responsible for slavery. He and they sing out "No Union with slaveholders," and refuse to vote. I admit our responsibility for slavery while in the Union, but I deny that going out of the Union would free us from that responsibility. There now clearly is no freedom from responsibility for slavery to any American citizen short of the abolition of slavery. The American people have gone quite too far in this slaveholding business now to sum up their whole business of slavery by singing out the cant phrase, "No union with slaveholders." To desert the family hearth may place the recreant husband out of the presence of his starving children, but this does not free him from responsibility. If a man were on board a pirate ship, and in company with others had robbed and plundered, his whole duty would not be performed simply by taking the longboat and singing out "No union with pirates." His duty would be to restore the stolen property. The American people in the Northern States have helped to enslave the black people. Their duty will not have been done till they give them back their plundered rights. . . . My position now is one of reform, not of revolution. I would act for the abolition of slavery through the Government—not over its ruins. If slaveholders have ruled the American Government for the last fifty years, let the anti-slavery men rule the nation for the next fifty years. If the South has made the Constitution bend to the purposes of slavery, let the North now make that instrument bend to the cause of freedom and justice. If 350,000 slaveholders have, by devoting their energies to that single end, been able to make slavery the vital and animating spirit of the American Confederacy for the last 72 years, now let the freemen of the North, who have the power in their own hands, and who can make the American Government just what they think fit, resolve to blot out for ever the foul and haggard crime, which is the blight and mildew, the curse and the disgrace of the whole United States.

WILLIAM GOODELL ARGUES THE ANTISLAVERY NATURE OF THE CONSTITUTION ON A VARIETY OF GROUNDS

William Goodell (1792–1878), like Douglass, considered the Constitution a potential weapon in the antislavery fight. An ardent publicist for a variety of reforms, Goodell combined his editorial fervor with his constitutional views and adduced therefrom the argument that the Constitution was not inevitably proslavery, but rather that the interstate commerce power and the guarantee of republican government gave the Congress adequate power to end slavery.

The simple question before the Court, is the power of Congress over the foreign and domestic slave *traffic*, and that question resolves itself into the question whether slaves are, in the

From William Goodell, *Views of American Constitutional Law, in its Bearing upon American Slavery* (Utica, N.Y.: Jackson & Chaplin, 1844), pp. 45–48, 57, 146–154.

eye of law, subjects of *commerce* at all. If they are, that commerce, with all other commerce, within the limits described, is under congressional control. So "strict construction" must decide, without regard to the bearing the decision may have on the tenure of slave property in general.

An objection has been raised, on the ground that the power to "*regulate* commerce" is not the power to *annihilate* commerce. The objection is groundless for two reasons.

In the first place, the prohibition of traffic in a particular commodity, and between certain specified localities or countries, is *not* an annihilation of commerce, but only a regulation of it. The making of the traffic in certain commodities contraband, does not annihilate commerce. The tariff of 1816, designed and operating to exclude the cotton fabrics of India, was not an annihilation of commerce.

But, in the second place, it has been decided by the Federal Courts that the power to regulate commerce *does* carry along with it the power to destroy, to prohibit, to annihilate commerce. By the long embargo, under Mr. Jefferson's administration, not only foreign commerce, but coast-wise commerce between the States, and even the fisheries, were expressly prohibited and substantially destroyed. And when some merchants who had been prosecuted for a breach of the embargo law, defended themselves by contesting the constitutionality of that law, and on this same plea that "the power to regulate commerce is not the power to annihilate commerce," no plea nor evidence was offered, on the part of the Government, to disprove the alleged fact, that commerce was annihilated by the embargo. The plea in Court against the defendants, was, that the power to regulate commerce, being an indefinite and unrestricted power, carried, of necessity, along with it the discretionary power, to prohibit all commerce. The plea was offered as a "strict construction" plea. The Court adopted it as such, declaring that they must be bound by the *words* and not by the *consequences* of the Constitution. Judgment was accordingly given against the defendants, and the embargo law was sustained.

To the uninitiated, it may appear somewhat remarkable that the same persons who cite the clause concerning "migration and importation" in illustration of the "compromises of the Constitution" in regard to slavery, (inasmuch as the power of prohibiting the slave-trade, was withheld as they say, from Congress, for twenty years)—should nevertheless contradict their own conclusions, by denying that now, after the twenty years are expired, the Congress possesses any such power? It was under *their own* construction of the Constitution, that the slave-trade was first tolerated, against the then prevailing sentiment of the country, till 1808, and under the same construction, it was then abolished, to a certain extent; and now that a further exercise of the *same* power is invoked, to complete the prohibition commenced in 1808 the constitutional power is denied on the ground that the clause does not touch slavery, at all! But "commerce with foreign nations" and commerce "among the several States" are placed on precisely the same footing, in the clause before us, under which the foreign slave-trade was abolished. In this we have another specimen of the trust-worthiness of the constitutional expositions, on the subject of slavery, that have *hitherto prevailed!* . . .

. . . We have incidentally adverted, already to the Constitutional provision that *"the United States shall guaranty to every State in the Union, a republican form of government."* . . .

. . . If slavery be contrary "to the *principles* of a republic," then slavery is anti-republican, and of course the United States have guarantied, to every State in the Union, an exemption from slavery. But the well "known principles of a republic" are—that "all men are created equal, and are endowed by their Creator with certain inalienable rights, among which are life, liberty and the pursuit of happiness." Any government not in accordance with these "principles" is not a republican government. . . .

Whether . . . we define a republic by its principles, its usages, its protection of human rights, or its sovereignty of the People, or of a majority of them, the slave States can not be called *republics.* . . .

. . . And whence the *binding authority* of laws, constitutions, and governments? You prove to me that a certain "compact" was made some fifty years ago, while I was an infant, or before I was born. You authenticate to me the *fact.* Very well. But how does that fact bind *me,* who had no part in the bargain? If, as is often said, the *whole* authority of civil government is founded in *"compact,"* how can that authority be binding on any persons except those by whom the compact was made? Suppose I do not choose to come into the "compact," what have its provisions to do with *me?* My being born in the country where the "compact" was made does not render me a party to the compact. I had a right to be born, when and where my Creator saw fit, and am not beholden to the makers of paper compacts for my right *to be* where Divine Providence has placed me, and to be a man, on my own proper account, and behoof. My good father or grandfather, (peace to their ashes,) may have signed the compact, as they had a right to do, if they saw fit. But they stood in their own shoes, and I stand in mine—as truly a man as either of them, with the same unimpaired powers—with the same high responsibilities to my Creator, to my country, and to my race, that they had. They had no power to make me less of an independent man, and a voluntary free agent, than they were, themselves. And they have not done it.

Thus, at least, men will reason, (and have reasoned,) when they wish to throw off the obligations, either of civil government in general, or the particular government they live under, or any enactments which they think oppressive, or which they dislike. And it might be very convenient to have something more logical to confute them with, than papers and precedents, something more august to overawe them than full bottomed wigs, (now grown into disuse,) something more satisfactory than gibbets, something more philosophical and more Christian than powder and ball, especially when wielded as *substitutes for the right*, instead of instruments of *suppressing the wrong*.

And most manifestly, civil government must have some other and higher authority than "*mere* compact" if we would claim for it the reverence due to "an ordinance of God."

"Social Compact" a Fiction, &c.

The date, moreover, and the locality of that great town-meeting of the human race, in which it was agreed to emerge from "a state of nature" and "enter civil society" with "a part of their rights surrendered for the better protection of the rest"—(as the old legend hath it,) is a matter that the paper and parchment records have never yet reached. The recent explosion of that wretched fiction of the old writers of civic romance, has left a vacuum in the theory of government, as existing in the literature of the age, which it is high time to fill up with *substantial truth,* if the high obligations of GOVERNMENT and of LAW are to retain any hold upon the ever progressive popular mind.

Who can tell us *whether there be* any such substantial truth to inculcate, unless our conceptions of government, of constitution and of law, can run back of mere libraries and precedents, of legislative enactments, of legal decisions, of conventional agreements, and fasten hold of SOMETHING of which all these are but the *exponents,* the *declarations,* the *expressions?*

Civil Government, a Science, &c.

In every other department of human activity and of human science, it is expected that the operator and the student should be able to fix his grasp upon *something in the form of fixed realities, besides* the mere papers and books that profess to give him *an account* of them. He is expected to examine *the things* for himself, and to use his parchments only as *means* to facilitate this examination. Why should the science of government be an exception? . . .

. . . And this opens before us another series of questions—which the present generation will have to decide upon, and in the decision settle the destinies of their country perhaps for ages to come. Their decision *will not alter the facts and principles* upon which they are called to decide. But it will fix the condition of the Republic, by determining its *adjustment* to those unchangeable principles and facts.

NATURE AND RELATIONS OF MAN.

The problem may be stated in some such queries as these —Is there, after all, any thing, in *the social nature of man,* in the *relations* of man to man, in the *duties* growing out of those relations, (duties therefore, imposed upon man by the author of his being,) which lay a foundation, (as they create a moral necessity) for such a science as that of CIVIL GOVERNMENT, a science as fixed and determinate, in the nature of things, as any of the other demonstrative sciences, based upon *"self-evident truths"* a science no more to be altered by parchments, or conventional arrangements, or precedents, than the sciences which enable the persons acquainted with them to traverse land and ocean by steam—a science which written constitutions, enacted statutes, and recorded decisions, can more or less correctly or incorrectly *describe* (or perchance contradict) *but can never alter nor change.*

Unless there be such a *science of legislation and of law,* which mankind can be *taught,* can *understand,* and can *apply,* then civil government itself becomes a cheat, and legislation becomes a farce, and jurisprudence becomes an usurpation, which the onward and rapid march of mankind must speedily detect, and woe to the conservators of a law and a government that shall prove themselves to be such contemptible shams, then. . . .

COMMON LAW, SECRET OF ITS POWER.

The volumes of the Common Law, doubtless, embodied and re-echoed as they are in our own Declaration of Independence, and in the Preamble of the Federal Constitution, technically so called, come the nearest to the instrumentalities we are seeking, of any thing within our reach. Our jurists, (aye, and our statesmen for the most part,) have heard of the *Common Law*, and have learned something of its authority and power. And the very soul of the Common Law is identical with the fundamental truths we would insist upon.

For *what is* the Common Law, the highest standard of appeal in our civil courts—the Common Law, that corrects hoary abuses, reverses judicial decisions, annuls statutes, revises charters, repeals parchments, abolishes. omnipotent parliaments with its presence, and annihilates royal prerogatives with a nod—the Common Law, that Luther like, looks confederate emperors in the face, and to their most authoritative mandates answers, calmly, "NO!" The Common Law that stepping into the Court of King's Bench, and taking up the slave code, avers, solemnly and decidedly that there is not power nor authority enough in the British Government, Kings, Lords, Commons, Judiciary and all, to make that iniquitous code, legal! That *says* this, and is *obeyed!*

From what source is this mighty and resistless power of the *Common Law* derived? Did King and Parliament that are overawed in its presence, at any time, enact the authority they hate, and before which they cower? When Common Law would present its credentials, does it show a commission signed by the dignified officials on the bench to whom it gives law, and whom it claims as its servants?

Or is it to the book makers, the compilers, the learned recorders, the writers, the printers, the publishers, or the hawkers, of Common Law maxims, that we must look, for the sources of the high authority with which they are clothed?

Let us open our eyes to the fact that the Common Law is superior, and paramount, and prior to all these—that she "teaches as one having authority, and not as the *scribes*"—the mere copyists or commentators of parchments—that she speaks in her own name, or rather, in the name of universal, essential, *uncreated, unalterable law,* in the other words, in the name of the most high and eternally supreme God. . . .

ONE UNIVERSAL LAW.

An expansion and purification of this idea of Common Law may introduce to us, the *one universal law*—the law of nature sometimes termed—under which all nations are placed—a law from which civilization and the social state does not release men—a law which it is the *sole business* of civil government to ascertain and enforce, in the *execution of justice, between a man and his neighbor.* "The rightful power of all legislation," says Thomas Jefferson, "is to declare and enforce only our *natural* RIGHTS *and* DUTIES, and take *none* of them *from* us. When the laws have declared and enforced all this, they have fulfilled their functions." This *universal* law, then, is the ONLY law. Whatever conflicts with this, is to be repudiated (as say likewise the writers on Common Law) "not as being *bad* law, but as being NO law!" Hence, nothing subversive of equity deserves the *name* of law, or is to to be *treated* as law, by any of the officers, the Judges, or the executors of law. There is, and there can be, no valid or binding law, at variance with justice or equity, either on earth or in heaven.

Source of Law, in the Divine Will.

Power belongeth unto God. All rightful rule and authority are from him. By bestowing social and moral existence on man, he has, of necessity, imprinted *the law* of that social and moral existence upon them. By giving them the *nature* they possess, he has bound them by *the law* of that nature. By establishing the *relations* they sustain to each other, he has indicated the *duties* they owe to each other. Among these duties is *the duty of the* COMMUNITY (not a select portion of them) to see that the rights of *each member* of the community is respected, and uninfringed. From the plagues of Egypt to the present hour, the universal history of the providential government of God, over the nations, attests this great truth that it is the MASSES and *not* the *officials merely*, of the nations, that God and nature hold responsible for the executing of *just judgment*. Fealty to *justice*, not to *parchments* is the constant burden of his requisitions.

Constitution of Government not Arbitrary.

If this be a truthful account of civil government, then the *Constitution* of civil government has a *foundation in nature*—that is to say, in the DIVINE WILL. It is an *existing matter of fact*, as much so as is the Constitution of the *human body*. Of the *latter*, the physiologist . . . may have given a more or less reliable account, in the books they may have written. Of the *former*, the Convention of 1787, may have traced, more or less correctly, the outlines, and indicated the appropriate details. In the former case, an individual, in the latter case, a convention, and afterwards an entire nation, assumed the responsibility of the statements. Both are statements and not *creations*, nevertheless. The Federal Convention, and "we the People of the United States" could no more *make* a Constitution of civil government, out of a cloth of our own fabric, and upon any principles that might suit our own selfishness or caprice—a Constitution that should be *valid* and *binding;* than ... an university of physiologists could *make*, at their own whim or pleasure, a constitution of the human body, that should, be binding upon all the anatomists and surgeons of a nation, or on all who should have occasion to contract their muscles, and move their limbs!—In both cases, it is *God* who has *made* the constitutions. All that men in either case can do, is to *learn*, to *teach*, and to *use* them.

As much as this, the *Common Law* says, when it denies that human authorities can make wicked and unjust laws, that can be binding and valid. As much as this, the *Declaration of Independence*, by obvious implication says, when it claims for the new Republic the power to "do all acts and things which independent States may, OF RIGHT, do." As much as this, the Preamble of the Federal Constitution recognizes, and the same is supposed in the provision to correct its own mistaken statements of "justice" by "amendments" of its provisions. . . .

. . . The time, however, can not be far distant, when these matters will be better understood—when legislative and judicial halls will be occupied in the rational task of *learning, declaring,* and *applying* to the affairs of men, the great principles of *eternal, immutable* LAW, rather than in vain attempts, either to CREATE, or to ANNUL it. To establish a *manufactory* and to commission *manufacturers of* LAWS for the government of the solar system, laws for the government of mineral, vegetable, or animal existences, chemical laws, or laws of hydrostatics; all this might pass for a rational amusement (as it seems indeed to have been the amusement of philosophers, before Lord Bacon's time) in the comparison with the still current usage of attempting to manufacture CONSTITUTIONAL LAW, the law by which the *social relations of man,* in political communities, must be governed! When shall the *inductive* instead of the constructive and hypothetical philosophy be applied to the science of *government!* When will men see that they can only *discover* and *obey,* not *construct,* the laws of the political world! That their paper constitutions can only *teach* and *declare,* not *originate,* the fundamental principles of a civil government!

To the case in hand. Human beings can no more construct a civil government, with binding authority over human beings, yet without the power to "execute judgment between a man and his neighbor," than they can construct a globe without the quality of roundness, or a cube without its six sides. Abortions and absurdities they may multiply as they please. "There *is no* authority but of God," and the authorities that *be* (that truly possess any binding authority) "are *ordained* of God." *These* "are a terror not to *good* works, but to the *evil.*" They are "the ministers of God" "attending continually upon this very thing," and on no other ground, and in no other character, can they rightfully claim to be recognized, or deserve the "tribute" of support.... *A Constitution of civil government, therefore, that tolerates slavery, is an absurdity that can not exist.*

ROBERT RANTOUL, JR., INTERPRETS THE CONSTITUTION STRICTLY AND CONCLUDES IT IS ANTISLAVERY

Unlike those who interpreted the commerce powers most broadly and thus made of the Constitution an antislavery vehicle, Robert Rantoul, Jr. (1805–1852) construed the Constitution strictly and thus contended that the Congress had no right to pass a fugitive slave bill. Running for election in Massachusetts as a Democrat and embarrassed by his party's support of the Fugitive Slave Act of 1850, he won election to the House of Representatives on this platform.

I belong . . . to that school which holds that the Constitution should be strictly construed, and its meaning strictly adhered to. And when I say this, I have at the same time a great veneration for all the compromises of the Constitution. We hear much of them. What are they? I sometimes hear people talk of the compromises of the Constitution in such a way that I think they would be much puzzled if they were to be asked what they are. There were compromises, the non-adoption of which would have prevented the Constitution itself from being adopted by the people. Leading members even went home in despair of effecting a Constitution acceptable to the people. And it was after they had gone, that certain compromises were adopted, which finally insured the acceptance of that instrument. . . .[1]

. . . Now when people talk about adhering to the compromises of the constitution, referring thereby to certain other things which are not compromises, which are not the agreement of two parties, in which each gives way a little for the sake of that which it esteems a greater good, but to those other things which are not alluded to in the Constitution, I should like to have them define what they mean. These which I have mentioned, it is necessary to adhere to.

From Robert Rantoul, Jr., *The Fugitive Slave Law. Speech . . . Delivered before the Grand Mass Convention of the Democratic Voters of the Second Congressional District of Massachusetts . . . April 3, 1851* (n.p.: n.p., [1851]), pp. 6–15.

[1] The compromises which Rantoul then defines are those concerning representation in the two houses of Congress, export and import taxes, apportionment for purposes of taxation, and the prohibition of the slave trade. [Eds.]

Therefore I go on to declare as to certain other clauses, that there are stipulations which are to be construed. And I propose now to construe them.

I come to the fourth article of the Constitution of the United States. In that I find all that is found in regard to the delivery of fugitive slaves. And I intend to ask, What does that language mean? Construe it by the same rules according to which the other clauses are construed. In the first place, the first section of the fourth article of the Constitution of the United States says, "Full faith and credit shall be given in each State to the public acts, records and judicial proceedings of every other State." Every State shall give full faith and credit to the public records of every other state. Does this grant power to any body? I see in the words that follow, what the makers of the Constitution thought on that subject. I see that they thought it did not grant the power to Congress, because they add language giving the power. What I have read is no grant of power to Congress. It is a prohibition to the States. It says, You shall not deny your belief in the truth of the public records of your sister States. If a court in South Carolina says a certain thing, you are to give full faith to it. That does not say that Congress shall do anything about it.—And the people of the United States did not understand that Congress had the power. The makers of the Constitution did not understand from the extract which I have read, that Congress had any power over the subject; and for this reason, that the close of the section gives to Congress the power which would have been needless had the preceding language conferred it. "And the Congress may, by general laws, prescribe the manner in which such acts, records and proceedings shall be proved, and the effect thereof." What need was there of adding this latter clause if the first was a grant of power? You may read this constitution through, and you will not find any words wasted. Every word means something. It was put there because it was necessary, and because the meaning would not have been there without it. I say that that first clause did not contain a grant of power; and the men who put it there knew it. They first say that faith shall be given; and then bestow on Congress the power in relation thereto. The powers not delegated to Congress are reserved to the States. That power would have been reserved to the States if not given to Congress in the last clause of this section. Can language make that clearer. I go to the next section.

SEC. 2. "The citizens of each State shall be entitled to all the privileges and immunities of citizens in the several States."

Very well! A colored man in Massachusetts goes out from our ports, and goes into one of the harbors of South Carolina. They do not give him the immunities of the citizen of the State. Does any southern man contend that Congress has the power to enforce that section? No! there is no power granted there. There is a declaration of a principle, but it does not say that Congress shall possess the power to enforce it. Therefore they say that South Carolina may make what laws she pleases, and the United States government can do nothing to prevent it. They adopt one rule for this clause, and another rule for another clause in the same section. But do I say that Congress has the power to enforce action in consonance with this clause, in the harbor of Charleston? No! I choose strict construction on all these clauses. I adopt the rule of strict construction in them all, and not a strict construction in one and a loose one in another.

The next clause is as follows: "A person charged in any State with treason, felony, or any other crime, who shall flee from justice and be found in another State, shall, on demand of the Executive authority of the state from which he fled, be delivered up, to be removed to the State having jurisdiction of the crime." Under that clause no serious difficulty has arisen. The States have given up criminals, and no State has of late years objected to it.

Then comes the next clause: "No person held to service or

labor in one State, under the laws thereof, escaping into another, shall in consequence of any law or regulation therein be discharged from such service or labor."

To whom is that directed? To the States or to Congress? To the States! It says, "no person shall be discharged by any law or regulation of the States." That is a regulation addressed to the States and not to the Union. And then it goes on to say, "But shall be delivered up on claim of the party to whom such service or labor may be due."

In the case of a person charged with crime, the rule is, that he shall be removed to the State having jurisdiction of the crime. Now, if the first part of this section is addressed to the States, then to whom is the subsequent clause addressed? For it does not go on to say Congress shall make the laws, but it says you shall deliver up. How can any person contend that one is addressed to the States and the other not?

One clause says they shall not make laws, and the next that they shall deliver up. I say that that last clause is as clearly addressed to the States as the first. And then I go back to the old rule laid down by our fathers, written by Samuel Adams in the Bill of Rights of Massachusetts, in which he says, "Every power, jurisdiction and right, shall remain with the people, unless specially delegated to Congress." Have these powers been delegated? [No! No!"][2] . . .

. . . Why, my friends, two sets of dangers have always threatened this government in the view of the people; one party has feared that it might fall to pieces; the other that it might become too strong. Which have we now most reason to apprehend? Is there any danger that our government will prove to be too weak? . . .

. . . It would be easy to illustrate in a thousand ways, the evils that may grow in the future history of the country out of

---

[2] The brackets in this selection appear, unless otherwise noted, in the original. [Eds.]

this disposition of the general government to encroach upon the rights of the States—to show that the fears of Thomas Jefferson, and Samuel Adams, and Patrick Henry, and Elbridge Gerry—fears of indefinite usurpation tending towards, and finally terminating in consolidated federal despotism, may perhaps some day be realized. I prefer to take this precise evil in order to illustrate the effect of this tendency. A law which is made by a State, is likely to be suited to what is to be done. The State of Massachusetts knows what her people can bear, and what they cannot bear. But if a law is to be made contrary to the sentiments of any State, it will be impracticable to carry it out in that State.

How does that apply to the question of slavery? Just in this way! The retaking of fugitive slaves is to be carried out, if any where, in a free State. Slaves do not, when they escape, stop in a Slave State. If fugitives are to be returned from any place, it is from a Free State. When Congress makes a law on the subject, it makes it against the very inmost sentiments of the souls of the people of the free States. ["Shame!" "Shame!"]

Is that a power likely by its exercise to tend to the perpetuation of the Union, by carrying out this law. I propose to perpetuate the Union by checking the power of the General Government, by confining it within its legitimate sphere of action, to those concerns upon which it may act for the common good, without arousing indignation and hatred in one section against the other; sometimes driving South Carolina to the brink of rebellion by the galling weight of unjust and intolerable taxation, and sometimes outraging all that is honest and patriotic in puritan Massachusetts, by levelling at a single blow all those bulwarks of liberty, which barons bold and sages grave in the olden time, and the Republicans who brought the Stuart to the block, with those who broke the yoke of the house of Hanover in later days, had labored, each in their generation since the twelfth century, to erect; which it is the proudest prerogative and boast of Britain that she possesses; and which constituted the richest inheritance that our fathers received from the mother island empire. I propose that the Federal power shall lift its iron heel from the neck of Massachusetts, and return to its appointed duty, and circumscribed routine. [Loud Cheers.]

But we are told that these are measures of conciliation, measures of peace. Enforce this law, and we shall have peace and quietness, it is said. How? Is one-third of the white people of the United States to dictate to the other two-thirds, and call their submission peace? I admit that these slave interests may set one part of the country against the other. It may so happen that difficulties will take place in either case, whether you legislate according to opinions almost universal, and moral feelings deeply rooted, and sanctioned by the religion of nine-tenths of the people of the North who possess either morals or religion, or whether you legislate according to notions which are common in all communities upon whom the institution of slavery has been entailed. But is it just as likely to cause difficulty when two-thirds of the whole people of the country are irritated as when only one third are irritated? [Applause.] I see no way of getting out of this difficulty, so straight-forward, so sure of its results, as it would be, if practicable, to go back to the old Democratic principle, of the strict construction of all constitutional grants of power; and finding no such power delegated, finding that it is not so nominated in the bond, to say the United States Government have nothing to do with this matter. [Cheering.]

But, sir and gentlemen, as this subject is one of great interest, and as the manner in which it has been most commonly discussed is different from the course I have pursued, allow me to go one step further. If it be granted, which I do not grant at all,—if it be granted that the United States government has the right to make a law upon this subject, under the fourth article, let us inquire what sort of a law it gives them a right to make; for that is a matter of great consequence. A man charged with crime shall on demand be delivered up! That is the law. What have you to ascertain before you give him up? Simply that he is *charged!* That means, that he is charged by some responsible person, on what a lawyer would call good and probable cause, upon which charge, so far substantiated, the executive of the State from which it is alleged that he fled, demands him, by a formal written requisition.

Where shall he be tried? Where he is charged! It is a privilege to the party charged with crime that he shall be tried where the crime is alleged to have been committed. This is inserted for the benefit of the person charged with crime. So that, if a person be charged with crime, let him go back to the place where it is alleged that the deed was committed, for there he can most easily prove his innocence. This is based on a very ancient principle of the English common law.

The question to be decided is, Is the man charged? Does a responsible man who would be convicted of perjury if it were not true, swear that he committed the crime? If so, we will take his oath and send the accused man back. We will take the requisition of the executive as proof that such a charge has been made. He does not have his trial where he is found, but only his preliminary trial there. The preliminary inquiry in such a case may be accomplished by a summary process, for it includes little more than the verification of the authority under which he is demanded, and proof of the fugitive's identity. It is not necessary to have a jury in Massachusetts to try a man who is charged with having committed a murder in New York. You could not conveniently give him a fair and full trial here. You, therefore, go through a summary process to determine whether it is necessary to send this man back.

I go next to the succeeding clause. I know that the men who made this Constitution knew what they were about, and did not put a single clause here, or a single word here, without meaning. There is no book in the English language, of which the construction is so plain, as the constitution of the United States. If a man comes to it with a sincere and honest heart, and will take the trouble to compare one portion with another, he cannot fail to come to a right conclusion.

We come, then, to the next section: "No person held to service or labor in one State under the laws thereof escaping into another, shall in consequence of any law or regulation therein be discharged, &c." There is a very extraordinary difference of language between this section and the preceding one. In that it was a "person *charged* with crime." There was probable cause to believe that he might be guilty. But in this section, is it a person *charged* with being held to service? a person that somebody swears was held to service? The Constitution tells you what it is: "No person held to service or labor, &c." If he is not *held*, he is not liable. "No person held to service or labor in one State, under the laws thereof, escaping into another, shall in consequence of any regulation therein, be discharged from such service or labor; but shall be delivered up, &c." Who shall be delivered up? The person "held." Not the person "charged," as in the case of a person *charged with murder*. It is not the person suspected, but it is the person "*held*." When? Not till it is found out whether he *be* held or not, I take it. [Repeated rounds of applause.]

But the person held to service or labor, "shall be delivered up on claim of the party to whom such service or labor may be due." The party who held him must prove that the service or labor is *due* and that he was *held*. How is this to be done? Is it to be done by a summary process? Did any man ever hear of such a thing except in relation to slavery? ["Hear! hear!"] Did any man ever hear that any question of liberty or property was finally disposed of by means of a summary process, except in relation to this subject of slavery?

We are told that we should submit. Now I do not go to a Southern State to tell them what they shall do, or what they shall not do. Let them provide for their own institutions as they please, but let them not come here and tell me that a man shall not have a trial by jury, and that he shall not only not have a jury trial here, but, perhaps, no where else. I do not admit any such doctrine here. [Cheers.]

Why, is it not quite clear how this question whether he be held to service or not, should be decided? What is the principle of the Constitution of the United States on that subject? For there is a principle laid down here. There is very little left out that ought to be in this Constitution. There is laid down here the rule that no man shall "be deprived of his life, liberty, or property, without due process of law." That is in the 5th article of the amendments of the Constitution of the United States.

Now I take it, if you seize a colored man,—or you may seize a white man under the operation of this law,—if you seize any man in Massachusetts under this fugitive slave law, the first question is, Shall he be deprived of liberty? You are not to take it for granted that he is a slave. All presumptions of law are in favor of liberty. It is a maxim older than Christianity itself, *"Presumitur pro libertate;"* that the presumption is always to be in favor of liberty. Now, if I say it was the maxim of ancient Rome before Christ was born, it is the maxim of Christian Europe, and of everybody, the world over, today; it is the maxim of the civil law of Europe, coming from the early ages of the Republic, through the Empire, and surviving the Empire, a system of law matured for twenty-five hundred years, into the most perfect embodiment of human reason to which the world has given birth; this law cried through all time, "All men are by nature free;" it is the great cry of Pagandom to Christendom, and Christendom echoes it back; it is the maxim of the common law of England; it is the maxim of the common law of Massachusetts; it is the maxim of the whole world, save only the slaveholding States of this Union. [Enthusiastic shouts of applause.] It is to be presumed that the man is free, from the fact that he is a man made in the image of God. [Renewed cheers.]

The image of God stamped upon him certifies him to be

free. [Cheers.] The human form divine with which he walks erect and proudly looks to heaven, certifies him to be free. [Intense sensation.] And when all Roman and all European, aye, Asiatic and American laws have decided he shall be free —when that is the universal law of the world, I will not agree that any miserable notion of a temporary expediency shall make me bow down to that very detestable, abominable, horrible, and wicked doctrine, that the color of a man shall establish the fact, or even furnish a presumption of the fact, that he is not free. [Cheers repeated for a considerable time.]

I go on then upon the Constitution of the United States, and I say this man found in the State of Massachusetts is presumed to be free; and therefore, when you seek to make a slave of him, the question is, Shall he be deprived of his liberty? He has his liberty. Shall he be deprived of it? The Constitution says he shall not be deprived of his life, liberty or property, without due process of law.

I admire the arrangement of those three words. I admire the putting of liberty between life and property. There are two schools on this subject: some who think life is worth more than property, some who think the life of a man is worth more than the shirt upon his back; and others who have a sacred regard for the dollars a man possesses, and believe that his purse is vastly more important than his person. If a man thinks that life is the more important of the two, then is liberty placed most appropriately by the side of it. If on the contrary he thinks property of the most importance, then liberty takes precedence even of that. Between property and life, it is in either case in a respectable position. [Applause.]

What is "due process of law?" Let me say why it was that that clause was put there. For all these safeguards are inserted in the Constitution by its framers, or by those who amended it, because they knew what had happened in the past. Men had been deprived of their lives, their liberty, and their property, without due process of law. They had in their minds the practices in the House of Stuart under James I, and Charles I, and in a degree under Charles II, and James II. Men's liberties had been taken away without due process of law, without trial by jury. This was accomplished by means of the Star Chamber, without trial by jury, without the confronting of witnesses.

In that Star Chamber, and also by means of certain other courts, the liberties of the citizens were taken away. Commissioners were also appointed, constituting irregular courts, not the courts of the king's bench, nor any other courts, with stated terms; but this appointment was effected by selecting certain individuals, fit tools of the tyrant. These would constitute a court, for the express purpose of trying a certain man. Commissioners were appointed who went down and tried the case without a jury, and without a public hearing and without confronting the witnesses. In that way men's liberties have been taken away. This was no new thing under the Stuarts. It had been done under the Tudors, under the Plantagenets, and even before the Plantagenets. This very ancient abomination, this hoary survivor of the iniquities of a thousand years had been among the causes of the civil wars between the monarch and the subject, in which British swords were sheathed in British hearts, till the genuine Norman nobility was almost exterminated from the land. It was denounced in all the Bills of Rights in the English language, and in charters before the English language was known, in Magna Charta, before Magna Charta, and perpetually in all proclamations of liberties afterwards.

When this article was added to the Constitution, those who did it meant to guard against these usurpations of power. Governments are the same in all ages, and these things might be done in our nation as well as elsewhere. No man shall "be deprived of life, liberty, or property, without due process of law." By due process of law, they meant in due process of proceeding in common law. It was the taking away of the trial by jury, it was the taking away of the *habeas corpus,* it was Star Chamber doctrine—it was all this against which they acted.

What was due process of law? That general examination of the Constitution, of which I have given you only a sketch, would show you what it was. To prevent any possible ambiguity, they said, in the seventh article of amendments, "In suits at common law where the value in controversy shall exceed twenty dollars, the right of trial by jury shall be preserved."

And they supposed when they had secured both criminal prosecutions and civil suits, that they had covered everything. They meant to cover all things, except well known and well defined proceedings in admiralty, proceedings in chancery, and also courts martial. They meant to include all save those exceptional cases, and they did not suppose that anybody would imagine that the trial of a man's liberty was one of these. The writ to ascertain whether a serf belonged to the lord who claimed him, is one of the oldest in the common law.

Will any one rise up and say that a man's liberty is not worth twenty dollars? If a man owes another eighteen or twenty dollars, and it costs a hundred dollars to get it, he would certainly better not have a jury to try the case. All sums below twenty dollars cannot be tried by a jury for this reason, viz., that it would cost more than that to try the case.

Some limit it was necessary to fix; and that amount was selected as the most appropriate. They never dreamed that any man's liberty would not be considered worth twenty dollars.

What is a man's liberty worth? Will the *owner* say it is not worth twenty dollars? If it be worth to the master five hundred dollars, is it not worth as much to the man himself? No slave would escape, no master would pursue him, no master would keep him, if he were not worth more than twenty dollars. But, "In suits at common law, where the value in controversy shall exceed twenty dollars, the right of trial by jury shall be preserved." Now the Supreme Court of the United States have decided (in the case of Lee against Lee) that a man's liberty is worth to him, in all cases, more than one thousand dollars, and that where there is no appeal unless the amount in controversy exceeds one thousand dollars, if the liberty of the party be brought in question, he shall have his appeal.

Due process of law is meant to distinguish the careful, guarded, strict, precise manner known to the English law, from the summary military process used in time of war. There can therefore be no doubt, that a person held to service is, by due process of law, entitled to his trial by jury. [Applause.]

There are other questions entitled to consideration, if I did not perceive that the hour is approaching at which a great portion of my audience will be obliged to leave the hall if they wish to reach their homes to night. [Cries of "Go on! go on!"]

I lay down two propositions: First, that the government have no jot or title of power, authorizing them to act for the rendition of fugitive slaves; and second, even if they had such a power, this clause would require that it should be exercised under due process of law, which due process of law includes a jury trial. [Applause.] A jury trial, where? "A person HELD to service shall be delivered up." Certainly, in the place where he is seized! He should be tried by an impartial jury. It is said, carry a man from Maine to Texas, and then he can have his trial. I should prefer not to run that risk if I were liable to be arrested. I would make it certain whether I had been held to service, before I ran the risk of perpetual servitude, by being carried into a slave State.

But that is not all. Suppose that every man who claims a fugitive slave were as wise as Solomon, and as upright as Sir Matthew Hale.[3] Suppose he were determined to give the

---

[3] Sir Matthew Hale (1609–1676), English jurist, specialist in criminal and common law. [Eds.]

alleged fugitive a fair trial in a Slave State.—What follows? Simply, that in the Slave-holding States, the rule of law is opposite to what it is here. Here he is a freeman till he be proved to be a slave. There he is a slave till he be proved to be a freeman.

The rule at the South is, that a colored man is a slave till he be proved free. He may be free and unable to prove it, because he has lost his free papers. He may be free because his mother and grandmother were free before him, and they might not be able to testify in a Southern court.

Suppose that they should always construe their laws fairly. Would you send a man back to a system of laws where a man is presumed to be a slave? ["No! no!"] And I say no! Never! Try a man where he is presumed to be free. [Cheers.]

SALMON P. CHASE ARGUES IN DEFENSE OF AN UNDERGROUND RAILROAD OPERATOR

Because there was a constant stream of fugitive slaves fleeing the South and because many Northerners assisted them in their flight, numerous suits were initiated by owners eager to retrieve their escaped property. Salmon Portland Chase (1808–1873) of Ohio defended several of these underground railroad travellers and their conductors. In his defense of John Vanzandt, an Ohioan sued by an irate slave owner, Chase argued that the condition of slave does not follow a man into a free state and that the Fugitive Slave Law of 1793 was unconstitutional. Finally he appealed to the Higher Law against slavery.

From Salmon Portland Chase, *Reclamation of Fugitives from Service; an Argument for the Defendant Submitted to the Supreme Court of the United States, at the December Term, 1846, in the Case of Wharton Jones vs. John Vanzandt* (Cincinnati: R. P. Donogh & Co., 1847), pp. 83–96.

What is a slave? I know no definition, shorter or more complete, than this: A slave is a person held, as property, by legalized force, against natural right. Slavery is the condition in which men are thus held. The law, which enables one man to hold his fellow man as a slave, making the private force of the individual efficient for that purpose by aid of the public force of the community, must necessarily, be local and municipal in its character. It cannot, speaking with strict accuracy, make men property, for man is not, by nature, the subject of ownership. It can only determine that within the sphere of its operation, certain of the people may be held and treated as property by others. It can punish resistance to the authority of the master, and compel submission to his disposal. But, if I may be allowed to introduce here the homely, but most forcible expression of the great poet of Scotland:—

"A man's a man, for a' that."

The law of the Creator, which invests every human being with an inalienable title to freedom, cannot be repealed by any inferior law, which asserts that man is property. Such a law may be enforced by power; but the exercise of the power must be confined within the jurisdiction of the state, which establishes the law. It cannot be enforced,—it can have no operation whatever,—in any other jurisdiction. The very moment a slave passes beyond the jurisdiction of the state, in which he is held as such, he ceases to be a slave; not because any law or regulation of the state which he enters confers freedom upon him, but because he *continues* to be a man and *leaves behind* him the law of force, which made him a slave. Even if the slave passes from one slave state into another, he is not held as a slave in the state to which he comes, by the law of the state which he has left. So far as that law is concerned, he is free; for he is beyond its reach. He may remain enslaved, or, more properly speaking, he may be re-enslaved under the law of the state he enters: or, that law may refuse to recognize the relation imposed on him by the foreign law, and then he will be absolutely free. There are familiar examples of this, in many slave states. The law of Virginia does not permit the enslavement of native American Indians brought into that state since 1691. Such a person, therefore, though a slave in another state, becomes free, on being brought into Virginia, for the law which enslaved him cannot follow him there. So, also, in other slave states, slaves brought into them, under certain circumstances or for certain purposes, become free. The law of the state, into which they are brought, refuses to lend its aid to their enslavement, and the law of the state, whence they came, cannot reach them, having no force in another jurisdiction.

If I am correct, then, in the position that the Government of the United States, cannot, under the constitution, create, continue, or enforce any such relation as that of owner and property, or,—what is, under the slave codes, the same thing,—of master and slave, between man and man, it must follow that no claim to persons as property can be maintained, under any clause of the constitution, or any law of the United States.

The clause in relation to fugitives from service is no exception to this remark.

Indeed, it may well be doubted, whether the majority of the convention regarded the clause as applicable, at all, to escaping slaves. The delegates from no state, except South Carolina, appear to have been anxious for any provision of the kind. And after it was introduced, various amendments were made ... with the express purpose, of excluding any implication that slavery was "legal in a moral point of view," and of adapting the language of the clause to "the obligations of free persons," and not to "the condition of slaves." It requires no great boldness, with the support of these facts, to affirm that the clause should be construed as providing only for the enforcement of the "obligations of free persons," and not for reconsigning men to the "condition of slaves."

Not insisting on this, however, nor waiving it, it seems to me quite certain, that this clause takes up and deals with no other relation than that of master and servant. It contains no recognition whatever, of any right of property in man. It establishes no rule in relation to negro or mulatto servants, which does not apply equally to white servants held by law. If, under the clause, a fugitive slave may be reclaimed, it is, not because he is a slave, but because he is a person held to labor. In that character, and only in that character, can he be reclaimed. After he has been brought back to the state where he was held to service, he resumes the condition, whether of servant, apprentice, involuntary servant, or slave, in which he was held prior to his escape: but while out of the state he is as free as any other person until reclaimed.

It follows from this, that any provisions which would be unconstitutional, in their application to other persons, are equally unconstitutional, in their application to escaping servants. Any immunities secured by the constitution to "persons" without distinction, belong, of right, to "persons" escaped from service.

So far as the act of 1793 authorizes the reclamation of servants, escaped into the *territories* of the United States, it is clearly unconstitutional. If a citizen of a territory cannot sue or be sued in the courts of the union, as a citizen of a state,— surely a person, escaped into a territory, cannot be reclaimed, under a clause, which authorizes, only, the reclamation of persons escaped into a state. It seems highly probable that no provision for the reclamation of servants escaping into a national territory was made, because the ordinance had already provided for such reclamation as to servants escaping from the original states. And this is made almost certain by the fact, that the constitution and the ordinance are almost contemporaneous documents, and the provision as to reclamation in the former, was taken, substantially, from the latter.

So far, also, as the act of 1793 undertakes to confer judicial powers on state magistrates, it is clearly void. The judicial power of the union, cannot, except in open breach of the constitution, be conferred on courts, not ordained and established by Congress, but ordained and established by state Legislatures;—not responsible to the general government, but responsible to the states only.

Besides, Congress, under the constitution, can appoint no federal officers whatever. By the second section of the second article it is made the duty of the President of the United States, with the advice and consent of the Senate, to appoint all judicial officers. Congress may, indeed, vest the appointment of inferior officers in the President alone, or in the courts of law, or in the heads of departments; but it can retain no such power to itself. Yet, if this act be constitutional, Congress can appoint federal officers, by thousands, at a breath; for, by this act, all, who then were or might afterwards become magistrates of counties, cities, and towns corporate, are constituted judges of the United States, with a vast and most important jurisdiction. It were mere waste of words to argue that the act, to this extent, must be unconstitutional. It is true that this court in the Prigg case, held that, in relation to claims of fugitives from service, state magistrates *may* act: but your honors were careful not to affirm that the state magistrates were clothed, by the law, with any judicial authority. If state magistrates act, their action must be justified, if at all, upon the ground that they are the *auxiliaries* of the master, in exercising *the power of recaption,* not under the law, but under the constitution. The magistrate must derive his authority from the master, not from the act of Congress.

I submit, further, that the act is unconstitutional, in all its leading provisions.

It authorizes seizure and confinement, by private force, without legal process. But the third clause of the fifth amendment of the constitution is in these words, "No person shall be deprived of life, liberty, or property, without due process of law." It is vain to say that the fugitive is not a person: for the claim to him can be maintained only on the ground that he is a person. It is vain to say that the amendment did not regard fugitives from service as persons within its intendment. Not only is there no authority for any such assertion, but it is directly contradicted by historical documents. The recommendation for this amendment came from Virginia, and, as proposed by her legislature, it provided that "no free man shall be deprived of life, liberty or property, but by the law of the land." Congress altered this phraseology, by substituting, for the words quoted, these: "No person shall be deprived of life, liberty, or property, without due process of law." Now, unless it can be shewn that no process of law at all, is the same thing as due process of law, it must be admitted that the act which authorizes seizure without process, is repugnant to a constitution which expressly forbids it. And this right to seize, and hold, and take before a magistrate constitutes the very essence of the act. Without this right, the act is of no avail whatever. If it fails in this, it fails altogether.

Mr. Justice Story, delivering the opinion of a majority of the court, intimated, in the Prigg case, that the master of an escaping servant might, at common law, retake him and reconvey him to the place whence he escaped, in the exercise of the right of reception. The learned Judge relied upon the authority of Blackstone; and Blackstone, in support of the proposition which he lays down, refers to no other authority than Roll, a reporter and author of the time of James the First, in the fifteenth year of whose reign, the last case of villeinage came before an English court. This, certainly, is not the highest authority for the middle of the nineteenth century, and for a country whose institutions are founded on the doctrine of personal liberty. But it seems to me quite clear that Blackstone never intended to sanction the doctrine imputed to him. He is speaking of the case where one has deprived another of his servant and wrongfully detains him, and not of an escaping servant at all. His obvious meaning is, that, in the case he puts, the master may retake the servant, with the servant's assent.

The condition, by which he limits the right of recaption, proves this: The master may retake, "so it be not in a riotous manner, or attended with a breach of the peace." And where was it ever held, since the days of villeinage, that it is not a breach of the peace in England, for a master to seize a servant, and compel him by force, to return to a service, which he has left? I affirm, boldly, that there is no such right of recaption, as is claimed, at common law, and no such right has been recognized in England since the days of villeinage. Mr. Hargrave, in the case of Somerset, stated, as an undeniable proposition that "the laws of England will not allow the servant to invest the master with an arbitrary power of correcting, imprisoning or alienating him." And there can be no recaption, against consent, without imprisonment. And Lord Hobart says: "The body of a freeman cannot be made subject to distress or imprisonment, by contract, but only by judgment." Certainly the constitution did not intend to confer any right of recaption on the masters of escaping servants, for every such recaption is a seizure and imprisonment without process, which the constitution expressly forbids.

But the amendment, prohibiting imprisonment or other privation of liberty, without process, is not the only clause of the constitution infringed by this act. It is equally repugnant to that provision, which declares that "the right of the people to be secure in their persons . . . against unreasonable searches and seizures shall not be violated." I ask, how can the people be subjected to seizures more unreasonable, than under this act of Congress? Even upon the unwarrantable assumption that the escaping servant has no rights, the act still violates this provision of the constitution. The claimant must necessarily select the object of seizure. He is not confined, by the act, to negroes, nor to slaves. He may seize any one, whom he chooses to claim as an escaping servant, and take him before a judge, or a magistrate, without authority except as the claimant's agent. He may be mistaken. He may intend to kidnap. No matter, he may seize, confine, transport; being responsible only in an action for a wrongful taking, if his victim shall ever be fortunate enough to find an opportunity to bring one. Surely, an act which authorizes seizure by private force, upon mere claim, violates that security from unreasonable seizure, which the constitution guaranties to the people.

The constitution, also, declares that, "In suits at common law, where the value of the matter in controversy, shall exceed twenty dollars, the right of trial by jury shall be preserved." Of what value is this provision, if Congress may, by legislation, provide a mode, in which every man, may, at the option of a slave claimant, be put upon trial of his liberty without a jury. Will it be said, that the value of a man or of his liberty is not mensurable by a pecuniary standard, and, therefore, that the constitutional guaranty does not apply? I answer, that if Congress cannot authorize the less, surely it cannot authorize the greater aggression upon individual right. Or, will it be said that the proceeding is not one at common law? I reply, where did Congress obtain the authority to authorize the enforcement of claims to services, in a mode at variance with the course of the common law? Not certainly from any grant in the constitution; for, not only does that instrument contain no such grant, but it expressly prohibits the mode of enforcing the claim, which Congress has adopted, namely, imprisonment without process. I insist, therefore, that Congress has no power to authorize the seizure and trial of any person without a jury. If Congress has such power in this case, then, in every other, where the constitution confers or guaranties a right, Congress may, without regard to constitutional restriction or limitation, adopt its own mode of enforcing that right, and the people must submit. If this be so, the constitution is waste paper, and we live under a despotism.

The provisions of the constitution, contained in the amendments, like the provisions of the ordinance, contained in the articles of the compact, were mainly designed to establish as written law, certain great principles of natural right and justice, which exist independently of all such sanction. They rather announce restrictions upon legislative power, imposed by the very nature of society and of government, than create restrictions, which, were they erased from the constitution, the Legislature would be at liberty to disregard. No Legislature is omnipotent. No Legislature can make right wrong; or wrong, right. No Legislature can make light, darkness; or darkness, light. No Legislature can make men, things; or things, men. Nor is any Legislature at liberty to disregard the fundamental principles of rectitude and justice. Whether restrained or not by constitutional provisions, there are acts beyond any legitimate or binding legislative authority. There are certain vital principles, in our national government, which will ascertain and overrule an apparent and flagrant abuse of legislative power. The Legislature cannot authorize injustice by law; cannot nullify private contracts; cannot abrogate the securities of life, liberty and property, which, it is the very object of society, as well as of our constitution of government, to provide; cannot make a man judge in his own case; cannot repeal the laws of nature; cannot create any obligation to do wrong, or neglect duty. No court is bound to enforce unjust law; but, on the contrary, every court is bound, by prior and superior obligations, to abstain from enforcing such law. It must be a clear case, doubtless, which will warrant a court in pronouncing a law so unjust that it ought not to be enforced; but, in a clear case, the path of duty is plain. I rejoice that I have the sanction of this Court to all these positions. . . .

I see not how the judicial enforcement of the claim to property in man can be at all reconciled with these principles; for that claim is admitted by all jurists, and by none more emphatically, than by those distinguished lawyers, whose opinions I have cited from the reports of slaveholding states, to be, not only unsupported by, but directly against natural right.

However this may be, I cannot doubt that the act of 1793, and much more the law of recaption, which has been thought to be contained in the constitutional provision relating to fugitives from service, fall within the very terms of one of the descriptions of unauthorized legislation given by this court, in *Calder* v. *Bull;* for they make a man the judge in his own cause, and, even more, the executioner of his own sentence. The act of 1793 authorizes the claimant to seize the defendant, without process; to take him, by force, before any magistrate he may select; to hold him, by force, while the magistrate examines the evidences of claim; to remove him, by force, when the certificate is granted. The defendant, thus seized and held by force, has no rights, under the law. The act affords him no opportunity to adduce evidence, and imposes no duty on the magistrate to hear it, if adduced. On the other hand, the claimant is allowed to make out his claim by affidavits, which, taken by himself and without cross examination, will always be partial, and, often, false. And, upon such evidence, while the defendant is under such duress and without any right to be heard, the magistrate is to decide. To complete the atrocious business, and leave no semblance of justice whatever to the transaction, the magistrate is entitled to no compensation for his services, under any law, state or federal; but is left to make such bargain with the claimant as he may. What is this, but to make the claimant, judge, jury and sheriff in his own cause, and to establish his will as law? What is it but to legalize assault and battery, and private imprisonment? I say fearlessly, that such acts of legislation as this, are subversive of the fundamental principles, on which all civil society rests. Let such acts be passed in relation to other claims. Let every man be authorized to enforce his demands in this summary manner. If he finds a horse, which he thinks his, in the possession of another, instead of resorting to due process of law, and the old fashioned replevin, let him seize the animal, take him before *his own hired magistrate,* and prove his claim by affidavits. If he claims the services of another, which that other will not perform, instead of suing him for breach of contract, let him drag his reluctant neighbor before his magistrate, establish his claim, and then remove him to his task. How long would society hold together, if this principle were carried into general application?

But I am not obliged to resort to any general principle of the natural law, however firmly established. I find firm footing in the constitution, and I take my stand upon its express provisions. The American People, speaking through the constitution, have forbidden Congress to enact, and this Court to enforce any law which authorizes unreasonable seizures, or privation of liberty without due process of law. This prohibition, in my humble judgment, nullifies the act of 1793.

XII

Argument for Political Action:

Regular Parties

THE MASSACHUSETTS ANTI-SLAVERY SOCIETY ADDRESSES MASSACHUSETTS ABOLITIONISTS ON THE SUBJECT OF POLITICAL ACTION

As antislavery enthusiasts began, in the late 1830's, to direct their attention toward politics, they asserted that political activity was a valid path to moral reform. The abolitionists eschewed, however, the formation of a political party. Rather they supported those candidates of the major parties who opposed slavery, and they brought constant pressure upon Congress to legislate against slavery wherever it could. The Address of the Massachusetts Anti-Slavery Society, which appears below, was signed by Francis Jackson (1789–1861), Boston merchant and philanthropist. It elucidates the needs for and the ways in which to carry out political action.

From Massachusetts Anti-Slavery Society, *An Address to the Abolitionists of Massachusetts, on the Subject of Political Action. By the Board of Managers of the Mass. A. S. Society* ([Boston?]: n.p., [1838]), pp. 2–20.

There are those who disapprove of every form of political action, on the part of abolitionists. They contend that our cause should be presented exclusively under its religious and philanthropic aspect; that it will be degraded and enfeebled at the North, by connecting it with politics,—while, at the South, our political efforts will rouse a more united and determined resistance to our objects.

We cannot yield to this reasoning. It proceeds, we think, upon a narrow view of the subject. Politics, rightly considered, is a branch of morals, and cannot be deserted innocently. Our moral convictions must follow us to the ballot-box. They are not less imperative on us as citizens, than as members of the church, or fathers of families. In each, we have nothing to do, but to carry out our highest idea, simply and fearlessly. If the public mind is misled or vitiated on the subject of politics,— if politics has come to be considered as a game played by the desperate and unprincipled for power or emolument, it must not therefore be abandoned to them. The worldly and corrupt would like nothing better, than that the good should retire, in fear or disgust, from this wide sphere of action. It seems to be our mission to substitute, in the minds of men, a new set of associations with the subject of politics. We believe that the tendency of the abolition efforts has, visibly, been to infuse more comprehensive principles into political bodies, and suggest to them purer motives of action, than have prevailed heretofore. Look at the dignified tone of the Reports and Resolves on Slavery and the Right of Petition, in several of the State Legislatures. Mark the high religious and moral stand assumed by Adams, Slade, Morris[1] and others, in Congress. It is worth noting that the abolitionists form the only great party, in our

---

[1] John Quincy Adams, see pp. 260–267. William Slade (1786–1859), Representative (Whig, Vermont), 1831–1843, one of the group of antislavery representatives. Thomas Morris (1776–1844), Senator from Ohio, (1833–1839), antislavery Democrat and opponent of a proposed Senate Gag Rule. [Eds.]

age, who, aiming at a wide social reform, and operating on and through social institutions, yet rest their efforts and their hopes professedly on religious ground;—on faith in God, and faith in the God-like in man. That slavery is a sin against God, has been our rallying-cry from the beginning; heard not merely from the pulpit, but in the courts of justice, the popular assembly, and the halls of government. Our strength lies, and we well know it, in the religious sentiment of men, recognizing a Christian brother in the crushed slave, and at once stimulating, emboldening and sanctifying the efforts for his deliverance.

To think of purposely keeping such a question—a question of essentially moral and religious character, but having important public bearings,—out of politics, is like the view some persons have, that religion belongs to the temple and the Sabbath, but is out of place in weekday life. Religion runs the risk of being sadly profaned, adulterated, caricatured, counterfeited, in encountering or mixing with the common business or amusements of men; but we nevertheless press it in among them. This is, after all, but a question of time. The subject of slavery must, obviously, sooner or later, enter deeply, into general politics. Slavery is itself the creature of law, that is of political action. It can only be finally destroyed, by the same power that gave it being.

We, however, value political action, chiefly as a means of agitating the subject. The great support of slavery,—without which it could not stand in the United States, two years,—is a corrupt public sentiment, among those who are not slaveholders. The current doctrine of the North is, that slavery is, indeed, an evil, and if southern society were to be reconstructed, slavery should, by no means, be introduced as an element; but that *in present circumstances, and with a view to probable consequences,* it cannot reasonably be expected of slaveholders to give up their slaves. This is what we suppose to be meant, by people's being opposed to slavery 'in the abstract.' . . .

. . . All we need for the overthrow of slavery is to gain the ear of the people. This is done by agitation; and never is agitation so thorough and effectual, as when it begins in the halls of legislation. We laugh to scorn the pomp and circumstance with which Mr. Calhoun, or Mr. Clay, or some other great slaveholding statesman, annually proclaims a final victory over fanaticism. Do they not see that our very defeats are triumphs to us? Have they yet to learn that revolutions never roll backwards? That our opposers are but erecting paper-ramparts, against the surges of an inswelling Atlantic? That their resolutions are but words? That a breath unmakes them, as a breath has made? They are only doing our work. The country has learned more of the dangerous tendencies of slavery, and of the desperate character and designs of its supporters, by the discussions in Congress, than we could have instilled directly for years. Again, in the mere process of signing a petition,—the simplest form of political action,—strength and clearness are added to the convictions of thousands. So much force and definiteness do our principles and feelings acquire, by expression; so much moral vigor does a man gain, by openly taking his side.

We cannot be justified in abandoning any wide field of action, be it moral, social, religious or political. There can be no vantage ground for the wrong side. The slavery question cannot, and ought not, we think, to be kept wholly disjoined from politics. It should not be made a mere political question, but the religious and moral sense of the people must speak out, on the subject, with precision and authority, to their political representatives.

Unquestionably that voice is to go forth, commanding the use of all moral, lawful and constitutional means to overthrow slavery. We believe the question of abolition is one, perhaps the only one, on which the North can be brought to unite. Our cause is, we think, destined to increase so rapidly, as to threaten political extinction to every public man here, who arrays himself against it. Instructions will go forth from the constituent bodies, that will command the obedience of northern representatives in Congress. When this is done, slavery must cease in the metropolis of the nation, and slavery in the States cannot long survive. We doubt not, before five years are gone, it will be the South, instead of the North, that will be disunited and vacillating. It does not belong to the character of their cause, or of the age and country we live in, that the South can long keep their ranks unbroken. Even now, there is no real unity of interest or opinion, between the farming and planting slave States.

Political action doubtless brings temptations and hazards; but so does any successful action. Success is itself dangerous. What then? shall we not aim at success? Shall a man seclude himself from the world, lest the world prove too strong for his virtue? As practical men we cannot proceed on these scruples. We cannot consent to forego the power to do good, from the apprehension that its possession may tempt us to use it for evil.

Is it then our purpose to recommend to abolitionists the formation of a distinct political party? So far from this, we think such a policy would be in the highest degree dangerous, if not fatal to the efficiency of our organization.—Our most intelligent friends, throughout the country, deprecate our assuming the character of a third political party. Such a course would be opposed to the well settled policy and wise example of the English abolitionists, who have always kept the political aspect of their cause subordinate to the religious. Remember that abolition was carried in England, mainly as a religious question.

If we were a political party, the struggle for places of power and emolument would render our motives suspected, even if it did not prove too strong a temptation to our integrity.

Make our cause mainly political, and it would be at once excluded from nearly every pulpit in the land.

If we were a distinct party, every member of it must vote for its candidates, however he might disagree with them on other important points of public policy. This would involve two great evils. The sacrifice thus demanded, being greater than we can reasonably expect most men to make, accessions to our party would be greatly retarded;—and, what is a more serious difficulty, divisions would inevitably arise among ourselves, growing out of the struggles of different sections of our own party, to secure the nomination of candidates of their peculiar sentiments. Whig abolitionists would ask for a whig candidate: the democrats of our party would insist on our nominating a democrat.

Experience seems to show, that under a free government, there cannot be at one time, more than two powerful political parties. The parties that now divide the country are active, zealous and strong. Years must elapse, if we should organize politically, before we could be any thing but an uninfluential minority.

Our position, as a small minority party in politics would be hazardous and perplexing. There is danger that low considerations of expediency would intrude upon our sense of eternal right.

Political adventurers, loud in their professions, unscrupulous in their means, would attach themselves to us. Disappointed men, who have been disowned by other parties, would come among us to use us as tools for their personal advancement, to disgrace us by their inconsistency, to lower our hitherto high standard of principle, and perhaps sacrifice us in the day of trial.

Belonging, as we now do, to the various political parties, we can readily work our principles in, among them. Our present political ties and sympathies give us a strong hold over our political associates. We should lose all this mode of influence, by withdrawing from them. Our withdrawal would be held equivalent to a declaration of war.

A new political organization would have, of course, the combined hostility of the old parties. It is now the interest of each to conciliate us, for the sake of our votes. Were those votes pledged to our own candidates, the other parties would have a common interest in crushing us.

To form a political party, on anti-slavery grounds, would involve a needless abandonment of our other political preferences, and therefore would imply, not merely that abolition is the *first,* but that it is the only public object, in which abolitionists feel interested. This is not true, and to produce such a state of feeling is as undesirable, as it would be impracticable.

To conclude this part of the subject, our true policy is not to turn party politicians, but in politics as elsewhere to stand firm by our principles, and let the politicians come to us.

Of each of the three forms of political action, petitioning, the interrogating of candidates for office, and suffrage, we have a few words to address to you.

We pray you not to weary in the work of petitioning the national and state legislatures. It is the anti-slavery petitions, mainly, that have unlocked the lips of our legislatures, on the subject of abolition, and slowly compelled the newspaper-press to recognize, and unwillingly to aid, our movements. The agitation, caused by the rejection of our petitions, has spread into every village. This simple mode of action marks our growing strength; indicates, definitely the people's will; enlightens our adversaries with the knowledge of our numbers; and is felt, by our representatives, as a great support in the discharge of their duty. Depend upon it, the time has come when the members of Congress, from this State, feel relieved, under their great responsibility, by their constituents holding a decided—aye, even a peremptory tone, on the subject of slavery.

We hope women will pour in their petitions to Congress, at its next session, in redoubled numbers. Let them thank God, and take new courage, for they have done great good. We feel deeply the value of the earnest labours of women, in our cause. All admit slavery is to be overthrown by a reformed public opinion; but public opinion is not composed of the opinion of either sex exclusively. In every christian and civilized community, self-devoted, intelligent women are among the most important sources of moral and religious influence. Grievously do they err, who deem lightly of the fact, that in the moral strife between freedom and slavery, the women of the North are with the abolitionists.

Your representatives in the next State Legislature, and for the Congress of 1839, are to be chosen the coming autumn. They should be seasonably interrogated, as to their opinions on the most important matters connected with our cause, on which they may probably be called to act. After some consideration, the Board have concluded to recommend, that the interrogatories to candidates be limited, for the present year, to the two following subjects:—The immediate abolition of Slavery in the District of Columbia; and the admission of new States into the union, whose Constitutions tolerate slavery.

Our Legislature, at its last session, resolved 'that Congress ought to take measures for the abolition of slavery, in the District.' This vague language can satisfy no one. *When* ought Congress to take these 'measures'?—what are the 'measures' that Congress ought to take? and how long a time are these 'measures' to occupy, before the slave is to be free? Remember, that the Senate and the House both refused to assert that Congress ought to immediately abolish slavery in the District, though this proposition was moved as an amendment. The resolution of the Legislature, as passed, would be accorded to, even by some slaveholders. It may mean apprenticeship,—it may import colonization. This State owes it to herself to speak out distinctly, that none may misunderstand or gainsay. She will be shorn of a portion of her moral power, till this is done.

The application of Florida, to be admitted as a slaveholding member of the Union is to be acted on, at no distant day— probably at the next session of Congress. You ought, therefore, to see to it that remonstrances against its admission as a slaveholding State, are presented early in the session. Our northern statesmen should be seasonably taught, that they must not in future misrepresent and betray the rights and principles of New England, as was done in the recent admission of Arkansas.

We request the officers of County Societies, within their respective limits, to see that the candidates for Congress and for the State Senate and House of Representatives are duly interrogated and their answers published in the local newspapers.

The questions should, of course, be in writing; and it seems better that they should be written and signed, not by the officers of societies *as such,* but, as far as practicable, by individual electors, political friends of the candidate interrogated. It is not advisable to ask any pledge from the candidate, but simply to inquire his present opinions. The questions to the State candidate may be, substantially, thus:

'Are you in favor of the passage of a resolution, by the State Legislature, declaring that Congress ought immediately to abolish slavery, in the District of Columbia?

'Are you in favor of the passage of a resolution, declaring that no new State ought to be admitted into the Union, whose Constitution tolerates slavery?'

The questions to candidates for Congress should run thus:

'Are you in favor of the passage of an act of Congress for the immediate abolition of slavery, in the District of Columbia?

'Are you opposed to the admission of any new State into the Union, whose Constitution tolerates slavery?'

A large school in politics, both in Great Britain and America, deny the right of instruction; principally on the ground, that if carried out, it would destroy the deliberative character of the representative body, and convert it into a mere instrument to register the edicts of the people. The practice, of exacting pledges from candidates, may be considered liable to similar objections. It is, however, sufficient to advert to the fact, that the presidential electors of all parties are uniformly chosen under an express pledge to vote for particular candidates, in order to shew, that no party has, in practice, scrupled to pledge its candidates. But in order to avoid any doubt or cavil on this point, we think it best to confine your inquiries, as we have already intimated, to the mere opinion for the time being, of the candidate. This you have a right to know; as without such knowledge it may often happen, that you cannot exercise intelligently your right of suffrage. It may be said, that a simple expression of opinion would, under the circumstances, be equivalent to a pledge. We deny that such is the fact, or that the thing is so understood. A pledge binds in all events. A previous expression of present opinion is not incompatible with keeping the mind still open to conviction, on listening to the opposing arguments. It is true, that a representative who should vote contrary to his previous professions, would find it necessary, before the next election, to satisfy his constituents that he came honestly by his new opinions; but this is certainly a very wholesome obligation, and one from which no honest man would desire exemption.

If it be objected, that these interrogatories may tempt candidates to belie their consciences for the sake of gaining votes, we reply, that to men of this easy virtue the whole action of society is full of temptation, but it cannot be suspended for their sakes. If the further objection be urged, that there is an indecorum in submitting to be thus questioned on the eve of an election, it is enough to reply, first, that as candidates are not usually nominated until the eve of an election, inquiries can be made at no other time; and, secondly, that inquiries of this nature, as they clearly imply confidence and not distrust, must be regarded rather as complimentary, than as derogatory to the candidate. We address him as an honest, straightforward citizen, and no man of genuine dignity of character will feel himself degraded, either in public or private life, by giving a plain answer to a plain question, where the inquirer has a right to the information asked. As to the fear of indecorum, like most overstrained modesty, it will be usually found symptomatic of conscious corruption within. Suppose you were about to engage a commander for your ship, a superintendent of your farm, an agent for your factory, and were to inquire his views as to the principles or details of the employment he was to undertake. Would you endure his insolence if he were to reply, 'I consider it undignified and improper to satisfy you on these points. You are at liberty to gain what information you can of my history and reputation, and thence to infer what are my views on the matter in question?' You would think, and probably but too justly, that he meant to cheat you. Will you bear such language from your political servants? No public man in this country is strong enough to sustain himself long, in this mode of defying the popular will. No party can do it. The right of the electors, to call for a frank disclosure of the opinions of candidates, on all subjects which may come within the scope of their official duties, has been expressly admitted by Martin Van Buren, Henry Clay, William H. Harrison, William Wirt, Edward Everett, and Marcus Morton[2] and by a host of other eminent statesmen. It is too late to question its validity. No man of plain integrity would shrink from the ordeal. The practice is eminently republican and useful. It is calculated to promote political honesty and open dealing, and to put an end to that double-faced and non-committal policy, by which politicians, of inferior abilities and low arts, sometimes crawl into power.

---

[2] Martin Van Buren (1782–1862), Senator from New York (1821–1828), Governor, New York, Vice-President (1833–1837), President (1837–1841), Democrat, Free Soil presidential candidate (1848). Henry Clay (1777–1852), Whig politician, Representative and Senator from Kentucky, presidential candidate (1824, 1832, 1840, 1844). William Henry Harrison (1773–1841), early leader in Indiana-Illinois territory, General in Indian Wars and in War of 1812, Representative (1816–1819) from Ohio, Senator (1825–1829), Whig, President (March–April 1841). William Wirt (1772–1834), author and lawyer, Anti-Masonic presidential candidate (1832), United States Attorney-General (1827–1829), Whig. Edward Everett (1794–1865), orator, clergyman, statesman, Representative (1825–1835), conservative on slavery question, vice-presidential candidate (1860) for Constitutional Union Party. Marcus Morton (1784–1864), Representative (1817–1821), Democratic leader in Massachusetts. [Eds.]

Your duties as voters are mainly negative. *Vote for no man, however estimable from general character and acquirements, who is not prepared to give a prompt, explicit, and satisfactory answer on the topics we have mentioned.* Be uncompromising on points of principle. Have no respect to persons. It is the secret of your strength, hitherto. Shew by your firmness, whether your heart is in your cause. Let not the fervor of political zeal, or the warmth of personal attachment, lead you to forfeit your character for resolution and consistency. Whoso loves father, or brother, or friend better than the truth, is not worthy of it.

We pray you to take no part, *as abolitionists,* in the nomination of candidates. Do not even vote, *by concert,* for candidates already in nomination. Let the act of voting be an individual act, but performed, by each voter, under a deep sense of responsibility. We are aware, that in many towns and districts, where you have considerable numerical strength, and where the answers of the regular political candidates may not be satisfactory, the temptation will be strong, to unite your forces upon a candidate of your own. We entreat you not to do this. Your example will be a dangerous one. On the other hand, do not stay away from the polls. Go, rather; and scatter your votes. This is the true way to make yourselves felt. Every scattering vote you cast, counts against the candidates of the parties; and will serve as an effectual admonition to them, to nominate the next time, men whom you can conscientiously support.

The candidates presented to your choice will, of course, be nominated either by the whigs or democrats. The most prominent individual of the whig party, and probably their next candidate for the presidency, is a slave-holder, president of that stupendous imposture, the Colonization Society, author of the fatal Missouri 'compromise,' and of the slavish resolutions against the abolitionists, lately passed by the Senate of the United States. On the other hand, the leader of the democratic party, 'the northern president with southern principles,' has deeply insulted this nation, by avowing his determination to veto any bill for the abolition of slavery in the District of Columbia, which may be passed by a majority of the people, in opposition to the wishes of the slave States.

No consistent abolitionist can vote for either of these individuals. It does not however follow, that he cannot vote for candidates for State offices or for Congress, who may be their friends and supporters. If the candidate before you be honest, capable, and true to your principles, we think you may fairly vote for him, without considering too curiously, whether his success might not have an indirect bearing on the interests of Mr. Clay or Mr. Van Buren. It is a golden maxim, 'Do the duty that lies nearest thee.' Vote for each man by himself, and on his own merits. If you attempt to make your rule more complicated, so as to include distant contingencies and consequences, it will be found perplexing and impracticable.

The independent course in politics, which we have recommended, supposes great prudence, disinterestedness, energy of purpose, and self-control, in those who are to adopt it. May you justify our confidence in you. Do your duty. Come out, in your strength, to the polls. Refuse to support any public man who trims, or equivocates, or conceals his opinions. Beware of half way abolitionists; and of men, who are abolitionists but once a year. Prove that you do not require the machinery of party discipline, to vote strictly according to your professed principles. Do this, and you will rapidly acquire a deserved influence. 'Such a party,' as Mr. Webster justly said, in speaking of the abolitionists, 'will assuredly cause itself to be respected.' Within the next two years, the friends of freedom might hold the balance of power, in every free State in the Union; and no man could ascend the presidential seat, against their will.

Our cause demands of us entire disinterestedness. We are not to desire power, for power's sake. Our prayers, and toil, and tears are not our own, but the slave's. We need circumspection. The attacks, that were formerly made on our principles and measures, are now turned upon our motives and personal characters. The corrupt and bitter portion of the newspaper press are beginning to discover, that the facts and arguments, in favor of our great doctrine of immediate emancipation, are irresistible, and are carrying conviction to almost every well informed and reflecting mind; and they are now trying to distort our motives, and blacken our reputations. This is making a false issue, but let it not too much disturb us. The true question for the public evidently is, Do we speak the truth? The inquiry, whether we are actuated by a right spirit, is, in reality, of very little comparative importance. The principle is all; the men nothing. Let God be true, and every man a liar.

Beware of forming alliances with any party. Enter into no stipulations in advance, for the disposition of a single vote. The party, or the press, or the politician that courts you most warmly to-day, will perhaps shew most malignance and treachery toward you, to-morrow. We have reason to be grateful to Heaven, that, thus far, we have so little to thank either of the great parties for. The leading presses on both sides, have done their best to outrage and insult us. There has been an eager competition between them, to purchase southern votes, by sacrificing the rights, and aspersing the character of the abolitionists. Even now, though it is seen by all persons of common sagacity, and is even generally admitted in private conversation, that our ultimate success is certain, the same treatment is, to a considerable extent continued. The class of trading politicians take no far-sighted views even for themselves, still less for their party,—least of all, for their country. They cannot wait for the slow returns of an honest and liberal policy. Their object is to meet the exigency of the moment, to carry the present point; like prodigals lavishing the resources of the future upon the passing hour; like gamblers trusting to chance or trick, to extricate them from the embarrassments they are aware must, by and bye, come.

This competition for southern votes, has saved us from the too dangerous friendship of either of the political parties. The President of the United States, had, (in his first message to Congress,) avowed himself the suppliant tool of the southern slaveholders, when the Whig merchants of New-York, determined not to be outbid, took occasion, in their address to the nation, to assure their southern brethren, that they were men, who 'thought the *possession* of property [not *its honest acquisition*]³ was evidence of merit!' and that persons of such sentiments, would be the last to disturb 'the peculiar property' of the south.

By counteracting forces like these, have we been providentially preserved from being absorbed by either of the political parties. With the fundamental principles of those parties, when properly understood, abolitionism has strong affinities. The idea of the whig party in this country is order, the supremacy of law, the sacredness of the person, the inviolability of property. Who has a stronger interest in these things than we? Who have suffered more than we, from anarchy and misrule? Who have pleaded more earnestly, for the right of every man to that which he produces by his own labor;—a right which is at the foundation of all property?—On the other hand, the great Democratic idea is Liberty, Reform, Progress, Equal Rights;—and are not these our very breath of life?

We are far from asserting, that these noble principles are actually embodied, in the leaders of either of our political parties. So far from this, the principles are in danger of being themselves brought into disgrace, by the selfish and inconsistent men, who pretend to represent them. Still, while these principles are, however imperfectly, represented in the struggle of the adverse parties, it is natural and right, that individ-

---

³ Brackets in the original. [Eds.]

ual abolitionists should range themselves, in these struggles, according as their political theories may incline them to take one or the other set of views. This must, however, be done in strict subordination to the interests of that hallowed cause, to which we have pledged our character and influence. Be assured, that not one man, in the very first ranks of the political parties, has any sincere attachment to your principles. Therefore, as you have little to hope for the abolition cause, from the sincere good will of the parties, as such, do not be driven to act with the one, or renounce the other, merely because, for some temporary purpose, the one side or the other happens, to-day, to treat you with unaccustomed consideration, or to heap upon you peculiar outrage and abuse. Circumstances may, for a while, induce the presses, of one or the other party, to conciliate you; but, depend upon it, there is, at bottom, but very little to choose between them. There is certainly no reason, thus far, why you should as a body, ally yourselves exclusively with either, but many and urgent reasons against it.

There is much, in the aspect of the times, to cheer us, in our political efforts. The danger of the admission of Texas is, probably, past. Thanks to the abolitionists, the free States have been roused to the disgrace and ruin of becoming a partner, in the crimes of that bloody and slave-trading Republic. Slavery in the United States, and slavery in Texas, will not be suffered to double their strength, by union. The gag resolution in Congress, has received its death blow, from the intrepid, illustrious and venerable Adams. The subject of slavery will henceforth be an open one, in that body. Within three years, we shall probably have a favorable report on slavery in the District, and in less than five, we have little doubt of witnessing its peaceful abolition.

Slavery once abolished in the District, what a vast accession of moral power is gained, both in the process, and from the result! Friends animated,—oppressors disheartened,—all consciences awakened! It is a gain to the cause of virtue every where. The spiritual atmosphere is purified. Each man draws freer breath into his soul. The Lord is seen indeed to reign. The testimony of the nation is thenceforth added to the general reprobation of slavery, and will help to shame it out of existence. Another illustrious proof is given, of the possibility of the highest public virtue.

Instead of calling on you to descend from these heights, from a fear that the elevation may make you giddy, we say to you, your only danger is in looking down. Keep your aims ever upwards, and there is no fear that your footing will not be firm.

JOSHUA R. GIDDINGS SUPPORTS ANTISLAVERY ACTION THROUGH MAJOR PARTIES

Men who had already made antislavery part of their political life but who had also come up through the ranks of the major parties did not lightly throw aside the party support which had made their careers possible. One such man was Joshua Reed Giddings (1795–1864), popular Representative from Ohio's antislavery Western Reserve. In 1842 he had resigned his seat in Congress after having been censured by the House for introducing on the floor material bearing on the Creole case. Standing immediately for re-election he was triumphantly returned to Congress. A Whig, Giddings found it necessary to justify his adherence to the party whose votes in the House had helped censure him. An antislavery supporter,

> he also found it necessary to justify his failure to support the antislavery Liberty Party. In a series of published letters he argued that effective antislavery action was possible only by supporting northern antislavery Whigs (like himself); that to vote for a Liberty Party candidate, who could not win, was indirectly, therefore, to vote for a proslavery Democrat.

MR. EDITOR: I have now stated, generally, the constitutional rights of the people of the free States concerning slavery, and have referred to some of the most prominent abuses to which those rights have been subjected. It remains for me to call the attention of my readers to the remedy. But this will at once suggest itself to the mind of every reader, and each will say that our remedy consists in a *united vindication of our rights;* that the real difficulty consists in our divisions, and our first efforts should be to unite the friends of northern rights. In order to do this, we must search out the cause of our division, and understand distinctly the point on which we separated. If I understand our Liberty men, they are anxious to maintain the rights of the free States, and they ask for nothing more. I speak upon the authority of many leading men of that party. I have never met with an intelligent man who asked or demanded any thing more than this; yet they say, "the Whigs have neglected a portion of our most important rights, and they feel it their duty to separate from them, and to form a distinct party, whose principal efforts are to be directed to the maintenance of such of our rights as have been neglected by the Whigs. It was not my intention, when I commenced these essays, to throw censure upon any class of men, nor is such my present object; I may, however, be permitted to say, that I think our

---

From Pacificus [Joshua Reed Giddings], *The Rights and Privileges of the Several States in Regard to Slavery; being a Series of Essays, Published in the Western Reserve Chronicle, (Ohio,) After the Election of 1842. By a Whig of Ohio* (n.p.: n.p., [1842]), pp. 13–14.

Liberty friends did not well "define their position" before they separated from us. For the correctness of this remark, I will refer to the recollection of the great mass of our people of all parties. At the time of separating from us, they had not clearly set forth to the world our rights, which had been trampled upon; nor did they state, with perspicuity, the abuses which they sought to correct. Neither did they definitely mark the boundaries, and limit the extent of the political reform which they were endeavoring to effect. On the contrary, there was a degree of obscurity pervading their objects. They professed opposition to slavery, and left the public to infer a design to invade the privileges of the slave States, instead of maintaining our own. This idea has rested in the minds of a large portion of our people, both in the free and in the slave States. It is true the charge was often denied; and it is equally true that the denial was not carried home to the minds of the great mass of our people; many of whom, to this day, really believe the object of the Liberty party to be an unconstitutional interference with the privileges of the slave States. But, so far as I have been able to learn their motives, and to analyze their views, I understand them to be simply the *preservation of our own rights;* the repeal of all acts of Congress, passed for the support of slavery or the slave trade; to separate the Federal Government, and the free States, from all unconstitutional connexion with that institution, and to leave it with the individual States, where the Constitution placed it. This, I believe, to be the boundary and farthest extent of their *political* intentions. If they entertain any other or farther views, I hope Judge King (the candidate of the Liberty party for Governor of Ohio) will state to your readers, through the Chronicle, the point on which I have failed to express their objects. I hope, also, that the editors of the Philanthropist and Emancipator will, through their respective papers, set forth definitely any error into which I may have fallen, in regard to the designs and objects of their party. But, for the present, taking these to be the definite limits to which they aspire, I will respectfully ask the Whigs, as a party, and the Liberty men, as a party, to show me the line of demarcation between them? Is there an individual in the whole Whig party of Ohio, or in the free States, that is willing to surrender a single right of our people? If there be such a whig, I have not met him. If there be a Whig editor, north of Mason and Dixon's line, who is willing to yield up any of the constitutional rights of the free States, I hope he will favor the country with his views; and that he will inform us distinctly *which part* of the Constitution we ought first to surrender. I speak with great confidence when I say, that I believe no such man can be found. Let the rights of the people of the free States, in regard to slavery, be fairly and distinctly pointed out, and there will be no want of firmness nor of patriotism to maintain them. It is true, however, that many Whigs have, and still do oppose the abolition of slavery in the District of Columbia; but they will assign to you, as the reason, that Congress *has not the constitutional power* to abolish it. If you then ask them if they are willing that Congress *should repeal its own laws,* for the support of slavery and the slave trade in that District, they will, at once, answer you in the affirmative. If you inquire whether they are willing to lend their influence, or their property, to support slavery, they will answer you that they detest the institution. If you interrogate them in regard to any other rights of the north, they will unhesitatingly assure you of their determination to sustain them.

If, then, our Whigs are willing to sustain *all* our rights, and our Liberty men have no further objects in view than the support of such rights, the question at once suggests itself, *why do they divide?* What principle separates them from each other? And it is a question of high and solemn import, which the writer would repeat in the ear of every Whig, every antislavery man, and of every lover of our free institutions, *why do you divide your political influence, and prostrate your polit-*

ical energies, while you agree in principle, and are laboring for the same objects?

We have the same interests to watch over, the same rights to maintain, and the same honor to protect. All these must receive our attention, or be left to those who, as a party, have uniformly lent themselves to the slave-holding influence. If we forget those rights, and spend our efforts in unmeaning contentions and useless quarrels with each other, will not our country hold us responsible? Our interests have been sacrificed; our rights have been trampled upon; our State has been disgraced, as I have heretofore shown. Yet we have divided our efforts, and separated from our political associates, and delivered the honor of our State to the keeping of a party who, forgetful of the dignity of freemen, have shown themselves willing to become the *catchers of slaves*, and to degrade themselves and their State by legislating for the sole purpose of robbing their fellow men of that liberty with which the God of nature has endowed them. But I desire to examine a little further the cause of our separation at the late election. The Whigs supported our tariff; our harbor improvements; the distribution of the proceeds of the public lands, with zeal and constancy. But our commerce with Hayti, the right of petition, the slave trade in the District of Columbia, received from them, generally, much less attention, although they were not neglected by a portion of that party. These latter subjects were deemed of paramount importance by a portion of our political friends; on these they bestowed their principal thoughts, and treated the others with comparatively little attention. In this manner each party felt that they were exerting their efforts upon subjects of vital interest to our country, and each considered the other as laboring in behalf of interests that were not worthy of the attention paid to them.

In this way each party became dissatisfied with the other. Here, then, is the precise point of division among our friends: not because either did *wrong*, but because each felt that the other was not sufficiently zealous in supporting *all* their interests. The division did not arise from any political sin of *commission*, but *for omitting some part of our duties*. The Democratic party has violently *opposed* those rights which Liberty men deem sacred. The Whigs were lukewarm in supporting them; and, on this account, our Liberty friends withdrew from us, and thereby delivered over our interests to the disposal of those whose bitterness against the rights of man can scarcely find utterance in our language. Having thus ascertained the cause, and the precise point of our separation, the remedy is plain. It consists simply in *doing our duty*—in maintaining our rights and interests, and firmly resisting all abuses; in placing ourselves upon the exact line of the Constitution, and temperately, but resolutely, opposing all encroachments upon our interests, our honor, or our constitutional privileges. I am aware that many of our editors and public men fear that the assertion and maintenance of our rights in regard to slavery, would drive from us our Whig friends in the slave States. If these fears were well grounded, they would form no good reason why we should surrender our constitutional rights, in order to *purchase* their adherence. This is the policy of the opposite party. They appear anxious to surrender up our rights, our interests, and our honor, for the purchase of southern votes. If the Whigs attempt to rival that party in *servility*, they must fail. The independent spirit, the high sense of honor, the patriotic sentiment of our Whigs, will not permit them to become subservient to the slaveholding interest. But the argument is not well-founded. Our southern Whigs are generally men of liberal and patriotic sentiments. They will not ask of us the sacrifice of our constitutional rights. On the contrary, they will be as willing to grant us the enjoyment of *all* our rights, as to demand the enjoyment of all their own. If they are not such men, they are unfit to be the associates of northern Whigs. It is, however, true, that they, as well as northern men, have not, heretofore, fully understood our rights, for the reason that we, ourselves, *dare not assert them;* and they, as well as northern men, have unconsciously voted and acted in opposition to the rights of the free States, under the impression that they were sustaining the Constitution. But when the attention of our southern and northern Whigs shall be directed to this subject; when they shall have fully investigated it, and shall understand the constitutional limits of slavery, I apprehend there will be no difference between them. It is, therefore, all important that public attention should be directed to this matter. Indeed, intelligence in regard to northern rights cannot be longer suppressed. A spirit of inquiry is abroad among the people, and it is increasing daily, and becoming stronger and stronger. A marked and palpable change has taken place in the public mind within the past year. In February last, almost the entire press united in the opinion that we were bound to support the coastwise slave trade of the south. At this time, who is willing to hazard his reputation by advocating such doctrine? Yet, with such examples before us, a portion of our press and of our public men, exhibit much timidity as to asserting and maintaining our constitutional rights. So long have the people of the north been accustomed to silent submission, when our rights have been invaded, that many of our editors, our statesmen and politicians, still appear to doubt the *safety* of an open, frank, and manly defence of our interests and our honor. It, however, needs no spirit of prophecy to foretell the downfall of any party, who has not the moral and political courage to maintain the rights and interests of the north. If the Whigs come forth to the defence of these interests, and maintenance of these rights, their success is not less certain than the continuance of time; and if the opposite party continue to *oppose* these rights and interests, their defeat is inevitable.

XIII

Argument for Political Action:

Third Parties

ARNOLD BUFFUM LAUDS
THE ANTISLAVERY THIRD PARTY

Dissatisfied with the rather meager results of questioning candidates, circulating and filing petitions, and of working in unorganized ways through the major parties, politically-minded abolitionists soon turned to more direct and systematic political action. The Liberty Party, founded in 1839, was the first distinctly antislavery political party. In 1840 and 1844 it ran as its presidential candidate, James G. Birney. Speaking in defense of the Liberty Party, Arnold Buffum (1782–1859), New England Quaker, first President of the New England Anti-Slavery Society, and a founder of the American Anti-Slavery Society, pointed up the advantages which
the new party had to offer.

From Arnold Buffum, *Lecture Showing the Necessity for a Liberty Party, and Setting Forth its Principles, Measures, and Object* (Cincinnati: Caleb Clark, 1844), pp. 8–15.

Having been a careful observer of the proceedings of the National Government for half a century—having witnessed its devotion for upwards of forty years to the Slaveholding interest, I have been led to look carefully over the acts of national legislation, and to examine minutely the operation and bearing of the measures which have been adopted, and I can arrive at no other conclusion, than that for the last *forty years*, every act of a national character, has originated with the Slaveholders, and has been adopted in a spirit of devotion to their interests, and of hostility to every other interest in our country. Thus OUR *national Government* has already been made, like the governments of Europe, an engine for building up an ARISTOCRACY in OUR country, which when once completely organized, will rob, not only the slaves on their own plantations, but also nine-tenths of the American people of *their* rights, and reduce *them* to the same wretched condition, which is now witnessed among the laboring population in Europe.

Notwithstanding the representation of the *property* of Slaveholders in the national government, we in the non-Slaveholding States, having nearly three-fourths of the popular vote of the nation, have a majority of 47 members in Congress, and the same majority in the Presidential Electoral Colleges: So that, were it not for the dough-faced servility of a portion of the representatives of freemen, in the Presidential election and in Congress, we might even now, have *our* rights protected, *our* welfare promoted, and all *our* elements of prosperity and sources of wealth successfully developed.

The remedy which we need, for the difficulties we now suffer, is to be found in the election of a President and members of Congress, who will *not* basely bow themselves down to the moloch of Slavery, but who will impartially administer the government on its true and original principles, for the promotion of the general welfare, and equally for the benefit of all who are subject to its power. The election of such men, is entirely within the power of the non-slaveholders of the country; and such men will be elected, just so soon as the non-slaveholders shall have been effectually aroused, to investigate and understand the arts of designing demagogues, who have heretofore but too successfully deceived the majority, into the support of Slave holding Aristocrats, or the sycophantic tools of the Slave power.

Within the last 42 years, Slaveholders have filled the Presidential office 34 years, and non-Slaveholders only 8 years. The office of Chief Justice of the Supreme Court, Speaker of the House of Representatives, President pro tem. of the Senate, Secretary of State, and most of the other departments of the Government, have been equally occupied and controlled by men, who from the nature of their *"peculiar in[s]titutions,"* are inevitably hostile to a laboring community of freemen.

Some of the measures which the Government has adopted, intended for the promotion of the Slave interest, have, by the ingenuity and enterprize of freemen, been so appropriated as to become productive of general benefit to the whole community, and to promote the prosperity and welfare of all; but when it has become evident, that an adherence to the existing order of things, would be productive of such *favorable* results, the policy has been changed, and measures which were operating thus beneficially, have been abolished; so that we have in the end been made deeply to suffer, in consequence of having conformed our business arrangements, to the operation of the acts of the Government.

When the Slaveholders have desired any measure of foreign or domestic policy, calculated to strengthen their power in controlling the action of the Government, or to promote their individual prosper[i]ty, they have always come up to the executive or legislative department of the Government, with an authoritative demand for compliance with their interests or wishes, and they have in no case been finally defeated. Every law has been passed, every measure adopted, at whatever sacrifice of all other interests it might require, which the

Slaveholders have demanded for their benefit. On the other hand, the interests of non-Slaveholders, have as invariably been unheeded; or what is still worse, the action of the Government has in many important cases, been *hostile* to the non-Slaveholding interest, without the anticipation of *benefit* to any body. No Measure of a general character, tending to *our* benefit, has been permitted to stand any longer than was *necessary* to answer some sinister purpose of the Slaveholders, or to operate upon our concerns, as the bait operates upon the fox, who is thereby beguiled into the well-concealed trap, which is then sprung upon him, whereby his foe is enabled to rob him of his skin. Such precisely has been the operation of our tariff laws, by which the citizens of the non-Slaveholding States, were induced to invest a hundred million dollars in manufacturing establishments, all to be swept away, by the springing of the Calhoun and Clay compromise trap upon them in 1833. Such too was the operation of two United States Bank charters, each running 20 years; just long enough for the people to conform their business arrangements to the operations of *"the Great Regulator;"* when by the demand of the Slaveholders, they were both forced to go *down,* that they might carry down with them the general prosperity of the people.

To these statements and charges, bold and sweeping as they are, I challenge an answer. If there is any politician, Whig, Democrat, or Tyler man, who can name *an instance* in which the Slaveholders have failed of obtaining a compliance with their interest and wishes, or in which any measure has been *adopted, carried out, and persevered in,* for the advancement of any of the other great interests of the country, I hope that through some medium, they will let the public know what it is. I call not for private contradictions of my statements; my allegations are publicly made, and the challenge for an answer is a public one; let the refutation be as public as are my charges, and then I will conclude, that the respondant has some confidence that he will be able to maintain his ground. I call not for mere declamation, or common party slang; but I call for facts, and I challenge the world to name the facts, in contradiction of the statements herein contained.

I call upon the leaders of the two great political parties, which have ruled the nation for the last forty years, to let the *people* know what *benefits they have derived* from the action of the Government, to support which, we have paid more than five hundred millions of dollars in taxes, of the earnings of the laboring people. For let the revenue of the Government be collected in what manner it may, whether by direct taxation, or indirectly, by the laying of duties on articles of consumption, the whole amount must be supplied by the productive industry of the country.

If any measures have been adopted by the Government, which were intended by *any portion* of those who voted for them, to promote the prosperity of the non-Slaveholders of the country, such measures have been suffered to remain in operation, *only* long enough to induce a change in individual pursuits in conformity to the encouragement thus held out by the Government, and then, they have been prostrated at the demand of the dealers in human flesh, and those who had trusted to the faith of the Government, have been prostrated with them.

The Slaveholders in all the States of our Union give but about two hundred and fifty thousand votes in popular elections; while the non-Slaveholders give more than two millions, being more than eight times as many as are given by the Slaveholders. Hence it is evident, that when the *true issue*, of *Slavery*, or *Liberty*, shall constitute the division line of political parties in our country, the *aristocratical* power will be entirely prostrated in the National Government, and the traffiickers in human flesh will be left to rely on State legislation alone, for the protection of their *"peculiar institution."* Then a President and a Congress will be elected, who will be neither Slave*holders*, nor the sycophantic tools of Slave*holders*. Our Government will then mark out and establish a systematic and permanent policy, and will conduct the affairs of the nation, in accordance with (not "the wishes of Slaveholders," but) the interests of freemen, and with the principles of the Declaration of Independence; giving stability and permanency to that cause, in which our forefathers embarked, when they declared it to be a self-evident truth, that all men are created equal, and endowed by their Creator with an unalienable right to be free, and to pursue their own happiness. The principles of a true democracy will then be practically applied in the administration of the Government; the rights of the people will then be maintained, and their welfare and prosperity will be so promoted, that the spirit of aristocracy will stand abashed, in despair of obtaining a royal diadem, or of effecting by any means the subjugation of the people. Then indeed will our institutions and our prosperity hold out to an admiring world, an irresistible invitation to demolish their thrones, dash their crowns in pieces, and build upon their ruins a temple of freedom, to guard the rights, and promote the happiness and welfare of the people.

Our whole object as a political party is, the inculcation and practical application of the great principles of human rights, derived from the charter given forth by the SUPREME LAW GIVER of the universe, when He created man in his own image, and gave to man universally the right to exercise dominion over all inferior beings in this world. We believe, that it is only by the faithful maintenance of these principles that any people can long retain their liberty, and enjoy the rights and privileges mercifully dispensed to *all*, by the common PARENT of us *all*. The practical application of these principles will put an end to all tyranny and oppression throughout the world, and secure to every human being the perfect enjoyment of the right to pursue his own happiness; restricted only by the divine prohibition of authority to trespass upon the happiness of others. . . .

. . . The American LIBERTY PARTY, is not, (as it is often denominated by our opponents) a *third* party. We are the true original American party, seeking to carry out the principles of our forefathers, as set forth in the declaration of Independence. These principles have for a long time been lost sight of, in the fog of the two great parties, which are contending with each other for the mastery, *not* for the promotion of the cause of liberty, but for the establishment of a domineering Oligarchy, and for the perpetuation of the old monarchical and aristocratical doctrine, that the well born and the rich have a right to tyranize over the poor, and to appropriate to themselves the product of their labor. . . .

. . . Some of our opponents, probably through ignorance, have represented it to be our intention *forcibly* to emancipate the slaves in the Southern States; we intend no such thing. We complain, that by the action of the national Government, and also of the governments of many of the non-Slaveholding States in *support* of Slavery, we are made participants in the crime of robbing men of their natural rights—we wish to absolve ourselves from such crime.

By the voluntary act of Virginia and Maryland, in ceding to Congress the District of Columbia, the institution of Slavery in that portion of those States, standing as it did *only* on State authority, would have fal[l]en to the ground, had not our *Northern* members of Congress yielded themselves as props for its continued support; and all we ask of them in regard to Slavery in that district—in Florida, and on the high seas, is, that they get out from under it, and let it fall of its own weight, as it assuredly must, when the national government no longer stands its god father and supporter.

In relation to Slavery in the States, politically we claim no right to interfere. So long as the people of the South may choose to hold a portion of their children in bondage, and traffic in them as they do in brute animals, they must do it; but we are not willing that men who plunder their *own* children of their rights, should rule over *our* children; we will not therefore support any Slaveholder for office in the government,—besides, regarding Slavery as the most grievous wrong that was ever inflicted by one man upon another, and as a palpable violation of the laws of God; and knowing that its existence in our country, has a powerful tendency to stifle every feeling of humanity—to annihilate every principle of justice—to drive morality from our land, and to build up a lordly aristocracy, which if unresisted would eventually establish itself in power, to the entire subversion of the liberties of the nation, we can but feel, that it is an object which should claim the untiring devotion of every patriot or philanthropist, to promote the speedy and entire abolition of the system. We should therefore be *criminal*, were we to neglect the use of all *legitimate* means for accomplishing this great object.

Slavery is a dark institution—it cannot stand before the light of truth; this the Slaveholders well know, and enact laws prohibiting the education of the oppressed. We believe however, that although they may keep the minds of their enslaved children, in a state of mental and moral darkness and degradation, the system cannot stand before that full blaze of intellectual and moral light, which is now being disseminated *among the free.*

The abolition of Slavery in our country, will be but an incidental result of the establishment of our principles; the practical adoption of which, in the administration of the government, is as necessary for the security of *our* rights, and the rights of *our* posterity, as for the security of the rights of the oppressed in the Southern States.

Such, fellow-citizens, are the principles, such the aim, of the Liberty men in our country. Against these principles, and this aim, are arrayed in unholy combination, the aristocratic enslavers of men, and through their influence, the existing administrations of the National and State Governments. These are sustained in their opposition, First, by the drunken mobocrats, whose arguments consist of rotten eggs, tar, feathers, and brick-bats. Secondly, by a majority of the Clergy and the Church; these have *no* arguments, but "stopping their ears against the poor,"—("Whoso stoppeth his ears at the cry of the poor, he also shall cry himself, but shall not be heard"— *Proverbs*, xxi:13) and on secretly circulating *slanderous falsehoods* against the prominent advocates of our cause!!! Thirdly, and strange to tell, by a small party of Abolitionists; they rely on either ignorant or intentional misrepresentations of our principles, motives and measures.

If any class of the above named opposers, are honest in their opposition, we invite them to meet us in the field of reason, argument and truth, and to debate with us the questions which divide us. We have in our ranks many, in various parts of the country, who hold themselves in readiness to discuss these questions, either orally or through the medium of the press. We ask for *open* opponents—*such as are not ashamed to subscribe their names* to their arguments that posterity may know that in *this* age of the world, they stood forth in opposition to the holy cause of liberty and human rights, as advocated by us. Let them show to the world, if they can, that our principles are unsound—that our measures are unwise— that our facts are unreal, or that the object which we seek, is unworthy of the efforts which it will cost. If they can successfully do this, then we must fall; but should they fail in the attempt, or should the conviction that we are right in all our propositions, prevent them from making the attempt, then let them, if they choose, continue as heretofore, to rely upon mobocracy and slander, and let the intelligence and the moral sense of the world decide, on which side lies the truth, and the best interests of mankind. Let every Patriot, every Philanthropist, every well-wisher to the happiness of our race, frown indignantly upon all attempts to stifle a discussion which has for its object the regeneration of the public sentiment of the world, and the abrogation of *all* the abuses which keep the mass of mankind in poverty, and tend to perpetuate among them, ignorance, degradation and vice. Let *all honest* men, unite in proclaiming the inviolability of human rights; and the spirit of despotism shall soon be driven from the world—man every where shall assume his true position, and standing in his native dignity, "redeemed, regenerated, and disenthralled," shall rejoice in the assurance, that his posterity to the latest generation, shall inherit and enjoy the blessing of RATIONAL LIBERTY.

WILLIAM GOODELL ENDORSES A MANY-PLANKED POLITICAL PLATFORM

There were those reformers, enthusiastic in the support of freedom, who found that a party, antislavery only, was too circumscribed. Seeking to achieve the total reform of American society through political action, they tried, therefore, to extend the Liberty Party to embrace free trade, antimonopoly, temperance, and a variety of other causes. The Address of the National Nominating Convention at Macedon, New York, written by William Goodell, reported the nomination of Gerrit Smith and Elihu Burritt for President and Vice-President on a universal reform platform.

From William Goodell, *Address of the Macedon Convention, and Letters of Gerrit Smith* (Albany: S. W. Green, 1847), pp. 3–8.

It is now nearly two years since this general outline of political principles and measures was definitely proposed by some of us, as a basis of associated political action, believing as we then did and still do, that the Liberty party, to which we belonged, was not only pledged to those general principles, but was also pledged, by its own original and oft-repeated promises, to apply those principles to all public questions, as the appropriate occasions should arise for their application. During the period that has intervened, although strong exceptions have been taken, and determined opposition manifested, to the course we had proposed, we have found no antagonists who have been willing to join issue with us on the *moral* question involved, whether the action proposed is, or is not, in accordance with the *right and the true in the abstract*. No one offers to show us, and few, if any, are prepared to affirm, that our principles and our measures are not RIGHT, EQUITABLE AND JUST. Our principles are the professed creed of the nation. They are loudly insisted on by Abolitionists in general, and by Liberty party men in particular. And not the first man among them has attempted to prove that the measures we propose are not legitimate deductions from those principles; that our application of them is not appropriate and proper, or that there is not occasion, in consequence of existing wrongs, that a remedy should be applied. It is almost universally admitted by them, as well as by a large portion of the community in general, that the wrongs we have enumerated are evils, and that it is desirable that they should be removed. Abolitionists in general, and Liberty party men in particular, have been accustomed to maintain, moreover, that it is always safe to do right, and safe as well as obligatory to do right at the present time—that it is morally wrong to defer doing right,—and that it is holding the truth in unrighteousness to acknowledge a truth in the abstract, and yet decline, on prudential considerations, reducing that truth to practice. On this ground it is, that Abolitionists persist in applying the epithet PRO-SLAVERY to that portion of the community, who while they acknowledge the moral wrong of slavery, excuse themselves on the ground of expediency, from reducing their convictions to practice, in the bestowment of their votes.

We cannot perceive why we are not bound to reason in the same manner and to act in accordance with the same considerations in respect to all other moral evils within the admitted sphere and province of political action. Admitting that chattel slavery is the greatest moral and political evil upheld and sanctioned by the government, (though the moral and political evils of intemperance are scarcely less,) we cannot feel ourselves, as moral and accountable beings, at liberty to undertake the mensuration and guaging of the moral and political evils upheld by the government, with a view of ascertaining which is greatest, and thus determining which moral evil we will select as our antagonist, and which we will enter into a truce with, at present, and virtually support, by not making opposition to it a test, in the bestowment of our votes. If those who wish to oppose, at the ballot-box, the licensing of the sale of intoxicating liquors, or the enactment of certain unjust and wicked laws which oppress the poor white man, may not for such objects, without moral wrong, and without becoming justly obnoxious to the charge of being pro-slavery, hold in abeyance their anti-slavery convictions and sympathies, bestowing their votes on pro-slavery law-makers, for the sake of preventing rum licenses and the enactment of unjust laws for oppressing poor white men, then we cannot see how, without moral wrong, we can hold in abeyance our temperance principles, or our convictions of the moral wrongfulness of corn laws, cloth laws, and other legislative devices for grinding the face of the poor, in order to bestow our votes on the opposers of chattel enslavement. Nor do we see the necessity, or the good policy of so doing. The most trustworthy opponents of chattel enslavement—indeed the only really trustworthy ones—are those whose opposition is founded on fixed moral principle, and impelled by simple-hearted benevolence and good will to mankind—men who are opposed to chattel enslavement, *because* it is morally wrong and inhuman, who are therefore opposed to rum-licenses, and to all other wicked and unjust acts of legislation, because they too are morally wrong and inhuman—men who will not stifle, nor compromise, nor hold in abeyance their moral convictions, either in the one case or in the other. To do otherwise would be choosing between the least of two moral evils, consenting to the one, but opposing the other, which we hold to be morally wrong, whether we select one or the other of the two moral evils for our antagonist.

To co-operate with a political party that refuses to array itself against any of the wicked and unjust acts of the government except chattel slavery, would be choosing the least of two moral evils. And we can perceive nothing more sagacious or more Christian like, in this process of choosing the least of two moral evils, than in the similar process of those whose political action, in their own apprehension, might be directed to the removal of all unjust and wicked legislation, *except* the legalizing of slavery. On the one hand, it might be pleaded that slavery is only ONE evil, and impossible, at present to be removed, so long as other similar and numerous evils are left to support it, while these are not too inveterate to be removed in detail, in the first place, thus preparing the way for the accomplishing of the more difficult task afterwards. On the other hand it might be pleaded, as indeed it is, that slavery is the greatest evil, the promoter, if not the source of all the rest; that it is the dictate of wisdom to unite our energies against this in the first place, and leave the rest to be attended to afterwards. It concerns us not to say which of these rival methods is marked with the greatest degree of falsehood and error. In neither of them can we discover the marks of true wisdom. Both methods we reject as contrary to true philosophy, sound morals, and practical good sense. The proclamation of neutrality in respect to one or more moral evils, amounting to a truce with them, and a co-operation with their supporters, is but a lame preparation for an onset with *another* moral evil, admitting it to be the parent and chief support of all the others. Such a policy resembles too closely—nay, is it not in substance, a proposition to enter into an alliance, offensive and defensive, with ALL the lesser devils of the pit, in the hope of decoying them into a successful campaign against the Prince and Father of them all? The friends of temperance were thus seduced, for a time, to hold a truce with the lesser demons of inebriation, the wine, the beer, and the cider, while they concentrated their energies against the Giant Fiend, Distilled Spirit. The result proved that a truce with the subalterns and privates of the army of intemperance, was a truce with the Commander-in-Chief of that army himself, and the World's history fails to furnish us with any other instance of better success in the attempt to cast out the Prince of the Devils by a truce or co-operation with his legions. . . .

. . . This notion that men have a moral right to select one field of moral, religious or benevolent effort, and on the ground of their activity in that department, withdraw themselves from open public sympathy and co-operation in *other* fields of moral, religious, or benevolent effort—that they may be neutral in respect to the existence of one class of moral evils, because they have concluded it best to expend all their energies against another class of moral evils, is one of the most subtle, delusive and mischievous of all the devices of the Arch Tempter. All men imagine they are discharging some of their duties, and most men think they are very faithful in the discharge of the duties they have selected as the most incumbent upon them, in the position they occupy. To take care of himself and his family, is the grand idea of duty with the sordid worldling. When other duties to God and mankind, growing out of other relations, are urged upon his attention, he is too much engrossed with his "one idea," to give heed.

One man is very earnest against prodigality—that is *his* "one idea,"—do not ask *him* to beware of penuriousness. Another is absorbed with the "one idea" of generosity—do not expect the virtue of frugality in *him*. He is occupied with *his* beau ideal of moral excellence. One man is strongly opposed to intemperance, and has he not a right to be neutral in respect to the vice of gambling? Highway robbers have plumed themselves on their almsgiving; and the man that bolts his door upon the houseless, thanks God that he has never defrauded any one. The very worst of men have selected something good, in which they may glory, and few are so abandoned as not to congratulate themselves that they are not so bad as some others. Precisely upon this principle the slaveholder claims the praise of hospitality and other kindred virtues, and bids defiance to the reprovers of his injustice. . . .

. . . It may be admitted that *voluntary societies,* selecting one distinct object, have been productive of some benefits. We do not allege that it is morally wrong to organize such societies, for the man that co-operates with one of them for the promotion of one good object, may at the same time, co-operate with another of them for another, and thus discharge in one, the obligations not discharged in the other. In supporting one of these societies, while its affairs are properly conducted, we do not necessarily neglect, much less oppose, any other good object. The case differs when, in attempting the promotion of one good object, a society loses sight of those moral affinities that bind together all good enterprises, and violates one class of obligations for the sake of discharging another. Thus a society that sanctions caste, in order to circulate Bibles, or that lends its sanction to slavery, in order to extend missions—or that thinks to convert the world without opposing all the world's vices—or that, in attempting to oppose licentiousness, is careful to take no notice of its strongest and deepest and most wide-spread entrenchments,—such societies, very evidently, while thus conducted, not only become the opponents of other good objects, but fail of fidelity to their own special trusts. An abolitionist that should content himself with that one department of benevolent or reformatory effort—an Anti-Slavery Society that should violate one class of moral obligations, in order to discharge another class—that should lead its members into a truce with other vices, and especially with other forms of oppression, as a means of abolishing chattel slavery, would become equally reprehensible, and undeserving of the public confidence.

We call attention to these plain considerations, in order to meet an objection against the course we propose, founded on the supposed teachings of experience in the use of our modern voluntary associations. We are admonished to take them as our models, and are particularly referred to the supposed secret of their efficiency, in the strictness with which they have confined themselves exclusively to one definite and distinct object; and because the Temperance Societies have done good by confining their attention to one distinct thing, we are told that a political party, to be efficient, must pursue a similar course.

To this argument we answer, in the first place, that the experiment of these voluntary associations falls far short of justifying the conclusion that they have always been conducted in the best manner, and that their success would not have been greater, had they taken more comprehensive views of the evils they undertook to remove. The Temperance enterprise, as already noticed, has suffered severely from the attempt to limit attention and effort within narrower bounds than the case demanded. The Missionary Society, too, in the same manner, has made still worse shipwreck, by too limited and technical a definition of its object. Scarcely a voluntary association can be mentioned, that has not fallen more or less into the same error, the present effect of which is sufficiently visible in their mutual rivalries and recriminations, and still more, in their all coming to a dead stand. The most experienced and observing men connected with those enterprises, to a great extent, are coming to look upon them as having passed their meridian, at least in their present shape, and partly because each one of them finds its wheels blocked by obstacles which the original plan of the society does not permit it to touch or to remove, and any thing like co-operation or mutual assistance, is, of course, out of the question, for the same reason. The Bible Society cannot assist the Abolitionists in giving Bibles to the slaves, because the Bible Society cannot go beyond its "one idea," as it would do, should it commit itself on the slave question. The Moral Reform Society, for the same reason, must make little or no allusion to the system of southern prostitution. The Temperance Society can have nothing to say of the theatres, gambling houses, and brothels, and licentious fashionable literature, that lead so many thousands to intemperance. And the Anti-Slavery Society can say nothing of any of the numerous systems of despotism and oppression by which the slave system is supported, and which it wields at pleasure, because each one of these falls short of "chattel" enslavement, and is not embraced in its "one idea." And not a few of these obstacles in the way of all our benevolent and reformatory societies have *no* particular society devoted to their eradication. We have no anti-gambling societies, nor free trade societies, and it would be a hopeless task to attempt organizing distinct societies for the removal of all such evils. The Churches, evidently, for the most part, take little cognizance of any of them, and the car of reformation stands waiting for some unknown power to remove the stumbling-blocks out of the way. . . .

. . . But we have a still further answer to the argument thus urged upon us. Had the example of the voluntary associations been never so faultless—had their success been never so satisfactory—had their interpretation and use of the "one idea" policy betrayed them into none of the inconsistencies, delinquencies and disasters which now, in many instances, mar their history, and cripple their energies, and disgrace their character, we have to submit that in stepping into the arena of *political* life, and thus attempting the discharge of the duties growing out of our relations to civil government, we pass altogether beyond the precin[c]ts of the *mere* voluntary association, and its maxims, though never so faultless within their legitimate field of application, are incompetent here, to guide us. The "one idea" of the seventh commandment may answer for the Moral Reform Society, but it does not follow that nothing else is requisite for the basis of a Christian Church. So the "one idea" of abolishing chattel slavery may suffice for the Anti-Slavery Society, but we must beg to be excused from admitting the inference that all the functions of civil government are exercised, and all its obligations discharged, by the simple abolition of chattel slavery, without the redress of any of its other abuses, the repeal of any other of its own unjust acts, the repression of any other species of crime. Because its penal code should prohibit and punish man-stealing, it does not follow that it should prohibit and punish nothing else. And just as broad and comprehensive as are the functions and duties of civil government, just so broad and comprehensive are the duties of free citizens and voters in their participation in the acts of the government. And just so broad and comprehensive, likewise, are the duties of any political association of voters and citizens uniting together in the nomination and support of all the officers by whom the government is to be administered.

Civil government is not a *mere* voluntary association of individuals, at liberty to enter into the engagement or not at their pleasure, and giving it a wider or a narrower scope at their option. And of course, political associations as above described, commonly called political parties, are not mere voluntary associations, at liberty to embrace within their objects, as much or as little as they think proper. . . .

. . . It is appalling to witness the inroads made upon the consciences and moral sensibilities of men, by the operation of the "one idea" theory, as it is commonly understood and applied. "As a Missionary Board," it seems, we can take no cognizance of God's commandments, out of the area that we have staked out for ourselves and occupied!—"As Temperance men," we can look no farther than "our pledge," whatever it may be, in avoiding and opposing intemperance!—To our "Anti-Slavery platform," we must welcome every body that cries out lustily against chattel slavery, wordwise, tho', at the very next opportunity, the orator may cast his vote for a slaveholder, or for a slaveholder's advocate, and may lend his aid to any other system of oppression, without forfeiting his reputation for a "great moral reformer."—As "Liberty party men," we have no right to inquire further concerning a proposed candidate for civil office than whether he can pronounce the shibboleth of "immediate emancipation."—Whatever moral duty or divine precept is urged upon our attention, we have only to ensconce ourselves within the narrow limits of our "one idea," whatever it may be—we have only to say that the distinct object of our favorite society or organization, or political party, did not include that particular duty or precept, and we make a merit of casting it to the winds! Just as though we expected to be judged, at the last final award, as members of a Missionary Board, or of a Temperance Society, or of an Anti-Slavery society, or of a Liberty party, and not rather AS MEN, with all the relations, responsibilities and duties of MEN, attaching to us, *not* in virtue of our own compacts, and pledges, and organizations, and platforms, all of our own devising, but in consequence of our moral natures, and of the relations which, so long as we remain men, we are obliged, whether we desire it or not, to sustain! . . .

. . . Let not our position be misunderstood—or mis-stated, as it has been. We do not say that our political party must provide for, or furnish an arena, for the discharge of all our moral duties. We only say that it must cover the ground of all of them that are appropriately political. This is only saying that all our political duties must be discharged.—We do not look to a political party, nor to political action, nor to civil government, to remove all moral and social evils. Far from it. We only look to them to do their proper work, along with other appropriate moral influences, for securing to all men, their original and essential rights. The field, tho' not without well-defined limits, is too broad for any one single political measure—any one legislative enactment. The most strenuous advocate for the narrow construction of our "one idea" would hardly venture to affirm, in so many words, that all the moral obligations resting upon our government could be discharged and fulfilled by the simple enactment of a statute abolishing chattel slavery.—But if the moral responsibilities of the government extend further than that limit, how can it be made to appear that the moral responsibilities of those who vote and who nominate the officers of the government do not extend farther?

Will it be said (it has been said) that a political party and an administration abolishing chattel slavery may be trusted, without further inquiry, to execute justice in all other respects? As well might it be affirmed that a man guiltless of burglary might therefore be safely entrusted with the reins of the government—that because a man had never robbed on the highway, was therefore upright enough for a judge, that whoever assists in rescuing a child from the flames, or a drowning man from the river, is entitled to implicit confidence as an arbiter between man and man! Let "practical men" inquire after the facts. The British Government that abolished chattel slavery in the West Indies is starving the people of Ireland, is crushing the operatives of Birmingham, is enforcing upon dissenters in England the payment of church tithes, is excluding large masses of the people from the right of suffrage, is building up a bloated aristocracy, is grinding the faces of the poor, is consenting to the oppression, by tariffs, of the lately emancipated West India negroes, is lending its aid to the importation of

East India coolies to compete with them, and reduce still lower their wages, entailing hopeless destitution upon both negroes and coolies, thus reviving, though without chattelhood, the closest possible resemblance to the slave trade!

If the opponents of chattel slavery in America are more comprehensive in their views of human rights, let it be shown by their promptly coming up to the position to which we invite them! If they are opposed to all other oppression as well as the oppression of human chattelhood, and if they are ready to act against both the one and the other, let them say so, and show their sincerity by their deeds. But if they *refuse* to do this when invited to do it—if they persist in claiming the privilege of bestowing their votes for the known supporters of the tariffs, monopolies, and class legislations, that are grinding the faces of the poor in our midst, for the emolument of the rich, let them cease urging the claim that the simple fact of opposition to chattel enslavement is proof positive that they may be safely entrusted with the protection of human rights. The merit of mere opposition to chattel slavery is becoming cheaper than it has been, and will be much cheaper still. The time hastens when, (by the elevation of a higher moral standard in politics than had before been attempted,) politicians of all parties, the most sordid and selfish, will be forced to come up, at least, as high as the level furnished by the Anti-Slavery Societies. This they will be glad to do, as a cover to their delinquencies in other respects. But the covering will become too narrow to hide them, and then, the mere merit of being anti-slavery, will avail a political party about as much as would, at the present time, the boast of legislation against sheep-stealing, or the glory of selecting candidates unsuspected of robbing henroosts. Those who rightly estimate and properly *feel* the inexpressible meanness and moral turpitude of baby-stealing, should be the last to claim for themselves and associates, any high degrees of humanity, moral discernment, regard to human rights, or competency to the task of defining and protecting them, on the mere ground of their readiness to treat baby stealing as a penal offence—their capacity to distinguish a man from a beast! High time were it for American citizens and their political parties to set up a higher standard of political trustworthiness than that which the oppressive British Government may claim.

When called upon to define the "one idea" to which we would render homage, we say that the great, all-comprehensive idea, with us, is the idea of pursuing, steadfastly and undeviatingly, wherever they are revealed to us, the TRUE and the RIGHT. In the department of Civil Government and of political responsibility, it takes the form of "THE PROTECTION OF HUMAN RIGHTS." This one idea we would honor by the prompt, impartial, and uniform application of it, to all classes of men, and the redress of all the wrongs of which Civil Government may take cognizance. With MORAL PRINCIPLE for our foundation and our polar star, we hope to shape our measures in accordance with them, desiring no other policy than adherence to the right.

CHARLES SUMNER EXPLAINS THE DUTIES OF MASSACHUSETTS DURING THE KANSAS-NEBRASKA CRISIS

The lack of success of the Liberty Party and of the Free Soil Party and the response of the North to the Kansas-Nebraska Act of 1854 led to the formation of another antislavery party. Charles Sumner, in his defense of the new Republican Party, denounced the parties of compromise and promoted a third party as the only means by which slavery and the slave power could be overthrown. Only the Republican Party, he urged, would interpret the Constitution so that its meaning would be consonant with the Higher Law.

. . . Our duties are manifest. First and foremost, the Slave Power itself must be overthrown. Lord Chatham once exclaimed, in stirring language, that the time had been when he was content to bring France to her knees; now he would not stop till he had laid her on her back. Nor can we be content with less in our warfare. We must not stop till we have laid the Slave Power on its back. [Prolonged cheers.][1] And, fellow citizens, permit me to say, not till then will the Free States be absolved from all political responsibility for Slavery, and relieved from that corrupt spirit of compromise which now debases, at once, their politics and their religion; nor till then will there be any repose for the country. [Immense cheering.] Indemnity for the past, and security for the future, must be our watchwords. [Applause.] But these can be obtained only when Slavery is dispossessed of its present vantage-ground, by driving it back exclusively within the limits of the States, and putting the National Goverment every where within its constitutional sphere, openly, actively and perpetually, on the side of Freedom. The consequences of this change of policy would be of incalculable and far-reaching beneficence. Not only would Freedom become national and Slavery sectional, as was intended by our Fathers; but the National Government would become the mighty instrument and spokesman of Freedom, as it is now the mighty instrument and spokesman of Slavery. Its power, its treasury, its patronage, would all be turned, in harmony with the Constitu-

---

From Charles Sumner, *Duties of Massachusetts at This Crisis. A Speech* . . . *Delivered at the Republican Convention at Worcester, Sept. 7, 1854* (n.p.: n.p., [1854]), pp. 3–5.

[1] The brackets in this selection occur in the original. [Eds.]

Argument for Political Action: Third Parties 441

tion, to promote Freedom. The Committees of Congress, where Slavery now rules, Congress itself, and the Cabinet also, would all be organized for Freedom. The hypocritical disguise or renunciation of Anti-Slavery sentiment would cease to be necessary for the sake of political preferment; and the slave-holding Oligarchy, banished from the National Government, and despoiled of its ill-gotten political consequence, without ability to punish or reward, would cease to be feared, either at the North or the South, until at last the citizens of the Slave States, of whom a large portion have no interest in Slavery, would demand Emancipation; and the great work would commence. Such is the obvious course of things. To the overthrow of the Slave Power we are thus summoned by a double call, one political and the other philanthropic; first, to remove an oppressive tyranny from the National Government, and secondly, to open the gates of Emancipation in the Slave States. [Loud applause.]

But while keeping this great purpose in view, we must not forget details. The existence of Slavery any where within the national jurisdiction—in the Territories, in the District of Columbia, or on the high seas beneath the national flag, is an unconstitutional usurpation, which must be opposed. The Fugitive Slave Bill, monstrous in cruelty, as in unconstitutionality, is a usurpation, which must be opposed. The admission of new Slave States, from whatsoever quarter, from Texas or Cuba, [applause] Utah or New Mexico, must be opposed. And to every scheme of Slavery, whether in Cuba, or Mexico,—on the high seas in opening the slave-trade—in the West Indies—the Valley of the Amazon,—whether accomplished or merely plotted, whether pending or in prospect, we must send forth an EVERLASTING NO! [Long continued applause.] Such is the duty of Massachusetts, without hesitation or compromise.

Thus far I have spoken of our duties in national matters; but there are other duties of pressing importance, here at home, which must not be forgotten or postponed. It is often said that "charity should begin at home." Better say, that *charity should begin every where*. But while contending with the Slave Power on the broad field of national politics, we must not forget the duty of protecting the liberty of all who tread the soil of Massachusetts. [Immense cheering.] Early in colonial history, Massachusetts set her face against Slavery. At the head of her Bill of Rights she solemnly asserted, that all men are born free and equal; and in the same declaration, surrounded the liberties of all within her borders by the inestimable rights of trial by jury and *Habeas Corpus*. But recent events on her own soil have taught the necessity of new safeguards to these great principles, —to the end that Massachusetts may not be a vassal of South Carolina and Virginia—that the Slave Hunter may not range at will among us, and that the liberties of all may not be violated with impunity.[2]

But I am admonished that I must not dwell longer on these things. Suffice it to say, that our duties, in National and State affairs, are identical, and may be described by the same formula: In the one case to put the National Government, in all its departments, and in the other case the State Government, in all its departments, openly, actively and perpetually, on the side of Freedom. [Loud applause.]

Having considered *what* our duties are, the question now presses upon us, *how* shall they be performed? By what agency, by what instrumentality, or in what way?

The most obvious way is by choosing men to represent us in the national government, and also at home, who shall recognize these duties and be ever loyal to them; [cheers] men who at Washington will not shrink from the conflict with Slavery, and also other men, who, at home in Massachusetts will not shrink from the same conflict when the Slave Hunter appears. [Loud applause, and cries of "good," "good."] But in the choice of men, we are driven to the organization of parties; and here the question arises, by what form of organization, or by what party,

---

[2] The reference is to the rendition of Anthony Burns. See p. lxxx. [Eds.]

can these men be best secured? Surely not by the Democratic party, as at present constituted; [laughter] though if this party were true to its name, pregnant with human rights, it would leave little to be desired. In this party there are doubtless individuals who are anxious to do all in their power against Slavery; but, indulge me in saying that, so long as they continue members of a party which upholds the Nebraska Bill, they can do very little. [Applause and laughter.] What may we expect from the Whig party? [A voice—Resolutions.] If more may be expected from the Whig party than the Democratic party, candor must attribute much of the difference to the fact that the Whigs are *out of power*, while the Democrats are *in power*. ["That's the talk," and long continued cheers.] If the cases were reversed, and the Whigs were in power, as in 1850, I fear that, notwithstanding the ardor of individuals, and the Resolutions of Conventions—[great laughter]—made, I fear, too often merely to be broken—the party might be brought to sustain an outrage as great as the Fugitive Slave Bill. [Laughter and applause.] But without dwelling on these things, (to which I allude with diffidence, and, I trust, in no uncharitable temper, or partisan spirit,) I desire to say that no party, which calls itself national, according to the common acceptance of the word, —which leans upon a slave-holding wing, [cheers] or is in combination with slaveholders,—[cheers] can at this time be true to Massachusetts. [Great applause.] And the reason is obvious. It can be presented so as to cleave the most common understanding. *The essential element of such a party, whether declared or concealed, is Compromise; but our duties require all constitutional opposition to Slavery and the Slave Power, without Compromise.* ["That's it," "good," "good."] It is difficult, then, to see how we can rely upon the Whig party.

To the true-hearted, magnanimous men who are ready to place Freedom above Party, and their Country above Politicians, I appeal. [Immense cheering.] Let them leave the old parties, and blend in an organization, which, without compromise, will maintain the good cause surely to the end. Here in

Massachusetts a large majority of the people concur in sentiment on Slavery; a large majority desire the overthrow of the Slave Power. It becomes them not to scatter their votes, but to unite in one firm, consistent phalanx, [applause] whose triumph shall constitute an epoch of Freedom, not only in this Commonwealth, but throughout the land. Such an organization is now presented by this Republican Convention, which, according to the resolutions by which it is convoked, is to cooperate with the friends of freedom in other States. [Cheers.] As *Republicans* we go forth to encounter the *Oligarchs* of Slavery. [Great applause.]

Through this organization we may most certainly secure the election of men, who, unseduced and unterrified, will uphold at Washington the principles of Freedom; and who also here at home, in our own community, by example, influence and vote, will help to invigorate Massachusetts. Indeed, I might go further and say, that, by no other organization can we reasonably hope to obtain such men, unless in rare and exceptional cases.

Men are but instruments. It will not be enough merely to choose those who are loyal. Other things must be done here at home. In the first place, all the existing laws for the protection of human freedom must be rigorously enforced: [applause, and cries of "good,"] and, since these have been found inadequate, new laws for this purpose, within the limits of the constitution, must be enacted. Massachusetts certainly might do well in following Vermont, which, by a special law, has placed the fugitive slave under the safeguard of trial by jury and the writ of *habeas corpus*. But a legislature true to Freedom, will not fail in remedies. [Applause.] A simple prohibition, declaring that no person, holding the commission of Massachusetts, as a Justice of the Peace, or other magistrate, should assume to decide a slave case, or to act as counsel of any Slave Hunter, under penalty of forfeiting his commission, would go far to render the existing Slave Act inoperative. [Applause.] There are not many, so fond of this base trade, as to continue in it when the Commonwealth has thus set upon it a legislative brand.

But besides more rigorous legislation, Public Opinion must be invoked to step forward and throw over the fugitive its protecting panoply. A Slave Hunter will then be a by-word and reproach; and all his instruments, especially every one who volunteers in this vileness, without any positive obligation of law, will naturally be regarded as a part of his pack, and share the ignominy of the chief Hunter. [Laughter and cheers.] And now, from authentic example, drawn out of recent history, learn how the Slave Hunter may be palsied by contrition. A most successful member of the Italian police, Bolza, whose official duties involved his own personal degradation and the loathing of others, has left a record of the acute sense which even such a man retained of his shame. "I absolutely forbid my heirs," says this penitent official, "to allow any mark of whatever kind, to be placed over the spot of my burial; much more any inscription or epitaph. I recommend my dearly beloved wife to impress upon my children the injunction, that, in soliciting any employment from the Government, they shall ask for it elsewhere than in the *executive police*, and not, unless under extraordinary circumstances, to give her consent to the marriage of any of my daughters with a member of that service." Thus testifies the Italian instrument of legal wrong. Let public opinion here in Massachusetts once put forth its Christian might, and every instrument of the Fugitive Act will feel a kindred shame. [Great applause.]

CHARLES FRANCIS ADAMS CONDEMNS THE KNOW-NOTHINGS

Distressed by the failures both of a simple antislavery party and of an antislavery party joined with a variety of other reform causes, some of the more opportunistic abolitionists turned hopefully to the popular Know-Nothing, Native American Party. Because its composition was an amalgam of anti-Catholicism, anti-foreignism, and a bigoted chauvinism, Charles Francis Adams (1807–1886), Boston lawyer, state legislator, later national Congressman and diplomat, condemned this move, which, he contended, would subordinate antislavery to a distinctly unworthy cause.

. . . There are other persons, I am sorry to add,—and the number in my own state, if not in others, is quite large, who have heretofore ranked among the most earnest friends of liberty,—whose course in joining this crusade has penetrated me with feelings of profound concern. It is of them, and them only, I would speak in the present connection. That they have acted under an honest belief that they are thus more fully carrying out their cherished principles, I do not permit myself to doubt. Suspecting, not without reason, that Romanism in America has been generally arrayed in opposition to their views, they have regarded an attack upon that as equivalent to the overthrow of one of the outposts of slavery in the free states. A few may have been precipitated into it by impatience at the obstacles interposed to the apparent progress of the direct antislavery movement, and by the attraction of the new patent for gaining ground by secrecy and surprises. Whilst I can understand and allow for all these inducements to leave the old path, I am not the less convinced that they have led to a serious mistake, the effects of which may be to postpone, at least for a time, our hopes of an early triumph. My reasons for this opinion must be very briefly given. They are these:—

1. There is no road so good to travel to get to an object as the straight road. Every turning, however slight at first, may, if

---

From Charles Francis Adams, *What Makes Slavery a Question of National Concern? A Lecture, Delivered, by Invitation, at New York, January 30, . . . 1855* (Boston: Little, Brown, & Co., 1855), pp. 32–40.

we follow it long enough, lead a very different way, from which it will not be easy to get back again to the right one. At best, the course of our friends is like descending from a clear, strong, well-fortified position, to a weaker, a less defined, and more extended one. As I have already remarked, the power of antislavery lies in the TRUTH. The more directly it can be kept before the world, freed from ambiguities and irrelevant associations of every kind; the more singly it can be presented to the mind, the more hold it will gain upon the public confidence. One great obstacle to its progress in the past has been the skilful use made by its enemies of the materials furnished by its own friends to fasten upon it burdens which it was under no call to bear. This error has been too often committed in every stage of the struggle, and has never been firmly enough resisted. "One thing at a time" . . . is equally applicable to measures of reform. Attacking the influence of a religious denomination of Christians is a process of itself somewhat novel in American politics, and introduces a complete change in those grounds of controversy which had been taken in the slave-question. And, as if this were not enough, another dispute is superadded upon the rights of foreigners to share in the councils of the country they have chosen to adopt; which is a second time diverting the public attention to a different decision upon a still different train of reasoning. On these questions, it is by no means unlikely that the slaveholders themselves might be found ranged on the same side with our friends. They have no sympathy with foreigners, a very large proportion of whom shun the territories worked by slave-labor, in order to settle, improve, and enrich the free states. They care little about Catholics as such, for the same reason. Why, then, are they not fit, if they choose it, to rush into the new movement, and control it, at least in their own states? But, if they **do**, what becomes of our old friends? Like the dog in the fable, who in snapping at the shadow lost his bone in the water, they will spend their strength upon inferior issues, whilst the slaveholder profits of the respite which he wants, to hide the progress of slavery out of sight of the people. For slavery does not diminish its power meanwhile. Every day's delay adds hundreds and thousands of dollars to the weight in the scale which must have its corresponding counterpoise on the side of freedom. I cannot but think, then, that antislavery men have got into the wrong place and into wrong company,—that is, if they honestly mean to do antislavery work.

2. But they will reply to this objection by urging that they can prevail in this new and very popular movement, and finally succeed in giving to it the impulse of their own opinions against slavery; and this will be a great help to the cause, worth working for: to which I would object the fact that they have divided the antislavery force by their action, and left a large share of it outside the inclosure which they have entered. If the whole, when united, was not strong enough to give an antislavery character to the whole people around them, how are the parts, when separated, likely to succeed better with proportionate numbers of that people? The most unfortunate consequence of this mistake is, that it impairs the unity of the antislavery action. Those who cannot consent to accept the new mode, for reasons wholly distinct from the slave-question, who spurn the bonds of secret obligations, or disapprove an indiscriminate crusade against foreign-born persons, must continue their labors in the former way, without any confidence in the co-operation of their old friends, however well-disposed these may be to aid them; whilst, on the other hand, they can do little to strengthen those within the new order in any emergency, because they have, with their eyes open, assumed a new obligation which covers what they plan from the public eye, and subjects it to become perhaps the contrary to what opposition to slavery would naturally require. The most honest and able champion of true antislavery principles must be dropped, if he is not within the charmed ring, and in his place must be put their most determined enemy, if the majority so decide. . . .

3. But it may be said that this difficulty can be avoided by joining the new organization in great force, in which case these excellent men will receive all the support their friends would be delighted to give them. But there is no proof that even this would avail in the new association, formed upon a strange basis, to place them exactly in the same prominent attitude which they occupy now as champions upon the old one. They are *opponents of slavery,* known as such the country over, representing those who have declared this to be their cardinal principle. How are they to gain any strength or honor by changing front, and announcing that thus far they have acted blindly and ignorantly,—that there was something else more important than slavery which they had overlooked and forgotten? They must first persecute the Irishman and the Englishman, the German, the Frenchman, and the Swede, disfranchise them, degrade them, turn them into beings scarcely above the grade of slaves; they must first wage a fierce religious war against the Catholic, native or stranger, to put him down; and, after they shall have succeeded in doing all that, they will be particularly fitted by their experience to take up the cause of the poor black slave. Moreover, I would venture to submit a question, how, by this variation of policy, they are going to stand in relation to the determined men who do not consent to turn aside, for any such considerations, to the right or to the left,—who nail their flag to the mast, and fight on, fight ever, in behalf of their old opinions and the policy to which they are pledged? Is not some consideration due to them whose principles have been tried over and over again, and have never been found wanting; who have not, for one instant, been led away, by the temptation of accidental advantage, to the substitution of any other object for the paramount question of liberty; who still stand where they have ever stood, more ready to take the lead in a moment of danger and desertion than when things looked more promising, and numbers indicated an earlier triumph? . . .

4. Furthermore: the assumption of an obligation of any sort,

which binds men to keep their movements secret, opens a question of morals of the most serious character, upon which antislavery men may reasonably entertain grave doubts, if not decided objections. Secrecy in political action implies one of two things,—either the object to be gained is not an honorable one, and therefore men are ashamed or afraid to avow it before the world; or else, supposing that object to be good, the means by which it is to be attained are to be used to gain an advantage by surprise over somebody. At best, it is no better than the warfare of the savage, who, in the thickness of the forest, or from the depth of a secret cave, aims his deadly rifle at the traveller, suspicious of nothing, who is following his straight road to his destination. I cannot withhold the opinion, that, under such a cover as this furnishes, the best public objects may at any time be degraded in the pursuit to a level with the worst: the very best men may be put far below the meanest. Even if the opposition to slavery could be made to triumph by such an agency, in my poor judgment the victory would be stripped of half its moral splendor in the process. We claim, as a class, to be honest, free-spoken, conscientious, God-fearing men, having nothing to conceal, and entertaining no malice to a single human being. We resist the slaveholders, because we feel the evils that flow from their devotion to a highly pernicious institution; but we do not seek to enter into any conspiracies against them. They are men, brethren, fellow-citizens, bone of our bone, flesh of our flesh, unduly biassed perhaps to countenance, perhaps to extend, what we consider fatal evils in public affairs, but at any rate conducting themselves manfully, and without disguises. I would treat them frankly in return. In the experience of a life now considerably beyond its prime, it has been my fortune to find those men most worthy of confidence, whether friendly or hostile, who are the most straightforward, and without concealments. They are the persons whose word I most rely upon in my private relations. They are the men whose action I can most surely count upon in public trusts. . . .

If I am correct in these opinions, then there are two errors of the first concoction which render the new movement in all its forms utterly repugnant to the true principles of opponents of slavery in America. I mean the secret obligation, and the absence of moral foundation in the discrimination set up between men. The first subjects the right of private judgment absolutely to the will of an accidental majority. The second involves the bad and the good, the innocent and the guilty, the industrious and the idle, alike in one common fate, which no act of their own incurs or can avert. The fugitive Protestants from the persecutions of Louis the 14th, instigated by the bigotry of his Jesuit confessor, many of whom came to America, and left behind them names honored ever since as among those of the best citizens, would have fared worse, in their day, than the convicts sent to the colonies in order to relieve the mother country from a burden by transferring it to them. This is not justice, nor humanity, nor even sound political economy. Emigration is one of the great moral agencies which is doing more than ever was done in any former age to change the face of the world; which is spreading the light of Christianity into the dark and benighted regions of all its various continents; which is even now stretching civilization along the western coast of North America, as it did, in the last two centuries, on the eastern; which is vivifying the deserts of Australia; which is humanizing the barbarism of Africa; and which is wearing away the prejudices of caste, even among the petrified institutions of the East. The exclusive bigotry, which seems now for the first time losing its hold in its remaining fastness,—the islands of Japan,—must not take its flight from there, only to settle down upon the banks of the Hudson or of the Mississippi, or to find a home upon the crests of the Alleghany or the Rocky Mountains. Such is the declaration of genuine philanthropy, which looks above the arbitrary and conventional demarcations of man's invention, and appeals to the mission of Christ as the great symbol of a revelation, that the good God above looks upon all men alike.

Upon no other foundation than this can the antislavery cause firmly repose. No aid nor true defenders can it obtain from among those who advocate proscription of any kind, merely on account of difference of race. The men who assumed that defence did it in behalf of a people originally torn from their native land, and brought to this against their will, who have ever since been deprived by force, not merely of civil rights, official distinctions, and social privileges, but of the fruits of their own labor, and of the secure enjoyment of their domestic affections. How can they continue their exertions, and, at the same time, countenance any other form of proscription bearing the remotest analogy to that of which they complain? How can they say to-day, that the slaveholder is a tyrant, who puts his heel on the neck of his slave, only because God made him of a different color from his own, and set him in Africa instead of in Europe; and to-morrow build a wall between themselves and others of their fellow-men, because God placed them, at the time of their birth, somewhere else than in the United States?

FREDERICK DOUGLASS DENOUNCES DISUNION AS A FUTILE ANTISLAVERY DEVICE

By the mid 1850's free Negroes in the North had become increasingly impatient with the impotence and splintering of the antislavery movement. Frederick Douglass expressed his impatience with those who shunned political action as well as with those who, he felt, watered down antislavery doctrine in free-soil and anti-extension campaigns. Small though it was, only the Liberty Party, in his mind, operated as an effective abolitionist group.

. . . I propose to speak of the different anti-slavery sects and parties, and to give my view of them very briefly. There are four principal divisions.

1st. The Garrisonians, or the American Anti-Slavery Society.

2d. The Anti-Garrisonians, or the American and Foreign Anti-Slavery Society.

3d. The Free Soil Party, or Political Abolitionists.

4. The Liberty Party, or Gerrit Smith School of Abolitionists.

There are others, and among them those conscientious men and women, principally of the Society of Friends, who may be called *"free labor people"*—since their remedy for slavery is an abstinence from slave produce. This Society formerly published in Philadelphia a periodical, called "The Non-Slaveholder," and kept open a store for the sale of free labor goods; and besides this, it promoted the growth of free cotton in several of the more Southern States. This Society is still in existence, and is quietly doing its work.

I shall consider, first, the Garrisonian Anti-Slavery Society. I call this the Garrisonian Society, because Mr. Garrison is, confessedly, its leader. This Society is the oldest of modern Anti-Slavery Societies. It has, strictly speaking, two weekly papers, or organs—employs five or six lecturers—and holds numerous public meetings for the dissemination of its views. Its peculiar and distinctive feature is, its doctrine of *"no union with slaveholders."* This doctrine has, of late, become its bond of union, and the condition of good fellowship among its mem-

---

From Frederick Douglass, *The Anti-Slavery Movement. A Lecture [Delivered] by Frederick Douglass before the Rochester Ladies' Anti-Slavery Society* (Rochester: Lee, Mann, & Co., 1855), pp. 29–35.

bers. Of this Society, I have to say, its logical result is but negatively, anti-slavery. Its doctrine, of "no union with slaveholders," carried out, dissolves the Union, and leaves the slaves and their masters to fight their own battles, in their own way. This I hold to be an abandonment of the great idea with which that Society started. It started to free the slave. It ends by leaving the slave to free himself. It started with the purpose to imbue the heart of the nation with sentiments favorable to the abolition of slavery, and ends by seeking to free the North from all responsibility for slavery, other than if slavery were in Great Britain, or under some other nationality. This, I say, is the practical abandonment of the idea, with which that Society started. It has given up the faith, that the slave can be freed short of the overthrow of the Government; and then, as I understand that Society, it leaves the slaves, as it must needs leave them, just where it leaves the slaves of Cuba, or those of Brazil. The nation, as such, is given up as beyond the power of salvation by the foolishness of preaching; and hence, the aim is now to save the North; so that the American Anti-Slavery Society, which was inaugurated to convert the nation, after ten years' struggle, parts with its faith, and aims now to save the North. One of the most eloquent of all the members of that Society, and the man who is only second to Mr. Garrison himself, defines the Garrisonian doctrine thus:

"All the slave asks of us, is to stand out of his way, withdraw our pledge to keep the peace on the plantation; withdraw our pledge to return him; withdraw that representation which the Constitution gives in proportion to the number of slaves, and without any agitation here, without any individual virtue, which the times have eaten out of us, God will vindicate the oppressed, by the laws of justice which he has founded. Trample under foot your own unjust pledges, break to pieces your compact with hell by which you become the abettors of oppression. Stand alone, and let no cement of the Union bind the slave, and he will right himself."

That is it. "Stand alone;" the slave is to "right himself." I dissent entirely from this reasoning. It assumes to be true what is plainly absurd, and that is, that a population of slaves, without arms, without means of concert, and without leisure, is more than a match for double its number, educated, accustomed to rule, and in every way prepared for warfare, offensive or defensive. This Society, therefore, consents to leave the slave's freedom to a most uncertain and improbable, if not an impossible, contingency.

But, *"no union with slaveholders."*

As a mere expression of abhorrence of slavery, the sentiment is a good one; but it expresses no intelligible principle of action, and throws no light on the pathway of duty. Defined, as its authors define it, it leads to false doctrines, and mischievous results. It condemns Gerrit Smith for sitting in Congress, and our Savior for eating with publicans and sinners. Dr. Spring[1] uttered a shocking sentiment, when he said, if one prayer of his would emancipate every slave, he would not offer that prayer. No less shocking is the sentiment of the leader of the disunion forces, when he says, that if one vote of his would emancipate every slave in this country, he would not cast that vote. Here, on a bare theory, and for a theory which, if consistently adhered to, would drive a man out of the world—a theory which can never be made intelligible to common sense —the freedom of the whole slave population would be sacrificed.

But again: "NO UNION WITH SLAVEHOLDERS." I dislike the morality of this sentiment, in its application to the point at issue. For instance: A. unites with B. in stealing my property, and carrying it away to California, or to Australia, and, while there, Mr. A. becomes convinced that he did wrong in stealing my property, and says to Mr. B., "no union with property

[1] Gardiner Spring was minister of the Brick Presbyterian Church in New York and a leading member of the benevolent empire of reformers. [Eds.]

stealers," and abandons him, leaving the property in his hands. Now, I put it to this audience, has Mr. A., in this transaction, met the requirements of stringent morality? He, certainly, has not. It is not only his duty to separate from the thief, but to restore the stolen property to its rightful owner. And I hold that in the Union, this very thing of restoring to the slave his long-lost rights, can better be accomplished than it can possibly be accomplished outside of the Union. This, then, is my answer to the motto, "No UNION WITH SLAVEHOLDERS."

But this is not the worst fault of this Society. Its chief energies are expended in confirming the opinion, that the United States Constitution is, and was, intended to be a slave-holding instrument—thus piling up, between the slave and his freedom, the huge work of the abolition of the Government, as an indispensable condition to emancipation. My point here is, first, the Constitution is, according to its reading, an anti-slavery document; and, secondly, to dissolve the Union, as a means to abolish slavery, is about as wise as it would be to burn up this city, in order to get the thieves out of it. But again, we hear the motto, "no union with slave-holders;" and I answer it, as that noble champion of liberty, N. P. Rogers,[2] answered it with a more sensible motto, namely—*"No union with slave-holding."* I would unite with anybody to do right; and with nobody to do wrong. And as the Union, under the Constitution, requires me to do nothing which is wrong, and gives me many facilities for doing good, I cannot go with the American Anti-Slavery Society in its doctrine of disunion.

But to the second branch of the anti-slavery movement. The American and Foreign Anti-Slavery Society has not yet departed from the original ground, but stands where the American Anti-Slavery Society stood at the beginning. The energies of this association are mainly directed to the revival of anti-slavery in the Church. It is active in the collection, and in the

---

[2] Nathaniel Peabody Rogers, see pp. 315–319. [Eds.]

circulation of facts, exposing the character of slavery, and in noting the evidences of progress in the Church on the subject. It does not aim to abolish the Union, but aims to avail itself of the means afforded by the Union to abolish slavery. The Annual Report of this Society affords the amplest and truest account of the anti-slavery movement, from year to year. Nevertheless, I have somewhat against this Society, as well as against the American Anti-Slavery Society. It has almost dropped the main and most potent weapon with which slavery is to be assailed and overthrown, and that is speech. At this moment, when every nerve should be strained to prevent a re-action, that Society has not a single lecturing agent in the field.

The next recognized anti-slavery body is the Free Soil party, *alias*—the Free Democratic party, *alias*—the Republican party. It aims to limit and denationalize slavery, and to relieve the Federal Government from all responsibility for slavery. Its motto is, *"Slavery Local—Liberty National."* The objection to this movement is the same as that against the American Anti-Slavery Society. It leaves the slave in his fetters—in the undisturbed possession of his master, and does not grapple with the question of emancipation in the States.

The fourth division of the anti-slavery movement is, the *"Liberty Party"*—a small body of citizens, chiefly in the State of New York, but having sympathizers all over the North. It is the radical, and to my thinking, the *only* abolition organization in the country, except a few local associations. It makes a clean sweep of slavery everywhere. It denies that slavery is, or *can* be legalized. It denies that the Constitution of the United States is a pro-slavery instrument, and asserts the power and duty of the Federal Government to abolish slavery in every State of the Union. Strictly speaking, I say this is the only party in the country which is an abolition party. The mission of the Garrisonians ends with the dissolution of the Union—that of the Free Soil party ends with the relief of the Federal

Government from all responsibility for slavery; but the Liberty Party, by its position and doctrines, and by its antecedents, is pledged to continue the struggle while a bondman in his chains remains to weep. Upon its platform must the great battle of freedom be fought out—if upon any short of the bloody field. It must be under no partial cry of "no union with slaveholders;" nor selfish cry of "no more slavery extension;" but it must be, "no slavery for man under the whole heavens." The slave as a man and a brother, must be the vital and animating thought and impulse of any movement, which is to effect the abolition of slavery in this country. Our anti-slavery organizations must be brought back to this doctrine, or they will be scattered and left to wander, and to die in the wilderness, like God's ancient people, till another generation shall come up, more worthy to go up and possess the land.

XIV

Argument against Political Action

WENDELL PHILLIPS VIGOROUSLY ESCHEWS POLITICAL ACTION

By 1840 the Garrisonians had disavowed political action. They were, in fact, on the threshold of their campaign to dissolve the Union, founded as it was upon a proslavery Constitution. Wendell Phillips (1811–1884), Boston's silver-tongued abolitionist orator and lifelong devotee of radical reforms, answered the question, *Can Abolitionists Vote or Hold Office?* with a thunderous No.

From Wendell Phillips, *Can Abolitionists Vote or Take Office Under the United States Constitution?* (*The Anti-Slavery Examiner* No. 13) (New York: American Anti-Slavery Society, 1845), pp. 9–29, 37.

Can an abolitionist consistently take office, or vote, under the Constitution of the United States?

1st. What is an abolitionist?

One who thinks slaveholding a sin in all circumstances, and desires its abolition. Of course such an one cannot consistently aid another in holding his slave;—in other words, I cannot innocently aid a man in doing that which I think wrong. No amount of fancied good will justify me in joining another in doing wrong, unless I adopt the principle "of doing evil that good may come."

2d. What do taking office and voting under the Constitution imply?

The President swears "to execute the office of president," and "to preserve, protect, and defend the Constitution of the United States." The judges "to discharge the duties incumbent upon them agreeably to the constitution and laws of the United States."

All executive, legislative, and judicial officers, both of the several States and of the General Government, before entering on the performance of their official duties, are bound to take an oath or affirmation, *"to support the Constitution of the United States."* This is what every office-holder expressly *promises in so many words.* It is a contract between him and *the whole nation.* The voter, who, by voting, sends his fellow citizen into office as his representative, knowing beforehand that the taking of this oath is the first duty his agent will have to perform, does by his vote, request and authorize him to take it. He therefore, by voting, impliedly engages to support the Constitution. What one does by his agent he does himself. Of course no honest man will authorize and request another to do an act which he thinks it wrong to do himself! Every voter, therefore, is bound to see, *before voting,* whether he could himself honestly swear to *support* the constitution. . . .

It is more than an oath of allegiance; more than a mere promise that we will not resist the laws. For it is an engagement to "support them"; as an *officer* of government, to carry them into effect. Without such a promise on the part of its functionaries, how could government exist? It is more than the expression of that obligation which rests on all peaceable citizens to *submit* to laws, even though they will not actively *support* them. For it is the promise which the judge makes, that he will actually *do* the business of the courts; which the sheriff assumes, that he will actually *execute* the laws.

Let it be remarked, that it is an oath to support *the* Constitution—that is, *the whole of it;* there are no exceptions. And let it be remembered, that by it each *one* makes a contract with the whole *nation*, that he will do certain acts.

3d. What is the Constitution which each voter thus engages to support?

It contains the following clauses:

Art. 1, Sect. 2. Representatives and direct taxes shall be apportioned among the several States, which may be included within this Union, according to their respective numbers, which shall be determined by adding to the whole number of free persons, including those bound to service for a term of years, and excluding Indians not taxed, *three fifths of all other persons.*

Art. 1, Sect. 8. Congress shall have power . . . to suppress insurrections.

Art. 4, Sec. 2. No person, held to service or labor in one State, under the laws thereof, escaping into another, shall, in consequence of any law or regulation therein, be discharged from such service or labor; but shall be delivered up on claim of the party to whom such service or labor may be due.

Art. 4, Sect. 4. The United States shall guarantee to every State in this Union a republican form of government; and shall protect each of them against invasion; and, on application of the legislature, or of the executive, (when the legislature cannot be convened) *against domestic violence.*

The first of these clauses, relating to representation, gives to 10,000 inhabitants of Carolina equal weight in the government with 40,000 inhabitants of Massachusetts, provided they are rich enough to hold 50,000 slaves:—and accordingly confers on a slaveholding community additional political power for every slave held among them, thus tempting them to continue to uphold the system:

... The second and the last articles relating to insurrection and domestic violence, perfectly innocent in themselves—yet being made with the fact directly in view that slavery exists among us, do deliberately pledge the whole national force against the unhappy slave if he imitate our fathers and resist oppression—thus making us partners in the guilt of sustaining slavery: the third is a promise, on the part of the whole North, to return fugitive slaves to their masters; a deed which God's law expressly condemns, and which every noble feeling of our nature repudiates with loathing and contempt.

These are the clauses which the abolitionist, by voting or taking office, engages to uphold. While he considers slaveholding to be sin, he still rewards the master with additional political power for every additional slave that he can purchase. Thinking slaveholding to be sin, he pledges to the master the aid of the whole army and navy of the nation to reduce his slave again to chains, should he at any time succeed a moment in throwing them off. Thinking slaveholding to be sin, he goes on, year after year, appointing by his vote judges and marshals to aid in hunting up the fugitives, and seeing that they are delivered back to those who claim them! How beautifully consistent are his *principles* and his *promises!* ...

OBJECTION II.[1]

A promise to do an immoral act is not binding: therefore an oath to support the Constitution of the United States, does not bind one to support any provisions of that instrument which

---

[1] The major section of this essay is organized as a series of objections to the nonpolitical-action position and of answers to those objections. [Eds.]

are repugnant to his ideas of right. And an abolitionist, thinking it wrong to return slaves, may as an office-holder, innocently and properly take an oath to support a Constitution which commands such return.

ANSWER. Observe that this objection allows the Constitution to be pro-slavery, and admits that there are clauses in it which no abolitionist ought to carry out or support.

And observe, further, that we all agree, that a bad promise is better broken than kept—that every abolitionist, who has before now taken the oath to the Constitution, is bound to break it, and disobey the pro-slavery clauses of that instrument. So far there is no difference between us. But the point in dispute now is, whether a man, having found out that certain requirements of the Constitution are wrong, can, after that, innocently swear to support and obey them, *all the while meaning not to do so.*

Now I contend that such loose construction of our promises is contrary alike to honor, to fair dealing, and to truthfulness—that it tends to destroy utterly that confidence beween man and man which binds society together, and leads, in matters of government, to absolute tyranny.

The Constitution is a series of contracts made by each individual with every other of the fourteen millions. A man's oath is evidence of his assent to this contract. If I offer a man the copy of an agreement, and he, after reading, swears to perform it, have I not a right to infer from his oath that he assents to the *rightfulness* of the articles of that paper? What more solemn form of expressing his assent could he select? A man's oath expresses his conviction of the rightfulness of the actions he promises to do, as well as his determination to do them. If this be not so, I can have no trust in any man's word. . . . The North makes a contract with the South by which she receives certain benefits, and agrees to render certain services. The benefits she carefully keeps—but the services she refuses to render, because immoral contracts are not binding! Is this fair dealing? It is the rule alike of law and common sense, that if we are not able, from *any cause,* to furnish the article we have agreed to, we ought to return the pay we have received. If power is put into our hands on certain conditions, and we find ourselves unable to comply with those conditions, we ought to surrender the power back to those who gave it. . . .

OBJECTION III.

I swear to support the Constitution, as *I understand it.* Certain parts of it, in my opinion, contradict others and are therefore void.

ANSWER. Will any one take the title deed of his house and carry it to the man he bought of, and let him keep the covenants of that paper as he says "he understands them?" Do we not all recognize the justice of having some third, disinterested party to judge between two disputants about the meaning of contracts? Who ever heard of a contract of which each party was at liberty to keep as much as he thought proper?

As in all other contracts, so in that of the Constitution, there is a power provided to affix the proper construction to the instrument, and that construction both parties are bound to abide by, or repudiate the *whole* contract. That power is the Supreme Court of the United States. . . .

. . . But, say some, our lives are notice to the whole people what meaning we attach to the oath, and we will protest when we swear, that we do not include in our oath the pro-slavery clauses. You may as well utter the protest now, as when you are swearing—or at home, equally as well as within the State House. For no such protest can be of any avail. The Chief Justice stands up to administer to me the oath of some office, no matter which. "Sir," say I, "I must take that oath with a qualification, excluding certain clauses." His reply will be, "Sir, I have no discretion in this matter. I am here merely to administer a prescribed form of oath. If you assent to it, you are qualified for your station. If you do not, you cannot enter. I have no authority given me to listen to exceptions. I am a servant—the people are my masters—here is what they require that you support, not this or that part of the Constitution, but 'the Constitution,' that is, the *whole*."

Baffled here, I turn to the people. I publish my opinions in newspapers. I proclaim them at conventions, I spread them through the country on the wings of a thousand presses. Does this avail me? Yes, says Liberty party, if after this, men choose to vote for you, it is evident they mean you shall take the oath as you have given notice that you understand it.

Well, the voters in Boston, with this understanding, elect me to Congress, and I proceed to Washington. But here arises a difficulty,—my constituents at home have assented—but when I get to Congress, I find I am not the representative of Boston only, but of the whole country. The interests of Carolina are committed to my hands as well as those of Massachusetts; I find that the contract I made by my oath was not with Boston, but with the whole nation. It is the *nation* that gives me the power to declare war and make peace—to lay taxes on cotton, and control the commerce of New Orleans. The nation prescribed the conditions in 1789, when the Constitution was settled, and though Boston may be willing to accept me on other terms, Carolina is not willing. Boston has accepted my protest, and says, "Take office." Carolina says, "The oath you swear is sworn to me, as well as to the rest—I demand the whole bond." In other words, when I have made my protest, what evidence is there that *the nation,* the other party to the contract, assents to it? There can be none until that nation amends its Constitution. Massachusetts when she accepted that Constitution, bound herself to send only such men as could swear to return slaves. If by an underhand compromise with some of her citizens, she sends persons of other sentiments, she is perjured, and any one who goes on such an errand is a partner in the perjury. Massachusetts has no right to assent to my protest—she has no right to send representatives, except on certain conditions. She cannot vary those conditions, without leave from those whose interests are to be affected by the change, that is, the whole nation. Those conditions are written down in the Constitution. Do she and South Carolina differ, as to the meaning? The Court will decide for them.

But, says the objector, do you mean to say that I swear to support the Constitution, not as I understand it, but as some judge understands it? Yes, I do—otherwise there is no such thing as law. This right of private judgment, for which he contends, exists in religion—but not in Government. Law is a rule *prescribed*. The party prescribing must have the right to construe his own rule, otherwise there would be as many laws as there are individual consciences. Statutes would be but recommendations if every man was at liberty to understand and obey them as he thought proper. But I need not argue this. The absurdity of a Government that has no right to govern—and of laws which have no fixed meaning—but which each man construes to mean what he pleases and obeys accordingly—must be evident to every one. . . .

. . . If we have a Constitution, let us remember Jefferson's advice, and not make it "waste paper by construction." The man who tampers thus with the sacred obligation of an oath,—swears, and Jesuit like, keeps "reserved meanings" in his own breast,—does more harm to society by loosening the foundations of morals, than he would do good, did his one falsehood free every slave from the Potomac to the Del Norte.

OBJECTION IV.

"The oath does not mean that I will positively do what I swear to do, but only that I will do it, *or submit* to the penalty the law awards. If my actions in office don't suit the nation, let them impeach me." . . .

... The Judge who, in questions of divorce, has trifled with the sanctity of the marriage tie—who, in matters of property has decided unjustly, and taken bribes—in capital cases has so dealt judgment as to send innocent men to the gallows—may cry out, "If you don't like me, impeach me." But will impeachment restore the dead to life, or the husband to his defamed wife? Would the community consider his submission to impeachment as equivalent to the keeping of his oath of office, and thenceforward view him as an honest, truth-speaking, unperjured man? It is idle to suppose so. Yet the interests committed to some of our officeholders' keeping, are more important often than even those which a Judge controls. And we must remember that men's ideas of right always differ. To admit such a principle into the construction of oaths, if it enable one man to do much good, will enable scoundrels who creep into office to do much harm, "according to *their* consciences." But yet the rule, if it be admitted, must be universal. Liberty becomes, then, matter of accident.

OBJECTION V.

I shall resign whenever a case occurs that requires me to aid in returning a fugitive slave.

ANSWER. "The office-holder has promised active obedience to the Constitution in every exigency which it has contemplated and sought to provide for. If he promised, not meaning to perform in certain cases, is he not doubly dishonest? dishonest to his own conscience in promising to do wrong, and to his fellow-citizens in purposing from the first to break his oath, as he knew they understood it? If he had sworn, not regarding anything as immoral which he bound himself to do, and afterwards found in the oath something against his conscience of which he was not at first aware, or if by change of views he had come to deem sinful what before he thought right, then doubtless, by promptly resigning, he might escape guilt. But is not the case different, when among the acts promised are some known at the time to be morally wrong? 'It is a sin to swear unto sin,' says the poet, although it be, as he truly adds, 'a greater sin to keep the sinful oath.'"

The captain has no right to put to sea, and resign when the storm comes. Besides what supports a wicked government more than good men taking office under it, even though they secretly determine not to carry out all its provisions? The slave balancing in his lonely hovel the chance of escape, knows nothing of your secret reservations, your future intentions. He sees only the swarming millions at the North ostensibly sworn to restore him to his master, if he escape a little way. Perchance it is your false oath, which you don't mean to keep, that makes him turn from the attempt in despair. He knows you only—the world knows only by your *actions,* not your *intentions,* and those side with his master. The prayer which he lifts to Heaven, in his despair, numbers you rightly among his oppressors.

OBJECTION VI.

I shall only take such an office as brings me into no connection with slavery.

ANSWER. Government is a whole; unless each in his circle aids his next neighbor, the machine will stand still. The Senator does not himself return the fugitive slave, but he appoints the Marshal, whose duty it is to do so. The State representative does not himself appoint the Judge who signs the warrant for the slave's recapture, but he chooses the United States Senator who does appoint that Judge. The elector does not himself order out the militia to resist "domestic violence," but he elects the President, whose duty requires, that a case occurring, he should do so.

To suppose that each of these may do that part of his duty

that suits him, and leave the rest undone, is *practical anarchy*. It is bringing ourselves precisely to that state which the Hebrew describes. "In those days there was no king in Israel, but each man did what was right in his own eyes.' This is all consistent in us, who hold that man is to do right, even if anarchy follows. How absurd to set up such a scheme, and miscall it a *government*,—where nobody governs, but everybody does as he pleases.

OBJECTION VII.

As men and all their works are imperfect, we may innocently "support a Government which, along with many blessings, assists in the perpetration of some wrong."

ANSWER. As nobody disputes that we may rightly assist the worst Government in doing good, provided we can do so without at the same time aiding it in the wrong it perpetrates, this must mean, of course, that it is right to aid and obey a Government *in doing wrong,* if we think that, on the whole, the Government effects more good than harm. Otherwise the whole argument is irrelevant, for this is the point in dispute; since every office of any consequence under the United States Constitution has some immediate connection with Slavery. Let us see to what lengths this principle will carry one. . . . According to this theory, the moment the magic wand of Government touches our vices, they start up into virtues! But has Government any peculiar character or privilege in this respect? Oh, no—Government is only an association of individuals, and the same rules of morality which govern my conduct in relation to a thousand men, ought to regulate my conduct to any one. Therefore, I may innocently aid a man in doing wrong, if I think that, on the whole, he has more virtues than vices. If he gives bread to the hungry six days in the week, I may rightly help him, on the seventh, in forging bank notes, or murdering his father! The principle goes this length, and every length, or it cannot be proved to exist at all. It ends at last, practically, in the old maxim, that the subject and the soldier have no right to keep any conscience, but have only to obey the rulers they serve: for there are few, if any, Governments this side of Satan's, which could not, in some sense, be said to do more good than harm. Now I candidly confess, that I had rather be covered all over with inconsistencies, in the struggle to keep my hands clean, than settle quietly down on such a principle as this. . . .

And let it be remembered that in dealing with the question of slavery, we are not dealing with extreme cases. Slavery is no minute evil which lynx-eyed suspicion has ferreted out. Every sixth man is a slave. The ermine of justice is stained. The national banner clings to the flag-staff heavy with blood. "The preservation of slavery," says our oldest and ablest statesman, "is the vital and animating *spirit* of the National Government."

Surely IF it be true that a man may justifiably stand connected with a government in which he sees some slight evils—still it is also true, even then, that governments *may* sin so atrociously, so enormously, may make evil so much the *purpose* of their being, as to render it the duty of honest men to wash their hands of them.

I may give money to a friend whose life has some things in it which I do not fully approve—but when his nights are passed in the brothel, and his days in drunkenness, when he uses his talents to seduce others, and his gold to pave their road to ruin, surely the case is changed.

I may perhaps sacrifice health by staying awhile in a room rather overheated, but I shall certainly see it to be my duty to rush out, when the whole house is in full blaze. . . .

OBJECTION IX.

If not being non-resistants, we concede to mankind the right to frame Governments, which must, from the very nature of man, be more or less evil, the right or duty to support them, when framed, necessarily follows.

ANSWER. I do not think it follows at all. Mankind, that is, any number of them, have a right to set up such forms of worship as they see fit, but when they have done so, does it necessarily follow that I am in duty bound to support any one of them, whether I approve it or not? Government is precisely like any other voluntary association of individuals—a temperance or anti-slavery society, a bank or railroad corporation. I join it, or not, as duty dictates. If a temperance society exists in the village where I am, that love for my race which bids me seek its highest good, commands me to join it. So if a Government is formed in the land where I live, the same feeling bids me to support it, if I innocently can. This is the whole length of my duty to Government. From the necessity of the case, and that constitution of things which God has ordained, it follows that in any specified district, the majority must rule—hence results the duty of the minority to submit. But we must carefully preserve the distinction between *submission* and *obedience*—between *submission* and *support*. If the majority set up an immoral Government, I obey those laws which seem to me good, because they are good—and I submit to all the penalties which my disobedience of the rest brings on me. This is alike the dictate of common sense, and the command of Christianity. And it must be the true doctrine, since any other obliges me to obey the majority if they command me to commit murder, a rule which even the tory Blackstone has denied. Of course for me to do anything I deem wrong, is the same, in quality, as to commit murder.

OBJECTION X.

But it is said, your theory results in good men leaving government to the dishonest and wicked.

ANSWER. Well, if to sustain government we must sacrifice

honesty, government could not be in a more appropriate place, than in the hands of dishonest men.

But it by no means follows, that if I go out of government, I leave nothing but dishonest men behind. An act may be sin to me, which another may sincerely think right—and if so, let him do it, till he changes his mind. I leave government in the hands of those whom I do not think as clear-sighted as myself, but not necessarily in the hands of the dishonest. Whether it be so in this country now, is not, at present, the question, but whether it would be so necessarily, in all cases. The real question is, what is the duty of those who presume to think that God has given them clearer views of duty than the bulk of those among whom they live?

Don't think us conceited in supposing ourselves a little more enlightened than our neighbors. It is no great thing after all to be a little better than a lynching—mobocratic—slaveholding—debt-repudiating community.

What then is the duty of such men? Doubtless to do all they can to extend to others the light they enjoy.

Will they best do so by compromising their principles? by letting their political life give the lie to their life of reform? Who will have the most influence, he whose life is consistent, or he who says one thing today, and swears another thing tomorrow—who looks one way and rows another? My object is to let men *understand me*, and I submit that the body of the Roman people understood better, and felt more earnestly, the struggle between the people and the princes, when the little band of democrats *left the city* and encamped on *Mons Sacer, outside*, than while they remained mixed up and voting with their masters, shoulder to shoulder. *Dissolution* is our *Mons Sacer*—God grant that it may become equally famous in the world's history as the spot where the right triumphed. . . .

. . . I admit that we should strive to have a *political* influence—for with politics is bound up much of the welfare of the people. But this objection supposes that the ballot box is the *only* means of political influence. Now it is a good thing that every man should have the right to vote. But it is by no means necessary that every man should actually vote, in order to influence his times. . . .

This objection, that we non-voters shall lose all our influence, confounds the broad distinction between *influence* and *power*. *Influence* every honest man must and will have, in exact proportion to his honesty and ability. God always annexes influence to worth. The world, however unwilling, can never get free from the influence of such a man. This influence the possession of office cannot give, nor the want of it take away. For the exercise of such influence as this, man is responsible. *Power* we buy of our fellow men at a certain price. Before making the bargain it is our duty to see that we do not pay "too dear for our whistle." He who buys it at the price of truth and honor, buys only weakness—and sins beside. . . .

. . . We come then, it seems to me, back to our original conclusion: that the man who swears to support the Constitution, swears to support the whole of it, pro-slavery clauses and all,—that he swears to support it *as it is*, not as it hereafter may become,—that he swears to support it in the sense given to it by the Courts and the Nation, not as he chooses to understand it,—and that the Courts and the Nation expect such an one in office to do his share toward the suppression of slave, as well as other, insurrections, and to aid the return of fugitive slaves. After an *abolitionist* has taken such an oath, or by his vote sent another to take it for him, I do not see how he can look his own principles in the face.

Thou that preachest a man should not steal, dost thou lie?

We who call upon the slaveholder to do right, no matter what the consequences or the cost, are certainly bound to look well to our own example. At least we can hardly expect to win the master to do justice by *setting him an example of perjury*. It is almost an insult in an abolitionist, while not willing to sacrifice even a petty ballot for his principles, to demand of the slaveholder that he give up wealth, home, old prejudices and social position at their call.

STEPHEN S. FOSTER IS SURE THAT REVOLUTION IS THE ONLY REMEDY

What the Garrisonians, for all their verbal gymnastics, had suggested was at most a dissolution of the Union. What Stephen S. Foster (1809–1881), as radical in politics as he was in the church, more pointedly asserted was that revolution was the only remedy. This implied, of course, the activism which John Brown would supply in 1859. But the fact remains that, for all the bombast, Foster's definition of revolution seemed to stop with a refusal to countenance the federal government, which, because it sanctioned slavery, implicated all its supporters in the peculiar institution.

We have now laid open before us the secret sources of the strength of the slave power. We see that power, feeble in itself, through the agency of the national government gathering into its hand the strength and resources of twenty millions of freemen, and employing them for its own aggrandizement. By means of this agency it lays its hand upon our pulpit, and it is dumb; upon the press, and it is silent; upon capital, and straightway, for the sake of its *per cent.*, it parts with its birthright; upon our literature, and forthwith it is self-emasculated. It commands our armies. It controls our treasury. It dictates law to our judges. It expounds the gospel to our churches. It has bound the conscience of the nation by an oath to participate in its crimes, and thereby rendered its opposi-

---

From Stephen Symonds Foster, *Revolution the Only Remedy for Slavery* (Anti-Slavery Tracts No. 7) (New York: American Anti-Slavery Society, n.d.), pp. 15–19.

tion impossible, or powerless. At its command we trample the law of God under our feet, and refuse to hide the outcast. Thus has it made us at once a nation of atheists and an empire of slaves.

Such is but a faint picture of the nature and strength of the evil with which, as abolitionists, we are called to grapple. Our contest is not with a few hundred thousand slave claimants, in distant States, but with a nation powerful in all the elements of physical strength and intellectual greatness. The enemy is at our own door. The entire government, from the president down to the humblest citizen in the retirement of private life, is, by the requirements of the Constitution, its protector, and is sworn to defend it, if need be, with the heart's blood. We lift our hand to succor the victim of the merciless man-hunter, and the bayonet, not of the Carolina planter, but of our next door neighbor, is thrust into our bosoms. We hasten the panting fugitive on his flight, and forthwith we find ourselves incarcerated within the walls of a prison built with our own money. We turn to the church for sympathy, and she brands us with the double infamy of fanaticism and infidelity. We, on the other hand, are few in number and limited in resources. And yet our only chance of success lies in being able to bring into the field and oppose to this mighty cordon of strength, behind which slavery has intrenched itself, a superior force. Where, then, lies our hope? Is it in political tactics? in the skilful manoeuvring of forces already committed by an oath to the slave power?

To the enlightened vision there is for this evil but one remedy. Our strength all lies in a single force—the conscience of the nation. All else is on the side of the oppressor. But conscience, that force of forces when properly instructed, is all, and always, on our side. It is to this element of strength, then, that our attention should be mainly directed. Our only hope is in being able to bring the conscience of the nation into active conflict with its present position, in respect to slavery, and thereby induce a radical change. . . . The Constitution requires of the general government the protection of slavery in such of the States as choose to retain it, with no power to regulate or abolish it. Hence the private citizen has no course left to him but either to aid in upholding the system, or renounce his allegiance to the government. His only choice is between slaveholding and revolution. By this subtle device of the slave power the whole country has been leagued in defence of the institution, and the north reduced to a mere subjugated province of the plantation. The heart of the church has been corrupted by it, the conscience of the country fettered, and our statesmen converted into sycophants fawning at the feet of the slave power. Here, then, is the seat of this terrible disease, and here especially must the remedy be applied. Our first great work is to cut this Gordian knot,—the Union,— and set free the northern conscience from the restraints of the constitutional oath. Till this is done, all other efforts will prove of little avail. There is no hope for the slave, nor the country, but in revolution.

So long as we fulfil our constitutional obligations to slavery, it will live, and extend its domain, in spite of freesoil and free democratic triumphs. To promise to fulfil them, with a different purpose in our hearts, is an act of fraud which will most certainly rob us of our moral power, and make us alike the prey and sport of our enemies. At present, we have little or nothing to do with the slave claimants. They are, of themselves, but a mere cipher. Our controversy is with the government which upholds the system, and makes it possible for the master to plunder his victim, and with a clergy and church who baptize such a government, and thank God for its existence, because, forsooth, it protects them and theirs, though at the same time it inflicts upon millions of their countrymen outrages such as find no parallel under the darkest despotisms of the old world —a government in whose capital stands the auction block for the sale of human flesh, and many of whose senators have acquired princely fortunes by robbing mothers of their babes. This sin of the government and of the church must be brought and laid at the door of every individual member of these corrupt bodies. They must be made to see and feel that they cannot remain in organizations which are employed in the commission of such atrocious crimes without being themselves partakers of the guilt. It is the presence, mainly, of the *seemingly* good in these corrupt organizations which gives them power to do the wrong. The vilest members of our government, if left alone, would stand aghast at its wickedness. But the presence of better men keeps them in countenance, the better class, meanwhile, excusing themselves with the belief that the villains who use and direct them will alone be held responsible for the results of their united action. Such delusion must be dispelled, and all the guilt, and blood, and fathomless abominations of slavery rolled upon the individual conscience of every man who consents to support a government which legalizes and protects it, or to fellowship a church which recognizes the members of such a government as ministers or followers of Christ. If we would succeed, our separation from slavery must be thorough and complete. "Come out from among them, and be ye separate, and touch not the unclean thing," is the voice of reason, as well as the language of Scripture.

The great anti-slavery lesson of to-day is, that support to institutions which protect or sanction slavery is slaveholding; and that uncompromising hostility to all such institutions is the only *genuine* anti-slavery. The time has gone by when lower ground than this can be safely occupied by any true friend of liberty. As well might we recognize a man who is in the daily use, in moderate quantities, of intoxicating drinks, as a genuine friend of temperance, as regard him as a true abolitionist who proffers his allegiance and support to a slaveholding government. The honesty of such a man we may not perhaps question; but in his influence, as well as by his position, he stands with the oppressor, and we should regard and treat him as an enemy of the slave. Freedom allows no compromises. The man who makes them is ill begotten, and can never inherit her estates. To consent to yield to the oppressor a single barleycorn is, in fact, to yield principle, and consequently to yield every thing. So we have always found it. So we always shall find it, till the law of God is reversed, and the corrupt tree brings forth good fruit. In every contest with evil, the highest ground is the strongest. Indeed, our only real strength is in planting our feet upon the absolute right, so that God can work with us and through us. He is no compromiser. He has no part or lot with those who abate one "jot or tittle" of his law to accomodate themselves to the institutions of wicked men. The idea of hedging slavery in within certain limits is morally absurd. It can be exterminated, but it can never be controlled. You can never say to it, "Thus far—but no farther." And that anti-slavery which seeks merely to confine it within its present limits, or within any limits, is utterly spurious and worthless. It is but a milder type of pro-slavery—a hybrid, or, more properly, a kind of varioloid, whose only grace is in comparison with the hateful disease to which it bears so close a resemblance, and for which it serves as a substitute. Talk of confining slavery? As well might you talk of regulating the cholera, or of confining the plague within certain limits, or say to intemperance, "In such and such localities seek your victims, and we will defend you there; but pass not those boundaries." The vices are not our servants. We have power to exterminate them, if we will, but we can never tolerate them, except to become our masters. A people whose moral standard will permit them to tolerate slavery any where are too weak to resist its most arrogant demands, under the pressure of temptations such as the slave power is always able to present.

If we would see our country free from the curse of slavery, we must begin the work of its abolition by applying to it the golden rule—the eternal law of absolute moral rectitude.

Our first work is with ourselves, to bring our own conduct within the requirements of this law, by assuming such a position towards the slaveholding institutions of the country as we should desire others to occupy were we the slaves; thus practically "remembering those in bonds as bound with them." Our next duty is to press its claims upon the conscience of our neighbor, and give him no rest till he also yields to its requirements. Anti-slavery, it must be remembered, is a reform as well as a revolution. It can progress only as the people are made better; and we can aid it only as we exert a healthful moral influence on those around us. The slaves can be delivered from their chains only by delivering their enslavers from their guilt. In the same proportion that the one is made morally better is the other made politically and socially free.

By means such as are here proposed must the moral sentiments of the country be renovated. When that shall have been done to any considerable extent, the time will have come to commence the work of reconstructing the government and remodelling the church. But it must be remembered, we cannot build without material; nor is it wise to commence the work till a moderate portion, at least, shall have been previously prepared. Let it be the aim, then, of every true friend of liberty to get ready the public mind; and in due time will appear a master-builder under the superintendence of whose tasteful and discerning eye will be reared an edifice worthy the highest love and admiration of a free and generous people. May God hasten the day when it shall be our happiness to hail for our beloved country a new State and a new Church, "wherein dwelleth righteousness."

XV

Emancipation and the War Power

ABRAHAM LINCOLN
DECREES EMANCIPATION

What the antislavery people themselves had been unable to accomplish was finally achieved under the impetus of civil war. Abraham Lincoln (1809–1865), himself more interested in the preservation of the Union than in the freeing of the slaves, found himself pushed by the tide of battle and the pressures for action on behalf of the Negro slaves to announce, on January 1, 1863, a general emancipation of all slaves in territory still held by southern armies. While students are quick to point out that no slaves were in fact freed by the proclamation, nevertheless the fact remained that a psychological and even moral victory of the first magnitude had been achieved by the President's action. The document is reproduced here as it first appeared in the Liberator.

Abraham Lincoln, "The [Emancipation] Proclamation," in *The Liberator*, January 2, 1863.

By the President of the United States of America.

A PROCLAMATION.

Whereas, on the 22d day of September, in the year of our Lord 1862, a Proclamation was issued by the President of the United States, containing, among other things, the following, to wit:—

That on the 1st day of January, in the year of our Lord 1863, all persons held as slaves within any State or designated part of a State, the people whereof shall then be in rebellion against the United States, shall be then, thenceforth and forever free; and the Executive Government of the United States, including the military and naval authority thereof, will recognize and maintain the freedom of such persons, and will do no act or acts to repress such persons, or any of them, in any effort they may make for their actual freedom; that the Executive will, on the first day of January aforesaid, by proclamation, designate the States and parts of States, if any, in which the people therein respectively shall then be in rebellion against the United States; and the fact that any State, or the people thereof, shall on that day be in good faith represented in the Congress of the United States, by members—chosen thereto at elections wherein a majority of the qualified voters of such State shall have participated—shall, in the absence of strong countervailing testimony, be deemed conclusive evidence that such State and the people thereof are not then in rebellion against the United States.

Now, therefore, I, ABRAHAM LINCOLN, President of the United States, by virtue of the power in me vested, as Commander-in-Chief of the Army and Navy of the United States, in time of actual armed rebellion against the authority and government of the United States, and as a fit and necessary war measure, do, on this first day of January, in the year of our Lord one thousand eight hundred and sixty-three, and in accordance with my purpose so to do, publicly proclaimed for the full period of one hundred days from the day first above mentioned, order and designate as the States and parts of States wherein the people thereof respectively are this day in rebellion against the United States, the following, to wit: Arkansas, Texas, Louisiana, except the parishes of St. Bernard, Placquemines, Jefferson, St. John, St. Charles, St. James, Ascension, Assumption, Terre Bonne, Lafourche, St. Mary, St. Martin and Orleans, including the city of New Orleans; Mississippi, Alabama, Florida, Georgia, South Carolina, North Carolina, and Virginia, except the forty-eight counties designated as West Virginia, and also the counties of Berkley, Accomac, Northampton, Elizabeth City, York, Princess Ann and Norfolk, including the cities of Norfolk and Portsmouth, and which excepted parts are for the present left precisely as if this proclamation were not issued.

And by virtue of the power and for the purpose aforesaid, I do order and declare, that all persons held as slaves, within said designated States and parts of States, are and hereafter shall be free, and that the Executive Government of the United States, including the military and naval authorities thereof, will recognize and maintain the freedom of said persons; and I hereby enjoin upon the people so declared to be free to abstain from all violence, unless in necessary self-defence. And I recommend to them in all cases when allowed, to labor faithfully for reasonable wages; and I further declare and make known, that such persons of suitable condition will be received into the armed service of the United States, to garrison forts, positions, stations and other places, and to man vessels of all sorts in said service. And upon this act, sincerely believed to be an act of justice, warranted by the Constitution upon military necessity, I invoke the considerate judgment of mankind and the gracious favor of Almighty God.

THE THIRTEENTH AMENDMENT ENDS SLAVERY IN THE UNITED STATES

Adopted December 18, 1865, this forty-three word amendment to the American Constitution did what the outpouring of millions of words from more impassioned spokesmen had failed to accomplish. Speedily ratified in the North, its ratification by returning Confederate states was also required as the prerequisite to their return to the Union. Thus simply after thirty-five years of the antislavery movement and four years of civil war was slavery ended. But still for the nation, for the Congress, and for the antislavery movement itself the other part of the crusade, equal rights for the Negro, was left unsettled. The amendment is reproduced here as it was published in the Liberator.

WILLIAM H. SEWARD, SECRETARY OF STATE OF THE UNITED STATES, TO ALL TO WHOM THESE PRESENTS MAY COME,
GREETING:

Know ye, that whereas the Congress of the United States, on the 1st of February last, passed a Resolution, which is in the words following, viz:

"A Resolution submitting to the Legislatures of the several States a proposition to amend the Constitution of the United States:

Resolved, by the Senate and House of Representatives of the United States of America, in Congress assembled, two-

---

"Official Proclamation [of the Thirteenth Amendment]," in *The Liberator*, December 22, 1865.

thirds of both Houses concurring, that the following article be proposed to the Legislatures of the several States as an amendment to the Constitution of the United States, which, when ratified by three-fourths of said Legislatures, shall be valid to all intents and purposes as part of said Constitution, viz:

ARTICLE XIII. SECTION 1. NEITHER SLAVERY NOR INVOLUNTARY SERVITUDE, EXCEPT AS A PUNISHMENT FOR CRIME, WHEREOF THE PARTY SHALL HAVE BEEN DULY CONVICTED, SHALL EXIST WITHIN THE UNITED STATES, OR ANY PLACE SUBJECT TO THEIR JURISDICTION.

SECTION 2. Congress shall have power to enforce this article by appropriate legislation."

And whereas, it appears from official documents on file in this Department, that the amendment to the Constitution of the United States, proposed as aforesaid, HAS BEEN RATIFIED by the Legislatures of the States of Illinois, Rhode Island, Michigan, Maryland, New York, West Virginia, Ohio, Missouri, Nevada, Indiana, Louisiana, Minnesota, Wisconsin, Vermont, Tennessee, Arkansas, Connecticut, New Hampshire, Maine, Kansas, Massachusetts, Pennsylvania, Virginia, South Carolina, Alabama, North Carolina—in all, twenty-seven States;

And whereas, the whole number of States in the United States is thirty-six;

And whereas, the before specially named States, whose Legislatures have ratified the said proposed amendment, constitute three-fourths of the whole number of States in the United States:

Now, therefore, be it known that I, William H. Seward, Secretary of the United States, by virtue and in pursuance of the second section of the act of Congress, approved on the 20th of April, 1818, entitled "An act to provide for the publication of the laws of the United States, and for other purposes, do hereby certify that THE AMENDMENT AFORESAID HAS BECOME VALID, TO ALL INTENTS AND PURPOSES, AS PART OF THE CONSTITUTION OF THE UNITED STATES.

Index

Adams, Charles Francis, xxxvii, lxxix, 445–452
Adams, John Quincy, xlv, xlvi, lviii, lxxv, 260–267
Admission of new slave states, 402–403, 441
Africa, 27–32, 48, 222
American and Foreign Anti-Slavery Society, xliii, liv, lv, lvi, lxxii, 148–163, 456–457
American Anti-Slavery Society, xxxii–xxxiii, xxxiv, xlii, l, liv, lv, lxxxi, lxxxiii, 65–71, 130–134, 191–196, 205–212, 453–456
American Colonization Society, xxvi–xxvii, 18–38, 206–207
American Convention for Promoting the Abolition of Slavery, 14–17
American Union for the Relief and Improvement of the Colored Race, xlix, lxix–lxxi
Amistad Case, lxxv
Anticlericalism, xlvii–l, 123–142, 249, 319
Anti-Slavery Convention of American Women, xli, lxxii
Antislavery lecturers, xl–xli
Antislavery press, xxxviii–xl
Atrocities, 86–91, 99–101, 216

Bacon, Leonard, xlviii, l, 111–114
Ballou, Adin, lxxii
Baptist Church, xlvii
Beecher, Charles, lxxvi
Beecher, Edward, lxi, 268–272

Beecher, Lyman, li
Benevolent societies, xxx–xxxi, 432–436
Benezet, Anthony, xxiv, 1–5
Biblical argument, 118–123
Birney, James G., xxxviii*n*., xxxix, xlvii, liii, lix, lxii, lxiii, lxvii–lxix, lxxiv, lxxxii, 43–49
Black Codes, lxi, lxviii, 307, 307*n*.
Blair, Francis P., Jr. (Frank), xxviii, 49–59
Boston Female Anti-Slavery Society, xxxvii, xli
Bowditch, Henry I., xli
Bowditch, William I., 343–348
British abolition movement, xxix–xxx, xxxv, 351
British West Indies, xxxvii, 47–48
Brown, William Wells, lxxiii
Buffum, Arnold, 418–427
Burleigh, Charles C., xxxviii*n*., 172–177
Burns, Anthony, "Rendition" of, lxxviii–lxxix, 251
Burritt, Elihu, 200–205, 427

Canada, lxix, 46–47, 196–200, 222
Caste, 287, 288, 291, 292
Channing, William Ellery, xxxix–xl, lvii, lx, 114–118, 240–245
Chapman, Maria Weston, xlix–l, li, lii, lxx, lxxiii, 205–212
Chase, Salmon P., xxvii, xi, lxiii, lxv, lxxvi, 384–394

487

Child, Lydia Maria, xxxviiin., xlvi, lv, lxxix, lxxxi, 86–91
Civil disobedience, lxxvi–lxxix
Civil liberties, xl, xlv–xlvii, 248–251, 257–297
Civil rights, lxvii–lxxiv, lxxxi, lxxxiv, 37, 195–196, 197–198, 243, 332–333, 373
(See also Racial equality)
Civil War, lxxxi, lxxxiii
"Clerical Appeal," xlix–l
Coles, Edward, xxv
Colonization, xxvi–xxviii, lxvii, lxxiv, lxxxii, 18–59, 196–200, 306–307, 316
Color prejudice (See Racial prejudice)
Colored conventions (See Negro conventions)
Colored National Convention (1853), 273–280
"Comeoutism," xlvii–l, 128–142, 190–191, 476–477
Compact theory of government, 363–364
Compensated emancipation, 166–171, 200–205, 209
Compromise of 1850, lxvi, lxxxiii
Congregational Church General Association of Massachusetts, xlix
Constitutional argument, xlv, lvii–lxii, lxxvi–lxxvii, lxxix, lxxxi, 70, 229, 241–242, 246–247, 273–274, 343–394, 461–462
Crandall, Prudence, xlii, lxx, 318
Creole Case, lvi, lvin.

Dawn community, lxix
Declaration of Independence, xxiv, lviii, lxxv, 216–217, 228, 233, 246, 281–282
Delany, Martin, lxxii, lxxxii, 319–330
Discrimination, racial (See Racial discrimination)

District of Columbia, slavery and slave trade, xliv, 183, 189–190, 231, 260–267, 402–403, 410–411, 414, 424, 441
Disunion, lx–lxi, lxv, lxxix–lxxxi, 222–223, 359–360, 453–456, 459–479
Douglass, Frederick, lv, lvi, lix, lxv, lxix, lxxiii, lxxxii, 314, 348–360, 452–458
Dred Scott Decision, lxvii, lxxix, lxxxiii
Due process, 380–384, 388–391

Earle, Thomas, lxii
Easton, Hosea, lxxxii, 330–335
Economic argument, xlii–xliv, 143–182, 247–248, 321–330
Economic boycott, xlii–xliii, 143–148
Education, xxxi, xli–xlii, lxviii, lxix, 41, 154–156, 197–198, 199, 210–211, 249, 280–297, 322–323
Elgin community, lxiv, 105n., 196–200
Ellsworth, William W., lxx
Emancipation, economic effects of, 169–171, 172–177
Emancipation Proclamation, lxxxi, 480–482
Emerson, George B., xli
Emigrant Aid Society, lxxx
Emlen Institute, xlii
Equality, racial (See Racial equality)
Extension of slavery in the territories, xliv, lxiv–lxvii, 231, 441

Fairfax, Ferdinando, xxvi
Finley, Robert, xxvi
Finney, Charles Grandison, xxix, lxxxii
Follen, Charles (Karl) T. C., lxi, 224–233
Forten, James, lxxxii, 36
Forten, James, Jr., lxxxii, 233–240
Foster, Abby Kelley, li–lii

Foster, Stephen S., xlviii, lv, lxxix, lxxxii, lxxxiv, 134–142, 474–479
Foster, Theodore, lxiv
Free labor, effect of slavery on, 158–159, 179–181
Free Negroes, 21–23, 27–32, 32–38, 43–49, 191–196, 273–280, 321–330
Free produce, xlii–xliii, 143–148, 211–212, 453
Free Soil Party, lxiv–lxvi
Frémont, John C., lxxxi
Friends, Society of, xxiv, xxvii–xxviii, xlii, xlvii, 1–14, 143–148, 453
Fugitive Slave Act (1793), lxviii, lxxiv, lxxvi, 384, 387–388, 393–394, 415
Fugitive Slave Act (1850), lxxvi, lxxviii, 441, 443
Fugitives, return of, lviii, lix, lx, lxxv–lxxix, 103–104, 123–128, 183, 209–210, 221–222, 240–244, 251, 346–347, 352–356, 372–394, 441–445, 461–462

"Gag Rule," xlv, lvi, 260–267
Garnet, Henry Highland, lxxiii, lxxx, lxxxii
Garrison, William Lloyd, xxviii, xxxi, xxxv–xxxvi, xliii, xlvi, xlviii, l, li, lii, liii, liv, lvi, lx, lxix, lxxii, lxxx, lxxxi, lxxxii, 38, 60, 65–71, 128–134, 323, 348, 453, 454
Garrisonians, xxxiv, xxxvi, xlviii–l, lii, liii, lix, lx, lxi, lxv, lxx, lxxxii, 343, 459–479
General welfare clause, lix
Genius of Universal Emancipation, xxviii, xxxi
Giddings, Joshua R., lvi–lvii, lxxvi–lxxvii, lxxxii, 411–417
Goodell, William, xxxvi, xxxviiin., lviii, lx–lxi, 360–370, 427–439
Gradualism, 1–17, 25, 72–75
Green, Beriah, xxxiii, xlv, lxi, 182–191

Grimké, Angelina (*See* Weld, Angelina Grimké)
Grimké, Sarah, li

Harper, Robert G., lxxxii, 18–32
Harpers Ferry, lxxxi
Hayden, Lewis, lxxviii
Helper, Hinton Rowan, xliv, 163–172
Henson, Josiah, lxxiii, lxxxii
Hicks, Elias, 143–148
Hicksite Friends, xlvii, 143
Higginson, Thomas Wentworth, lxxvii, lxxviii, lxxx, lxxxi
Higher Law, lxi, lxii, lxvii, lxxv, lxxvi, lxxvii, 240–245, 249, 368, 385, 392–394, 478
Hodges, Charles E., lxxix
Holley, Myron, liii, lxii
Hopkins, Samuel, xxvi
Howe, Samuel Gridley, lxxviii
Humanitarianism, xxix–xxxi
Hunter, David, lxxxi

Immediatism, xxviii–xxxii, xxxv–xxxvii, 60–85
"Infidelity," applied to abolitionists, 128–134
Interrogating candidates, lii, 403–405
Interstate commerce power, lviii, 360–362
"Irrepressible Conflict," 177, 181

Jackson, Francis, 395
Jay, William, xxix, xxx, lviii
Jefferson, Thomas, xxiv, xxvi, 218, 301–303
Jerry Rescue, lxxviii

Kansas, lxxx, lxxxi
Kansas-Nebraska Act, lxvi
Kelley, Abby (*See* Foster, Abby Kelley)
Kimball, Horace, xxxvii
King, William, lxxxii, 105n., 196–200
Know-Nothing Party, 445–452

490 Index

Land prices, effect of slavery on, 164–171
Lane Debates and debaters, xxxiv, lxxxii
Lane Seminary, xxxiv
Leavitt, Joshua, xxvii, lxv
LeMoyne, Francis, lvii
Liberator, xxxi, xxxviii, 322
Liberia, xxvi, 48
Liberty Party, liii, lvii, lxii–lxiv, lxv, 412–416, 418–439, 457–458
Licentiousness, 91–93, 137–138
Lincoln, Abraham, xxviii, lxxxi, 480–482
Loring, Ellis Gray, liii, lv, lxxvii
Lovejoy, Elijah P., xxxix, 268–272, 318
Lowell, James Russell, 310–315
Lundy, Benjamin, xxviii, lxxxii, 38

McDuffie, George E., 151, 151n., 237
Macedon Convention, 427–439
McHenry, Jerry, lxxviii
Madison, James, xxvii, 352–354
Mahan, John B., 318
Manifest Destiny, 54–56
"Man-stealing," 137–139
Manufacturing, effect of slavery on, 156–158
Manumission, private, 20–21, 28–29, 38–43
Marshall, John, xxvii
Martyrdom, xxxix, 219
Massachusetts Anti-Slavery Society, liii, 225, 395–411
(*See also* New England Anti-Slavery Society)
May, Samuel, Jr., xliii, lvi, lxv
May, Samuel Joseph, xxvii, liii, lxxviii, 65
Methodist Episcopal Church, xlvii, 135
Mexican War, lxiv
Mob violence, xxxii, xxxix, xli, 135–136, 257, 268–272, 317–318
Monroe, James, xxvii, 53–54

Municipal doctrine of slavery, lviii, lxvii

Nashoba, xxv, 38–43
Nat Turner's Rebellion, xxv, xxxi
Native American Party, 445–452
Nativism, 226–229, 445–452
Natural law, lxi, 114–118, 224–256, 362, 365–370
Natural rights, lxi, lxxvi, 36, 114–118, 213–218, 224–256, 261–262, 273, 281–282, 385–386
Negro conventions, lxvii–lxviii, lxxiv, lxxx, 273–280
Nell, William C., lxxiii
New England Anti-Slavery Convention, lv–lvi, lxxx, 212–223
New England Anti-Slavery Society, xxxii, xli, lxxii, 60–64
(*See also* Massachusetts Anti-Slavery Society)
New York Anti-Slavery Society, xxxii
Non-resistance, li-lii, lxxx, lxxxi
Non-slaveholders, effects of slavery on, xliii–xliv, 148–172
Northwest Ordinance, xxiv, lxxvi

Oberlin College, xxxiv, xlii
Organized Negro communities, lxix, 38–43, 196–200

Parker, Theodore, xliii, lxxviii, lxxxi, lxxxii, 246–256
Pennsylvania Hall, xli, 318
Perfectionism, li
Petition campaign, xliv–xlv, li, lii, lvi, 189–190, 231, 260–267, 396–397, 401–402
Phelps, Amos A., xxvii, l, lxxv, 71–85
Philanthropist, xxxix
Phillips, Wendell, xli, xliv, lv, lx, lxxvii, lxxxi, lxxxii, lxxxiv, 339, 459–479
Phoenix Society, xlii
Pillsbury, Parker, lxxxii

Political action, lii–liv, lvi–lvii, lxii–lxvii, 207–209, 248, 395–479
Population, effect of slavery on, 152–154
Practical action, xxxvii–xxxviii, xli–xlvii, lxxx, 182–221, 321–322
Prejudice, racial (See Racial prejudice)
Presbyterian Church, l
Prigg v Pennsylvania, lxxiv–lxxv, 388, 389
Purvis, Robert, lxviii, lxxxii

Quakers (See Friends, Society of)
Quincy, Edmund, lv, lxxxii, 223

Races, segregation of, xxviii
Racial discrimination, lxviii, 276, 298–342
Racial equality, lxi, lxvii–lxxiv, 215, 273–280, 298–342
(See also Civil rights)
Racial prejudice, lxviii, lxxi–lxxiv, 7, 10–12, 19–21, 45–48, 51, 56–59, 183, 192, 214–215, 225–226, 232, 236, 296–297, 298–342
Racial segregation, lxx–lxxiii, 210–211, 280–297, 336–342
Randolph, John, xxv
Rankin, John, lxxi, 87–88, 118–123
Rantoul, Robert, Jr., lix, lxxvii, 370–384
Refugee Home Society, lxix
Religious argument, xxiv, xxix, xxxiii, xlvii–xlviii, lxiv, lxvi, 1–14, 111–142, 185–186, 214–215, 304–308, 311–312
Remond, Charles Lenox, lxxiii, lxxxii, 314, 335–342
Republican government, Constitutional guarantee of, lix, 362
Republican Party, lxvi–lxvii, 439–445
Revivalism, xxix, xxxiv, lxxxii
Revolution, lx, lxxix–lxxxi, 298, 308–309, 474–479

Roberts Case, lxxi, 280–297
Rogers, Nathaniel P., xxxviii*n.*, 315–319, 456

Sabbath observance, 194–195
Segregation, racial (See Racial segregation)
Sentiment, argument from, 86–110, 123–128
"Separate but equal" idea refuted, 285–287, 291–293
"Seventy," The, xxxiv
Seward, William H., xliv, xlv, lii, lvii, lxi, lxiii–lxiv, lxxv, lxxvi, lxxviii, lxxxi, 177–181, 483–485
Sharp, Granville, xxiv
Sims, Thomas, Case, lxxvii, 251
Slade, William, xlvi, xlvi*n.*
"Slave power conspiracy," xliv, lxiv–lxv, 183, 419–421, 474–479
Slave rebellion, xxv, 220–221, 243–245, 308–309, 347–348, 351–352, 461–462
Slave trade, lviii, lx, 1–5, 15–16, 146–148, 251–252, 344–346, 350–351, 360–362, 413
(See also District of Columbia, slavery and slave trade)
Slavery in the ancient world, 300–303
Smith, Gerrit, xxvii, xxx, xli, xlii, lxxxi, lxxxii, 257–260, 427
Stewart, Alvan, lxii
Storrs, Charles B., xxxiii*n.*
Stowe, Harriet Beecher, 105–110
Stowell, Martin, lxxviii–lxxix
Strader, Gorman, and Armstrong v. Christopher Graham, 44
Strict construction, lix, 370–384
Sumner, Charles, xliv, xlvi, lxv, lxxi, 280–297, 439–445

Tappan, Arthur, xxvii, xxx, xxxii, xlvi, lxxxii
Tappan, Charles, xlix
Tappan, John, xlix

Tappan, Lewis, xxx, xxxii, liii–liv, lxiii
Temperance, 192–193
Texas, annexation of, xliv, lx, lxiv, 410
Third parties, lxii–lxvii, 399–401, 418–458
(*See also* Liberty Party, Free Soil Party, Republican Party, Know-Nothing Party)
Thirteenth Amendment, lxxxi, 483–485
Thome, James A., xxxvii, lxxxii, 91–93
Thompson, George, xlvi, xlvi*n*., lxxx, lxxxii, 319, 319*n*., 350
Thompson, Waddy, 265*n*., 267
Thornton, William, xxvi
Three-fifth ratio, lviii, lix, 344, 350, 461–462
Transcendental argument, 115–118
Turner, Nat, lxxxii
(*See also* Nat Turner's Rebellion)

Underground Railroad, lxx, lxxv
Union (*See* Disunion)
Universal reformism, l–lii, lxiii, 427–439
Utica Convention, xli, 257

Van Buren, Martin, lxv
Van Zandt Case, lxxvi, 384–394
Vashon, J. B., 38
Vice, abstention from, 193
Voluntary societies (*See* Benevolent societies)

Walker, David, lxxiv, lxxxii, 298–310
War power, lix, lxxxi, 352, 480–482
Washington, Bushrod, xxvii
Wattles, Augustus, xlii
Weld, Angelina Grimké, xliii, li
Weld, Theodore Dwight, xxxiii–xxxiv, xxxix, xl, xlv, li–lii, lv, 94–102
Western Reserve College, xxxiii–xxxiv
Wheaton, James, lxxi
Whittier, John G., xxxviii*n*., 65, 102–104, 123–128
Wilberforce community, xxviii, lxix
Women's rights, l–li, liv, lxi, 229–231, 401–402
Woolman, John, xxiv, 5–14
Wright, Elizur, Jr., xxxiii*n*., l
Wright, Frances, xxv, 38–43
Wright, Henry C., li, lxxix

THE AMERICAN HERITAGE SERIES

THE COLONIAL PERIOD

Adams, John *The Political Writings of John Adams: Representative Selections* AHS 8 George A. Peek, Jr.
The English Libertarian Heritage: From the Writings of John Trenchard and Thomas Gordon in The Independent Whig *and* Cato's Letters AHS 32 David L. Jacobson
The Great Awakening AHS 34 Alan Heimert, Perry Miller
Puritan Political Thought AHS 33 Edmund S. Morgan

THE REVOLUTIONARY ERA

The American Revolution as a Democratic Movement AHS 36 Alfred Young
The Antifederalists AHS 38 Cecelia Kenyon
Early American Libertarian Thought: Freedom of the Press from Zenger to Jefferson AHS 41 Leonard W. Levy
Franklin, Benjamin *The Political Thought of Benjamin Franklin* AHS 64 Ralph Ketcham
Paine, Thomas *Common Sense and Other Political Writings* AHS 5 Nelson F. Adkins

THE YOUNG NATION

Calhoun, John C. *Disquisition on Government and Selections from the* Discourse AHS 10 C. Gordon Post
Channing, William Ellery *Unitarian Christianity and Other Essays* AHS 21 Irving H. Bartlett
Democracy, Liberty, and Property: The State Constitutional Conventions of the 1820's AHS 43 Merrill D. Peterson

The Federal Convention and the Formation of the Union of American States AHS 19 Winton U. Solberg
From the Declaration of Independence to the Constitution: The Roots of American Constitutionalism AHS 6 Carl J. Friedrich, Robert G. McCloskey
Gallatin, Albert *Selected Writings* AHS 40 E. James Ferguson
Hamilton, Alexander *Papers on Public Credit, Commerce, and Finance* AHS 18 Samuel McKee, Jr., J. Harvie Williams
Hamilton, Madison, and Jay on the Constitution: Selections from the Federalist Papers AHS 7 Ralph H. Gabriel
Jefferson, Thomas *The Political Writings of Thomas Jefferson: Representative Selections* AHS 9 Edward Dumbauld
Social Theories of Jacksonian Democracy: Representative Writings of the Period 1825–1850 AHS 1 **Joseph L. Blau**
The Writings of Justice Joseph Story AHS 45 Henry Steele Commager

THE MIDDLE PERIOD

The Antislavery Argument AHS 44 Jane and William Pease
Lincoln, Abraham *The Political Thought of Abraham Lincoln* AHS 46 Richard Current
The Radical Republicans and Reconstruction AHS 47 Harold Hyman

THE LATE NINETEENTH CENTURY

Bryan, William Jennings *The Mind and Thought of William Jennings Bryan* AHS 52 Ray Ginger
The Forging of American Socialism: Origins of the Modern Movement AHS 24 Howard H. Quint
Late Nineteenth-Century American Liberalism AHS 26 Louis Filler
The Populist Mind AHS 50 Norman Pollack

THE TWENTIETH CENTURY

Addams, Jane *The Social Thought of Jane Addams* AHS 69 Christopher Lasch
The American Writer and the Great Depression AHS 63 Harvey Swados

Negro Protest Thought in the Twentieth Century AHS 56
  Francis Broderick, August Meier
New Deal Thought AHS 70 Howard Zinn
The Progressives AHS 54 Carl Resek
Roosevelt, Theodore *The Writings of Theodore Roosevelt*
  AHS 53 William H. Harbaugh
The Supreme Court: Law Versus Discretion AHS 72 Wallace Mendelson
Wilson, Woodrow, *The Political Thought of Woodrow Wilson*
  AHS 68 E. David Cronon

TOPICAL VOLUMES

The American Economic System: Representative Selections
  AHS 27 Massimo Salvadori
American Military Thought AHS 75 Walter Millis
The Churches and the City AHS 61 Robert Cross
Freedom of the Press: 1800–1965 AHS 74 Harold L. Nelson
Nonviolence in America: A Documentary History AHS 60
  Staughton Lynd

THE EVANS LIBRARY
FULTON-MONTGOMERY COMMUNITY COLLEGE
2805 STATE HIGHWAY 67
JOHNSTOWN, NEW YORK 12095-3790